RENEWALS 458-4574
DATE DUE

AMERICAN FOREIGN POLICY IN A GLOBALIZED WORLD

AMERICAN FOREIGN POLICY IN A GLOBALIZED WORLD

EDITED BY
David P. Forsythe
Patrice C. McMahon
Andrew Wedeman

Routledge
Taylor & Francis Group
New York London

Library
University of Texas
at San Antonio

Published in 2006 by
Routledge
Taylor & Francis Group
270 Madison Avenue
New York, NY 10016

Published in Great Britain by
Routledge
Taylor & Francis Group
2 Park Square
Milton Park, Abingdon
Oxon OX14 4RN

© 2006 by Taylor & Francis Group, LLC
Routledge is an imprint of Taylor & Francis Group

Printed in the United States of America on acid-free paper
10 9 8 7 6 5 4 3 2 1

International Standard Book Number-10: 0-415-95397-9 (Softcover) 0-415-95396-0 (Hardcover)
International Standard Book Number-13: 978-0-415-95397-9 (Softcover) 978-0-415-95396-2 (Hardcover)
Library of Congress Card Number 2005031290

No part of this book may be reprinted, reproduced, transmitted, or utilized in any form by any electronic, mechanical, or other means, now known or hereafter invented, including photocopying, microfilming, and recording, or in any information storage or retrieval system, without written permission from the publishers.

Trademark Notice: Product or corporate names may be trademarks or registered trademarks, and are used only for identification and explanation without intent to infringe.

Library of Congress Cataloging-in-Publication Data

American foreign policy in a globalized world / edited by David P. Forsythe, Patrice McMahon and Andrew Wedeman.
   p. cm.
Includes bibliographical references and index.
ISBN-13: 978-0-415-95396-2 (hardback)
ISBN-13: 978-0-415-95397-9 (pbk.)
   1. United States--Foreign relations--2001- 2. Bush, George W. (George Walker), 1946---Political and social views. 3. Globalization--Political aspects. 4. Unilateral acts (International law) I. Forsythe, David P.,1941- II. McMahon, Patrice C. III. Wedeman, Andrew Hall, 1958-

E902.A468 2006
327.73009'0511--dc22   2005031290

Taylor & Francis Group
is the Academic Division of Informa plc.

Visit the Taylor & Francis Web site at
http://www.taylorandfrancis.com

and the Routledge Web site at
http://www.routledge-ny.com

Contents

Acknowledgments	vii
Introduction: Sustaining American Power in a Globalized World PATRICE C. McMAHON AND ANDREW WEDEMAN	1
1 Doctrinal Unilateralism and Its Limits: America and Global Governance in the New Century JOHN GERARD RUGGIE	31
2 Article 2(4) on the Nonuse of Force: What Were We Thinking? EDWARD C. LUCK	51
3 Sovereign Inequality and Hierarchy in Anarchy: American Power and International Society JACK DONNELLY	81
4 American Security, the Use of Force, and the Limits of the Bush Doctrine JON WESTERN	105
5 The Bush Doctrine and Multilateral Institutions KAREN A. MINGST	123
6 American Public Opinion and Foreign Policy: Did the September 11 Attacks Change Everything? OLE R. HOLSTI	141
7 Supervising America's Secret Foreign Policy: A Shock Theory of Congressional Oversight for Intelligence LOCH K. JOHNSON	173
8 American Policy toward Enemy Detainees in the War on Terrorism DAVID P. FORSYTHE	193

9 Democracy Promotion and
   American Foreign Policy:
   Afghanistan, Iraq, and the Future   215
   MARK PECENY

10 Draining Swamps and Transplanting Values:
   Nation Building and the American Military   241
   CONRAD C. CRANE

11 The United States and Europe:
   Explaining the Transatlantic Bond   261
   ROBERT J. LIEBER

12 The Bush Doctrine in Asia   287
   MEL GURTOV

13 The Bush Doctrine and Democracy Promotion
   in the Middle East   313
   MAHMOOD MONSHIPOURI

   Contributors   335

   Index   339

Acknowledgments

This book was made possible through the generosity of G. E. Hendricks, an alumnus of the University of Nebraska–Lincoln (UNL). Hendricks had a lively interest in American politics and was especially concerned about the limitations on public discussion during the McCarthy era of the early 1950s. So in the period 1949–1957 he gave the Nebraska Foundation a substantial sum of money to be used to address "current controversial political questions in a nonpartisan, unbiased manner."

With the support of the G. E. Hendricks fund, in April 2005 we brought to the UNL campus a number of distinguished commentators on American foreign policy for a two-day conference—the nineteenth meeting held in the Hendricks series. We subsequently invited other experts to join this group to contribute to *American Foreign Policy in a Global World*. Quite clearly contemporary American foreign policy is controversial, principally because of the Bush "doctrine" of preemptive, unilateral war and its application to Iraq. There is no doubt that these strategic orientations, along with other assertions of American unilateralism and exceptionalism, have sparked intense controversies at home and abroad. We and our coauthors have certainly tried to address, in a nonpartisan, unbiased fashion, Bush foreign policy and whether it is sustainable in an interdependent and integrated world. We have attempted to remain committed to the values articulated by Hendricks.

We are especially grateful not only to the Hendricks fund but also to the UNL Department of Political Science, which administers the Hendricks Fund. Jack Comer, chair of the department, was most supportive, as was Helen Sexton, the department's administrative assistant. We are also grateful to the Cooper Foundation and the E. N. Thompson Forum on World Issues for sponsoring Dr. John Ruggie. Also lending cheerful support was Kim Weide, the events coordinator for the UNL College of Arts and Sciences, along with Carrie Althoff, Evan Litrell, and Carrie Heaton. It was a pleasure to work with Robert Tempio, Richard Tressider, and Stephanie Drew of Routledge.

David P. Forsythe
Patrice C. McMahon
Andrew Wedeman

Introduction: Sustaining American Power in a Globalized World

PATRICE C. McMAHON AND ANDREW WEDEMAN

Throughout the 1990s the United States seemed to defy both history and international relations theory.[1] Its resources were unrivaled, and the concentration of power in its hands unprecedented. Its military might, economic vitality, and cultural influence, alongside its willingness to provide global public goods augured—at least to some—a fundamental transformation in world politics. The unipolar structure of the international system, however, did not translate into "the end of history" or even to a more peaceful world order. Nor did it mean that the sole superpower would respond to international crises alone; with notable exceptions, multilateralism was the means of choice for the United States. Some use of U.S. power proved controversial, as when Russia and China objected to and sought to condemn the North Atlantic Treaty Organization (NATO) bombing of Serbia in 1999 as led by Washington, D.C. But in the 1990s there was not a broad and vigorous challenge to U.S. primacy.

In hindsight, these observations about the nature of the post-Cold War world proved short lived, if not wholly mistaken. After the attacks on New York City and Washington, D.C. on September 11, 2001, the George W. Bush administration adopted a profoundly different approach to the use of American power resources. Articulated formally in 2002, the Bush administration's grand strategy emphasized American unilateral power and the right to preemptive attack. As the 2002 National Security Strategy explains, "We must adapt the concept of imminent threat to the capabilities and objectives of today's adversaries ... To forestall or prevent such hostile acts by our adversaries, the United States will, if necessary, act preemptively."[2] Thus, a decade after the end of the Cold War, the United States began behaving like a traditional great power. It defined its national interests more narrowly (while asserting that what was good for the United States was also good for the rest of the world) and viewed its overarching conventional military strength as a means to accomplish its goals.

Discussions of the U.S. position in the world, its expansive ambitions, and unipolarity have produced a number of noteworthy books, many of which compare America's power to previous empires or provide theoretical justifications for why a unipolar system cannot last. Although this project draws on these debates, it focuses centrally on contemporary foreign policy behavior, its defining characteristics, and, most importantly, its effects. How is the foreign policy of the George W. Bush administration different from previous governments? What role, if any, have domestic actors played in facilitating these foreign policies? Has the administration succeeded in making the U.S. homeland secure or in accomplishing its other declared priorities? Finally, how has this turn in foreign policy affected the role of the United States in different regions of the world?

This book seeks to answer these questions, specifically—as posed particularly in the chapter by John Gerard Ruggie—whether doctrinal (i.e., ideological) unilateralism is sustainable in a globalized world. This and following chapters provide theoretical, historical, and geographical examinations of these questions. Although differing in their emphasis, the chapters contain a fairly consistent thesis: While the U.S. resources remain substantial, Washington's ability to shape outcomes in the world is challenged, if not undermined, by its expansive foreign policy goals and exceptionalist approach to international relations, as well as fundamental changes in the global system. The United States does continue to display primacy of many forms of coercive power, but the authors of this book mostly question the fungibility, if not longevity, of these resources. In fact, most authors—even when taking notice of the Bush administration's achievements—question whether the United States can continue to convert military and economic resources to preferred outcomes when acting in an essentially unilateral manner.

Given the centrality of the concept of power in this project, this chapter begins with a definition and brief discussion of American hegemony. We then look at the primary source of U.S. power: its military capabilities. Although it is frequently assumed that the United States enjoys overwhelming military superiority and that its dominant position is unlikely to be challenged in the near term, measuring military power is not a simple matter of counting beans. Military capabilities are only one part of the formula and, as security analysts are likely to point out, must be considered in the context of a state's national security requirements and its intentions. A seemingly vast supply of military might can, in fact, mask weakness if the demands on that military power are greater than available resources. Or, as international relations scholars assert, one state's overwhelming concentration of power might provoke other states into balancing against it. This chapter puts American power in context and analyzes its sustainability by focusing on the consequences of Bush's foreign policy, particularly regarding the Iraq War. The chapter concludes with an overview of the volume.

Hegemonic Power

Though power is a central concept in international relations theory, it is rarely defined and notoriously difficult to measure. Here we lay out the conception of power underlying the chapters that follow.

Scholars like David Baldwin and Joseph Nye have delineated the dimensions of states' power and the means for measuring influence in international politics. Drawing on *social power* literature, Baldwin argues that (1) power is a relationship rather than a property; (2) the bases of power are many and varied; and (3) power is multidimensional and varies in scope, weight, domain, and cost.[3] Put simply, power is a type of causal relationship emerging from a variety of resources but must be considered in terms of issues and actors (or scope and domain). Only by adopting what is referred to as a "policy-contingency framework" that specifies who is trying to get whom to do what can analysts approximate a state's power.[4]

Most contemporary discussions of states' power begin with Robert Dahl's behavioral explanation of power, or the ability of one state to get another to do what it would not otherwise have done.[5] However, Peter Bachrach and Morton S. Baratz argue there is a "second face" of power that is not always clearly visible: the ability to set the agenda and mobilize influence through international institutions. Understanding the exercise of power thus requires some analysis of why certain issues are considered important to the international community while others are not.[6] During the Cold War, the United States extensively influenced international institutions and led by example. It thereby implicitly set the tone for what was deemed important and legitimate to the international community, which is precisely why several contributors in this volume reflect on American attitudes and policies toward international organizations, human rights, and democracy promotion. Doctrinal unilateralism, or the desire to go it alone from ideological belief rather than pragmatic calculation, on the part of the Bush administration, however, has the potential to seriously damage this face of power for the United States—especially when large numbers of the international community, including important states, do not share Washington's assumption that what is good for the United States is automatically resulting in good for the rest of the world.

Drawing on these insights about the complexity of power, scholars also acknowledge and emphasize another aspect of state power: the ability not only to effect specific outcomes and to shape international agendas but also to influence perceptions and preferences.[7] Drawing on the Gramscian notion of hegemony, this latter, even more obscured manifestation of power, confers on some great powers a broad measure of legitimacy. As Ruggie argues, legitimacy can only be conferred by others. As Jack Donnelly argues in his chapter, it is important to situate the United States in the society of states and to recognize that the society of states has from time to time endorsed not only the idea of sovereign equality but also all sorts of unequal arrangements impinging on state sovereignty. As Donnelly shows, many situations reflecting inequality of status have been endorsed as legitimate. Referred to by Nye as "soft power," this capability to elicit consent allows states to shape outcomes to their liking because their values are attractive to others. U.S. soft power, alongside its material resources and its willingness to develop a dense network of international institutions devoted to the public good, meant that, beyond the communist camp, for much of the Cold War the United States did not need to coerce others to change behavior or affect outcomes. Until the George W. Bush administration took office, international institutions, decision-making procedures, and dominant values reflected and usually advanced American interests.[8]

Though the individual authors of this book may disagree about the distinctiveness of Bush's foreign policy or its implications for American power, they implicitly agree that American power is based on both certain material resources and an array of intangible, political assets. In a globalized world, which is to say in an interdependent world, soft power resources are increasingly separate from and beyond the government's total control. In fact, in a theme highlighted in the first substantive chapter by Ruggie, the emergence of a multiplicity of actors from below and above the nation-state has led to a greater diffusion of soft power. This suggests that whereas globalization mostly bolstered U.S. power during the Cold War, today it is no longer certain if transnational corporations or intergovernmental or nongovernmental organizations will continue to strengthen or even look kindly on the United States.

Regardless of whether a state exerts its power directly, indirectly, or through the socialization of values, a state's power is usually associated with the possession of certain tangible resources. Historically and theoretically, a great power's most important resource is its military capability because of the anarchic nature of international politics and the self-help environment it engenders. Yet, as Kenneth Waltz noted, "military muscle does not guarantee political influence."[9] Karen Mingst, quoting John Gaddis, points out in her chapter that muscle is not brains: Measuring a state's power requires not only an analysis of its capabilities but also some reading of its will and intentions and wisdom in policy choice. Throughout the 1990s, what surprised most observers of international politics was the noticeable lack of will on the part of U.S. leaders—Republicans and Democrats alike—to use the country's resources to exercise primacy or to dominate outcomes. Although rhetoric did not always match reality, even the language used by Presidents George H. W. Bush and Bill Clinton avoided accentuating U.S. dominance or unilateral means, opting instead for phraseology that called for "a new world order" or "assertive multilateralism." Such behavior seemed to signify that despite the structural changes in the international system, this alone was insufficient to predict behavior, and the United States did not always seek to exploit or assert its power in unilateral ways. When George Bush used unilateral military power in 1989 to control the situation in Panama, or when Clinton used limited military strikes in places like the Sudan and Afghanistan, neither tried to elevate such unilateralism to a global doctrine, as compared to a particular response to a pressing particular problem.

American primacy of hard power is not really new.[10] Coming out of World War II, the United States had the opportunity to construct new international institutions and to structure the international system in ways that might have established it as an imperial power. Unlike previous great powers, the United States used its resources in an unusual, if not exceptional, way. While containing the Soviet Union, it simultaneously worked with other countries to build a new set of relationships based on trust and transparency. The chapter by Edward C. Luck reminds us that the United States took the lead in writing Article 2, paragraph 4 into the United Nations (UN) charter, supposedly restricting the use of force, including by Washington, to defend against armed aggression.

American power was widely seen as hegemonic, especially outside the communist camp, because it elicited widespread support. The core of that power may have been hard in the sense of the capability to coerce. But there was also much soft power because of consent derived from multilateral cooperation. Mingst develops this point well. Rather than crudely dominating other states, the United States tried to work with them in ways that recognized their interests, empowering its allies and constructing a durable and reasonably well-accepted international order.

The chapter by Robert J. Lieber reminds us not to be too rosy in our recollections. During the Cold War, Washington's relations with Europe were often strained and even tumultuous. Developing countries were often particularly unhappy with the economic arrangements that derived from the decisions of the global north. But in relative terms, especially in dealing with important allies, Washington was reasonably sensitive to the needs of others.

It must be emphasized that the United States did all of this at the apex of its material power by restraining its own ambitions and committing its resources to the security and benefit of others. Without ever losing sight of its own national self-interest, the United States tried to reassure its allies that it would neither dominate nor abandon them.[11] In practice, it tried to put its allies at ease by creating an array of international organizations and sector-specific regimes. This, then, is the crucial difference between the United States and similarly situated great powers: after 1945 the United States was an institution builder that constructed a negotiated international order based on mutually acceptable principles.[12] Unlike the Soviet Union, which projected its power primarily through coercion and intimidation, U.S. power was bolstered through a jumble of overlapping international organizations and multilateral institutions manifesting some genuine consent by member states. At least formally, relations among states were based on generalized principles of conduct without regard to the interests of the parties or the specific situation.[13] Thus, to a degree neither history nor theory had anticipated, America's power was both constructed and constrained by international institutions created by the United States. Donnelly reminds us, however, that many of these international arrangements formalized a special, exceptional position for the United States and other presumed great powers, such as permanent membership entailing the veto in the UN Security Council and special voting rights in the World Bank and International Monetary Fund.

With bipolarity's demise, debates over the future of American power and its hegemonic position returned. Many predicted that given the structural changes in the international system, the concentration of power resources in the hands of the United States simply could not last. Realist theorists assumed that other states would form an alliance to offset U.S. primacy of hard power. The first decade of unipolarity proved otherwise; in fact, throughout the 1990s American power resources only increased—in military, economic, and even political terms.[14] Economically, the American economy outperformed both its European allies and Japan, and its military dominance became more pronounced, with the United States spending more on military expenditures than all other major powers combined. Most unexpectedly, international acceptance of American power and leadership, though challenged, did not decline significantly.

This apparent malfunction of the "balance of power" was largely the result of the foreign policy behavior of U.S. presidents during these years and even into the twenty-first century. It seemed, at least for a while, as if American leaders understood the tenuous nature of the position of the United States, the need for restraint, as well as the costs of relying on the country's coercive power to affect outcomes. At least for a while, structural position did not alter the behavior of the United States significantly. Perhaps the Soviet Union's imperial overstretch had convinced George H. W. Bush of the importance and cost-effectiveness of building coalitions and winning international support. Certainly, Bush relied on international institutions, allies, and diplomacy extensively, using these resources successfully to build one of the largest and broadest coalitions in history before attacking Iraqi forces occupying Kuwait in January 1991. Still, as had been true historically, the senior Bush used unilateral power in the Western Hemisphere—as already mentioned, in Panama in 1989.

Subsequently, U.S. humiliation in Somalia in 1993 demonstrated the limits of American power. Subsequently, the Clinton administration seemed to embrace a new multilateralism that sought to avoid the commitment of American ground forces by relying more heavily on airpower and the provision of logistic support for ground operations by allied forces, as was the case in the Balkans. Despite this putative shift to multilateralism, the commitment of U.S. forces to overseas security operations slowly increased, and by the late

1990s it appeared to some that U.S. military forces, whose overall size had decreased after the end of the Cold War, were stretched increasingly thin.[15]

During the 2000 presidential election, George W. Bush suggested that although realist principles and national self-interest would define the administration's foreign policy, so too would humility and the judicious use of American power. He said, "If we are an arrogant nation, they'll view us that way, but if we're a humble nation, they'll respect us."[16] At least initially, the Bush administration used America's resources circumspectly. It reduced U.S. military forces abroad and adopted a lower profile role in many parts of the world, while simultaneously backing away from a host of international commitments and multilateral organizations. For a time, the Bush team apparently realized that hegemonic power works best and is most durable when noticed least.[17]

As most of the authors in this volume acknowledge, the terrorist attacks on the World Trade Center and the Pentagon, however, brought forth a different and distinct tendency within the Bush administration and changed the way it viewed and interacted with the world. Within less than a year, an ambitious foreign policy agenda was under way, some of which had been discussed, in fact, before the 2001 attacks. Because of the attacks, President Bush did not face some of the domestic political constraints that had encumbered his father or Clinton, even though, as Ole R. Holsti's chapter confirms, there has been a surprising amount of continuity in how domestic institutions operate and their influence on foreign policy. What did change decisively were the administration's goals and means. Rather than continue to pull back American power, Bush now embraced a policy that stressed the active, even anticipatory, use of hard power to remake the international system and to protect American national interests from a new and amorphous enemy. Initially, the policy known as the Bush doctrine produced dramatic successes, as the United States and its allies toppled the Taliban regime in Afghanistan and the U.S. military made short order of the Hussein regime in Iraq. After 2003, however, things seemed to go sour. The American-led coalition began to fray and fragment as the United States found itself bogged down in an unexpectedly difficult insurgency in Iraq, unable to find a seemingly intractable problem of a nuclear-armed North Korea and faced with the threat of a nuclear weapons crisis with Iran. In these cases, in fact, the Bush administration appeared to incline toward multilateralism. Today, paradoxically, even though no new superpower has emerged to challenge it, the viability of the American claim to hegemony appears at risk.

Coercive Power

The Bush administration's belief in the utility of preemption and unilateralism flows directly from an assumption of overarching American strategic supremacy, an assumption that seems well founded. However, this assumption only works if one sees military power as a property and not as just one component in a complex relationship that must be fungible to affect certain actors in specific situations. In 2004, U.S. military spending accounted for an estimated 49 percent of global defense spending, up from 40 percent in the late 1980s (see Fig. I.1).[18] Spending by American allies and friends accounted for an additional 20 percent. Spending by Russia, meanwhile, fell from 9.4 percent in 1988 to just 1.4 percent in 2003. Chinese spending increased significantly, but even at its expanded level it accounted for only 3.4 percent of global defense spending.[19] The two surviving members of the so-called axis of evil—North Korea and Iran—combined with Iraq's apparent replacement, Syria, accounted for 2.8 percent. In raw dollar terms, therefore, the United States greatly outspends potential adversaries.

Measuring power in terms of defense spending is, of course, problematic because personnel costs vary wildly, as do the security challenges facing individual powers. North Korean soldiers are, for example, paid a pittance compared to American soldiers, and whereas North Korean security concerns are effectively limited to its immediate region, the United States has global security interests. But moving away from crude aggregates to more sophisticated measures based on military hardware and capabilities only reinforces the impression of American strategic dominance.

The United States maintains the second largest military in the world, with nearly 1.5 million men and women serving on active duty and an additional 1.25 million in the reserves (see Table I.1). China's military is larger, with 2.25 million on active duty and 500,000 in its reserves. What distinguishes the

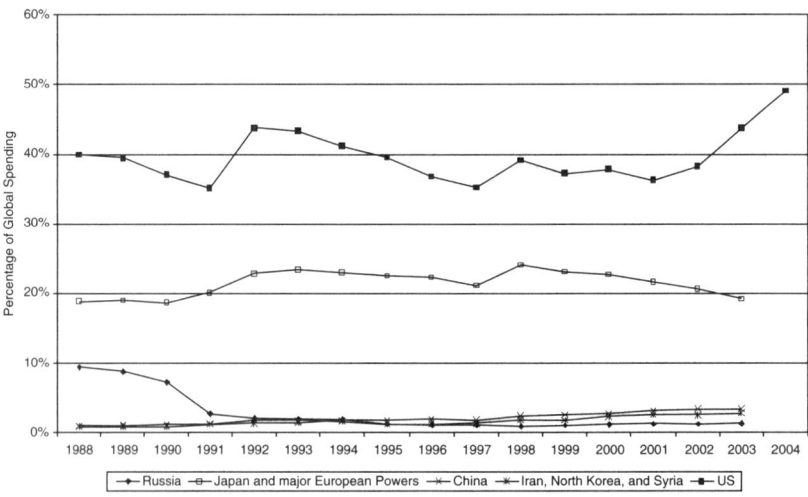

Fig. I.1 Military expenditure. Source: Stockholm International Peace Research Institute, Military Expenditure Database available at http://www.sipri.org/GlobalSecurity.org.

Table I.1 Size and Strength of Selected Armed Forces, 2003

	United States	Russia	China	North Korea	Iran	Syria
		Total Armed Forces				
Active	1,427,000	960,000	2,250,000	1,082,000	540,000	319,000
Reserves	1,237,000	2,400,000	550,000	665,000	350,000	354,000
Strategic Forces						
Nuclear Warheads	4,530	5,483	250	6	0	0
SLBMs*	432	216	12	0	0	0
ICBMs*	550	735	30	0	0	0
Ground Forces						
Army	485,000	321,000	1,700,000	950,000	350,000	215,000
Marine Infantry	174,400	7,500	10,000	0	2,600	0
Reserves	698,000	0	0	0	120,000	0
Battle Tanks	8,023	21,930	7,180	3,500	2,035	4,500
Fighting Vehicles	20,919	25,975	4,500	2,500	650	3,700
Artillery	1,547	20,746	15,200	10,400	2,755	2,060
Naval Forces						
Ballistic Submarines	16	13	1	0	0	0
Attack Submarines	35	35	67	26	3	0
Carriers	12	1	0	0	0	0
Cruisers	27	7	0	0	0	0
Destroyers	49	14	21	3	0	0
Frigates	30	10	42	0	3	2
Naval Attack Aircraft	1,176	0	248	0	0	0
Air Forces						
Bombers	203	197	180	3	0	0
Fighters/Fighter Bombers	2,968	1,514	1,666	507	270	422

* SLBM=Submarine Launched Ballistic Missile System; ICBM=Intercontinental Ballistic Missile System.
Source: International Institute for Strategic Studies, *The Military Balance, 2003–2004* (London: Oxford University Press, 2003).

American military from others is not so much its size but rather its combination of size and quality. American forces are generally better equipped and trained than other armed forces. For example, whereas all American fighter and fighter-bomber aircraft were advanced third-generation aircraft (from the 1970s and 1980s), 39 percent of fighters and fighter bombers flown by the People's Liberation Army Air Force (PLAAF) were first generation (from the

1950s), 52 percent were second generation (from the 1960s), and only 9 percent were advanced third generation—a mere 284 fighters. Fully half of the North Korean Air Force consisted of 1950s-era MiG-17s and MiG-19s, and 37 percent were 1960s-era MiG-21s, MiG-23s, or SU-7s. In all, North Korea had only sixty-five planes built after 1970. American pilots were also better trained. American fighter pilots average 190 flight hours a year. Chinese pilots flew half as many hours. Syrian pilots averaged about thirty, North Korean pilots twenty, and Russian pilots fifteen. Moreover, a decade of enforcing no-fly zones over Iraq have provided American pilots with real-world combat experience. Senior American officers are veterans of the 1991 Gulf War and hence have war-fighting experience.

Advanced technology gives U.S. forces an additional edge. Integrated command, control, and communications (C3) systems link American forces in ways that allow for the rapid concentration of firepower and forces on the battlefield. Ground units can, for example, call in fire support, air strikes, and armored reinforcements. Airmobile infantry can be moved quickly to reinforce beleaguered points or to exploit tactical opportunities. Massed airpower, meanwhile, allows American forces to establish air superiority, to provide tactical air support for ground units, and to strike the enemy's rear areas. This combination permits U.S. forces to mount rapid-moving, high-intensity operations designed to knock opposing forces off balance, to isolate and defeat combat elements, and to strike deeply into their rear.

A second factor setting the American military apart is its tremendous force-projection capability. American ground and air forces already are permanently forward deployed in Europe and Northeast Asia, and the American blue water navy allows it to control the sea. From its overseas bases, forward-deployed amphibious forces, and bases in the continental United States, American military power can be projected into most parts of the world with remarkable speed. Within a matter of hours, long-range strategic bombers and sea-launched cruise missile can begin striking targets anywhere in the world. Special operations elements and tactical air units can begin deployment within days. Within two weeks a lightly equipped airborne division can be deployed, along with carrier battle groups and marine expeditionary forces. If their heavy equipment and supplies have been prepositioned, regular ground force—including heavy-armored units—can deploy by air and marry up with their equipment. Fully equipped divisions can also be sea-lifted into the region. The U.S. military anticipates that it can deploy two heavy-armored divisions within thirty days and two more divisions within seventy-five days.[20] In a matter of months the United States can amass a sizable force to conduct high-intensity offensive operations in most parts of the globe.

Potential challengers, on the other hand, have limited force-projection capabilities. China, for example, currently has a large army but lacks the amphibious assault capability to mount a major operation across the Taiwan

Straits (though it does have the ability to launch a potentially crushing missile attack on Taiwan). North Korea can launch a massive ground attack on South Korea but can only attack Japan using missiles. Iran could strike at American forces deployed in Iraq but not elsewhere. The asymmetry of force-projection capabilities thus means that whereas the United States can take the fight to other countries, potential enemies cannot take the fight to U.S. homeland. This does not mean that countries such as China or North Korea lack military power. With their large militaries they in fact possess considerable defensive power and perhaps even a short-range offensive capability. Nor does their lack of conventional offensive power imply they cannot strike back using unconventional means such as terrorism. But in strategic terms the United States is an offensive power, whereas its potential adversaries are defensive powers.

Moreover, the massive American strategic arsenal gives it the ability to unleash a devastating nuclear attack anywhere on the globe. The U.S. nuclear arsenal of over 4,000 warheads is only matched in quantitative terms by Russia, which currently has nearly 5,000 warheads.[21] China with 250 warheads or North Korea with six could inflict a blow to the United States, but not one of the same magnitude the United States could deliver in return—assuming of course they could strike major urban concentrations in the United States. Although China's thirty intercontinental ballistic missiles (ICBMs) can reach the United States, neither North Korea nor Iran has long-range missiles. Even if North Korea and Iran were to develop missiles with sufficient range to strike the United States, they are unlikely to ever achieve the ability to launch a disarming first strike, meaning that use of their nuclear weapons would precipitate a massive and utterly devastating retaliatory strike. The threat of massive retaliation, in turn, negates the offensive utility of their nuclear weapons. As Daniel Ellsberg argued many years ago, if the almost certain result of launching a nuclear strike is a devastating counterstrike, then the utility of striking in the first place is essentially zero.[22] That does not, of course, rule out their use. But it means that such a strike would be an act of suicidal desperation, not strategic opportunism, because the severe asymmetry of nuclear capabilities ensures the United States would suffer much less proportionately that any would-be attacker.

In sum, the United States currently joys a sizeable advantage in terms of raw military might. No anti-status quo, revisionist power has the combination of high-quality military forces and the force-projection capability that would make it either a superpower or, more specifically, an offensive-capable superpower. The leading revisionist powers generally have large but relatively poorly equipped forces that provide a robust defensive capability and a limited short-range offensive capability. The preponderance of American battlefield power, however, means that if a revisionist power were to mount an offensive operation against its neighbors, American forces could swiftly deploy for a counterattack. Possession of nuclear weapons by certain rogue states alters the calculus to the extent that it provides them with the capability to deter the United States. This capability is thin, however, because these rogues are likely to acquire a rudimentary strategic capability insufficient to allow them to challenge the status quo, except to the extent that they could bluff the United States into retreat or passivity when faced with aggression.

Sustainability of Hegemonic Power

In an abstract vacuum, American military superiority appears more than sufficient to provide U.S. hegemonic power. But military power must always be measured in relative, not absolute, terms, and the costs of maintaining and using military power must be carefully evaluated to appreciate the opportunities foregone in making such choices. As argued in this section, the tremendous edge in military power the United States enjoyed prior to the War on Terror—which seemed to justify the Bush Doctrine in 2002—eroded rather quickly as the war progressed because in projecting American power globally, the Bush Doctrine substantially increased the demands on American military power. The extent to which demands have grown much more rapidly than supply in fact gives rise to new questions about whether the United States now has sufficient power to achieve its national security goals (to say nothing of its ability to continue supporting global public goods). Moreover, Bush's domestic economic agenda, with its emphasis on tax cuts, has produced a situation in which American defense spending now depends in part on the sale of U.S. government securities to foreign investors and thus creates a form of financial dependency not associated with the idea of hegemonic power. Finally, there is the problem of credibility as initial justifications for the war in Iraq disappear and nation building faces daunting obstacles.

Military Power

In the short term, the ongoing insurgency in Iraq has undeniably diminished the extent of American strategic dominance. In very simple terms, the deployment of large number of troops in Iraq has tied down a sizable portion of both the regular and reserve forces. During summer 2005, the United States had approximately 160,000 to 170,000 troops deployed in Operation Iraqi Freedom and an additional 20,000 in Afghanistan.[23] In total, these two operations tied down less than a tenth of total American military power. Yet the demands on American ground forces are not limited to the seven divisions currently involved in combat operations. Deployed units rotate on an approximately annual basis. Returning units require six months to a year to rest, refit, and retrain before they can be considered fully combat ready.[24] Units preparing to deploy also need to undergo a period of training and preparation. Conventional military wisdom suggests, therefore, that it takes a total of four units to sustain one unit in the field.[25]

The impact of the War on Terror is reflected in the state of the army's units of operation, which, roughly speaking, are brigade-equivalent combat units.[26] As of May 2005, of the thirty-nine regular army units currently operational, eighteen were deployed, seventeen were preparing for deployment, and three had recently returned from deployment (see Table I.2). Nine of the thirty-nine National Guard brigades were deployed, two were preparing for deployment, eleven had recently returned from deployment, including two that had become exempt from further mobilization (see Table I.3).[27] In short, the regular army is almost fully committed to the War on Terror, with the overwhelming bulk of its forces engaged in counterinsurgency operations in Iraq, and just under a third of the National Guard is committed to the War on Terror. The Marine Corps is also heavily committed to the Iraq conflict, with approximately one of its four divisions and 26,000 Marines deployed in Iraq.

Table I.2 Status and Location of U.S. Army Units of Operation, May 2005

Status	Afghanistan	Germany	Iraq	Korea	Total
Deployed	2	1	15	1	19
Preparing to Deploy	3	0	14	0	17
Recently Deployed	0	0	3	0	3
Total	5	1	32	1	39

Source: Based on Globalsecurity.org, "Where Are the Legions?" http://globalsecurity.org/military/ops/global-deployments.htm.

Table I.3 Status and Location of National Guard Brigades, May 2005

Status	Afghanistan	Balkans	Iraq	Sinai	Total
Deployed	0	1	1	7	0	9
Partially Deployed	0	0	0	0	1	1
Preparing for Deployment	0	1	0	1	0	2
Mobilization Eligible	1	0	0	0	0	1
Recently Redeployed	0	1	5	3	0	9
Mobilization Exempt	2	0	0	0	0	2
Inactive	15	0	0	0	0	15
Total	18	3	6	11	1	39

Source: Based on Globalsecurity.org, "Where Are the Legions?" http://globalsecurity.org/military/ops/global-deployments.htm.

In the grand scheme of things, the physical cost of the war in terms of American casualties has been limited. As of mid-August 2005, 2,066 Americans had been killed in Iraq or Afghanistan (over 90 percent of them since President Bush declared major combat operation over) and 14,414 wounded.[28] The war in Iraq has created increasingly serious problems with recruitment and retention. In February 2005, the army fell 27 percent short of its recruiting target.[29] It failed to reach its goal by 32 percent in March, and in April it fell 43 percent short.[30] Despite a narrowing of the shortfall in May to a 25 percent gap and a small surplus in June and July, total enlistments were likely to be off 10 percent for the army's 2004–2005 recruitment cycle.[31] The Marine Corps also fell short of its monthly goals beginning in January 2005, when it missed its target by 3 percent.[32] New enlistments fell 6 percent short in February, 2 percent in March, and 9 percent in April.[33] In March, the Army Reserve missed its goal of 1,600 new enlistments by 46 percent; as of April 2005 total annual recruitment was expected to fall short by 10 percent.[34] The National Guard was expected to fall 25 percent short of its objectives.[35] Retention problems have also increased as the Iraq War has continued. The impact on retention is difficult to measure because stop-loss regulations prevent soldiers assigned to units deployed or preparing for deployment from leaving the military at the end of their enlistments; one study estimates, though, that the war could lower retention by 22 percent for the National Guard and 15 percent for the regular army.[36]

A combination of falling recruitment and retention rates thus creates a double squeeze on U.S. ground forces. Because neither American naval nor airpower is as heavily committed to security operations as its ground forces, the U.S. still has considerable force-projection power and hence the ability to mount offensive military operations. In the event of a crisis, moreover, ground units slated for deployment to Iraq or Afghanistan would be sent elsewhere. Another major commitment of American ground forces would likely stretch American power dangerously thin, where two major ground operations could not be sustained for more than a short period. Finally, an abstract danger exists that the strain of fighting open-ended guerrilla wars could result in the sort of serious deterioration in the quality of American forces similar to that caused by the Vietnam War.

Economic Power

The War on Terror has been much more costly than expected. Whereas the Bush administration initially claimed that the combined cost of the war in Afghanistan and Iraq would be around $50 billion and much of the cost would be covered by Iraqi oil money, by 2005 the United States had spent $280 billion and was spending roughly $5 billion every month on military operations in Iraq and $900 million in Afghanistan.[37] The Congressional Budget Office (CBO) estimated in 2005 that total costs could reach over $450 billion over the next decade—assuming that the intensity of American involvement decreases progressively over time and that costs fall from $94 billion in 2006 to around $50 billion a year by the end of the decade.[38] These figures are the supplemental costs imposed by the War on Terror and do not include the regular cost of sustaining U.S. power. According to the Defense Department, regular military spending will rise from $375 billion in fiscal year (FY) 2004 to $402 billion in FY2005, $416 billion in FY2006, reaching $488 billion by FY2009.[39] In other words, the United States now spends about a half trillion dollars each year to sustain its military, with roughly more than 15 percent of the total going to fund ongoing combat operations; that figure is likely to increase to close to $550 billion by the end of the decade. In addition to these costs, the United States will also spend about $40 billion a year on homeland security.

While military spending has grown, tax cuts passed shortly after Bush took office in 2001 have erased the $230 billion surplus President Clinton handed over when he left office. By 2004, the gross federal budget deficit was $576 billion, according to the CBO, and the national debt had increased from $5.78 trillion in September 2001 to $7.75 trillion in May 2005.[40] As of 2005, the CBO projects the deficit to gradually decrease. Nevertheless, even assuming that annual deficits decrease, the total national debt will continue to grow for the foreseeable future, and as it grows the cost of financing the debt will increase (see Table I.4). Servicing the debt will, in fact, likely consume at least 15 percent of federal revenues each year and could constrain future increases in defense spending, particularly if the cost of the War on Terror does not decrease.[41] Some in Washington have already expressed concerns that the United States might not be able to afford the new advanced weapon systems that ensure its military edge.[42]

Compared to the size of the American economy, the deficit may not appear particularly large, roughly 5 percent of the gross domestic product (GDP);

Table I.4 Congressional Budget Office Deficit Projections (billions of dollars)

	FY2005	FY2006	FY2007	FY2008	FY2009	FY2010	FY2011
Gross deficit[a]	539	487	477	473	463	461	370
Net deficit	365	298	268	246	219	201	95
Estimated debt	4,296	4,661	4,959	5,227	5,475	5,693	5,988
Estimated debt service	322	350	372	392	410	427	442
Service/Revenues (%)	15.7	15.8	15.8	15.6	15.4	15.2	14.4

[a]The gross deficit is the simple difference between revenues and expenditures. The net deficit includes monies siphoned out of the Social Security surplus and transfers from the postal service. In theory, at least, transfers from the Social Security surplus are actually loans and hence must be paid back.

Source: Congressional Budget Office, "The Budget and Economic Outlook: Fiscal Years 2006 to 2015," http://www.cbo.gov.

hence, the funding the War on Terror should not strain the United States or threaten American hegemony. Complications, however, could arise from who holds the debt. Historically, the United States has financed a third of its annual debts by selling treasury bills to foreign investors. During most of the 1990s, Japan was the major buyer of these bills, followed by Great Britain and other members of the western alliance. In recent years, however, China has emerged as a major purchaser, using part of the dollars it earns from it trade surplus with the United States to buy U.S. government securities. In early 2003, it surpassed Great Britain as the second largest holder of U.S. public debt. By late 2004, China held over 10 percent of the total treasury debt owned by foreigners and close to 5 percent of the publicly held debt (see Table I.5). In total, China bought $243.5 billion worth of U.S. government securities between 2001 and 2004—over 10 percent of the new debt incurred since the beginning of the War on Terror.[43] Because the United States continues to run a large trade deficit with China, attempting to shift borrowing to domestic capital markets would likely prove difficult and could result in a significant increase in domestic interest rates.

Increased dependence on the Chinese to finance federal expenditures, including defense expenditures that exceed domestic revenues, places the United States in a complicated situation: Unlike Japan or Great Britain, which are long-time U.S. allies, China has never been part of the western alliance. In its early days, in fact, the Bush administration identified China as a potential rival. During the 2000 campaign, Bush called it "a competitor, not a strategic partner."[44] Other members of his administration, including those identified as "neo-cons," took a harder view. Deputy Secretary of State Paul Wolfowitz, for example, flatly stated that he considered China "the major strategic competitor and potential threat to the United States."[45] Condoleezza Rice described China as a "potential threat to stability in the Asia-Pacific region," a rising power that "resents the role of the United States." She went on to say that "this

Table I.5 Total U.S. Debt and Ownership of Debt (billions of dollars)

Date	Total	Held by Public	Foreign	Percent Foreign	China	Percent Foreign China	Percent Public China
1996	5,294.3	3,734.1	1,294.4	34.67	46.6	3.60	1.25
1998	5,580.2	3,721.1	1,288.9	34.64	46.4	3.60	1.25
2000	5,689.0	3,409.8	1,202.6	35.27	46.9	3.90	1.38
2002	6,339.8	3,540.4	1,203.7	34.00	102.9	8.55	2.91
2004	7,529.3	4,295.5	1,930.8	44.95	194.5	10.07	4.53

Sources: Department of the Treasury, Bureau of the Public Debt, "The Public Debt Online," http://www.publicdebt.treas.gov; U.S. Department of the Treasury, Office of Domestic Finance, "Quarterly Refunding Charts," http://www.treas.gov/.

means that China is not a 'status quo' power" and was hence a "strategic competitor," not a "strategic partner."[46]

After 9/11, the administration quickly dropped its anti-Chinese rhetoric and embraced China as a member of the global war on terror. Subsequently, after North Korea responded to its classification as a member of the axis of evil and talk of preemptive regime change by reactivating its nuclear weapons programs, the Bush administration looked to Beijing to leverage Pyongyang. However, Beijing has not stepped into the role cast for it by Washington policymakers. Instead of immediately ratcheting up the pressure on Pyongyang by shutting off the flow of crude oil and applying the diplomatic strong arm, Beijing signaled Washington that it ought to provide Pyongyang with assurances the United States will not seek regime change in return for a North Korean pledge to suspend further nuclear weapons development. Far from bowing to American hegemony, Beijing has in fact sought to leverage American weakness to its advantage, much to the chagrin and annoyance of the Bush administration, which sees Beijing's lack of action as contributing to the ongoing standoff.[47]

Three other factors contribute to tensions between the U.S. and Beijing. First, China's trade surplus with the United States continues to grow, generating increasingly shrill demands for actions to restrict and tax Chinese exports.[48] Second, the situation in the Taiwan Straits remains unstable. Beijing, on the one hand, enacted a new Anti-Succession Law, which at least on the surface threatens war if Taiwan declares independence; at the same time, it has been courting the Taiwanese opposition in a two-track effect to create pressure on Taipei to accept talks on reconciliation and to undermine and isolate President Chen Shui-bian. Washington, which formally espouses a "one China" policy but practices a "one China, one Taiwan" policy in which it seeks to maintain relations with both Beijing and Taipei, thus finds itself mired once more in the complicated and irresolvable dispute between the rival Chinas. Third, Sino-Japanese relations have soured in recent years as China has sought to establish itself as a regional power and has opposed a similar role for Japan, which has long been the main strategic partner of the United States in northeast Asia. Rising nationalism in both China and Japan has created an increasingly tense situation, which recently exploded into a massive anti-Japanese demonstration in China.

The situation in East Asia highlights the complex realities facing the United States and the constraints on American power. On the one hand, the United States seems to have few palatable options in dealing with North Korea. North Korea's ability to launch a conventional strike against South Korea likely checkmates any possible military action designed to take out North Korea's nuclear program, thus forcing the United States to rely on a multilateral diplomatic strategy. Its allies in that multilateral effort, however, do not necessarily share the Bush administration's grand strategic agenda and are increasingly at odds with each other. At the same time, the United States is heavily dependent on these same countries to finance its budget deficit. In much the same manner, the United States faces complex challenges in dealing with Iran, which also seems to have read the axis of evil message as a call to acquire nuclear weapons as a hedge against an American-backed regime change. Here too, the United States has the military capability to launch air and missile strikes against suspected weapons facilities but faces the possibility that Iran might retaliate against American forces in Iraq. A preemptive attack would also face stiff opposition from the Europeans and Russians.

Viewed relative to the demands placed on it, in sum, American power is more constrained than it appears in the absolute terms laid out in the preceding section of this chapter. Even with a sizable portion of its ground forces committed to operations in Iraq and Afghanistan, the United States retains a formidable capability to mount air and naval attacks. However, barring a significant reduction in the number of ground forces deployed in Iraq or a costly and—given increasing shortfalls in recruitment—difficult expansion of its ground forces, it now lacks the military wherewithal to mount the sort of preemptive war it launched against Iraq in March 2003. American power is further constrained by the fact that it is dependent on foreign financing of U.S. debt to sustain existing levels of defense spending. Simply by ceasing to buy treasury bills, countries like China or others opposed to a hypothetical preemptive war could squeeze the United States, forcing it to (1) cut back on politically sensitive domestic spending; (2) raise taxes, which the Bush administration is loathe to even consider; or (3) resort to inflationary fiscal policies. In a rather fundamental sense, therefore, American power is not truly autonomous because sustaining current levels of defense spending depends in part on the willingness of foreigners—including some whom members of the Bush administration view with considerable suspicion—to buy and hold American debt.

Political Power

The War on Terror has siphoned off American military power to fight the Iraqi insurgency and has forced the United States to rely on foreigners to fund its military effort. In addition, the manner in which the Bush administration chooses to conduct the war has undermined American power in less tangible, though equally significant, ways. Even before 9/11, Bush exhibited what some in the international community saw as the arrogance of a self-conscious and self-engrossed hegemon. Whereas the United States under the first Bush and Clinton seemed to shy away from assuming the role of global strongman and paramount leader, members of the new Bush administration seemed much more assertive. From the beginning the second Bush's rhetoric and behavior suggested a diminished commitment to the international order constructed by the United States during the Cold War that at times seemed to border on an outright distaste for multilateralism. Even before Bush was elected, for example, his main foreign policy adviser, Condoleezza Rice, made it clear that although the United States would not use its military force for national advantage, a future Bush administration would also look cautiously at the demands of international organizations because it would proceed from the firm ground of the national interest—not from "the interests of an illusory international community."[49] Once in office, President Bush demonstrated his administration's lack of interest in supporting, let alone underwriting, many of the international institutions the country built after World War II. In short order, he pulled the United States out of the Kyoto Protocol, unilaterally abrogated the Anti-Ballistic Missile Treaty, tacitly withdrew from the Comprehensive Test Ban Treaty (which the United States signed but never ratified), rejected the biological weapons convention, and withdrew from negotiations about the International Criminal Court.

For a time, the Bush administration's go-it-alone posturing seemed to disappear in the immediate aftermath of 9/11, as it focused on building a broad coalition to fight terror. Indeed, in the few months following the terrorist attacks, the president received much praise from abroad for his patience. In reality, the nature of the administration was masked temporarily by the spontaneous emergence of a broad antiterror coalition and immediate international recognition of the U.S. right to strike back against Al-Qaeda, its Afghan allies, and the loose confederation of terrorists associated with Osama bin Laden. Even as it talked publicly about international coalitions and collective defense against terror, behind closed doors members of the Bush administration were formulating a new American grand strategy, which has become known popularly as the Bush Doctrine. The new strategy assumes that global stability requires the maintenance of a unipolar international system dominated by the United States, free of potential challengers.[50] In the nuanced language of the formal doctrine, "The U.S. national security strategy will be based on a distinctly American internationalism that reflects the union of our values and our national interests. The aim of this strategy is to help make the world not just safer but better."[51]

Fighting terror was, of course, a central part of the new doctrine. But rather than stress the elimination of groups such as Al-Qaeda, the new doctrine claimed that the United States had a right to take action not only against "imminent threats" but to take "… anticipatory action to defend ourselves, even if uncertainty remains as to the time and place of the enemy's attack. To forestall or prevent such hostile acts by our adversaries, the United States will, if necessary, act preemptively."[52]

Preemption, according to the authors of the doctrine, included the right to force regime change designed to rid the international system of anti-status quo states. As bluntly articulated by Assistant Secretary of Defense Wolfowitz, It's not just simply a matter of capturing people and holding them accountable, but removing the sanctuaries, removing the support systems, ending states who sponsor terrorism."[53]

The extent to which the Bush administration saw itself as unfettered by the international community and by the multilateralism that had characterized American foreign policy during previous administrations was evident in the run up to the 2003 attack on Iraq. Determined to overthrow Saddam Hussein, the administration was clearly reluctant to even consult with organizations such as the United Nations, which some in the administration saw as an impediment in the war on terror. And it was only under considerable pressure from Tony Blair and others that Bush agreed to new arms inspections and later sent Colin Powell to New York in an attempt to convince the security council that Hussein's possession of weapons of mass destruction, support for international terrorism, and gross violation of human rights justified war. When the international community balked, Bush pressed ahead, with some members of his inner circle and his partisan allies seeming to go out of their way to express their utter contempt for those refusing to stand with the United States. In their view, the United States had the right—perhaps even a duty—to lead without regard for the views of others.

The bitterness and rancor accompanying the Iraq war's opening did not, ultimately, shatter the long-standing western alliance or trigger the formation of a new anti-American bloc. But it clearly left the United States weaker in intangible ways. As noted earlier, Nye argues a soft dimension to power derives from the willingness of others to recognize a state's legitimate right to lead. In the aftermath of 9/11, there was little question that the world grieved for the United States. Virtually without exception, people around the world—even in the Middle East where support for Islamic fundamentalism had been rising—sympathized with Americans' pain and not only conceded the United States the right to strike back but also even expressed a willingness to support it.

The attack on Iraq rapidly dissipated support for the new aggressive American foreign policy, even among some of the country's most faithful long-term western allies. The most significant changes were in the views of the United States as a country. In Great Britain, those holding favorable views of the United States fell from 75 percent in summer 2002 to 48 percent in March 2003, while those having very unfavorable views increased from 4 percent to 16 percent.[54] In France, whose government opposed the invasion, favorable views of the United States fell from 63 percent to 31 percent; in Germany, whose government also opposed the war, views fell from 61 percent to 25 percent. The percentage of those expressing very unfavorable views, meanwhile, jumped from 8 percent to 22 percent in France, from 4 percent to 30 percent in Germany, and from 4 percent to 16 percent in Great Britain. Moreover, many of those polled believe the United States does what it wants, with little consideration of the opinions of other countries. In fact, fully

84 percent of those surveyed in France in 2004 and 61 percent of those surveyed in Germany said the United States acts with little to no attention to their interests. In the Islamic world, anti-Americanism surged to new highs, inflamed in part by graphic images of the suffering of innocent Iraqis caught up in the crossfire and by the concurrent intensification of the conflict between Palestinians and Israeli forces in the occupied territories.

Despite some recovery in the wake of the January 2005 elections in Iraq, support for the United States has never recovered to nearly the level it had been in late 2001. At the same time, the decline in American favorability abroad has led to a widening gap between foreign and American perceptions of U.S. behavior, with more than 75 percent of all Americans and nearly all those identifying as Republicans believing that U.S. foreign policy takes into account other nation's interests.[55]

Yet declining support for American foreign policy or even negative images of the United States do not mean that American soft power has crumbled. As Nye points out, soft power derives not only from attitudes toward not only a government's action but also cultural and social factors beyond a government's control. In these areas, it is less clear that American soft power is waning. As evidenced by popular revolutions in Armenia, the Ukraine, Lebanon, and Kyrgyzstan, there is widespread support for democratization and political liberalism, which are key elements of American foreign policy. Although there had not been a significant deepening of hostility toward Americans or violence directed against Americans abroad, some opinion polls suggest that favorable views of Americans are also on the decline. In 2002, for example, some 80 percent of those polled in Great Britain and 71 percent in France had a favorable view of the American population; two years later, this dropped to 70 percent in Great Britain and just over 50 percent in France. In fact, in every single country polled, the positive image of American people has declined. Numbers such as these and the results of other polls have thus led some to argue that the stereotypes of Americans as arrogant, self-indulgent, hypocritical, and unwilling or unable to engage in cross-cultural dialogue are now pervasive and deeply rooted.[56] This, indeed, may say something about the lure of American culture and soft power.

In fact, although Americans and global opinion embrace common values, American soft power remains intact even as the credibility of the Bush administration has decreased sharply.

The Bush Policies in Practice

History often provides the best guide for understanding and evaluating current policies. The first three chapters of this volume, by John Gerard Ruggie, Edward C. Luck, and Jack Donnelly, use history and international relations theory to explain and differentiate current U.S. policies from previous administrations. Ruggie focuses on the historical and theoretical roots of America's exceptionalism and exemptionalism, arguing that these factors combined to structure both American foreign policy behavior and the international system after 1945. In his complementary analysis on the UN charter's proscription on the unilateral use of force, Luck shows that despite its overwhelming military advantage at the end of World War II, the United States wrote in legal constraints on the use of that power, a factor which helps explain why the United States did not act as a stereotypical great power. He shows that while the U.S. government at that time was not completely and single-mindedly committed to Article 2(4), its articulation of that norm expressed its hopes for the postwar world. Using the English School of International Relations theory, Donnelly looks at how hegemonic power is constructed. In this view, states are not billiard balls interacting in a vacuum but are part of a society of states, and accepted state practices structure global politics. Donnelly shows that despite sovereignty's supposed equality for all states, forms of inequality and hierarchies were not uncommon throughout history. All three authors place an emphasis on the central part multilateralism and negotiated arrangements have played in the past, which sets the stage for an evaluation of the pronounced unilateralism of George W. Bush's foreign policy.

Not only have the principles governing U.S. foreign policy changed, according to the more focused analyses of Jon Western and Karen A. Mingst, but its conduct has also been greatly altered by the demise of *defensive realism,* or the belief that national security was best achieved through primarily defensive means. Western argues that although the Bush administration has indeed eliminated hostile regimes in Afghanistan and Iraq, the application of the Bush Doctrine has ignored, if not sparked, other threats posing significant dangers to the United States and has fueled growing anti-Americanism. Whereas Mingst recognizes the United States has always used a mixture of multilateralism and unilateralism in its foreign policy, she finds that the Bush administration has identified a broad array of enemies and has crafted foreign policy in absolute terms. She argues that Bush policy seeks not only to deter terrorism or to remove a select set of tyrants but also is bent on transforming the international system. These grandiose ends are matched by an often strident emphasis on unilateral means; hence, the United States has forgone benefits of multilateralism and has incurred greater risks.

Focusing on the home front and the impact of domestic structures in the United States, Ole R. Holsti finds that even though 9/11 set the stage for the Bush administration's adoption of a new grand strategy, this event did not fundamentally transform some of the constraints that have in the past militated against an expansive foreign policy.[57] Based on extensive survey data from both the pre- and post-9/11 period, Holsti finds surprising continuity, rather than differences, in American opinions on foreign affairs. He finds that the 9/11 attacks have not pushed Americans toward isolationism or a retrenchment from the world. On the contrary, the public remains highly pragmatic and skeptical of unilateralism and imperial primacy.

Loch K. Johnson, on the other hand, finds that Congressional oversight in general, and especially supervision of the U.S. intelligence establishment, remains lax. Thus, at least in the short term, Congress is not a very powerful constraint for the Bush administration because of party loyalty.

If some scholars are right in thinking that the United States has averted imperial overreach in the past because of its domestic institutions, then these chapters are insightful. Without directly saying so, they suggest that any costly shifts in foreign policy on the part of the Bush administration are not likely to last. Continuing difficulties in Afghanistan and Iraq are likely to show up in increased congressional disquiet and willingness to tighten oversight as a reflection of skeptical public opinion. At the time of this writing, public opinion polls were showing precisely this increased domestic concern.

Conrad C. Crane and Mark Peceny evaluate two of the most pressing challenges facing the Bush administration: nation building and democracy promotion. Drawing on historical examples of state stabilization and reconstruction, with particular focus on military roles and missions, Crane highlights the numerous difficulties involved in transplanting liberal democratic values and institutions, especially to non-Western societies such as Afghanistan and Iraq. He argues that the American military is not structured to perform such operations and is reluctant to act as a state builder; in addition, American civilian agencies lack the resources to assume responsibility for such operations. Peceny's chapter brings together international and domestic politics, asserting that even though the United States may instrumentally promote democracy as a means to justify military intervention to a domestic audience and its allies, local actors frequently recognize the value of embracing the cause of democracy. Consequently, efforts to promote democracy often produce some degree of political liberalization and limited electoral competition but rarely lead to fully consolidated democracy. Focusing on human rights and enemy detainees, David P. Forsythe shows that in its determination to eliminate terrorism, the Bush administration has violated many human rights and humanitarian standards that previous administrations endorsed. In the process, the Bush team lost the high moral ground, and much soft power, in its war on terrorism and made its relations particularly with the Arab–Muslim world much more difficult.[58]

Robert J. Lieber, Mel Gurtov, and Mahmood Monshipouri examine three regional challenges to U.S. power: Europe, Asia, and the Middle East. According to Lieber, a long list of disputes notwithstanding, predictions about an imminent divorce between the United States and Europe are premature. In his view, Europe's lack of unanimity on foreign and security policy and a shared interest in transatlantic cooperation as well as common values will require a continuing partnership between the United States and Europe. Whereas

Lieber is optimistic about the western alliance, Gurtov sees the United States facing mounting challenges in Asia. He argues that (1) the appearance of a united front in the war on terror masks potentially compromising alignments with repressive leaderships in Central Asia, Pakistan, and Indonesia; (2) relations with China are likely to turn sour because of U.S.–Japan military cooperation, U.S. arms sales to Taiwan, and U.S. deployments in Central Asia; and (3) U.S. handling of North Korea endangers its relationships with long-standing allies. Monshipouri too is skeptical about the ability of the U.S. effort to stabilize the Middle East. Despite a groundswell of support for democratic reforms, the deep roots of Middle Eastern authoritarianism, suspicion of American motives, a complex and shifting political context, and the lack of any sort of workable blueprint suggest that progress will be slow and uncertain. Moreover, he argues that democratic reforms in the region must be accompanied by a settlement of the Palestinian–Israeli and broader Arab–Israeli conflicts.

The challenges to American power are not, of course, limited to those emanating from the various regions covered in this volume. The continually morphing crisis in sub-Saharan Africa has created a zone of instability and chaos stretching across the continent. Despite the tragic human toll of a series of bloody civil wars, the Bush administration has opted for a strategy of benign neglect, intervening only when the chaos threatens to spiral out of control and even then making only minimal, short-term commitments of U.S. power. In other instances such as the Darfur genocide, it has opted for a plodding, ad hoc multilateral approach of the very sort it has denounced as an ineffectual alternative to decisive unilateral action. Its major policy initiative, the Millennium Challenge, promised $10 billion in aid to the continent, but Congress has appropriated only $3 billion, of which a mere fraction has actually been spent.[59] In cold strategic terms, mayhem, death, and poverty in Africa—no matter how tragic—need not threaten the security of the United States; moreover, when prioritized against more pressing dangers the Bush administration's decision to push the continent to the back burner may represent a rational allocation of scarce resources.

At the time of writing, it is much less certain that the Bush administration can similarly ignore emerging threats in Latin America. Despite increased assistance and support from the United States, Columbia continues to suffer from the destabilizing effects of *narcoterrorism*. Narcotics traffickers have also emerged as a dangerous destabilizing force in parts of northern Mexico. Bolivia and Ecuador teeter on the verge of internal upheaval. More critically, the United States has become locked into a standoff with Venezuelan President Hugo Chavez. Covert efforts to encourage regime change have failed. With oil prices already hovering around $60 a barrel, with the possibility they could rise to $70, a deepening of the crisis could trigger a serious international oil crisis and an economic crisis in the United States: With between 52.5 and

77.8 billion barrels in know reserves, Venezuela has the seventh largest proven reserves of oil, is the seventh largest oil provider in the world, and is the fourth largest exporter to the United States, providing nearly 13 percent of U.S. oil needs.[60]

Compared to the challenges to American power in the Middle East, Asia, and Europe, the demands emanating from Africa and Latin America are more abstract, amorphous, and potential. In the interest of brevity, we have therefore opted to omit separate chapters on these regions. It is important to note that even though the demands on American power in these regions may be less than in other regions, they cannot be isolated: The sum of demands affects the sustainability of U.S. power. Thus, even though endless instability and grinding poverty in Africa may not be a direct threat to U.S. security and most of the worst-case scenarios in Latin America may never come to fruition, new demands from these regions could suddenly and unexpectedly undermine U.S. hegemony.

Conclusion

In the wake of 9/11, many people argued that everything had changed. The Cold War became history, and the world entered a new era: the global War on Terror, in which the United States appeared to have unequalled power. Moreover, the attacks on the World Trade Center and the Pentagon rallied the American people behind a global assault on the enemies of civilization and brought forth a vast Global Coalition against Terrorism. Means and will, therefore, came together to an extent not seen since Pearl Harbor, and in short order, the coalition of the willing decapitated the regime in Afghanistan and launched a global campaign against Al-Qaeda and its Taliban allies. The American military colossus then turned on Iraq and in a matter of weeks had obliterated the Iraqi army and had stormed into Baghdad, forcing Saddam Hussein to hide in a hole in the ground. Having driven out all before them, hard line neoconservatives in Washington began talking about taking the fight to Syria and Iran.

Four years later, the triumph of the early days of the War on Terror has faded. American forces remain embroiled in a nasty, deadly, and—at least to some—intractable insurgency in Iraq. The grand antiterror coalition has fragmented and shrunken. Osama bin Laden remains at large, free to periodically taunt the United States and to praise the most bloodthirsty elements of the Iraqi insurgency. A new generation of Jihadists has reportedly rushed to the central front in the War on Terror in hopes that they can turn Iraq into America's Afghanistan and inflict a crushing blow to the crusader-Zionist alliance. In Afghanistan, the Taliban has slowly reemerged from the ashes of its defeat to once again threaten coalition forces. Despite some potential progress in summer 2005, the North Korean mess remains unresolved. Iran not only continues to refuse to curtail its nuclear program but also has recently lurched away from reform and back toward conservative Islam. In the United States, American support for the Iraq war is declining.[61] Amid new pessimism, the *New York Times* responded to the Bush administration's June 28, 2005, attempt to rally support for the war effort by asking, "How many more times over how many years" will the president "have to deliver the same message of patience and resolve?"[62] Far from dictating outcomes, the United States seems only able to cope.

In a sense, this volume seeks to answer a fundamental question: Why, given its great preponderance of coercive power—power not only unrivaled by any other state or potential combination of states in the existing international system but also unprecedented in history—has the United States been unable to shape outcomes in the manner envisioned by strategic planners in Washington? This is not to say that the Bush administration has failed or that the United States faces defeat in the War on Terror; on the contrary, the current administration has succeeded in radically reshaping the international system since 9/11. What is clear, however, is that the application of American power has achieved much less than it seemed capable of in the immediate wake of 9/11.

The authors in this volume demonstrate what the power literature advances: that power is not a property but a relationship; it is relative and not absolute, and the use of power comes at a cost. Arrayed against any single threat or a finite set of threats, American resources appear overwhelming, but when compared to a variety of demands in different sectors and with some consideration of opportunity costs, American power suddenly seems less impressive. What our analysis of the post-9/11 period highlights—and perhaps we should reiterate—is that coercive capability is not power, and it is certainly not hegemonic power. Power is a complex relationship comprised of a combination of force, diplomacy, economic resources, and an almost undefinable thing called *soft power*. Contrary to what Mao Zedong claimed, power does not grow out of the barrel of a gun. Clearly the gun matters, as does the person wielding it, but the gun and its holder are merely two parts of a more complex dynamic.

The power that really matters to the lone superpower—hegemonic power—emerges from its ability to convince others it wields the gun in a legitimate manner that serves not only its own self-interest but also that of the larger group. American unipolarity has failed to live up to expectations because its unipolar position has not been successfully married to leadership. In the immediate post-9/11 months, the United States led and hence was powerful. But since the end of the Afghan operation, its command and leadership has diminished, and its military might has proven to be a second-best substitute. Sustaining American hegemonic power is then less a matter of continuing to generate the military resources that have given the United States strategic dominance in crude terms than a matter of ensuring American power does not rest on military might alone.

Notes

1. Josef Joffe, "Defying History and Theory: The United States as the 'Last Remaining Superpower,'" in *America Unrivaled: The Future of the Balance of Power,* ed. G. John Ikenberry (Ithaca: Cornell University Press, 2002), 155–80.
2. "The National Security Strategy of the United States of America" (September 2002), http://www.whitehouse.gov/nsc/nss.pdf.
3. David A. Baldwin, *Paradoxes of Power* (New York: Basil Blackwell Inc., 1989), 2–4; Joseph Nye, Jr., *The Paradox of American Power* (New York: Oxford University Press, 2002).
4. Ibid., 131–146.
5. Robert Dahl, *Modern Political Analysis* (Upper Saddle River, NJ: Prentice Hall, 1991), 29.
6. See Peter Bachrach and Morton S. Baratz, "Two Faces of Power," *American Political Science Review* 56, no. 4 (December 1962): 947–952; Bachrach and Baratz, "Decision and Nondecisions: An Analytical Framework," *American Political Science Review* 57 no. 3 (September 1963), 632–642.
7. Stephen Lukes, *Power: A Radical View* (London: Macmillan, 1974), 24.
8. See Joseph S. Nye, *The Paradox of American Power* (Oxford: Oxford University Press, 2002), 8–12l; Nye, *Bound to Lead: The Changing Nature of American Power* (New York: BasicBooks, 1990), 32–35.
9. Kenneth Waltz, *Theory of International Politics* (New York: McGraw-Hill, 1979), 130.
10. There is a long-standing debate about whether the United States was in fact a hegemonic power prior to 1991. For more on this, see Christopher Layne, "The Unipolar Illusion: Why New Great Powers Will Rise," *International Security* 17, no. 4 (Spring 1993), 4–14.
11. Ikenberry, "Democracy, Institutions, and American Restraint," in *America Unrivaled* (see note 1), 215.
12. Joffe, "Defying History," 155.
13. John G. Ruggie, "The Anatomy of an Institution," in *Multilateralism Matters: The Theory and Praxis of an Institutional Form,* ed. Ruggie (New York: Columbia University, 1993), 11.
14. Ikenberry, "Introduction," in *America Unrivaled* (see note 1), 1.
15. This shift in strategy has been called a "retrenchment," even though the number of overseas military operations was actually higher than in the latter days of the Cold War. See Charles A. Kupchan, "Hollow Hegemony or Stable Multipolarity?" in *America Unrivaled* (see note 1), 82–90.
16. Cited in Michael Hirsh, "Bush and the World," *Foreign Affairs* 81, no. 5 (September–October 2002), 41.
17. Michael Mastanduno, "Incomplete Hegemony and Security Order in the Asia-Pacific," in *America Unrivaled* (see note 1), 186.
18. Based on data from Stockholm International Peace Research Institute (SIPRI), Military Expenditure Database, http://www.sipri.org.
19. Chinese defense spending is based on SIPRI's estimate of total spending. Official spending is considerably lower. Other sources, including the International Institute for Strategic Studies (IISS) and the U.S. State Department, estimate total Chinese defense spending to be at least twice that estimated by SIPRI. Even if we use these higher estimates, the fact remains that China spends a fraction of what the U.S. spends. See the International Institute for Strategic Studies *The Military Balance* (London: Oxford University Press), various years; and U.S. State Department, Bureau of Verification and Compliance, *World Military Expenditures and Arms Transfers, 1999–2000.*
20. Globalsecurity.org, "Readiness," http://globalsecurity.org/military/agency/army/readiness.htm.
21. Under the terms of the 2002 Treaty on Strategic Offensive Reductions both are supposed to cut their total arsenal to between 1,700 and 2,200 by 2012. Treaty text available at Bureau of Public Affairs, "Treaty between the United States of America and the Russian Federation on Strategic Offensive Reductions," http://state.gov/t/ac/trt/18016.htm#1.
22. Daniel Ellsberg, "The Crude Analysis of Strategic Choices," *American Economic Review* 51, no. 2 (May 1961), 472–78.
23. At the time of this writing, the American force in Iraq consisted of 73,000 regular army soldiers; 17,000 army reservists; 37,000 national guard; 26,000 marines; and 17,000 Air Force personnel and sailors.
24. "Testimony of the Joint Chiefs of Staff before the Committee on Armed Services, United States House of Representatives, Regarding the Fiscal Year 2005 National Defense Budget

25. Peter Hatemi, "The U.S. Military: Over-deployed and Under-manned: Who Ya Gonna Call … Up?" (unpublished paper Department of Political Science, University of Nebraska–Lincoln, May 2004), 4.
26. See also Lynn E. Davis and others, *Stretched Thin: Army Forces for Sustained Operations* (Santa Monica, CA: Rand Corporation, 2005).
27. Units are limited to 24 months of active service, after which they can only be reactivated in the event of a full-scale mobilization.
28. "Operation Iraqi Freedom U.S. Casualty Status," http://www.defenselink.mil/news/casualty.pdf. Approximately 190 soldiers from other members of the coalition were reported dead, along with at least 2,900 Iraqi national guard and police; see iCasualties, "Iraq Coalition Casualty Count," http://icasualties.org/oif/IraqiDeaths.aspx. Between 160 and 200 private security contractors have also died; see Daniel Bergner, "The Other Army," *New York Times Magazine*, August 14, 2005, p. 29. Estimates of Iraqi civilian casualties range from 23,600 to 26,700; see "Iraq Body Count," http://www.iraqbodycount.net/. Rough estimates by the Brookings Institution suggest that some 45,000 Iraqi insurgents have died or were captured as of July 2005; see The Brookings Institution, "Iraq Index," July 2005, available at brookings.edu/fp/sabana/index.pdf.
29. Tom Shanker, "Army Likely to Miss 2 Recruiting Goals, Review is Planned." *New York Times*, March 24, 2005.
30. Jamie Wilson, "US Army Cuts Tour of Duty as Recruitment Declines," *The Guardian*, May 14, 2005.
31. Eric Schmitt, "For First Time in Months, Army Meets its Recruiting Goals," *New York Times*, June 30, 2005; "Army Recruiting Continues to Lag," *Associated Press*, June 9, 2005; "Army Reaches July Goal," *Associated Press*, August 10, 2005. The army, however, decreased its monthly target from 8,000 to 6,700 in May.
32. Robert Burns, "Marines Fall Short of Recruiting Goal," *Associated Press*, 2/3/05 and Jim Miklaszewski, "Army, Marines Miss Recruiting Goal Again," *MSNBC News*, 5/10/05.
33. "Army Recruiting Down for Third Month in a Row," *Agence France Presse*, 5/3/05.
34. "Army Still Missing Recruiting Targets," *Chicago Tribune*, April 1, 2005.
35. Rowan Scanborough, "Army Falls Short of Recruiting Goals by 6 percent," *Washington Times*, April 7, 2005. As of July 2005, the National Guard had reached its recruiting targets only twice in nineteen months. That month, it fell 20 percent short of its goal; see "Army Reaches July Goal, *Associated Press*, August 10, 2005.
36. Hatemi, "The U.S. Military," 31–33.
37. Supplemental appropriations totaled $13.6 billion in fiscal year (FY) 2001, $17.2 billion in FY2002, $78.6 billion in FY2003, $88.1 billion in FY2004, and $82.0 billion in FY2005; see Congressional Budget Office (CBO), "The Budget and Economic Outlook," August 2005, available at cbo.gov/showdoc.cfm?index=6609&sequence=0.
38. Amy Belasco, "The Costs of Operations in Iraq, Afghanistan, and Enhanced Security," *CRS Report for Congress* no. RS21644, March 2005.
39. Department of Defense, "National Defense Budget Estimates for FY2006," available at http://www.mil/comptroller/defbudget/FY2006/FY2006_greenbook.
40. Bureau of the Public Debt, "The Public Debt Online," http://www.publicdebt.treas.gov/opd/opd.htm.
41. Estimated interest costs assumes debt service costs equal to the 7.5 percent cost level of 2004. In fact, service costs have averaged 9.5 percent over the past fifteen years. At that higher rate, debt service would consume approximately 20 percent of federal revenues.
42. The Department of Defense, for example, has reportedly begun to consider whether it might have to scale back planned purchases of the DDX Zumwalt destroyer, the F-35 Joint Strike Fighter (the replacement for the mainstay F-16), and the F-22 Raptor stealth fighter. Mark Mazzetti, "Pentagon May Scrap Jet Plans," *LAT*, July 27, 2005.
43. Government Accounting Office (GAO), "International Trade: Treasury Assessments Have Not Found Currency Manipulation, but Concerns about Exchange Rates Continue," GAO-05-351, April 19, 2005, 34.
44. Governor George W. Bush, "A Distinctly American Internationalism," Speech at the Ronald Reagan Presidential Library, Simi Valley, California, November 19, 1999.

45. "Testimony of Paul Wolfowitz before the U.S. Senate Committee on Commerce, Science, and Transportation," September 17, 1998, p. 3, available at http://commerce.senate.gov/hearings/0917wol.pdf.
46. Condoleezza Rice, "Promoting the National Interest," *Foreign Affairs* 79, no. 1 (January–February 2000), 56; Robert Kagan, "Viva What Difference?" *Washington Post*, September 24, 2000, B07.
47. At points, the standoff has degenerated into an exchange of insults. In late April 2005, for example, Bush called Kim Jong-il a "tyrant" and a "dangerous person" and Secretary of State Rice branded North Korea an "outpost of tyranny." The North Koreans responded by calling Bush a "hooligan," "philistine," and "dictator." China rebuked Bush saying that he ought to measure his words more carefully, but the White House, in turn, shrugged off China's criticism. Pyongyang also called Assistant Secretary of State John Bolton "human scum." "North Korea Says Its Expects No Solution to Nuclear Standoff While 'Hooligan' Bush in Office" *Associated Press*, April 30, 2005; Jean-Louis Dorbles, "Bolton Brouhaha Bruises Bush," *Agence France Presse*, May 13, 2005.
48. GAO, "International Trade," 34. In July 2005, China removed one point of contention by revaluing the *renminbi*, but by only a fraction of what critics believe to be its total undervaluation.
49. Ibid., 62.
50. Michael E. O'Hanlon, Susan E. Rice, and James B. Steinberg, "The New National Security Strategy and Preemption" (Brookings Institution policy brief no. 113, December 2002).
51. "National Security Strategy," 1.
52. Ibid., 15.
53. http://www.pbs.org/wgbh/pages/frontline/shows/iraq/etc/cron.html. Moderates like Colin Powell distanced themselves from Wolfowitz's remarks.
54. The Pew Global Attitudes Project, "A Year after Iraq," http://pewglobal.org.
55. The number of Americans holding favorable views of key European countries (the United Kingdom, Germany, and France), meanwhile, declined from 74 percent in 2002 to 65 percent in 2004, while the number holding favorable views of Turkey, Morocco, Pakistan, and Jordan fell from 34 percent in 2002 to 29 percent in 2004. http://pewglobal.org/reports/pdf/206.pdf.
56. Peter G. Peterson, "Public Diplomacy and the War on Terror," *Foreign Affairs* 81 no. 5 (September–October 2002), 75.
57. For more on this, see Jack Snyder, *Myths of Empire: Domestic Politics and International Ambition* (Ithaca, NY: Cornell University Press, 1991).
58. On domestic institutions and foreign policy, see Synder, *Myths of Empire*, 255–304.
59. "Bush Aid Initiative for Poor Nations Faces Sharp Budget Cuts and Criticism," *New York Times*, June 17, 2005.
60. U.S. Department of Energy, Energy Information Administration, *International Energy Annual, 2000*, http://www.eia.doe.gov/iea/contents.html.
61. According to CNN/*USA Today*/Gallop polls, whereas 72 percent of those surveyed in March 2003 favored the war, by June 2005, the number had fallen to 39 percent. Polls conducted by ABC and the *Washington Post* show the number of those saying the war was worthwhile had declined from 70 percent in April 2003 to 46 percent in June 2005. Data available at http:// www.pollingreport.com.
62. Richard W. Stevenson, "Staying the Course," *New York Times*, June 29, 2005, A8.

1
Doctrinal Unilateralism and Its Limits: America and Global Governance in the New Century

JOHN GERARD RUGGIE

This chapter assesses the shift toward American unilateralism during the first administration of President George W. Bush and what it means for global governance. I am not interested in routine unilateral acts, which are a standard practice of states, especially when taken in self-defense. The particular form of unilateralism that concerns me here is the doctrinal belief that the use of American power abroad is entirely self-legitimating, requiring no recourse to the views or interests of others and permitting no external constraints on its self-ascribed aims. By global governance, in turn, I mean the constellation of treaty-based and customary international law, shared norms, institutions, and practices by which the international community as a whole seeks to manage its common affairs.

Are America and global governance on a collision course? If so, how did that come to be? And what are the consequences—for the United States and for the rest of the world?

This chapter has two aims, the first of which is to place the resurgence of American doctrinal unilateralism into its historical and conceptual contexts, in the hope that doing so will help us to understand it better. The second goal is to argue that, despite the vast power asymmetries that exist between the United States and the rest of the world, especially in the military realm, it is not as easy as it may seem at first blush for the United States to sustain such a unilateralist posture today. One major reason, ironically, is the success of America's own post-World War II strategy of creating an integrated global order, inhabited by a diversity of state and nonstate actors and based on the animating principles—if not always the practice—of democracy, the rule of law, and multilateralism. Thus, the United States is locked in a struggle today not only with its allies and other states but also with the results of its own creation—and, in that sense, with its own sense of self as a nation.

On Change and Continuity

Diplomatic History, the official journal of the Society for Historians of American Foreign Relations, published a roundtable discussion recently about what is new and what is not in the foreign policy of President George W. Bush, focused in particular on its unilateralism.[1] Melvyn Leffler, a realist by orientation and whose introductory essay is the focal point for the debate, stresses elements of continuity: Samuel Flagg Bemis, Leffler reminds us, described Theodore Roosevelt's interventions in the Caribbean and Central America as *protective imperialism.* "... The wise men of the Harry Truman administration worked brilliantly to forge alliances, but they never foreswore the right to act unilaterally ... When they perceived threats, especially in the Third World, U.S. officials during the Cold War did not refrain from acting unilaterally"—Leffler notes Vietnam in particular. Even President Bill Clinton is said to have followed course, continuing to build up America's military might and to preserve "the right to act unilaterally and to strike preemptively." What did change during the first Bush administration, Leffler concludes, is that the existential threat posed by 9/11 led policymakers to permit the assertion of American ideals and principles, such as liberty and democracy promotion, to trump the "careful calculation of interests [that] is essential to discipline American power and temper its ethnocentrism." But he finds ample historical precedent for that tendency as well at previous points of major crisis.[2]

Other contributors to the roundtable criticize Leffler from both sides. One charges him contentiously with not identifying and explaining yet a deeper, and different, source of continuity: *"choosing* a war nearly every generation seem[s] to be part of *core U.S. national identity."*[3] Most of the others accuse him of overlooking critical discontinuities. Says one, "If policy has only been recalibrated [by the Bush administration] rather than changed, why are we discussing [it] in these papers and why are so many foreign policy historians and analysts expressing concern?"[4]

As illuminating as this debate may be, ultimately it remains unsatisfactory because the narratives it presents are conceptually thin, and its core analytical elements are underspecified. Thus, I propose to view the issue of American unilateralism through somewhat more refined lenses, thereby constructing some building blocks of an argument that should permit a more systematic assessment of recent trends in U.S. foreign policy—and their sustainability in the years ahead.

American Exceptionalism

As a nation, America was not only born free, Robert Keohane once remarked; it was also "born lucky."[5] For much of its history before the turn of the twentieth century, the United States—far removed from the constant jostling of European power politics, heavily self-sufficient, able to grow into continental scale, protected by oceans on either side and adjoined by relatively weak and usually friendly neighbors to the north and south, and a magnet attracting a constant inflow of newcomers eager to make a fresh start—luxuriated in the posture described by John Quincy Adams of being "the well-wisher to the freedom and independence of all … the champion and vindicator only of her own."[6] Thus, America's traditional aversion to "entangling alliances," first expressed in George Washington's farewell address, flowed naturally from its geopolitical constitution.[7] By 1823, the United States felt sure enough of itself for President James Monroe to enunciate the doctrine that the United States would view as "an unfriendly disposition" any European intervention in the Americas, though until the end of the nineteenth century the British navy, for reasons of its own, undoubtedly played a greater role in safeguarding the Monroe Doctrine than did the United States itself.

By the turn of the century, however, the world was closing in on the United States. On September 5, 1901, President William McKinley delivered a major address on America's new role in the world at the new century's first world's fair in Buffalo, New York. "God and men have linked nations together," he said. "No nation can longer be indifferent to any other."[8] The very next day, at the same place, McKinley was assassinated, making Theodore Roosevelt (or TR as he was known) the nation's president. TR picked up on McKinley's theme and carried it a step further a few months later in his first State of the Union message: "The increasing interdependence and complexity of international political and economic relations," he declared, "render it incumbent on all civilized and orderly powers to insist on the proper policing of the world."[9] The dilemma, however, was how to interest an unconcerned country—the Congress as well as the public—in that mission.

For the McKinley and Roosevelt administrations the issue initially was quite unproblematic: The United States would have to behave like other great powers, for the simple reason that it, like the European great powers, was affected by and in turn helped shape the global balance of power. It alone would decide when and how to act abroad in accordance with its self-defined interests. And so McKinley took the country on a brief imperialist fling following the Spanish–American War of 1898, fought on flawed if not false premises; he also annexed Hawaii and the Philippines while making a protectorate of Cuba. For his part, TR instigated the creation of the state of Panama and built the isthmus canal, and he issued a corollary to the Monroe Doctrine, whereby the United States claimed the right to intervene in the affairs of its southern neighbors. For good measure, TR sent the entire American fleet on a symbolic around-the-world cruise to demonstrate that the United States had arrived as a global player.

But the "fever of imperialism," as David Fromkin describes it,[10] died down quickly, stymied by Congressional purse strings and declining public interest, though interventions in Central America and the Caribbean continued in response to real and imagined threats to the security of the canal and the sanctity of American investments. In short, while the United States was becoming increasingly powerful, conventional *raison d'état* as a basis for global engagement held little allure for the American people, who refused to see their nation as a normal great power, doing what great powers supposedly did.

Teddy Roosevelt was frustrated by this lack of interest in global engagement, but in the process he also discovered one promising way to mobilize the country behind that agenda—by tapping into strains of American exceptionalism.[11] Searching for the right formula, he invoked, with equal enthusiasm, a mixture of piety, patriotism, and jingoism—so much so that, in John Milton Cooper's biography of TR and Woodrow Wilson, it is a toss-up who ends up the "priest" and who the "warrior."[12] Thus, Roosevelt was the first American leader to propose a league of nations as early as 1914, calling it a "World League for the Peace of Righteousness" and saying that it would work like that familiar American institution, "a posse comitatus."[13]

Wilson, of course, went considerably further, promising to make the world safe for a whole panoply of American values and to enshrine that promise in a new international system—thereby generating the doctrine that still bears his name. When Wilson asked Congress on April 2, 1917, to declare war on imperial Germany, he stated solemnly that if America must shed blood, it would be "for the things which we have always carried nearest our hearts—for democracy, for the right of those who submit to authority to have a voice in their own governments, for the rights and liberties of small nations, for a universal dominion of right by such a concert of free peoples as shall bring peace and safety to all nations and make the world itself at last free."[14] But with geography and neutrality no longer able to protect the United States and World War I having demonstrated that the balance-of-power system was doomed to failure, Wilson concluded that to achieve these aims "we must have a society of nations" built on premises the American people could recognize as their own.[15]

And so, via the route of American exceptionalism, the world got its first general-purpose multilateral institution, the League of Nations—albeit without U.S. membership. Conventional wisdom has it that Wilson's plans were stymied by the lure of isolationism. The reality is a good deal more complex. According to Lawrence Gelfand, a highly regarded Wilson scholar, "existing evidence, essentially the considered judgment of seasoned politicians and journalists in the fall of 1918 and well into the spring of 1919, pointed toward solid public support for American membership in the League of Nations."[16] Moreover, there were barely more than a dozen hard-core irreconcilables in the Senate who were opposed to U.S. membership in a league of any form. Henry Cabot Lodge, chair of the Foreign Relations Committee, was prepared to vote for the League and to deliver enough Republican votes to ratify the treaty, provided that Wilson accepted Lodge's reservations. In essence, they came down to this nonnegotiable issue: in Lodge's words, to "release us from obligations which might not be kept, and to preserve rights which ought not to be infringed."¹⁷ But this was not isolationism; it was unilateralism. Wilson's inability or unwillingness to compromise, coupled with his rapidly declining health that cut short his campaign for the League, doomed the effort.¹⁸

Isolationism was not the cause of treaty's defeat, then; it was its consequence. But the two were often hard to distinguish. For example, Senator William Borah, one of the few isolationist leaders seriously interested in foreign affairs, sounded very much like Lodge when he insisted that the United States "does propose ... to determine for itself when civilization is threatened, when there may be a breach of human rights and human liberty sufficient to warrant action, and it proposes also to determine for itself when to act and in what manner it shall discharge the obligation which time and circumstances impose."¹⁹ The trouble was that, until the direct attack on Pearl Harbor twenty-seven months into World War II, no international threat was ever deemed to pass that threshold.

As a result, for Franklin Roosevelt (also known as FDR), the key postwar challenge was to overcome the isolationist legacy of the 1930s and to ensure sustained U.S. engagement in achieving and maintaining a stable international order. He, like Wilson and TR before him, recognized that the American people needed an animating vision beyond the mere dictates of balance-of-power politics—the failure of which had dragged America into two world wars in the span of a single generation. Thus, FDR, too, framed his plans for winning the peace in terms he believed would resonate with the public: creating an American-led order based on relatively modest forms of constitutionalism: that is, rules and institutions promoting human betterment through provisions for a collective security organization grafted onto a concert of power; stable money and free trade; human rights and decolonization; and an international civic politics beyond the domain of states through active engagement by the private and voluntary sectors.

FDR's postwar plans were tempered by a far greater pragmatic appreciation of domestic and international political realities than Wilson had exhibited. Moreover, they were intended not only to secure American engagement abroad but also to safeguard the aims and achievements of the New Deal at home. That combination of commitments yielded the United Nations (UN), including its socioeconomic agencies, the Bretton Woods institutions, negotiations on an international trade organization (which produced the General Agreements on Tariffs and Trade, or GATT, later folded into the World Trade Organization), and, in due course, the transnational expansion of U.S. corporations and civil society organizations.

And so it went on into the beginnings of the Cold War. When Soviet vetoes in the UN Security Council blocked the effective use of the UN in the late 1940s, Truman took the concept of collective security regional in Western Europe where the need to respond to the Soviets was greatest, creating the

North Atlantic Treaty Organization (NATO). It is worth recalling today that leading unilateralists at the time opposed NATO's core commitment, and why.

In the Senate, Robert A. Taft of Ohio, known as Mr. Republican, voted against NATO despite being a strident anticommunist because, he said, "I do not like the obligation written into the pact which binds us to come to the defense of any country, no matter by whom it is attacked and even though the aggressor may be another member of the pact."[20] That is, Taft objected precisely to the multilateral character of NATO's security commitments, the very feature differentiating it from all previous alliances in history.[21] George Kennan, the author of America's postwar containment strategy vis-à-vis the Soviets, protested for the same reason. Both preferred specific bilateral alliances as needed based on what Keenan called "particularized" rather than "legalistic–moralistic" commitments, which is how he saw NATO.[22]

But the "unis" lost and the "multis" won.[23] Because they did, a North Atlantic security community gradually came into being: a grouping of states among which the recourse to war as a means to settle differences is unthinkable—a mission backed by every subsequent administration from Dwight Eisenhower on down and that may well be America's single most important achievement ever in the international arena.

Like Leffler, I have identified elements of continuity in American foreign policy since the United States became a world power, but my thread of continuity is quite different from his. At critical junctures when the international order was being remade, U.S. leaders from TR to Wilson and from FDR to Truman have espoused international arrangements—multilateral arrangements—they believed resonated with the American public by reflecting core elements of America's own self of sense as a nation and that would help sustain, therefore, constructive U.S. engagement in the affairs of the world. Presidents George Bush and Bill Clinton drew on a similar ideational repository to frame their visions for world order at the end of the Cold War.[24] The transformational effects of those arrangements are unfolding still.

Debates about these issues among international relations scholars often get bogged down on several closely related questions. One is whether these leaders really meant what they said or merely invoked certain rhetoric and images for instrumental reasons. For the purposes of the present discussion this question is fundamentally irrelevant, because by acting on their rhetoric and images they created a reality that otherwise would not have existed. For example, the indivisible or collective security guarantees in NATO—that an attack on one would be considered an attack on all—created a different reality in Europe than two or three bilateral alliances would have done; one needs only to compare Europe with East Asia today to appreciate the difference.[25]

Another question has to do with power: the United States, it is frequently said, did what it did because it could. But this is a mere truism. Its profound limitations become clear when one considers that no other power of comparable magnitude would have done the same things. Nazi Germany was not about to construct a liberal international economic order or to advance the cause of human rights had it won the war, nor were the Soviets, had they ended up on top. Indeed, even the United Kingdom would have done some things differently, especially with regard to maintaining colonialism and imperial preferences.[26]

That brings us, finally, to the hoary subject of interests. Yes, the United States fully pursued its interests as determined by its political leaders. But by virtue of its power it had available to it a fairly broad repertoire of means by which to pursue those interests. I have suggested that the ideational factor of American identity—the nation's sense of exceptionalism—shaped how interests were defined and pursued. Broadly speaking, and unusual for a great power, the United States created a rule-based system that encouraged not only acquiescence but also active participation by other and lesser powers, who saw their own interests taken into account and were given an institutionalized hearing in the system's management. It goes without saying that the United States, in Leffler's words, "preserved the right" to act unilaterally—and some of its lesser foreign policy successes occurred when it did so act, including U.S.-sponsored coups from Iran to Chile; U.S. support for military dictators and other forms of autocracy; and the long and deeply divisive Vietnam War. But insofar as the U.S.-created multilateral order enjoyed widespread legitimacy abroad, America's "soft power" resources remained plentiful.[27]

American Exemptionalism

So far, I have suggested that the promotion of multilateralism at key moments in the twentieth century reflected and drew upon a sense of American exceptionalism, helping to constitute the post–World War II international order. But this narrative is incomplete. For, from the very outset of the postwar era, the United States also has sought to insulate itself from the domestic blowback of some of the multilateral instruments it created, especially in the area of human rights and on the question of international jurisdiction. I call this American *exemptionalism*.[28]

Whereas the executive branch traditionally drove the exceptionalist agenda, the exemptionalist resistance to its domestic effects has been anchored in Congress, where it has typically been framed in terms of protecting such core features of the U.S. Constitution as the separation of powers or states' rights against federal treaty-based incursions. Indeed, serious constitutional issues are at stake in relation to international treaties and, even more so, to the proliferation of customary international law, which have sparked lively and highly productive debates among legal scholars and practitioners in the past several years.[29] The immediate driver of exemptionalism after World War II, however, was the domestic politics of race relations.

In drafting the UN charter, for example, the United States introduced language reaffirming faith in fundamental human rights. But because the support of southern Democrats was critical to the charter's ratification by the Senate, the need to keep Jim Crow laws beyond international scrutiny obliged the United States to balance that reaffirmation by adding what became Article 2(7): "Nothing contained in the present Charter shall authorize the United Nations to intervene in matters which are essentially within the domestic jurisdiction of any state."[30] No international judgment would be passed, in other words, on so-called separate but equal education for black children or on state lynch laws—under which less than 1 percent of lynch murderers were ever tried. The United States could vote for the Universal Declaration of Human Rights in the UN General Assembly in 1948 because it was a statement of aspirations, which created no binding legal obligations and required no ratification.

Race also was at the root of a backlash against the UN Genocide Convention, negotiated by the executive branch. During debates on the convention, Raphael Lemkin—a State Department official and a Jew who invented the term genocide and was the intellectual force behind the convention—found himself in the unenviable position of testifying that genocide occurred only when intent existed to exterminate an entire group, whereas "those who committed lynchings lacked this requisite motivation."[31] Not swayed, the Senate in 1954 nearly adopted the Bricker Amendment, which would have reduced significantly the president's treaty-making powers.[32] Eisenhower just managed to dodge this bullet but in return was forced to withdraw from further efforts to ratify the genocide convention and other UN rights covenants. As a result, the United States only ratified the Genocide Convention in 1989; the International Covenant on Civil and Political Rights in 1992; and the Convention Against Torture as well as the Convention on the Elimination of All Forms of Racial Discrimination in 1994, all with reservations severely limiting—indeed, mostly negating—their domestic legal effects.[33]

During the Cold War, presidents from Truman to Ronald Reagan sought to minimize the international embarrassment resulting from exemptionalism, especially regarding human rights, often acting through executive agreements or other such means. The United States was, after all, in a contest vis-à-vis the Soviets for the hearts and minds of people throughout the world. Washington was especially concerned that the non-white third world not tilt toward the communist cause. So although such presidents as John F. Kennedy might have been slow to embrace fully the need for change on racial issues at home, they were acutely concerned to manage the fallout from domestic racism abroad.[34]

A half-century after the Bricker Amendment, race is no longer the driver behind exemptionalism that it once was. Today it is animated by a more diffuse set of social issues including abortion, capital punishment, gay rights, gun control, unfettered property rights, and, thus, opposition to environmental regulations—coupled with distrust of government and even more so of international institutions and treaties. But the geographic locus of exemptionalism has not moved far. A look at an electoral map of the United States today suggests that the core of red-state America resides in the old isolationist regions of the Midwest and mountain states and in the deep South, which had forced the coupling of the postwar multilateralist agenda with exemptionalism in the first place, before its conversion away from the political coalition FDR had constructed toward the Republican Party, partly as a result of the racial and cultural turmoil of the late 1960s that became the basis for Richard Nixon's so-called southern strategy.[35]

Doctrinal Unilateralism Today

Signs of a resurgent doctrinal unilateralism go back to the first Reagan administration: withholding assessed contributions to the United Nations; walking away from the International Court of Justice when it ruled adversely in *Nicaragua v. the United States;* rejecting the Law of the Sea Treaty negotiated over many years by presidents of both parties; attacking the Bretton Woods institutions; expressing deep ambivalence about nuclear deterrence, as opposed to superiority, as well as about arms control; and justifying these policy postures by virtue of America's special provenance as the shining "city on a hill," an exemplar to others. But in his second term both Reagan and his foreign policy advisers steered back closer to the postwar norm, even urging Congress to pay to the UN arrears the United States had accumulated in his first term.

Inspired by and hoping to sustain the Reagan revolution, as it was then known, conservative think tanks such as the American Enterprise Institute (AEI) and the Heritage Foundation from the 1980s on began to develop a doctrinal basis for a new American unilateralism to undermine and dismantle the postwar consensus. The doctrine came in two related parts: the unfettered use of American power abroad coupled with a radical exemptionalism of the United States from the international normative sphere.

As John Bolton wrote not long before he left AEI to join the George W. Bush administration as a senior State Department official, "the harm and costs to the United States of [globalists] belittling our popular sovereignty and constitutionalism, and restricting both our domestic and our international policy flexibility and power are finally receiving attention."[36] The UN has been a leading target of this attention for daring to pronounce on such questions as when the use of force may or may not be legitimate.[37] But the European Union is also seen as posing a serious danger, not only because it has, according to Jeremy Rabkin, "many practical ramifications for U.S. policy. But it also presents a clear ideological alternative"—above all, by its members adhering to more active social policies while agreeing to pool aspects of their sovereignty to achieve their everyday policy aims.[38] Adds Bolton, presumably referring to the International Criminal Court, "Not content alone with transferring their own national sovereignty to Brussels, [the EU has] also decided, in effect, to transfer some of ours to worldwide institutions and norms."[39]

The exemptionalist component of the new unilateralist doctrine kicked in first, in the form of a "new sovereigntist" defense of American institutions against alleged international encroachment.[40] Rabkin writes, in a somewhat circular fashion, "because the United States is fully sovereign, it can determine for itself what its Constitution will require. And the Constitution necessarily requires that sovereignty be safeguarded so that the Constitution itself can be secure."[41] The practical steps that follow from this axiom include rejecting multilateral treaties, declaring illegitimate a good deal of what is said to be customary international law, diminishing the role of multilateral institutions, and above all delegitimating the International Criminal Court—going so far as to punish smaller and weaker countries that do sign up to it, even to the detriment of other U.S. foreign policy objectives such as drug interdiction and co-opting their militaries.[42]

These policy preferences began to prevail in Congress after the 1994 midterm elections, when Republicans took control of both houses of Congress. That election had been nationalized by means of a common Republican platform termed "Contract with America," which claimed, among other things, that "the Clinton administration appears to salute the day when American men and women will fight, and die, 'in the service' of the United Nations."[43] The Senate subsequently rejected the Comprehensive Test Ban Treaty and made it clear that it would not ratify the international inspections provisions of the biological weapons convention. A straw poll in that chamber indicated that the Kyoto protocol would face a similar fate, even before George W. Bush rejected it altogether. Clinton did not dare submit the International Criminal Court statute for ratification, knowing that it was dead on arrival. And withholding UN dues became transformed from a targeted policy instrument in the Reagan years to a common Congressional pastime. Bolton noted these developments approvingly: "Recent clashes in and around the United States Senate indicate that the Americanist party has awakened."[44]

After the election of Bush in 2000, the new unilateralism moved into the White House as well, and with it the second part of the doctrinal shift: proclaiming the view that the use of American power abroad is entirely self-legitimating, determined solely by U.S. interests, neither requiring nor welcoming any form of external accountability. The administration's new national security strategy expressed the aim of perpetual U.S. military predominance while also promulgating the highly controversial concept of *preventive*, in contrast to *preemptive*, warfare.[45] The strategy document assigned no role to multilateralism and, indeed, acknowledged no serious need for international support. The administration risked the NATO alliance to fight an elective war in Iraq on flawed premises and before other means had been exhausted. And its aggressive treatment of prisoners of war, who were placed in a legal limbo that seemed deliberately designed to escape the provisions of the Geneva conventions, raised serious questions abroad about America's commitment to the rule of law.

Some scholars, including Leffler, often cite the terrorist attacks on 9/11 to explain this shift. 9/11 did represent a profoundly different type of threat and vulnerability for America, but many of the administration's policy postures preceded the attacks, so they can hardly have been the cause. Another popular argument, especially in the run-up to the Iraq War, is the unprecedented power gap between the United States and everyone else. In the transatlantic context, as Robert Kagan put it evocatively, Americans are from Mars, and Europeans are from Venus.[46] The United States is militarily powerful; Europe, in relative terms, is weak. So it is axiomatic that America would use force and project power to pursue its interests, downplaying norms and institutions, while Europe stresses diplomacy and writes checks. America is unilateral because it can be; Europe favors multilateralism because it must. But this reasoning is deeply flawed.

About the power asymmetry there can be no dispute. The United States now spends nearly as much on its military as the rest of the world combined, yet that still consumes less than 5 percent of its gross domestic product. The gap in technology and combat experience is even greater. Policy differences inevitably will result from an asymmetry of this magnitude, but permissive conditions do not constitute causal factors. Yes, the United States can do many of the things Kagan and other neoconservatives ascribe to it, including prosecuting what some among them have happily described as a policy of "democratic imperialism"—reminiscent of Bemis's characterization of some of TR's policies. But it follows that it neither must nor will do those things by virtue of its power differential alone.

Consider the fact that, for all practical purposes, the transatlantic power gap was as great in the 1990s as it is a decade later. When the Soviet Union imploded, the American neoconservative commentator Charles Krauthammer already heralded the advent of what he called "the unipolar moment."[47] Then-secretary of state Madeleine Albright hectored the allies and the United Nations at every opportunity that the United States was "the world's indispensable nation."[48] And Hubert Védrine, French foreign minister at the time, coined the term *hyperpuissance* to express the unique extent of American hegemony even then.[49] Yet transatlantic grumbling was not appreciably worse than in earlier times. And everyone—including the German Red-Green coalition government—was on board for the U.S.-led Kosovo intervention that arguably had less legal justification going for it than the war against Iraq.

The difference is doctrinal. When the Clinton administration reminded the world of America's indispensability, it invariably did so in the context of values and policy objectives broadly shared but not achieved without active U.S. involvement—be they opening global markets, promoting nuclear threat reduction, fielding robust peacekeeping missions, or sustaining the Middle East peace process. Even American triumphalism in the 1990s—and there was plenty of it—celebrated a shared achievement: the victory of free markets and democratic governance against an adversary the West collectively had combated for much of the twentieth century.

These doctrinal differences, in turn, reflect a deeper political reality. The liberal internationalism on which the postwar consensus ultimately rested has fared no better in recent years than its domestic counterpart: it has lost the war of ideas just as it has lost elections. And doctrinal unilateralism, unlike exemptionalist impulses throughout the Cold War, is unrestrained by the existence of any major countervailing power. Or is it?

Transnational Civic Politics

It is well beyond the scope of this chapter—or my expertise, for that matter—to speculate about the emergence of any countervailing military challengers to the United States down the road, be they other states or the further proliferation of and collaboration among terrorist networks. But I do want to address briefly certain forms of transnational social power: new platforms and channels of transnational action the U.S. state cannot fully control, which are deeply entwined with American society itself and which in considerable measure represent the success of America's own postwar international agenda. They include the spread of democracy and the rule of law, more robust norms in areas ranging from human rights to the use of force, international institutions like the UN, and the fact that nonstate actors such as nongovernmental organizations and transnational firms are increasingly involved in the promotion and production of global public goods. As a result of these developments, even as doctrinal unilateralism has sought to disembed the United States from postwar multilateral norms and frameworks, the very system of states slowly is becoming embedded within an increasingly mobilized and institutionalized global public domain, and subject to a rudimentary transnational civic politics.[50] We see evidence of this at work in several recent developments, including the highly contentious Iraq War and its aftermath, as well as the fight over Kyoto.

I draw three lessons from Iraq for the purposes of this discussion. First, Iraq demonstrates the fact that there is no automatic relationship between power and international legitimacy—and that legitimacy matters. One state can amass force, but only others can endow its deployment with legitimacy. The United States ignored that rule in Iraq and has paid the price in blood and treasure, with little meaningful help even now from anyone but the British, and they desperately wanted the cover of a second Security Council resolution before going to war.

It is true that the successful use of force can produce legitimacy over time, when and if opposition collapses. The U.S. "quarantine" of Cuba during the 1962 missile crisis may well have been illegal (an interference with shipping on the high seas) and perhaps unwise (drawing a line in the ocean and then leaving it up to the Soviets to decide on peace or war).[51] But it ended up producing agreement and deference, including from all members of the Organization of American States except for Cuba. However, there is nothing automatic about this process. Soviet control over the Baltic states and Eastern Europe during the long Cold War did not lead to international legitimacy in the view of many important actors, which contributed to the ultimate collapse of the Soviet empire.

And attaining legitimacy is not simply a mechanical exercise, such as counting votes in the UN Security Council. After all, the council did not authorize NATO's Kosovo campaign, yet U.S. allies and arguably even the UN itself regarded that as a legitimate act. When Russia presented a draft resolution condemning NATO's bombing, the council voted it down by 12–3, thus in a backhanded way belatedly conferring legitimacy on the bombing campaign.

Instead, legitimacy typically emerges out of a process of persuasion in which the relevant others look for evidence that power, especially military force, is used in pursuit of broadly shared aims and in accordance with broadly accepted norms. In Iraq the United States failed to persuade much of the international community on (1) the most serious weapons of mass destruction charges; (2) stopping the weapons inspections; (3) the concept of preventive war; and (4) marginalizing the political role of the UN. Indeed, it is little remembered that, apart from a threatened French veto, the United States was unable to garner eight votes on a UN Security Council that included some of the world's poorest and therefore presumably most susceptible countries—precisely because other states viewed Iraq as a test case for preventive warfare and they had no desire to endorse any such notion.[52] Thus, although the United States is powerful enough to go to war and to succeed in major combat operations on its own, it is not so powerful as to compel others to buy into or support its mission.[53] Only others can do that. That is one lesson from Iraq.

A second lesson from Iraq is that as the number of democracies in the world continues to increase, so too will the demand for not only internal but also external accountability of states. Neoconservative pundits like William Kristol and Robert Kagan are among the most vocal advocates of democracy promotion abroad. Yet in their vigorous advocacy of and support for the Iraq War, they expressed little more than contempt for public opinion abroad, not appreciating the indivisible link between the two.

In the run-up to the war the United States had the most trouble not with authoritarian states or kleptocracies but with other democracies—and not only in "old Europe" France and Germany, as Secretary of Defense Donald Rumsfeld put it so indelicately, but also in Canada, Chile, Mexico, and Turkey.[54] Neither neoconservative pundits nor unilateralist members of Congress may care what people elsewhere think of the United States. But leaders of other democracies must be concerned with what their own people think about them if they are to survive politically. Very few such leaders will risk siding with the United States when two-thirds or more voters in their countries oppose U.S. policy. And reputable polls have shown that favorable attitudes toward the United States in most countries surveyed have sunken to all-time lows.[55]

In sum, America's success at promoting democracy abroad has the inexorable effect of constraining the United States from deviating too far from international norms if it desires or needs the help of others—or of imposing significant costs on the United States if it chooses to go it alone.

But America's Iraq problems did not stop with other states and their publics, and therein lies the third lesson. The American state is increasingly bumping into the interests of the U.S.-based global business community. During the Iraq War, the *Financial Times* reported that "big American consumer brands such as Coca-Cola, McDonald's, and Marlboro are paying a price as boycotts spread from the Middle East to the rest of the world, especially Europe."[56] In 2004, Control Risks Group, a thoroughly mainstream British business risk consultancy, described U.S. foreign policy as "the most important single factor driving the development of global [business] risk. By using U.S. power unilaterally and aggressively in pursuit of global stability, the Bush administration is in fact creating precisely the opposite effect."[57] At some point, the corporate sector can be expected to resist the imposition of these costs.

Beyond the Iraq War, climate change politics illustrates similar points and also highlights the role of nongovernmental organizations. When Bush rejected the Kyoto protocol, several major oil companies lobbied the U.S. Congress for voluntary greenhouse-gas limits. Shell and BP were among them, both of which enjoy carefully cultivated "green" images, have instituted company-wide emissions reductions programs, have invested heavily in alternative energy sources, and have feared suffering competitive disadvantages. So, too, was Enron, hoping to become a major player in an expanding global emissions trading market.[58] European activist groups, for their part, organized a boycott of Esso, a subsidiary of ExxonMobil, one of Kyoto's most determined opponents. Now that Kyoto is in force without U.S. adherence, Jeffrey Immelt, chief executive officer of GE, an American company whose merger with another U.S. firm was blocked by the European Commission and who therefore understands well the consequences of operating a global firm in conflicting regulatory environments, has called for a consistent transatlantic policy on producing cleaner energy: "For us to remain competitive, we simply cannot navigate a regulatory maze that forces us to tweak and modulate every product and process to suit individual regulatory regimes at their whim." Moreover, Immelt laments the fact that, as a result of policy failure by the United States, "the U.S. has watched Europe and others advance, strengthening their economies and security."[59]

Likewise, the number of shareholder resolutions demanding climate change risk policies from American companies doubled in just one year, while lawsuits were filed against the federal government as well as firms. Swiss Re, one of the world's largest insurers, requested information from all energy-intensive firms for which it provides liability coverage, regarding whether they have a carbon accounting or reporting system in place and how they intend to meet their obligations under Kyoto or any similar such instrument—implying that rates and even coverage could be affected.

Meanwhile, in the governmental arena fully half of all U.S. states by now have introduced so-called son-of-Kyoto bills, aiming to build state-based frameworks for regulating CO_2 emissions, and the automakers are suing California to invalidate its proposed regulations. Environmental groups support the campaign hoping that it will generate industry demands for uniform federal standards rather than face a proliferation of individual states' standards. Adding to the transnational mix, Canada has adopted California's targets. Actions such as these in and of themselves are no substitute for a viable climate treaty. But they do alter the structure of incentives and the political balance of power in this space so that sooner rather than later any U.S. administration will have to come to grips with climate change by means of a binding global instrument.

These and other cases like it demonstrate that the transnational manifestations of American exceptionalism continue to survive—and in some respects thrive—even as its exemptionalist counterpart currently is in the ascendancy at home.

Conclusion

Two Americas stand astride the global stage today: America the exceptionalist and America the exemptionalist; the legacy of institutionalized multilateralism and the new assertion of doctrinal unilateralism. The unfolding of the dialectic between the two will have a fundamental impact on the future evolution of global governance. When Bush sent Bolton to the United Nations, many observers concluded that the game was up. But putting aside symbolism and transaction costs, Bolton probably can do less serious damage at the UN than in the Department of State.

In other respects, early in its second term the Bush administration exhibited signs of modifying some previous stances. Finding itself largely alone in a struggle in Iraq that continues to be far more challenging than anticipated has imposed enormous costs in American treasure and lives, generating growing disaffection among the American public and making it less likely that the Iraq campaign will become the legitimizing affirmation of the administration's new doctrine. Bush and his new foreign policy team, firmly led by Secretary of State Condoleezza Rice, seem more solicitous of the European allies and are working well with them on the Iran nuclear file. The administration also is cooperating with regional allies and China in dealing with the North Korean nuclear threat. It opposed Congressional efforts to begin yet another round of withholding UN payments linked to the oil-for-food scandal. And perhaps most significant in some respects, the administration permitted the UN Security Council to refer the Darfur genocide to the International Criminal Court, thereby adding to the court's stature despite having spent the previous four years maligning and undermining it.[60]

In broader Republican circles, Newt Gingrich, former house speaker and an architect of the party's 1994 "Contract with America," cochaired a congressionally mandated bipartisan commission in 2005 that urged serious U.S. engagement with the UN, based on its assessment of American interests.[61] And in 2004 Kagan, the neoconservative commentator of "Mars and Venus" fame published an article acknowledging, albeit grudgingly, the United States faced a crisis of international legitimacy that adversely affected the successful conduct of foreign policy.[62]

The asymmetry of American power, especially military power, is truly extraordinary—perhaps unprecedented. But its efficacy is bounded and becoming more so, not only because other states get in the way but also because the very system of states is becoming embedded in a broader global public domain and subject to an emerging transnational civic politics. Nowhere is this truer than among the world's democracies, America's closest affinity group.

Unilateralism as routine state practice is a permanent feature of international life, especially in cases of genuine self-defense. But I have suggested that the recent American doctrinal version of it is unsustainable in our interconnected and institutionally pluralistic world. American exceptionalism itself, in the form of linking a special U.S. identity and role to a multilateral world order, has contributed mightily to restraining its exemptionalist counterpart.

Notes

1. "Diplomatic History Roundtable: The Bush Administration's Foreign Policy in Historical Perspective," *Diplomatic History* 29 (June 2005).
2. Melvyn P. Leffler, "9/11 and American Foreign Policy," *Diplomatic History* 29 (June 2005), 398, 399, 401, 403, and 413, respectively.
3. Walter L. Hixson, "Leffler Takes a Linguistic Turn," *Diplomatic History* 29 (June 2005), 420, italics in original.
4. Anna Kasten Nelson, "Continuity and Change in the Age of Unlimited Power," *Diplomatic History* 29 (June 2005), 437.c
5. Robert O. Keohane, "Associative American Development, 1776–1860," in *The Antinomies of Interdependence: National Welfare and the International Division of Labor*, ed. John Gerard Ruggie (New York: Columbia University Press, 1983), 90. The following paragraphs draw on an earlier discussion in Ruggie, *Winning the Peace: America and World Order in the New Era* (New York: Columbia University Press, 1996), ch. 1. Also see Fareed Zakaria, *From Wealth to Power: The Unusual Origins of America's World Role* (Princeton, NJ: Princeton University Press, 1998).
6. Walter LaFeber, *The American Age: United States Foreign Policy at Home and Abroad since 1750* (New York: Norton, 1989), 80.

7. Felix Gilbert, *To the Farewell Address: Ideas of Early American Foreign Policy* (Princeton, NJ: Princeton University Press, 1961).
8. David Fromkin, *In the Time of the Americans: The Generation that Changed America's Role in the World* (New York: Knopf, 1995), 23.
9. Robert Dallek, *The American Style of Foreign Policy* (New York: Oxford University Press, 1983), 34–35.
10. Fromkin, *In the Time of the Americans*, 12.
11. See further Seymour Martin Lipset, *American Exceptionalism: A Double Edge Sword* (New York: Replica Books, 1998); Charles Lockhart, *The Roots of American Exceptionalism: Institutions, Culture, and Policies* (New York: Palgrave Macmillan 2003); and Anatol Lieven, *America Right or Wrong: An Anatomy of American Nationalism* (Oxford: Oxford University Press, 2004).
12. John M. Cooper, Jr., *The Warrior and the Priest: Woodrow Wilson and Theodore Roosevelt* (Cambridge, MA: Harvard University Press, 1983). Henry Kissinger, in contrast, follows the two stereotypes of Roosevelt the realist and Wilson the liberal in *Diplomacy* (New York: Simon & Schuster, 1994).
13. Cooper, *Warrior and the Priest*, 281.
14. Thomas J. Knock, *To End All Wars: Woodrow Wilson and the Quest for a New World Order* (New York: Oxford University Press, 1992), 121–122. Also see Cooper, *Breaking the Heart of the World: Woodrow Wilson and the Fight for the League of Nations* (New York: Cambridge University Press, 2001).
15. Knock, *To End All Wars*, 97.
16. Lawrence E. Gelfand, "The Mystique of Wilsonian Statecraft," *Diplomatic History* 7 (Spring 1983), 89.
17. Knock, *To End All Wars*, 258. If Gelfand's assessment is right, then Lodge's opposition to the treaty simply may have been motivated in part by fear of grave partisan disadvantage for the Republicans if Wilson won.
18. For good discussions of the political intricacies and dynamics within Congress, see Cooper, *Breaking the Heart of the World*; and the earlier but still valuable Lloyd E. Ambrosius, *Woodrow Wilson and the American Diplomatic Tradition* (New York: Cambridge University Press, 1987).
19. Manfred Jonas, *Isolationism in America* (Ithaca, NY: Cornell University Press, 1966), 7.
20. Robert A. Taft, *A Foreign Policy for Americans* (Garden City, NY: Doubleday, 1951), 88–89.
21. The institutional differences between bilateral alliances and collective security can be put schematically: in both instances, state A is pledged to come to aid of state B if B is attacked by C. In a collective security scheme, however, A is also pledged to come to the aid of C if C is attacked by B. Consequently, as Hudson points out, "A cannot regard itself as the ally of B more than of C because theoretically it is an open question whether, if an act of war should occur, B or C would be the aggressor. In the same way B has indeterminate obligations toward A and C, and C toward A and B, and so on, with a vast number of variants as the system is extended to more and more states." G. F. Hudson, "Collective Security and Military Alliances," in *Diplomatic Investigations*, ed. Herbert Butterfield and Marin Wight (Cambridge, MA: Harvard University Press, 1968), 176–177.
22. Anders Stephanson, *Kennan and the Art of Foreign Policy* (Cambridge, MA: Harvard University Press, 1989), 140. In his memoirs, Kennan recalled that he had favored a dumbbell arrangement, but one in which the two sides of the Atlantic would be linked not by a treaty but merely by a U.S.–Canadian guarantee of assistance in case of Soviet attack. George F. Kennan, *Memoirs: 1925–1950* (Boston: Little, Brown, 1967), 406–407.
23. The reasons are too complex to elaborate fully here, but they included the critical fact that the idea of a U.S.-led UN collective security system had converted prewar isolationist figures like Arthur Vandenberg (R-Mich), Chairman of the Senate Foreign Relations Committee, to the internationalist cause, and when that system turned out not to work as planned he led the campaign for NATO in the Senate. See Lawrence S. Kaplan, *NATO and the United States: The Enduring Alliance* (Boston: Twayne Publishers, 1988).
24. Lack of space prohibits a further discussion here, but see Ruggie, "The Past as Prologue? Interests, Identity, and American Foreign Policy," *International Security* 21 (Spring 1997), 89–125.
25. See Christopher Hemmer and Peter J. Katzenstein, "Why Is There No NATO in Asia? Collective Identity, Regionalism, and the Origins of Multilateralism," *International Organization* 56 (Autumn 2002), 575–607.

26. Ruggie, "Multilateralism: The Anatomy of an Institution," *International Organization* 46 (Summer 1992), 561–598.
27. On the legitimacy of the postwar multilateral order, see Ruggie, "Multilateralism"; G. John Ikenberry, "Is American Multilateralism in Decline?" *Perspectives on Politics* 1 (September 2003), 533–550; and Edward Luck's chapter in this volume. On soft power, see Joseph S. Nye, Jr., *Soft Power: The Means to Success in World Politics* (New York: Public Affairs, 2004).
28. For a discussion in the context of human rights, see Ruggie, "American Exceptionalism, Exemptionalism and Global Governance," *in American Exceptionalism and Human Rights,* ed. Michael Ignatieff (Princeton, NJ: Princeton University Press, 2005).
29. The conventional liberal internationalist view has been challenged most notably by Curtis A. Bradley and Jack L. Goldsmith, "Customary International Law as Federal Common Law: A Critique of the Modern Position," *Harvard Law Review* 110 (February 1997) 816–976; Bradley and Goldsmith, "U.N. Human Rights Standards and U.S. Law: The Current Illegitimacy of International Human Rights Litigation," *Fordham Law Review* 66 (November 1997) 319–370; Goldsmith, "Should International Human Rights Law Trump U.S. Domestic Law," *Chicago Journal of International Law* 1 (Fall 2000) 327–340; and Bradley, "International Delegations, the Structural Constitution, and Non-Self-Execution," *Stanford Law Review* 55 (May 2003) 1557–1596. For a rejoinder, see Harold Hongju Koh, "Is International Law Really State Law?" *Harvard Law Review* 111 (May 1998) 1824–1861; and Koh, "On American Exceptionalism," *Stanford Law Review* 55 (May 2003) 1476–1527.
30. Carol Anderson, *Eyes Off the Prize: The United Nations and the African American Struggle for Human Rights, 1944–1955* (New York: Cambridge University Press, 2003), ch. 1; and Ruth B. Russell, *A History of the United Nations Charter* (Washington, DC: Brookings, 1958), ch. 39. The Soviets and many other states were happy to have the provision included.
31. Anderson, *Eyes Off the Prize,* 228.
32. It was so called for the Ohio Republican who first introduced it in 1951. In addition to the existing ratification requirement of a two-thirds Senate supermajority, the amendment would have required subsequent implementing legislation by both houses of Congress and approval by all state legislatures. A weakened substitute fell one vote short of the required two-thirds. Natalie Hevener Kaufman, *Human Rights Treaties and the Senate: A History of Opposition* (Chapel Hill: University of North Carolina Press, 1990), ch. 4. The amendment would not have affected executive agreements or congressional–executive agreements.
33. Successive administrations largely counted on the domestic political process, including the courts, to achieve progress in these matters. See Koh, "On American Exceptionalism."
34. See Mary L. Dudziak, *Cold War Civil Rights: Race and the Image of American Democracy* (Princeton, NJ: Princeton University Press, 2002); and Thomas Borstelmann, *The Cold War and the Color Line: American Race Relations in the Global Arena* (Cambridge, MA: Harvard University Press, 2001).
35. The shift actually began with George Wallace's independent campaign in 1968, which split the white Southern vote and helped deliver the White House to Nixon. Dan T. Carter, *The Politics of Rage: George Wallace, the Origins of the New Conservatism, and the Transformation of American Politics* (New York: Simon & Schuster, 1995).
36. John R. Bolton, "Should We Take Global Governance Seriously?" *Chicago Journal of International Law* 1 (Fall 2000), 206. Bolton was senior vice president of AEI, became undersecretary of state for Arms Control and International Security Affairs, and is currently serving as U.S. ambassador to the United Nations on a recess appointment by President Bush.
37. I was personally chastised by Bolton when, as assistant secretary-general of the United Nations, I voiced concern in early 1999 over the fact that U.S. intelligence agencies had piggybacked onto UN weapons inspections in Iraq to gather targeting information intended, presumably, for a decapitation strike on the Iraqi leadership. My concern was not with protecting Saddam Hussein or his henchmen; I wanted to point out that it would be tough convincing other countries in the future to accept UN weapons inspections if they could not be counted on to be impartial and stick to their mandate. Thundered Bolton in response, "It is a fundamental and irreparable error to argue that UNSCOM was ever intended to be impartial or strictly technical …What if instrumentalities of the United Nations were used for American intelligence objectives? What if the information obtained were used for activities outside of UNSCOM's mandate, or any other UN mission? If true, these are facts of life that the United Nations, the secretary general, and everyone else should get used to." Bolton, "The UN Secretary-General versus the United States," *Human Events,* February 5, 1999, 26.

38. Jeremy Rabkin, "Is EU Policy Eroding the Sovereignty of Non-member States?" *Chicago Journal of International Law* 1 (Fall 2000), 273.
39. Bolton, "Should We Take Global Governance Seriously?" 221.
40. Peter J. Spiro seems to have coined the term in his critique, "The New Sovereigntists: American Exceptionalism and Its False Prophets," *Foreign Affairs* 79 (November–December 2000), 9–15.
41. Rabkin, *Why Sovereignty Matters* (Washington, DC: American Enterprise Institute, 1998); also see Rabkin, "International Law vs. the American Constitution," *National Interest* 55 (Spring 1999), 30–41.
42. On the last of these, see Juan Forero, "Bush's Aid Cuts on Court Issue Roil Neighbors," *New York Times,* August 19, 2005, 1.
43. Ed Gillespie and Bob Schellhas, eds., *Contract with America* (New York: Times Books, 1994), 109.
44. Bolton, "Should We Take Global Governance Seriously?" 206.
45. Preemptive warfare has a well-established international legal pedigree but requires imminence of threat and proportionality of response. After the Iraq War, the administration shifted its rhetoric onto the normatively safer preemptive grounds, but it continued to have a difficult time establishing that the threat the United States faced from Iraq was imminent. On the difference between and respective implications of the two, see Francois Heisbourg, "A Work in Progress: The Bush Doctrine and Its Consequences," *Washington Quarterly* 26 (Spring 2003), 75–88; and Anthony Arend, "International Law and the Preemptive Use of Military Force," *Washington Quarterly* 26 (Spring 2003), 89–103.
46. Robert Kagan, "Power and Weakness," *Policy Review* 113 (2002), 3–28.
47. Charles Krauthammer, "The Unipolar Moment," *Foreign Affairs* 70 (1990–1991), 23–32.
48. As the *Toronto Star* put it shortly after her appointment as secretary of state, "It so happens that the phrase 'indispensable nation,' first minted by the new U.S. Secretary of State Madeleine Albright, is now used constantly by American officials and commentators to describe the overarching role of the United States in the contemporary world. [It] is triumphalist and irritating—which doesn't mean that it isn't apt. From Bosnia to Haiti, only the U.S. has the will and means to address major global problems." Richard Gwyn, "Annan Shows He's Much More than 'the U.S. Choice,'" *Toronto Star,* December 27, 1996, A31.
49. Hubert Védrine, *Face à l'Hyper-puissance* (Paris: Fayard, 2003); the original essay by that title was published in 1995.
50. For a more sustained discussion, see Ruggie, "Reconstituting the Global Public Domain: Issues, Actors, and Practices," *European Journal of International Relations* 10 (December 2004), 499–531.
51. We now also know that the decision was even more risky than was thought at the time; whereas Kennedy believed the Soviets had not yet deployed missiles on Cuba, they in fact had, thus giving them a much greater retaliatory capability than was assumed.
52. I base this judgment on interviews with council members at the time, including some of America's closest friends.
53. The contrast between the Bush administration's unilateralism in Iraq and the Truman administration's mixture of unilateralism and multilateralism in the Korean War is informative. When confronted with the North Korean invasion of South Korea, Truman unilaterally ordered American forces into the war but immediately sought UN sanction for its actions. Having obtained that approval, the Truman administration proceeded to fight the war as a UN/multilateral operation, even though American commanders de facto controlled its conduct. Truman was thus able to legitimate the defense of South Korean by convincing other nations that their collective security depended on curbing aggression in Northeast Asia. As Western argues in this volume, a similar contrast can be drawn between the elder Bush's patient construction of a broad coalition in the case of the Gulf War and the younger Bush's unilateralist turn in Iraq.
54. In a press conference Rumsfeld tried to dismiss French and German opposition to the administration's Iraq policy by claiming they represented old Europe and that "new Europe" countries like Poland and others supported the United States. At least they did in limited ways and for a limited time.
55. See, for example, the Pew Global Attitudes Project, *What the World Thinks in 2003* (Washington, DC: Pew Research Center for the People & the Press, 2003). Also see Steven Kull, "It's Lonely at the Top," *Foreign Policy* 149 (July–August), 36: "A new poll of nearly 24,000 citizens from 23 countries, conducted the international polling firm GlobeScan and the

program on International Policy Attitudes at the University of Maryland, suggests that the tectonic plates of world opinion are shifting. People around the world are not only turning away from the United States; they are starting to embrace the leadership of other major powers."

56. Richard Tomkins, "Anti-war Sentiment Is Likely to Give Fresh Impetus to the Waning Supremacy of U.S. Brands," *Financial Times,* March 27, 2003, 19.
57. Quoted and summarized in Stephen Fidler and Mark Husband, "Bush Foreign Policy 'Is Creating Risks for U.S. Companies,'" *Financial Times,* November 11, 2003, 11.
58. Andrew C. Revkin and Neela Banerjee, "Energy Executives Urge Voluntary Greenhouse-Gas Limits," *New York Times,* August 1, 2001, C1.
59. Jeffrey Immelt, "A Consistent Policy on Cleaner Energy," *Financial Times,* June 29, 2005, 17.
60. The United States abstained on the resolution, thereby allowing it to be adopted.
61. United States Institute of Peace, *American Interests and UN Reform: Report of the Task Force on the United Nation* (Washington, DC: USIP, 2005).
62. Kagan, "America's Crisis of Legitimacy," *Foreign Affairs* 83 (March–April 2004).

2

Article 2(4) on the Nonuse of Force: What Were We Thinking?

EDWARD C. LUCK

While these great states have a special responsibility to enforce the peace, their responsibility is based upon the obligations resting upon all states, large and small, not to use force in international relations except in the defense of law. The responsibility of great states is to serve and not to dominate the world.[1]

> President Harry S. Truman
> First Speech to Congress, April 16, 1945

In its capacity as declaration, the Charter states principles which its Members accept as binding ... Members are to "refrain in their international relations from the threat or use of force against the territorial integrity or political independence of any state, or in any other manner inconsistent with the Purposes of the United Nations."[2]

> Secretary of State Edward R. Stettinius
> Report to the President on the Results of the San Francisco Conference, June 26, 1945

Recently ... Secretary-General Kofi Annan publicly proclaimed that only the United Nations Security Council can legitimately authorize the use of force in international affairs. Now, I came out of my chair when I read that myself ... Now I think the world of Kofi Annan, but I just wonder if ... his doctrine infringes on the sovereignty of individual members of the United Nations to pursue policies that are in their national interest.[3]

> Senator Jesse Helms
> Chair, Senate Foreign Relations Committee, January 21, 2000

From the beginning, America has sought international support for our operations in Afghanistan and Iraq, and we have gained much support. There is a difference, however, between leading a coalition of many nations, and submitting to the objections of a few. American will never seek a permission slip to defend the security of our country.[4]

> President George W. Bush
> State of the Union Address, January 20, 2004

Once a seemingly forgotten provision of the United Nations (UN) charter, Article 2(4) has become one of the principal irritants in the troubled relationship between the United States and the United Nations. Fourth of the seven principles that are to guide the actions of "the Organisation and its Members," it reads simply that "all Members shall refrain in their international relations from the threat or use of force against the territorial integrity or political independence of any state, or in any other manner inconsistent with the Purposes of the United Nations."[5] Secretary-General Kofi Annan, most member states, and rafts of international legal scholars take these words to preclude the threat or employment of force except either (1) when explicitly authorized by the Security Council acting under chapter VII or (2) in response to an armed attack as permitted under Article 51. Successive American presidents and any number of congressional leaders, however, have rejected such a strict and literal interpretation. U.S. national security and the constitutional prerogatives and responsibilities of the president and Congress, they assert, cannot be held hostage to the whims of fourteen other member states serving on the Security Council.

During the Cold War years, with Security Council action repeatedly blocked by deep political divisions within its ranks, the question of whether to seek the council's blessing for the use of force was usually moot. With a revitalized and increasingly activist council in the post-Cold War era, however, there has been renewed interest among many member states and within the secretariat regarding the rules on the use of force constraints embodied in Articles 2(4) and 51. Developments in UN doctrine and in the larger strategic balance have helped to push these concerns to center stage. As the last two UN secretaries-general have underlined, the United Nations no longer contemplates the possibility of organizing or overseeing international military action to enforce the decisions of the Security Council, as provided for by the provisions of chapter VII of the UN charter.[6] This task is to be left to coalitions of willing member states, as authorized by the council. In military terms, moreover, the world is becoming increasingly unipolar, as the capacity to project and sustain force around the world lies primarily in U.S. hands. The growing asymmetries in military capacity have been reflected, not surprisingly, in disparate interpretations of international norms on the use of force.

The debate over these divergent readings of the charter's use of force provisions came to a head with the decisions of the United States, the United Kingdom, and their coalition partners to use force to topple the regime of Saddam Hussein in Iraq in March 2003, despite their failure to gain the Security Council's blessing. As a political, if not legal, matter, the coalition's concerted campaign to achieve the council's authorization for the use of force attested to the legitimizing value of such a resolution.[7] But U.S. leaders, as they have so often in the past, dismissed the claim that the lack of Security Council endorsement made the coalition action illegal under the constraints imposed by Article 2(4) or the standards of state practice under customary international law. In the wake of the indecisive but highly dramatic debate in the Security Council over the use of force in Iraq, the secretary-general warned against "the unilateral and lawless use of force." He declared, furthermore, that the world body had come to a "fork in the road" at "a moment no less decisive than 1945 itself, when the United Nations was founded."[8] In response, he launched his High-Level Panel on Threats, Challenges, and Change, whose December 2004 report sought to pose a new formula capable of meeting the concerns of both sides of the debate.[9] Its proposals in this regard, while well received in some quarters, have been firmly rejected by the Bush administration, congressional leaders, and various American commentators.[10]

This chapter does not seek to resolve the legal debate surrounding Article 2(4) and the use of force provisions of the charter, instead leaving that task to more competent legal scholars.[11] Instead, it looks to the origins of 2(4) in an effort to understand what the UN's founders—particularly American policy-makers—had in mind. This inquiry begins with a puzzlement. Judging by recent commentary, even by the stance of Democratic as well as Republican presidents, one would assume that (1) the charter's restraints on the use of force were imposed on reluctant U.S. negotiators as part of the trade-offs required to gain broad international acceptance of other provisions in the charter more favorable to U.S. values and interests and (2) the U.S. accepted 2(4) because its inherent right of self-defense was reinforced by Article 51. Yet such was not the case. Similar restrictions on the use of force were included in the earliest plans for postwar international organization produced by the Franklin D. Roosevelt (FDR) administration, though self-defense language was not added until the last minute in San Francisco at the insistence of the Latin American delegations, not the United States.[12] Throughout the international negotiations at Dumbarton Oaks and San Francisco on the shape of postwar institutions, the United States was a leading advocate for a blanket restraint on the unilateral use of force. That posture stirred virtually no dissent in Congress, the bureaucracy, or public commentary. Why? What has changed?

This chapter considers a series of five explanations for this apparent contradiction in American thinking:

1. *Idealism:* Presidents FDR and Harry Truman and their postwar planners, determined to do everything possible to prevent a third world war in the twentieth century and convinced of the need for a bold departure from the patterns of the past, including the weak provisions of the League Covenant, were convinced that a renunciation of the use of force for political purposes was a *sine qua non* for building the new postwar order. In essence, their logic was dictated by their larger strategic vision and by the sweep of their rhetoric. There were certainly lots of presidential statements in those years that confirm, at least on the rhetorical level, that 2(4) fit neatly into the global vision being projected by the United States at the time. The fact that there was relatively little public debate about use of force questions—at least during the period when the provisions of the charter were being negotiated and then sold to the Senate and the American public—is suggestive that there is something to this model, but the lack of debate would support some of the other models as well.
2. *Cynicism:* For all of their high-flying rhetoric about such things, many of Washington's foreign policy professionals were both skeptical about the prospects for the new world body and dismissive of such bold promises of restraint. They put much more stock—and devoted far more attention—to retaining the veto than to 2(4). A careful look at the U.S. interpretation of the Kellogg-Briand Pact of 1928 suggests that a similar pattern was at work. On the surface, the United States and other major powers renounced the use of force, but their reservations and interpretations of the pact gutted it of any operational content. In essence, it was agreed that the pact would not preclude the proactive, even preventive, defense of their interests around the world. According to this model, the lack of debate or concern about the consequences of 2(4) reflected the assumption of many well-placed Americans that the implications of 2(4) for U.S. foreign policy were inconsequential at most.
3. *Exceptionalism:* In some ways a variant of models one and two, American exceptionalism has proven extraordinarily durable as a tenet of the American worldview from the earliest days in part because it embraces both the idealism of model one and the cynicism of model two.[13] Under this model, the notion that 2(4) might actually place constraints on U.S. foreign policy and security choices barely occurs to U.S. policymakers and opinion leaders. American values are seen as the world's values and American interests as the world's interests. Article 2(4) was needed to discourage others with potentially dark designs, not the United States, which was to play a custodial role in the UN system, to borrow Michael Reisman's term.[14] The UN was to be our institution: a place to get others on board the U.S. bandwagon,

not where they would try to mount roadblocks in our way. The big worry in this regard was just the opposite, i.e., that others would try to use the Security Council to commit U.S. forces to missions without congressional authorization. In the focus on this scenario, little attention was paid to the potentially blocking role of the council when the United States was considering the use of force.

4. *Realism:* Realists, seeing 2(4) in the context of chapter VII and the UN's potential as the hub of a larger collective security system, would have understood its restraints on the unilateral use of force as having life only if the rest of the system was working. As part of a broader notion of collective security, restraint on the part of individual states within the system would be expected. But if the machinery of chapter VII proved to be stillborn, as turned out to be the case, then it would be both unfair and illogical to demand that 2(4) should be mandatory on its own. The Cold War, in this regard, changed everything. With the Security Council perpetually deadlocked, member states had no choice but to band together in regional security arrangements when possible and to rely on their own devices when not. In terms of international political dialogue, at least, the provisions of 2(4) seemed to have been largely forgotten by all sides until the end of the Cold War. In a historical context, Mike Glennon has a point when he asserts that the insistence on respecting 2(4) in the debate over the use of force in Iraq looks like the exception, not the rule.[15] As I have argued elsewhere, Security Council members who pressed the illegality of the use of force in Iraq, yet did not stand up for the implementation of earlier chapter VII measures in Iraq, must bear some responsibility for the impossible situation in which the UN found itself.[16] They ended up championing one part of the charter package even as they weakened another: pursuing multilateralism à la carte, much as the United States has so often done.

5. *Domestic politics:* Another interpretation would look to domestic political dynamics and constitutional restraints. The permissive political environment at that point, encouraged and shaped by a massive, determined, and skillful public relations campaign by the Franklin Roosevelt and Truman administrations, precluded serious questioning of this and other key provisions of the charter. Nonetheless, the U.S. negotiations at San Francisco were determined not to repeat the controversies over an allegedly open-ended commitment to use force that had blocked Senate support for doomed American participation in the League of Nations. Therefore, they preferred charter language that was, in their view, nonbinding both on the obligation to use force and on the restraints against its use. With the veto in their pocket, they could assure wavering senators that U.S. sovereignty concerning

the employment of U.S. force had not been compromised either way. As so often, in the end the U.S. attitude toward the provisions of Article 2(4) shifted from deep ambivalence to profound indifference.

None of these models, of course, provide a sufficient explanation, nor are they mutually exclusive. Most of the UN's architects incorporated elements from several of these perspectives in their thinking and planning. Each of these models, however, appears to provide a necessary piece of a more complete and complex picture of why American views of 2(4) have changed so dramatically over the years.

Idealism

The Charter of the United Nations was conceived, shaped, negotiated, and signed during wartime. In September 1939, more than two years before the United States entered the world conflict, FDR declared that "it seems to me clear, even at the outbreak of this great war, that the influence of America should be consistent in seeking for humanity a final peace which will eliminate, as far as it is possible to do so, the continued use of force between nations."[17] In the president's view, convening the founding conference while fighting was still going on would produce a better, more ambitious, and more enlightened document than had been the case with the Covenant of the League of Nations. The latter, tied to a controversial peace treaty, was negotiated at a time when postwar spoils and vengeance were much on the minds of the victors and when it was harder to maintain their sense of unity and common purpose. If a central recurring theme could be found in the pronouncements of the UN's founders, it was that they were determined not to replicate the mistakes of the League's creators. With the still-unfolding horrors of World War II before them, the delegates gathering in San Francisco would be more likely to strive to produce a quantum leap in the nature of interstate relations and in the quality, strength, and reach of the world organization that would seek to manage those relationships.

The laws of cognitive dissonance would ensure that every effort would be made to produce institutions worthy of the enormous human and material sacrifices being made in the war effort. Aiming high, it was widely believed, would avoid the letdown and disillusionment that had accompanied the stillbirth of the League. As Truman reminded the delegates at the opening of the San Francisco conference, "we who have lived through the torture and tragedy of two world conflicts must realize the magnitude of the problem before us."[18] To underline this linkage between the sacrifices of war and the organization of peace, FDR had insisted that the new organization adopt the name—United Nations—of the antifascist wartime allies. At the closing of the conference, Truman assured the delegates, "You have won a victory against war itself.

It was the hope of such a Charter that helped sustain the courage of stricken peoples through the darkest days of the war. For it is a declaration of great faith by the nations of the earth—faith that war is not inevitable, faith that peace can be maintained."[19]

Secretary of State Edward R. Stettinius, Jr., who led the U.S. delegation at San Francisco, captured the spirit of idealism well in his report to Truman on the results of the conference: "The first function of the Charter is moral and idealistic: the second realistic and practical. Men and women who have lived through war are not ashamed, as other generations sometimes are, to declare the depth and the idealism of their attachment to the cause of peace. But neither are they ashamed to recognize the realities of force and power which war have forced them to see and endure."[20] Leaders, in other words, had to be idealistic to capture the spirit, determination, and expectations of peoples still at war but yearning for a better, more peaceful future. As Stettinius emphasized, the charter aimed to provide moral guidance as well as an idealistic vision. Only peace-loving countries could join. On returning from Yalta, FDR told Congress that at San Francisco "we all hope, and confidently expect, to execute a definite charter of organization upon which the peace of the world will be preserved and the forces of aggression permanently outlawed."[21] Stettinius praised the charter's "dual quality as declaration and as constitution." As a declaration, it "constitutes a binding agreement by the signatory nations to work together for peaceful ends and to adhere to certain standards of international morality."[22]

Justice was a core theme of Truman's addresses to the opening and closing of the founding conference. As the delegates assembled, he asserted that "the world has experienced a revival of an old faith in the everlasting moral force of justice."[23] More specifically, he concluded, "the sacrifices of our youth today must lead, through your efforts, to the building for tomorrow of a mighty combination of nations founded upon justice for peace." In closing the conference, he asserted that "by their own example the strong nations of the world should lead the way to international justice. That principle of justice is the foundation stone of this Charter."[24]

In terms of international politics and the quest for security, it could no longer be business as usual. Upon returning from Moscow and the conclusion in November 1943 of a key foreign ministers' declaration, Secretary of State Cordell Hull foresaw a time when "there would no longer be any need for spheres of influence, for alliances, for balance of power or any other of the special arrangements through which, in the unhappy past, the nations strove to safeguard their security or to promote their interests."[25] With similar words and the same buoyant spirit, on returning from Yalta FDR told Congress that "the Crimean Conference was a successful effort by the three leading nations to find a common ground of peace. It spells, it ought to spell, the end of the system of unilateral action and exclusive alliances and spheres of influence and balance of power and all the other expedients that have been tried for centuries, and have always failed."[26] He warned that in some liberated areas "queer ideas of 'spheres of influence' which were incompatible with the basic principles of international collaboration" had begun to grow. In his first speech to Congress as president, only nine days before the opening of the San Francisco conference, Truman spoke of the prospects for a better future: "In bitter despair, some people have come to believe that wars are inevitable. With tragic fatalism, they insist that wars have always been, of necessity, and of necessity wars always will be. To such defeatism, men and women of good will must not and can not yield. The outlook for humanity is not so hopeless."[27] At the opening session he told the delegates, "We can no longer permit any nation, or group of nations, to attempt to settle their arguments with bombs and bayonets." Rather than "accept the fundamental philosophy of our enemies, namely, that "Might Makes Right' ... We must, once and for all, reverse the order, and prove by our acts conclusively that Right Has Might."[28]

In this new, reformed era, even the most powerful states would need to accept restraints on their use of force. In April 1944, Secretary of State Hull declared that a postwar organization "must be based upon firm and binding obligations that the member nations will not use force against each other and against any other nation except in accordance with the arrangements made."[29] He did recognize, however, that those arrangements must include "institutions and procedures" for calling a force "into action to preserve peace." As Truman told Congress and then repeated in his opening address at San Francisco, "Nothing is more essential to the future peace of the world than continued cooperation of the nations which had to muster the force necessary to defeat the conspiracy of the Axis powers to dominate the world. While these great states have a special responsibility to enforce the peace, their responsibility is based upon obligations resting upon all states, large and small, not to use force in international relations except in the defense of law. The responsibility of great states is to serve and not to dominate the world."[30]

In closing the conference, he cautioned that "we all have to recognize—no matter how great our strength—that we must deny ourselves the license to do always as we please." Militarily powerful nations, he continued, "have no right to dominate the world ... That is why we have resolved that power and strength should be used not to wage war, but to keep the world at peace, and free from the fear of war."[31] One of the leading academic experts of that time, Clyde Eagleton of New York University, contended that "what we now have to do is to make the use of force the monopoly of international government, and forbid its use by any state against another." Rather than allow states alone to claim that their use of force was in self-defense, he continued, now the UN could provide "the impartial judge" to make such a determination.[32]

Failure to accept both the constraints and obligations spelled out in the charter would have dire consequences in the Manichaean world painted by

FDR and Truman. The latter's prose was particularly vivid, when in his first speech to Congress, he warned that without sound international organization "the rights of man on earth cannot be protected" and "the entire world will have to remain an armed camp. The world will be doomed to deadly conflict, devoid of hope for real peace."[33] At the opening plenary in San Francisco, he cautioned that "with ever-increasing brutality and destruction, modern warfare, if unchecked, would ultimately crush all civilization. We still have a choice between the alternatives: the continuation of international chaos, or the establishment of a world organization for the enforcement of peace."[34] Moreover, he went on to admonish the delegates, "if we should pay merely lip service to inspiring ideals, and later do violence to simple justice, we would draw upon us the bitter wrath of generations yet unborn." At the final conference session, he claimed that "if we had had this Charter a few years ago—and above all, the will to use it—millions now dead would be alive. If we should falter in the future in our will to use it, millions now living will surely die."[35]

As idealistic as these sentiments sound today, they were based on classical notions of cooperative international security, whether through a concert of major powers as practiced in Europe for much of the nineteenth century, a collective security system as envisioned by Woodrow Wilson but imperfectly realized in the League of Nations, or an extension of a wartime alliance as in FDR's notion of the United Nations. Under each of these arrangements, the members were to avoid the precipitous or capricious use of force and, at the very least, to consult with each other before taking military action. FDR, with a clear strategic concept of how to structure the postwar world, was hardly naive. From the time of the declaration by the United Nations, less than two months after the United States entered the war, the notion that the Big Four—the United States, the USSR, the United Kingdom, and China—would win the war and then ensure the peace afterward was central to U.S. planning for the postwar world.[36] FDR's vision was hardly egalitarian, for these "four policemen," later with the addition of a liberated France, were to have special powers and prerogatives—as well as responsibilities—in the new Security Council.[37] Under Article 53(1), regional groups undertaking enforcement action against "any enemy state" would be exempt from the requirement to get prior authorization from the Security Council.[38] The provisions to discourage the unilateral use of force were to help perpetuate both the unity of the Big Four (later Five) and their dominance over the rest of the membership and any external aggressors.

So this was a decidedly practical strain of idealism on the part of the American planners, but they were hardly alone. Though the nonuse-of-force paragraph came from the U.S. draft, it was "strongly supported by the British as well as the Soviet delegations" at Dumbarton Oaks, according to an American account of the meetings.[39] There, it was the Chinese delegation that urged further elaboration of the rather broad principles agreed on by the United

States, United Kingdom, and Soviet Union during the first round of discussions. In particular, they were concerned about the implications of the prohibition on the use of force "in any manner inconsistent with the purposes of the Organization," language from the initial American draft and the basis for what was to become Article 2(4) of the charter. They wanted reassurance that this clause would not limit a nation's right to self-defense and wondered what would prevent states from justifying any decision to use force as an effort to forward the organization's broad purposes.[40] Once their hosts underlined that the principle would not apply to self-defense, but that other uses of forces would have to be authorized by the Security Council, the Chinese delegation relented.

At that stage, of course, the assertion in Article 51 of the "inherent right of individual or collective self-defense" had not been added to the draft charter, and the valid concerns of the Chinese would be echoed by Latin American representatives at San Francisco. At the time, however, Stettinius characterized the Chinese emphasis on principles as "extremely idealistic."[41] In retrospect, it is remarkable that neither the American nor British delegates at Dumbarton Oaks appreciated the full import of the Chinese challenge or made any effort to patch this very significant gap in the charter's provisions on the use of force. The incident would seem to confirm either the force of FDR's vision and the idealistic bent of the founders or the core cynicism behind the enunciation of such sweeping principles.

Cynicism

The lack of high level attention to the nonuse of force provision at any point in the process of conceptualization, development, negotiation, and ratification of the charter is remarkable. This oversight lends credence to explanations based on cynicism or exceptionalism. The nonuse of force stricture stirred virtually no controversy in the United States in the early to mid-1940s. During the Senate Foreign Relations Committee hearings on the charter in July 1945, not a single question was voiced about this provision. As noted already, the earliest planning documents on postwar organization prepared by the State Department or interagency groups included similar language. Judging from accounts of the various discussions of these plans and provisions with Presidents FDR and Truman or with Secretaries of State Hull and Stettinius, the topic either never came up or was not considered consequential enough to be included in the notes of the sessions. When first briefing the U.S. delegation for San Francisco about the draft charter agreed on at Dumbarton Oaks, Leo Pasvolsky underlined "that a good many provisions of the proposals had not been criticized and that little attention would have to be paid to these provisions."[42] Among these was the paragraph on the nonuse of force. Clearly Truman was not worried about congressional or public reactions, since, as already quoted, he included a relatively bald and bold version of the 2(4) constraint in his first speech as president to Congress and again, nine days later, in his address to the opening plenary at San Francisco.

Idealists, of course, would not question a provision so close to their conception of how the world ought to be. Cynics, on the other hand, would readily dismiss such attempts to radically alter historic patterns of interstate behavior through pious declarations of principle. From their perspective, it might not be worth the effort to deign to refute such inconsequential assertions. For graphic and ultimately tragic evidence of the emptiness of such paper commitments, they only had to cite the Kellogg-Briand Pact of 1928 (The Pact of Paris), which had grandly renounced war as an instrument of national policy. The product of American–French collaboration and known by the names of their respective foreign ministers, the treaty sought to unite "the civilized nations of the world" and to perpetuate "the peaceful and friendly relations now existing between their peoples." Among the parties were Germany, Italy, and Japan, the very axis powers whose aggression would soon ignite the second world war. Tellingly, Senator Tom Connally's initial reaction to the Dumbarton Oaks wording that was to become Article 2(4) was dismissive. To him, "this was just another statement of the Kellogg-Briand Pact."[43]

For the purposes of this chapter, what is most relevant and interesting is how the parties, including the United States, chose to interpret and apply the pact's provisions. In presenting the treaty to the Senate Foreign Relations Committee, Secretary of State Frank B. Kellogg was blunt about the limited character of the agreement. He stressed, first, that he "was not willing to impose any obligation on the United States. I knew that was out of the question." Second, he suggested that it was "incomprehensible" to expect any country to "sign a treaty which could be construed as taking away the right of self-defense if a country was attacked." Third, it was "left entirely to that government" to determine if it was acting in self-defense. And fourth, "the right of self-defense is not limited to territory in the continental United States … It means that this Government has a right to take such measures as it believes necessary to the defense of the country, or to prevent things that might endanger the country; but the United States must be the judge of that, and it is answerable to the public opinion of the world if it is not an honest defense; that is all."[44] In other words, this amounted to an early rationalization for preventive war three-quarters of a century before the George W. Bush administration returned to the theme.

Kellogg, with apparent approval, went on to quote a similarly narrow interpretation by the British government. According to London, "there are certain regions of the world the welfare and integrity of which constitute a special and vital interest for our peace and safety … interference with those regions can not be suffered. Their protection against attack is to the British Empire a measure of self-defense." The French took a similar line, emphasizing the need to meet their obligations under the covenant, the treaties of Locarno, and various treaties of alliance.[45] As Edwin Bouchard aptly phrased it at that time, "far from constituting an outlawry of war, they constitute the most definite sanction of specific wars that has ever been promulgated."[46] Seventeen years later, in the run-up to San Francisco, acting Assistant Secretary of State Joseph C. Grew cabled U.S. embassies in Paris, London, Moscow, and Chungking to spread the reassuring word that the Dumbarton Oaks language on the nonuse of force posed "no conflict" with the Soviet–French Alliance, the Act of Chapultepec, or similar regional security arrangements.[47]

The conceptual dilemmas created by these nuanced, even debilitating, interpretations of the pact (and of the similar Dumbarton Oaks language) were not lost on leading scholars and commentators of the time. According to Eagleton, for example, "Kellogg's interpretation of the Pact of Paris, recognizing to each state the right to determine what constitutes an act of self-defense, complicated the problem. At the same time, public opinion more vigorously than ever condemns aggression."[48] The noted legal scholar Hans Kelsen, writing before the San Francisco conference, pointed out that the Dumbarton Oaks language that "the employment of force is allowed only as a collective action for the realization of the purposes of the Organization" was "accommodated to the provisions of the Kellogg Pact."[49] In their definitive commentary on the charter's provisions, Leland M. Goodrich and Edvard Hambro contended that the reference to "in their international relations" in Article 2(4) would not "prohibit the use of force in suppressing colonial disorder."[50] They also pointed to the U.S. position on the Greek Frontier Incidents case when it came before the Security Council: "The failure of the Security Council to act did not preclude individual or collective action by the states willing to act, so long as the action taken was in accordance with the general purposes and principles of the United Nations."[51] In their view, "this raises the question whether the threat or use of force in the exercise of the right of self-defense to meet a danger short of 'armed attack' would be consistent with 'the Purposes of the United Nations.'"[52]

Given these ambiguities, it is hardly surprising that some members of Congress have taken a broad view of the latitude given to U.S. defense decision making under Article 2(4). The testimony of John Foster Dulles, an active member of the U.S. team at San Francisco, during the Senate Foreign Relations Committee's hearings on the charter raised further doubts about the reach of 2(4). Dulles, once a student of and then aide to Woodrow Wilson at the Paris peace conference that produced the League of Nations Covenant, had been the chief foreign policy adviser to Republican presidential candidate Thomas Dewey in 1944 and later became secretary of state under President Dwight Eisenhower. He told the committee in 1945, "There is nothing whatsoever in the Charter which impairs a nation's right of self-defense. The prohibition against the use of force is a prohibition against the use of force for purposes inconsistent with the purposes of the Charter. Among the purposes of the Charter is security."⁵³ If the senators accepted Dulles' interpretation of 2(4)—and none questioned it during the hearings—then its ban on the unilateral use of force would have seemed no more potent than what was in the Kellogg-Briand Pact. It is hard to imagine the U.S. government—or any other for that matter—deciding to use force in situations deemed not to advance national security. As noted earlier, whereas the members of the committee neglected to pose a single question about 2(4), they did seek, and regularly received, assurances that nothing in the charter would inhibit the United States in its hemispheric defense responsibilities under the Monroe Doctrine.

The broad public support for the charter and the carefully orchestrated campaign by the FDR and Truman administrations to rally favorable public, nongovernmental organization, and editorial commentary ensured relatively quick and largely unquestioning Senate approval. At Dumbarton Oaks, the American, Soviet, and British conceptions of the principles to guide the organization had proven similar and noncontroversial.⁵⁴ According to the account of the New Zealand delegation to San Francisco, the statement of principles did not receive much attention there either. "As a result of vigorous chairmanship and a very firm limitation of discussion the chapter was passed by the committee in a few hours without alteration of the proposals made by the subcommittee."⁵⁵ The task of organizing the Senate Foreign Relations Committee hearings on the UN charter fell to the able Dean Acheson, then assistant secretary but in 1949 to become Truman's secretary of state. He reported that it was one of his easier tasks, but one for which he felt little personal enthusiasm: "Although I had nothing to do with the planning of the United Nations Charter or the negotiations at Dumbarton Oaks in Washington or the conference in San Francisco that led to its adoption, the management of the hearings before the Senate Committee on Foreign Relations regarding its ratification fell within my field of responsibility. I did my duty faithfully and successfully but always believed that the Charter was impracticable. Moreover, its presentation to the American people as almost holy writ and with the evangelical enthusiasm of a major advertising campaign seemed to me to raise popular hopes which would only lead to bitter disappointment."⁵⁶

The intensity of the FDR and Truman drives to ensure the United States would be fully aboard the second effort in the twentieth century to build a new global security structure no doubt discouraged other officials in Washington, D.C., from voicing their reservations. Indeed, some senators also questioned the rush to ratification without a full discussion of key charter provisions.⁵⁷ Acheson, moreover, was hardly alone in his doubts and concerns. A month before the charter was signed, acting Secretary of State Grew, no less, commented in a private memorandum that the provisions of the veto would leave the UN "powerless to act against the one certain enemy, Soviet Russia," leaving the UN's "power to prevent a future world war . . . but a pipe dream."⁵⁸

Americans were not alone in interpreting the application and scope of Article 2(4) rather narrowly. At the October 1944 Moscow conference of the foreign ministers of the chief allies, Soviet foreign minister Vyacheslav M. Molotov doggedly pressed his partners on whether the restrictions on the use of force would have to apply to the establishment of naval and air bases a larger country might establish in a smaller one. In response, Secretary of State Hull replied, "This article was in the nature of a self-denying act on the part of the large nations to allay the suspicions of the smaller countries in regard to the use of superior force."[59] Though no doubt meant to reinforce the new norm, Hull's explanation sounded more like the description of a political trade-off than of a new binding legal principle. Still, the U.S. approach may not have been sufficiently cynical for some of its partners. The Earl of Halifax, London's ambassador in Washington and leader of the British delegation for much of the San Francisco conference, described Americans as follows: "faith in the magic of large words; an enthusiastic belief that the mere enunciation of an abstract principle is equivalent to its concrete fulfillment; a tendency to overlook the practical difficulties that obstruct the easy solution of current problems; above all, a constant disposition to prefer the emotional to the rational approach."[60]

Upon returning from the Yalta summit prior to the opening of the San Francisco conference, British Prime Minister Winston Churchill told the House of Commons that "there is nothing at all" in the new agreement to deal with aggression by the great powers. This gap would not be addressed at San Francisco, he continued, because Yalta "does prescribe for a differentiation between the treatment of the greatest powers in these matters and of the smallest powers." To try to do otherwise, he cautioned, "would be foolish" given the differences "between great and small, between the strong and the weak in the world." He warned against trying to attain "a hopeless ideal."[61] So although Article 2(4) may be worded in sweeping and universal prose, its enforcement by the Security Council would be selective, conditioned by the voting requirement of concurrence among the five permanent members [see Article 27 (3)]. Once again, the dictates of power politics would trump the declaration of grand principles.

Exceptionalism

In conceiving, assembling, negotiating, and selling the charter, American planners and leaders did not seem to be the least concerned that the prohibitions on the use of force could apply to U.S. actions. Twice in the last three decades, the United States had been called upon to overcome its reluctance and to supply the forces that would tip the balance in favor of its allies—the new Security Council's other permanent members—in the two world wars. The cautions of Article 2(4) hardly seemed to be intended for a nation that had emerged from the grip of isolationism only a few years before. This plank, after all, was produced by American planners, who were undoubtedly confident that it was much more necessary to inhibit countries other than their own. It would have been reasonable to assume that Congress and a wary public—not charter principles—would be the primary brake on military adventurism by the United States. As discussed in greater detail in this section, congressional and executive branch leaders were far more concerned that the UN might try to compel, instead of restrict, the use of U.S. forces than attempt to restrict their use.

The long-standing tendency toward exceptionalism in American thinking, furthermore, identified U.S. interests with global interests and conflated U.S. principles and values with universal ones.[62] Consciously or subconsciously, American postwar planners were inclined to believe that what was good for the United States was good for the United Nations, if not the world. The fact that the world body began as an alliance with the United States at its center, not as a universal body, no doubt acted to confirm such exceptionalist assumptions. The tone of Secretary of State Stettinius's report to Truman on the results of San Francisco is suggestive in this regard. In discussing Article 2(4) and the restrictions on the use of force, he commented that "the standards of conduct of this country permit us to assume this obligation with no hesitation."[63]

Others expressed similar sentiments. Reportedly, the whole notion of having a chapter of the Dumbarton Oaks proposals devoted to principles came from the British side and was intended to "give the smaller states some satisfaction."[64] Referring to the four-power Moscow declaration of October 1944, British foreign minister Anthony Eden told his Soviet and American counterparts that "his Government believed it inconceivable that any of the powers represented at the conference would use their armed forces or establish bases in territory of other states except for the purposes envisaged by the Declaration."[65] Though American exceptionalism was the most pronounced variety, the convening powers as a whole exhibited a kind of group sense of exceptionalism both through the permanent status they assigned themselves in the Security Council and through the rules and principles they laid down for others to meet if they wanted to join the alliance turned world organization. By definition, according to Article 4(1) of the charter UN members were to be "peace-loving." The primary threats to international peace and security, therefore, were most likely to come from nonmembers.

In addition, it is telling that a leading Republican, John Foster Dulles, was the most sanguine about how little the charter's principles, rules, and procedures would affect the conduct of U.S. foreign and security policy. In a robust defense of the charter, he reassured the Senate Foreign Relations Committee that "the document before you charts a path which we can pursue joyfully and without fear." He continued, "Under it we remain the masters of our own destiny. The Charter does not subordinate us to any supergovernment. There is no right on the part of the United Nations Organization to intervene in our domestic affairs. There can be no use of force without our consent. If the joint adventure fails, we can withdraw."[66] The use of force provisions, in his view, were a plus because they gave Washington a veto over the actions of others. He failed to address the possibility that others might use the same rules to try to restrict U.S. security options.

The prevailing assumption among U.S. decision makers — that the Charter was to be based on American norms and models of government — added another set of blinders. Unlike the distant and flawed League, this was to be a world body inspired and designed largely by Americans, negotiated and to be based on American soil. We would teach, others would learn. In reporting to Congress on his recent trip to Yalta, President Roosevelt confided that "I spent a good deal of time in educating two other nations of the world in the Constitution of the United States."[67] In his first speech as president to Congress, Truman claimed that "the entire world is looking to America for enlightened leadership to peace and progress." Asserting that "America has become one of the most powerful forces for good on earth," the president called on all Americans to "live up to our glorious heritage" and to "assist suffering humanity back along the path of peaceful progress."[68] He certainly did not sound like a leader worried about the UN telling him when he could and could not use force for what he believed to be the common good.

These messianic and exceptionalist impulses fed the common notion that the architecture, principles, and procedures of the new world body would reflect American institutions as well as values. In reporting to the president on the characteristics of the charter, for instance, Secretary of State Stettinius compared the functions of the Security Council, International Court of Justice, and General Assembly to the three branches of the federal government, as follows: "On the frontiers of democratic society—not least upon the American frontiers—the instruments of order have always been, in one form or another, an agency to enforce respect for law with moral and physical power to prevent and suppress breaches of the peace; a court in which the differences and disagreements of the citizens could be heard and tried; and a meeting place where the moral sense of the community could be expressed and its judgments formed."[69]

Commander Harold E. Stassen of the U.S. Navy, the one military figure on the U.S. delegation, told the assembled delegations at San Francisco that the Security Council would act as a police officer and as a jury would do in the United States. He also suggested that there were similarities in the processes for developing the UN charter and the U.S. Constitution.[70] Similar comparisons between the domestic and international order had been made when membership in the League was being considered.

Acheson and other realist critics found it easy to deride such strained analogies, which in Acheson's view amounted to "a grand fallacy." One could not "apply to external affairs the institutions and practices of legislative procedure in liberal democracies." Nor should one assume that "among peace-loving peoples—and all others should be or had been suppressed—violence could and would be superseded by reason." He disdained "the true believer, of whom Arthur Vandenberg was to become one of the most vociferous."[71] Yet, as noted previously, Acheson did not raise these qualms publicly when the Senate was deciding whether to give its advice and consent to the charter. The notion that the UN would be something of a global clone of its principal founder was a powerful argument at a time when the president's first concern was to avoid Woodrow Wilson's mistakes so that he could bind the United States to the UN as closely and permanently as possible. To suggest that the UN and United States might part company someday over a decision in Washington to use force would have been to sound a most unwelcome, unanticipated, and discordant note.

Realism

Realism, as well, had its place in postwar planning. The renunciation of the use of force contained in Article 2(4) might appear hopelessly idealistic on its own and out of context. But as part of the larger fabric of commitments, obligations, and capacities envisioned in the charter, its place in the postwar security structure assumed a certain logic. By spring 1943, according to Hull FDR's conception of a global security system based on the combined military prowess of the "four policemen" began to drive postwar planning.[72] That same year, Walter Lippmann published his influential realist critique of prewar U.S. policies, *U.S. Foreign Policy: Shield of the Republic.* In it, he took William Howard Taft and Wilson to task for neglecting strong alliances and national defense in deference to an unrelenting idealism. "In them," Lippmann wrote, "the idealism which prompts Americans to make large and resounding commitments was combined with the pacificism which causes American to shrink from the measures of force that are needed to support the commitments."[73]

FDR had learned these lessons well. He was determined neither to repeat Wilson's errors nor to permit Congress once again to shortchange U.S. defense preparedness following the conclusion of the war. Under his conception, the new world security organization built on American military might aid security alliances—not supplant them. Collective restraint required collective security. In December 1943, in his cover letter to the president presenting the State Department's outline plan for the new organization, Hull noted that

> The entire plan is based on two central assumptions:
>
> First, that the four major powers will pledge themselves and will consider themselves morally bound not to go to war against each other or

against any other nation, and to cooperate with each other and with other peace-loving states in maintaining the peace; and

Second, that each of them will maintain adequate forces and will be willing to use such forces as circumstances require to prevent or suppress all cases of aggression.[74]

As Stettinius reported to Truman a year and a half later, "the whole scheme of the Charter is based on this conception of collective force made available to the Organization for the maintenance of international peace and security."[75] The nonuse of force clause, in that regard, was intended to be one plank in a much broader and more robust security architecture. Without the other pieces it could not stand alone. As the *New Republic* opined, the founders were creating "a practical device, suited to the realities of the situation, rather than an idealistic dream put on paper."[76]

Two points were so widely accepted among the founders that it apparently did not seem necessary to enunciate them or explicitly refer to them in the Dumbarton Oaks draft. First, the pledge of the nonuse of force could not preclude the inherent right of self-defense, which was a well-established tenet of international law. Second, the implementation of Article 2(4) would depend on the extent the other security provisions in chapters VI, VII, and VIII of the charter would prove effective. Writing in 1946, Grayson Kirk, professor at Columbia University, member of the U.S. delegation at Dumbarton Oaks, and executive officer of the Third Commission at San Francisco dealing with the Security Council, noted that, although the Dumbarton Oaks draft was silent on "how far might a state go in resorting unilaterally to the use of force" in self-defense, "it could be deduced from the nature of the projected organization that the inherent right of self-defense had not been abandoned."[77] According to Eagleton, the new organization must "have the power to change existing legal or factual situations" and "the physical force with which to compel conformity with its decisions. When this is done, it will be possible to forbid the use of force by states."[78] In other words, when the other pieces of the new security structure were in place—not before—compliance with Article 2(4) could be expected.

Over the course of a few months, Dulles's views on the implications of Article 2(4) shifted remarkably. This transition from alarm to indifference helps explain why the paragraph ended up attracting so little controversy, or even interest, among senators and private citizens alike. When first presented to the U.S. delegation during its preparations for San Francisco, the series of principles agreed at Dumbarton Oaks were deemed by Dulles to be "extremely dangerous,"[79] as "they gave the illusion of security through sweeping commitments" and created "a false illusion."[80] He went on to remind his colleagues that even the United States was not "prepared to settle all disputes by peaceful means." By the end of the San Francisco conference, however, he apparently was reassured that these dangerous gaps and illusions had been addressed satisfactorily. As he told the Senate Foreign Relations Committee, "At San Francisco, one of the things we stood for most stoutly, and which we achieved with the greatest difficulty, was a recognition of the fact that that doctrine of self-defense, enlarged at Chapultepec to be a doctrine of collective self-defense, could stand unimpaired and could function without the approval of the Security Council."[81] Two points are worth noting here. One is Dulles's rather loose and permissive interpretation of the charter's provisions on the use of force and on enforcement measures by regional arrangements and agencies. Also, Dulles was one of a very few U.S. officials to express even private concern about the restrictions of 2(4) in the absence of Article 51's specific invocation of the inherent right of individual and collective self-defense. Other delegations to San Francisco, however, found the draft wording of 2(4) produced at Dumbarton Oaks inadequate. The way their concerns were addressed at the world conference—through clarifications as well as amended language—apparently met Dulles's doubts as well.

The Dumbarton Oaks language was both stark and simple: "All members of the Organization shall refrain in their international relations from the threat or use of force in any manner inconsistent with the purposes of the Organization." A resolution of the Inter-American Conference on Problems of War and Peace, held in Mexico City in late February and early March 1945, however, called for "amplifying and making more specific the enumeration of the principles and purposes of the Organization."[82] Bolivia, Brazil, Mexico, and Paraguay called for a more explicit recognition of the principles of respect for territorial integrity, noninterference, and political independence of member states.[83] Australia, New Zealand, and several other states added their voices to this growing chorus at San Francisco.[84] The strongly held Latin American position stemmed from two somewhat contradictory worries: the first fueled by past interventions by their powerful northern neighbor and the second from concern about extra-hemispheric security threats that could not be met collectively if great power (particularly Soviet) vetoes in the Security Council thwarted action under the Monroe Doctrine. A generation earlier, of course, the latter scenario helped to undermine support in the U.S. Senate for the League of Nations, and this was a continuing worry to Dulles and many other Washington strategists and legislators in 1945.

The mini-revolt of the Latin American delegations at San Francisco threatened to disrupt the positive atmosphere so carefully engineered by FDR and Truman, while renewing the divisive debates of 1942–43 over the relative advantages of global versus regional approaches to organizing collective security.[85] At the same time, however, the regional debate also helped to clarify the range of assumptions about self-defense and the use of force held both within the U.S. delegation and among the other governments represented at San Francisco.

Within the U.S. team, Dulles contended that nothing in the Dumbarton Oaks proposals would limit self-defense, and Pasvolsky concurred, asserting that, should any permanent member veto enforcement action when required in this hemisphere, "we would go ahead and use force to suit ourselves (and the Peace League would be all through)."[86] Eventually the U.S. delegation took the lead in drafting Article 51, on "the inherent right of individual or collective self-defense if an armed attack occurs against a Member of the United Nations, until the Security Council has taken measures necessary to maintain international peace and security," to meet the concerns of its southern neighbors.

For the U.S. delegation, however, it is evident that this new language was viewed essentially as a confirmation of preexisting and inherent rights that had not been compromised in any way by the nonuse of force clause agreed at Dumbarton Oaks.[87] When the U.S. team first reviewed the Dumbarton Oaks proposals, Leo Pasvolsky affirmed, in response to a query by Vandenberg, that "the right of self-defense existed but that there was an obligation to notify the Council. If the Council failed to act immediately then a country was free to act. He considered that self-defense was implicit in the document but inquired how it could be spelled out. He stated that no suitable language had yet been found."[88] Nevertheless, the addition of Article 51 did come in handy at times. By the end of the day, Pasvolsky was able to tell the Senate Foreign Relations Committee that "as long as the Organization functions, the Monroe Doctrine does not need to come into play" for both institutions were based on the principle of nonintervention. Should the UN fail to maintain international peace and security, on the other hand, he reassured the senators, "this contingency is covered by the provisions for self-defense, which are stated in article 51."[89]

The U.S. delegation in San Francisco was determined to keep "the scope of obligations" not to use force under 2(4) relatively narrow. Regarding some of the proposed amendments to the Dumbarton Oaks language, Stassen, seconded by Dulles, cautioned against any new language that "would prevent necessary action by Member states when the veto power of the Organization was used arbitrarily." He asserted that "so long as the veto power remained, he would stand against enlarging the scope of the obligations" under 2(4).[90] At first, the U.S. delegates were unenthusiastic about the proposals from a number of states (noted previously) to add references to territorial integrity and political independence to the wording of 2(4).[91] Eventually they agreed to the Australian amendment along these lines, apparently for two reasons. First, the idea had received broad support among other delegations and had cleared the subcommittee dealing with principles unanimously.[92] And second, it must have seemed far more palatable—to the delegates and potentially to the U.S. Senate—than a parallel New Zealand suggestion (discussed in the next section) that all members pledge to protect the political independence and territorial integrity of each member state.⁹³ Indeed, after one of the subcommissions had approved the New Zealand amendment, the United States and other major powers convinced it to reverse its decision and to adopt the Australian draft instead.⁹⁴

The U.S. delegation rejected Norway's proposal, on the other hand, to clarify 2(4) by stating that no force should be used "if not approved" by the Security Council.⁹⁵ Dulles argued that "this was a very bad recommendation because it was contrary to the provision concerning self-defense," and Stassen moved its disapproval.⁹⁶ Norway and other smaller states, still unhappy with the lack of precision in the Dumbarton Oaks wording, proposed substituting "provisions of this Charter" for "purposes of the Organization."⁹⁷ Again the United States balked. Stassen claimed that "the revision would constitute an unnecessary restriction upon the right of the member states to use force consistent with the purposes of the Organization." According to Dulles, the right of self-defense "was dependent on the original wording of Principle 4 which made possible the use of force by member states." In Stassen's view, the use of the word *provisions* "would necessitate supervision by the Security Council over the use of force by the member states."⁹⁸ Dulles suggested, moreover, that the smaller states should recognize "that it would be contrary to their interest and to the principle of regional collaboration for defense if they were to oppose the old wording." Neither proposal survived the intergovernmental subcommittee dealing with charter principles.⁹⁹

The outbreak of the Cold War within a few short years of the signing of the charter underlined just how realistic and practical such a narrow reading was of the constraints imposed by 2(4). With the Security Council hampered by deep divisions among the permanent members and repeated Soviet vetoes, Washington officials and the American public alike began to have grave misgivings about whether the world body could ever live up to its initial promise as an effective international security mechanism.¹⁰⁰ The worries related both to the control of atomic weapons—which did not exist when the charter was being conceived, negotiated, and signed—and to threats to regional stability, peace, and security. In June 1946, less than a year after the charter was signed, Bernard Baruch underlined the urgency of overcoming or circumventing blockages to Security Council action in dealing with atomic threats if his plans for nuclear disarmament were to be realized: "There must be no veto to protect those who violate their solemn agreements not to develop or use atomic energy for destructive purposes. The bomb does not wait upon debate. To delay may be to die. The time between violation and preventive action or punishment would be all too short for extended discussion as to the course to be followed."¹⁰¹

As Baruch feared, the Security Council has never proven itself capable of dealing with either the vertical or horizontal dimensions of nuclear proliferation. The nuclear arms race—the most imminent threat to human security ever devised—proceeded over the course of four decades of Cold War under its own rules, doctrines, and logic without reference to the machinery, purposes, or principles laid out so carefully in the charter. As Moscow, Washington, and other capitals developed their strategies for nuclear deterrence and defense, it is doubtful that the provisions of 2(4) even entered their thinking. "The search for security through the United Nations, through regional defense arrangements, and through attempts to regulate armaments," Acheson ruminated years later, "seems even more baffling today than it was when it appeared to be the supreme problem of two decades ago."[102]

Writing in 1949, Leland M. Goodrich and Edvard Hambro, veterans of the founding conference from the United States and Norway, respectively, ruefully concluded that "the inability of the Security Council to act effectively in the discharge of its responsibilities because of disagreements among its permanent Members, together with the development of the atomic bomb, has created a situation, not envisaged at San Francisco, in which a more liberal exercise of the right of self-defense seems necessary. The provisions of the Charter, not too clear in their meaning in any case, are being interpreted to justify action which now seems necessary to meet situations which the regular organs and procedures of the United nations have proven incapable of handling in a satisfactory manner."[103] Over the course of a few years following the founding of the world body, the United States developed a series of regional security arrangements to resist what it deemed to be encroachments aided, inspired, or implemented by one of the other "four policemen."

In each case, the regional alternatives were presented as efforts to carry out the intent, if not always the letter, of the charter. For example, in presenting the Truman Doctrine, which was aimed at assisting Greece and Turkey, to Congress in 1947 Truman contended that "in helping free and independent nations to maintain their freedom, the United States will be giving effect to the principles of the Charter of the United Nations."[104] Likewise, the Vandenberg Resolution of 1948 asserted that it was the sense of the Senate that the United States should pursue the "progressive development of regional and other collective arrangements for individual and collective self-defense in accordance with the purposes, principles, and provisions of the Charter."[105]

Though such doctrines no doubt represented rather liberal interpretations of what was allowed under the use of force provisions of the charter, they do appear to largely coincide with the realist understandings of Articles 2(4) and 51 voiced by the U.S. delegation at San Francisco. The flexible reading of the charter's provisions also permitted the often beleaguered world body to survive four decades of divisive, polarizing, and often brutal Cold War among its core founders. Under a less political and pragmatic and more legal and literal reading of 2(4), the UN should have gone out of business by its fifth birthday, following the invasion of South Korea, if not earlier. A. L. Goodhart of Oxford University, writing in 1957 of the Suez Crisis, queried "whether the limitation of force to self-defense against an armed attack is a reasonable and practical provision in a world in which the United Nations has not itself been able to carry out its duty to prevent threats of aggression and other breaches of the peace." Although not offering a definitive conclusion, he opined that "it is not certain how the United Nations can continue to be effective if it insists that so impractical a doctrine is an essential part of its existence."[106]

Domestic Politics

In shaping the charter's security and use of force provisions, U.S. planners and leaders had the luxury of working within a far more flexible and permissive political environment in terms of public and congressional attitudes than the one that faced Wilson and the League. In part, as pointed out already, FDR and Truman had learned a lot from Wilson's mismanagement of the Senate and tardy courting of public support.[107] Efforts to make this a truly bipartisan project were aided by early consultations with members of Congress from both sides of the aisle by (1) the selection of a politically diverse U.S. delegation for San Francisco; (2) the holding of the conference during wartime; (3) a concerted campaign to spur broad support from the public and civic organizations; (4) FDR's immense popularity; and, ultimately, (5) his untimely death on the eve of San Francisco, which transformed the realization of the world body into his legacy.

Acheson, who orchestrated the Senate hearings, found this to be the "easiest of all" the tasks he undertook as assistant secretary of state for Legislative Affairs and Conferences given the "popular steam behind the Charter."[108] Not surprisingly, Connally, chair of the Senate Foreign Relations Committee, discovered that "the overwhelming majority of witnesses wanted the charter. The Gallup Poll found the country in favor by twenty to one. And the members of the Senate Foreign Relations approved it twenty-one to one."[109] When other arguments failed to work, the charter's advocates never tired of reminding senators that the inability of the League to prevent the ongoing world war might have resulted, in part, from the Senate's failure to approve U.S. participation. "At one point during the wrangling," Connally proudly recounted, "I pointed to the Senate chamber wall and thundered, 'They know that the League of Nations was slaughtered here in this chamber. Can't you see the blood?—There it is on the wall.'"[110] Apparently, collective institutional guilt worked just fine. Though tactically brilliant and remarkably successful in the short term, with only two dissenting votes in the Senate on the charter, the very intensity of the pro-charter campaign discouraged a careful review of many of its potentially consequential provisions, including Article 2(4). Knowing the unfavorable odds at that point, the would-be opponents of the UN laid in wait for a more propitious time to begin chipping away at its weaker points.[111] As noted earlier, the significance of 2(4) from an American perspective was undermined by the Senate's disinterest in it. It never received a proper review.

The Republican and Democratic platforms of 1944 were uniformly enthusiastic about the development of postwar organization, but in each case the emphasis was on the collective use of force, not on the renunciation of its unilateral use. The Republicans called for "effective cooperative means to direct peace forces to prevent or repel military aggression."[112] The Democrats, for their part, stressed the need "to have such forces available for joint action when necessary. Such organization must be endowed with power to employ armed forces when necessary to prevent aggression and preserve peace."[113] In August 1944, the Republican presidential candidate, Thomas Dewey, did criticize the notion that four big powers should dominate the world, but a series of discussions between his chief foreign policy adviser, John Foster Dulles, and Secretary of State Cordell Hull soon produced a convergence of views.[114] The U.S. delegation in San Francisco included a number of military advisers, and the Truman administration made sure it obtained the approval of the joint chiefs of staff, in writing, of the new charter. In their view, "the military and strategic implications of this draft charter as a whole are in accord with the military interests of the United States."[115]

Despite all of these good omens, one issue had, more than any other, scuttled American participation in the League and could have threatened to do the same with the charter if not handled adroitly. As Vandenberg said in discussing with Secretary of State Hull the progress of the Dumbarton Oaks conference, "I would never consent that our delegates on the new 'League' Council should have the power to vote us into a major military operation (tantamount to declaring war) without a vote of Congress as required by the Constitution."[116] The U.S. representative to the UN, in his view, should be free to veto proposals for the joint use of force, because "our Constitution clearly lodges the exclusive power to declare war in the Congress. Frankly, I do not believe the American people will ever agree to lodge this power anywhere else."[117]

As Vandenberg's comments made crystal clear, the U.S. delegation was determined to avoid another Article X debacle, in which Henry Cabot Lodge, Elihu Root, and other opponents of the covenant were able to cast it as creating an open-ended obligation to guarantee the territorial integrity and political independence of all members of the League.[118] Actually, the obligation, if any, was to participate in the deliberations of the League's council, which lacked enforcement powers and was intended to operate by consensus. The skeptics claimed, however, in true exceptionalist fashion that for the United States a moral commitment was equivalent to a legal one.[119] The right of veto in the UN's Security Council, of course, was seen as the essential first line of defense against unwanted obligations. As Connally argued in the floor debate on the charter, the veto provision "is a source of strength for the Charter in that it gives absolute assurance to each of the Big Five that they will not be asked to use their armed forces in some military enterprise in which they do not concur."[120] Moreover, as Hans Kelsen commented following the Dumbarton Oaks meetings but before San Francisco, "there is no provision analogous to that of Art. 10 of the Covenant by which each member of the League is obliged to respect the territorial integrity and existent political independence of all the other members." This, in his view, was advantageous in that the new Charter "is not to be burdened with a guarantee of the territorial status quo."[121]

Some smaller delegations, however, apparently missed the old Article X. On the eve of the San Francisco conference, the Australian minister of external affairs, Herbert Vere Evatt, complained that "there is no express positive guarantee of either the territorial integrity or the political independence of members, comparable with Article X of the League Covenant."[122] New Zealand went further, proposing that a new paragraph be introduced following what would become 2(4), as follows: "All members of the Organization undertake collectively to resist every act of aggression against any member."[123] Though the United States and the other major powers blocked acceptance of this amendment in a subcommission vote, New Zealand pressed it in the full Commission I, falling just short of the required two-thirds support (26 to 18). Its delegation cited the inequities of the veto and permanent membership, while asking, "What guarantee of safety are the small Powers to get in return for the heavy commitments they are to undertake"? In addition "this proposal appeared to the New Zealand delegation to go to the very core and kernel of any system of collective security. If no such system of mutual insurance was included in the Charter the organization being set up in San Francisco might, when tested, prove to be a container without content."[124]

The United States argued strenuously against this addition, claiming that it could jeopardize Senate consent to the ratification of the charter and was "reminiscent of certain features of the Covenant which had made that document unacceptable to the United States."[125]

Conclusion

This episode illustrates a key contradiction in the U.S. approach to Article 2(4) and the nonuse of force principle. If the charter was to define a true collective security system, then the nonuse of force rule should have been tied to a collective commitment to use force to resist aggression against any member, as New Zealand had insisted. But the United States was not about to make such an open-ended commitment, both for sound strategic reasons and because the constitutional system of separation of powers had given Congress, not the executive, the authority to declare war. In the end, the United States seemed to want to have it both ways. As with multilateral decision making and global collective security, the U.S. approach to Article 2(4) was selective, ambivalent, and tentative. This was undoubtedly true for the other major powers as well, for none appeared ready to accept the kinds of commitment smaller states like New Zealand would have ideally preferred.

For the United States, however, the ambivalence appeared to run deeper. In the mid-1940s, at least, the flame of idealism burned brighter in the United States than elsewhere. As Gladwyn Jebb of the British delegation noted ruefully on returning home from San Francisco, "On arriving back in this country after ten weeks' absence at San Francisco, the British official is struck by the widespread lack of interest in this country in all questions connected with the World Organization. America is another world. There the question is anxiously debated in all sections of the community. Sometimes rather unrealistically, it is true; but, generally speaking, the approach is one of constructive criticism and tempered enthusiasm ... Here, on the other hand, if anybody can be induced to talk about the subject at all, it is in a mood of disillusionment, not unmixed with cynicism."[126]

Cynics were certainly well represented among American experts and bureaucrats as well, but in the White House and at the top of the State Department idealism and exceptionalism, conditioned at times by a healthy dose of realism, seemed to exert a stronger pull on those seeking to chart the course of the postwar world. As Stettinius sagely suggested, war has that effect on people. The idealism and exceptionalism that made the U.S. champion Article 2(4), however, were never fully reconciled with the demands of realism and domestic politics that robbed it of much of its content. Today, with idealism at ebb, 2(4) is at best a faint echo of what some had hoped—and others had feared—in 1945.

Notes

1. Available at http://www.trumanlibrary.org/ww2/stofonio.htm.
2. Charter of the United Nations: Report to the President on the Results of the San Francisco Conference by the Chairman of the United States Delegation, the Secretary of State (Washington, D.C.: U.S. Department of State, June 26, 1945), p. 13.
3. Hearing, The Future of U.S.–UN Relations: Visit of the U.S. Senate Committee on Foreign Relations to the United Nations," January 20–21, 2000, Senate Hearings, 106–777, 106th Cong., 2nd sess., 56.
4. President George W. Bush, "State of the Union Address," January 20, 2004. Available at http://www.whitehouse.gov/news/releases/2004/01/20040120-7.html.
5. United Nations Charter, Article 2(4), Chapter I: Purposes and Principles. Available at http://www.un.org/aboutun/charter.
6. Secretary-General Boutros Boutros-Ghali, "Supplement to an Agenda for Peace: Position Paper of the Secretary-General on the Occasion of the Fiftieth Anniversary of the United Nations" (A/50/60-A/1995/1, January 3, 1995), 18–19, paras. 77–80; and Secretary-General Kofi Annan, "Renewing the United Nations: A Programme for Reform" (A/51/950, July 14, 1997), 36, para. 107.
7. Nevertheless, as this author has argued elsewhere, the United States seems to have put less stock in the importance of attaining UN endorsement for the use of force than do some other member states. Edward C. Luck, "The United Sates, International Organization, and the Quest for Legitimacy," in *Multilateralism and U.S. Foreign Policy: Ambivalent Engagement*, ed. Stewart Patrick and Shepard Forman (Boulder, CO: Lynne Rienner Publishers, 2002), 47–74.
8. Press Release (SG/SM/8891, GA/10157, September 23, 2003).

9. United Nations, *Report of the Secretary-General's High-Level Panel on Threats, Challenges and Change, A More Secure World: Our Shared Responsibility* (New York: United Nations, 2004), 62–67, paras. 183–209.
10. Among the latter, see Michael J. Glennon, "Idealism at the UN," *Policy Review*, no. 129 (February–March 2005), 3–14; in Sven Biscop and David Mindleoff, eds., *Power to the System: The UN High-Level Panel and the Reinvigoration of Collective Security: Conference Proceedings* (Brussels: Royal Institute for International Relations), forthcoming, 2006.
11. There is a vast literature on the subject. For a useful summary of the literature, see Christine Gray, *International Law and the Use of Force*, 2d ed. (Oxford: Oxford University Press, 2004), especially ch. 2, "The Prohibition of the Use of Force." For provocative critiques of efforts to outlaw force, see John R. Bolton, "Is There Really 'Law' in International Affairs?" *Transnational Law and Contemporary Problems* (University of Iowa College of Law) 10 no. 1 (Spring 2000), 1–48; and Michael J. Glennon, "Why the Security Council Failed," *Foreign Affairs* 82 no. 3 (May–June 2003), 16–35.
12. For example, in the State Department's outline plan for postwar organization, presented to Franklin Roosevelt in December 1943, the first "principal obligation of a member state" was "to refrain from the use of force or threat to use force in its relations with other states and from any intervention in the internal affairs of other states, except in performance of its obligations to contribute to the enforcement procedures instituted by the Executive Council." U.S. Department of State, *Postwar Foreign Policy Preparation, 1939–1945* (Washington, DC: U.S. Government Printing Office, 1949), 576–81, app. 33 (hereafter cited as State Department, *Postwar Foreign Policy Preparation*). Four months later, in the department's "Possible Plan for a General International Organization," states were to "be required (a) to settle disputes by none but peaceful means, and (b) to refrain from the threat or use of force in their international relations in any manner inconsistent with the purposes envisaged in the basic instrument of the international organization." Ibid., 582–91, annex 35.
13. For a fuller account of the evolution of American exceptionalism and its historical holding power, see Luck, *Mixed Messages: American Politics and International Organization, 1919–1999* (Washington, DC: Brookings Institution Press for the Century Foundation, 1999).
14. W. Michael Reisman, "The United States and International Institutions," *Survival* 41 no. 4 (Winter 1999–2000), 62–80.
15. Glennon, "Why the Security Council Failed," 22.
16. "Making the World Safe for Hypocrisy," *New York Times*, March 22, 2003, 11.
17. Cordell Hull, *Memoirs of Cordell Hull*, vol. 2 (New York: MacMillan Co., 1948), 1625.
18. U.S. Department of State, *President Truman's Address to Opening Session of United Nations Conference on International Organization at San Francisco, April 25, 1945*. Available at http://www.trumanlibrary.org/whistlestop/study_collections/un/large/
19. U.S. Department of State, *Address at Final Plenary Session of the United Nations Conference on International Organization, June 26, 1945*. Available at http://www.trumanlibrary.org/publicpapers/viewpapers.php?pid=73.
20. U.S. Department of State, *Charter of the United Nations Report to the President on the Results of the San Francisco Conference by the Chairman of the United States Delegation, The Secretary of State, June 26, 1945* (Washington, DC: Department of State, 1945), 12 (hereafter cited as State Department, *Charter of the UN Report to the President*).
21. "President Roosevelt's Report to Congress on the Crimea Conference," *New York Times*, March 1, 1945, 12.
22. U.S. Department of State, *Charter*, 12.
23. U.S. Department of State, *President Truman's Address*.
24. U.S. Department of State, *Address at Final Plenary Session*.
25. Hull, *Memoirs*, 1648.
26. "President Roosevelt's Report."
27. Address before Joint Session of Congress.
28. U.S. Department of State, *President Truman's Address*.
29. Hull, *Memoirs*, 1651.
30. Address before Joint Session of Congress.
31. U.S. Department of State, *Address at Final Plenary Session*.
32. Clyde Eagleton, "Aggression and War" (Preliminary Report and Monographs, Commission to Study the Organization of Peace), reprinted in Robert E. Summers, "Dumbarton Oaks," *Reference Shelf*, 18 no. 1 (New York: H. W. Wilson Co., 1945), 26.

33. Address before Joint Session of Congress.
34. U.S. Department of State, *President Truman's Address*.
35. U.S. Department of State, *Address at Final Plenary Session*.
36. Robert C. Hilderbrand, *Dumbarton Oaks: The Origins of the United Nations and the Search for Postwar Security* (Chapel Hill: University of North Carolina Press, 1990), 15–16.
37. Forrest Davis, "Roosevelt's World Blueprint," *Saturday Evening Post*, April 10, 1943, 20–21, 109–110.
38. The term *enemy state,* according to Article 53(2), "applies to any state which during the Second World War has been an enemy of any signatory of the present charter." Going even further, it is asserted in Arthur Vandenberg's papers that "it was generally agreed that any nation or nations would, after the war, have complete freedom to take action to prevent any resurgence of aggression by the Axis states." Arthur H. Vandenberg, Jr., ed., *The Private Papers of Senator Vandenberg* (Boston: Houghton Mifflin Co., 1952), 186.
39. Memorandum by the Assistant Chief of the Division of International Security and Organization (Orie B. Gerig) and the Executive Secretary of the Policy Committee (Charles W. Yost), November 20, 1944, *Foreign Relations of the United States* (Washington, DC: Government Printing Office, 1944), 903 (hereafter cited as Gerig and Yost memo).
40. Hilderbrand, *Dumbarton Oaks*, 237.
41. Ibid., 236.
42. Minutes of the Fifth Meeting of the United States Delegation, Washington, April 9, 1945, *Foreign Relations of the United States* (Washington, DC: U.S. Government Printing Office, 1966), 218 (hereafter referred to as Minutes of the Fifth Meeting).
43. Ibid., 224.
44. Testimony of Secretary of State Frank B. Kellogg, Hearings before the Committee on Foreign Relations, United States Senate, 70th Cong., Part 1, December 7, 1928, on the General Pact for the Renunciation of War Signed at Paris, August 27, 1928. Available at http://www.yale.edu/lawweb/avalon/kbpact/kbhear.htm.
45. Edwin Bouchard, "Renunciation of War," Address to the Williamstown Institute of Politics, August 22, 1928.
46. Ibid.
47. Telegram, The Acting Secretary of State to the Ambassador in the United Kingdom (Winant), March 8, 1945, in *Foreign Relations of the United States*, 111–12.
48. Eagleton, "Aggression and War," 25.
49. Hans Kelsen, "The Old and the New League: The Covenant and the Dumbarton Oaks Proposals," *American Journal of International Law* 39 no. 1 (January 1945), 66.
50. Leland M. Goodrich and Edvard Hambro, *Charter of the United Nations: Commentary and Documents*, 2d ed. (Boston: World Peace Foundation, 1949), 103.
51. Ibid., 106.
52. Ibid.
53. Hearings before the Committee on Foreign Relations, United States Senate, the Charter of the United Nations, 79th Cong., 1st sess., July 9–13, 1945 (Washington, DC: U.S. Government Printing Office, 1945), 650 (hereafter referred to as Senate Hearings, UN Charter).
54. Hilderbrand, *Dumbarton Oaks*, 85.
55. Department of External Affairs, *Report on the United Nations Conference on International Organization by the Rt. Hon. Peter Fraser, Chairman of the New Zealand Delegation* (Wellington: Department of External Affairs, 1945), 22 (hereafter referred to as External Affairs, *New Zealand Delegation*).
56. Dean Acheson, *Present at the Creation: My Years in the State Department* (New York: W. W. Norton & Co., 1969), 111.
57. Luck, *Mixed Messages*, 254–260.
58. Hilderbrand, *Dumbarton Oaks*, 254.
59. Hull, *Memoirs*, 1299–1300.
60. Earl of Halifax, "Memorandum on the Great Powers, August 9, 1945," *British Documents on Foreign Affairs: Reports and Papers from the Foreign Office Confidential Prints*, pt. 3, series 50, vol. 5 (Frederick, MD: University Publications of America, 1998), 324.
61. Robert E. Summers, *Dumbarton Oaks* (New York: H. W. Wilson Company, 1945), 132–33.
62. Luck, *Mixed Messages*, 1, 16–17, 56–57.
63. Report to the President on the Results of the San Francisco Conference, 41.

64. Gerig and Yost memo, 903. Also see Gladwyn Jebb, "Reflections on San Francisco," Memorandum to Foreign Office, July 25, 1945, para. 4, *British Documents on Foreign Affairs* (see note 54), 318.
65. Hull, *Memoirs,* 1299–1300.
66. State Department, *Charter of the UN Report to the President,* 641.
67. "President Roosevelt's Report" (see note 16).
68. Address before Joint Session of Congress. Today, President George W. Bush sounds every bit as messianic. In his January 2004 State of the Union address, for example, he stressed that "America is a nation with a mission, and that mission comes from our most basic beliefs ... Our aim is a democratic peace ... America acts in this cause with friends and allies at our side, yet we understand our special calling: This great republic will lead the cause of freedom." State of the Union Address, January 20, 2004. (See note 4.)
69. Report to the President on the Results of the San Francisco Conference, 17. He went on to identify a fourth need: for a mechanism to draw on knowledge and experience to address pressing economic and social problems (e.g., ECOSOC).
70. *The United Nations Conference on International Organization, Selected Documents* (Washington, DC: U.S. Government Printing Office, 1946), 540–41.
71. Acheson, *Present at the Creation,* 112.
72. Hull, *Memoirs,* 1642–43. Also see Davis, "Roosevelt's World Blueprint."
73. Walter Lippmann, *U.S. Foreign Policy: Shield of the Republic* (Boston: Little, Brown & Co., 1943), 31.
74. State Department, *Postwar Foreign Policy Preparation,* 576–77.
75. Report to the President on the Results of the San Francisco Conference, 41.
76. "Editorial: The Dumbarton Oaks Plan," *New Republic* 111, 17, October 23, 1944, 510–511.
77. Grayson Kirk, "The Enforcement of Security," *Yale Law Journal* 55 no. 5 (August 1946), 1091–92.
78. Eagleton, "Aggression and War," 26.
79. Minutes of the Fifth Meeting, 224. To avoid confusion, it should be noted that, in the Dumbarton Oaks proposals, chapter 1 lists the purposes of the new organization and chapter 2 its principles. The charter, however, includes both in chapter 1, with Article 1 enumerating purposes and Article 2 principles.
80. Minutes of the Sixth Meeting of the United States Delegation, Washington, April 10, 1945, in ibid., 230.
81. Senate Hearings, UN Charter, 650.
82. Inter-American Conference on Problems of War and Peace, *Resolution 30 on the Establishment of a General International Organization,* Mexico City, February 21–March 8, 1945 (Mexico: Ministry of Foreign Affairs, 1945), 18.
83. Ibid., 44–46.
84. Ruth B. Russell, *A History of the United Nations Charter: The Role of the United States, 1940–1945* (Washington, DC: Brookings Institution, 1958), 673–75.
85. For informative accounts of this episode, see ibid., 693–704; Stephen Schlesinger, *Act of Creation: The Founding of the United Nations* (Boulder, CO: Westview Press, 2003), 175–92; Townsend Hoopes and Douglas Brinkley, *FDR and the Creation of the U.N.* (New Haven, CT: Yale University Press, 1997), 192–98; and Thomas M. Campbell, *Masquerade Peace: America's UN Policy, 1944–1945* (Tallahassee: Florida State University Press, 1973), 164–75.
86. The quote is Vandenberg's account of Pasvolsky's comments. Vandenberg, *Private Papers,* 189.
87. For a summary of the deliberations of the U.S. delegation on the final wording of Article 51, see *Foreign Relations of the United States,* 816–20. (See note 37.)
88. Ibid., 230.
89. Senate Hearings, UN Charter, 304.
90. *Foreign Relations of the United States,* 344.
91. Ibid., 374–75.
92. United Nations Conference, Selected Documents, 485. (See note 70.)
93. Leo Pasvolsky said as much. Ibid., 726; also see 747–48; and Parliament of the Commonwealth of Australia, *United Nations Conference on International Organization, Report by the Australian Delegation* (Canberra: Government of the Commonwealth of Australia, 1945), 28, para. 142 (hereafter referred to as Parliament, *Report by the Australian Delegation*).
94. Russell, *A History of the United Nations Charter,* 673.

95. United Nations Conference, Selected Documents, 485.
96. *Foreign Relations of the United States*, 751.
97. Ibid., 1162.
98. Ibid., 1163.
99. United Nations Conference, Selected Documents, 486.
100. Luck, *Mixed Messages* 106, 201–05, 266–67.
101. Kirk, "The Enforcement of Security," 1091. Acheson reported similar worries in the State Department at that point. Acheson, *Present at the Creation*, 155.
102. Acheson, *Present at the Creation*, 331–32.
103. Goodrich and Hambro, *Charter of the United Nations*, 107.
104. Address of the President of the United States before a Joint Session of Congress, Recommending Assistance to Greece and Turkey, March 12, 1947, http://www.trumanlibrary.org/whistlestop/study_collections/doctrine/large/index.php.
105. Senate Resolution 239, 80th Cong., 2nd Sess., June 11, 1948.
106. A. L. Goodhart, "Some Legal Aspects of the Suez Situation," in *Tensions in the Middle East*, ed. Philip W. Thayer (Baltimore: Johns Hopkins Press, 1958), 259.
107. See, for example, Schlesinger, *Act of Creation*, 17–31; Hoopes and Brinkley, *FDR and The Creation of the U.N.*, 1–11, 55–63, 123–32; and Thomas M. Franck, *Nation against Nation: What Happened to the U.N. Dream and What the U.S. Can Do about It* (New York: Oxford University Press, 1985), 7–20.
108. Acheson, *Present at the Creation*, 109.
109. Tom Connally, *My Name is Tom Connally* (New York: Thomas Y. Crowell Co., 1954), 285.
110. Ibid., 285–86.
111. Luck, *Mixed Messages*, 254–260. A British diplomat in Washington came to a similar conclusion that there was more latent opposition to the charter than met the eye at that point. J. Balfour, Memorandum on United States Attitudes to World Organization, August 21, 1945, in *British Documents on Foreign Affairs*, 331.
112. Summers, "Dumbarton Oaks," 101.
113. Ibid., 102.
114. Hull, *Memoirs*, 1686 and 1691; and Hoopes and Brinkley, *FDR and the Creation of the U.N.*, 161–62.
115. *United States Foreign Relations*, 1431.
116. Vandenberg, *Private Papers*, 116.
117. Ibid., 117.
118. Luck, *Mixed Messages*, 164–70.
119. For a particularly cogent statement along these lines by Elihu Root, see Philip C. Jessup, *Elihu Root, 1905–1937* (New York: Dodd, Mead & Co., 1938), 378.
120. *Congressional Record*, 79th Cong., 1st Sess., July 25, 1945, 8017.
121. Kelsen, "The Old and the New League," 83.
122. Parliament, *Report by the Australian Delegation*, annex C, 63.
123. The United Nations Conference on International Organization, Selected Documents, 556–57.
124. External Affairs, *New Zealand Delegation*, 25.
125. Russell, *History of the United Nations Charter*, 674–75.
126. Gladwyn Jebb, "Reflections on San Francisco," July 25, 1945, in *British Documents on Foreign Affairs*, 317.

3

Sovereign Inequality and Hierarchy in Anarchy: American Power and International Society[1]

JACK DONNELLY

What are the implications of unrivaled American power for the shape of twenty-first-century international relations? This chapter focuses on elaborating the conceptual resources required for any adequate answer to this question. Rather than use *empire* to cover most systematic inequalities between states I explore multiple forms of *hierarchy in anarchy*[2] and diverse practices of *sovereign inequality*—concepts that most mainstream perspectives, unfortunately, find deeply paradoxical, if not simply self-contradictory.

My argument is rooted in the English School of international theory, which stresses the institutional structure of the society of states, rather than its material structure, considered from a broad comparative–historical perspective.[3] Such a focus, I argue, is essential for thinking accurately and deeply about the nature of American power and its impact on international order and (in)equality.

I begin by defining *empire* as a point of reference to compare other forms of hierarchy and inequality. "Hierarchy in Anarchy" shows that anarchy and hierarchy, rather than opposites, can and regularly do coexist, resulting in a variety of forms of hierarchy in anarchy. The next three sections explore the principal varieties of sovereign inequality in Westphalian legal practice, emphasizing the fact that sovereign equality has always coexisted with no less important elements of formal sovereign inequality. The sixth section lays out nine historical models, including empire, of hierarchical international societies. These concepts and models are then applied to interpreting the contemporary "American colossus" and "Iraq." I argue that whether our purpose is to understand the world or to change it, we must appreciate the nature and variety of international inequalities. And, for better or worse, the concepts of hierarchy in anarchy and sovereign inequality—but not empire—are essential today to sound theory and practice.

Empire

This chapter is concerned with exploring the varieties of hierarchy and inequality. Empire is a useful starting point both because it is so commonly referred to today and because it specifies an extreme version of hierarchical inequality against which other forms can be compared.

Empire derives from the Latin *imperium*, meaning, roughly, legitimate authority or the right to rule, as in the formula *imperium populi Romani* (the "empire" of the Roman people). *Imperium* was translated from the Greek *arche*, "rule," and provided "something approaching a notion of sovereignty"[4]—which was its principal use in modern English through the eighteenth century.[5] The *Oxford English Dictionary* cites Blackstone: "The legislature … uses … empire … to assert that our king is … sovereign and independent within these his dominions."

As the Republic gave way to the Empire, *imperium* was similarly transformed. "At least from the second half of the first century AD., *imperium Romanum* is used as we would use 'Roman Empire.'"[6] *Imperium* gradually came to be fused with both the *imperator* ("emperor") and the entity ruled. The revived (Holy) Roman Empire likewise linked power, person, and polity. These senses also are deeply rooted in English: "supreme and extensive political dominion; esp. that exercised by an 'emperor'" and "an extensive territory (esp. an aggregate of many separate states) under the sway of an emperor or supreme ruler."[7]

Today we use *sovereignty* for the right to rule. Emperors are figures of history or fantasy. But we still need a term to describe an extensive polity incorporating diverse, previously independent units, ruled by a dominant central polity. This definition is broadly consistent with those of the leading comparative students of empire.[8]

Empires are composite polities knit together and defined by the imperial core. The core polity rules over, rather than simply influences, the subordinated polities. Although most contemporary states are composite in origin—consider Spain, France, the Netherlands, Italy, Nigeria, India, Indonesia—empires retain their composite character long after they are well established. Unlike federal states, in which more equal polities create a new superordinate composite, empires arise from the dominance of an established core polity that constructs and then defines the imperial composite.

Michael Hardt and Antonio Negri[9] creatively redefine empire as an amorphous, uncentered global network, ostensibly in response to an emerging, qualitatively different form of political domination. Here I restrict myself to *empire* in the traditional sense of composite core-periphery polities defined by the predominance of the core. In other words, I only deal with conceptions of empire to which the adjective *American* might apply.

This excludes fundamentally nonterritorial and nonpolitical accounts of *empire* that equate it with the spread of capitalism or globalization. Although understanding such processes is certainly important, equating them with *empire* simply means that we need another language to think about traditional empires, which are also the subject of lively and important contemporary discussions that merit consideration. That is my focus here.

Imperial polities may be units within a broader nonimperial international system (as in nineteenth-century Europe) or centralized hierarchical international societies. Descriptions of the Roman Empire as "a pacified zone" or "a dangerously disjointed polity policed by widely dispersed Roman legions"[10] also fit many other historical empires. It is in this later sense—Rome, Alexander, or Athens rather than China, Russia, or Britain—that many contemporary analysts worry about or look forward to an American empire.

Hierarchy in Anarchy

Before reviewing the historical record of international hierarchy and inequality, a brief general discussion of anarchy and hierarchy is necessary.

Anarchy and Hierarchy

Hierarchy and anarchy are typically treated as an exhaustive and mutually exclusive dichotomy; that is, all political orders are described, as a rough first approximation, as either anarchic or hierarchic.[11] This understanding encourages equating hierarchy with empire,[12] thus significantly impeding even acknowledging, let alone understanding, nonimperial forms of inequality.

Anarchy indicates the absence of government: literally, without a leader (*archos*) or rule (*arche*). Kenneth Waltz, consistent with ordinary usage, defines *hierarchy* as "relations of super- and subordination" in which "actors are formally differentiated according to the degrees of their authority, and their distinct functions."[13] It is immediately evident, though, that anarchy and hierarchy are not mutually exclusive. Both superordination and differentiation of authority and functions, which define hierarchy, may arise from sources other than government. Hierarchy can exist in anarchy.

The opposite of anarchy is, literally, *archy*: government, political authority; *empire* in the old sense of rule; *sovereignty*. Hierarchy misleadingly directs our attention to higher authority. It is the absence of governmental authority that defines anarchy. But anarchic international society is full of other forms of authority, inequality, and functional differentiation.

Realists typically argue that in anarchic orders "authority quickly reduces to a particular expression of capability."[14] To the extent that is true, it is a contingent empirical matter, not a logical consequence of anarchy. Horizontal authority is a pervasive feature of contemporary international relations, most notably in the form of treaty obligations. A few international actors, such as the United Nations (UN) Security Council and the World Trade Organization, even have (limited but significant) vertical authority over sovereign states. And these forms of hierarchy and inequality simply are not reducible to capabilities. Conversely, those who hold sovereign authority in national polities may do so largely through raw power. Consider, for example, Guatemala in the early 1980s or any of the various failed states of the post-Cold War era. The degree of authority, the mix between superordinate and coordinate authority, and the relationship between authority and capabilities are contingent empirical issues in anarchic and nonanarchic orders alike.

Polarity, Hierarchy, and International Order. Figure 3.1 presents a simple typology of anarchic international orders, geared toward thinking about empire and its alternatives. Rather than the conventional distinction between bipolar and multipolar orders—that is, two or more great powers—I distinguish orders with one and more than one great power; that is unipolarity and multipolarity in a literal but nonstandard sense of that term. International orders are further distinguished by the extent of hierarchy—that is, whether there are substantial elements of superordinate authority.

Quadrant I covers multipolar orders with little hierarchy. The powerful balance and the weak bandwagon in an environment with little functional differentiation and largely horizontal authority; this has been the principal focus of mainstream IR theory. My focus is on the other three quadrants.

		AUTHORITY	
		Coordinate	**Superordinate**
POLARITY	**Multipolar**	I (balance of power) [inter-war Europe]	II (concert, protection) [Concert of Europe]
	Unipolar	III (preponderance) [post-Cold War]	IV (hegemony, empire) [Athens, Rome]

Fig. 3.1 Hierarchy in anarchy: polarity, authority, and international order.

Quadrant II encompasses multipolar orders with significant elements of superordinate authority. Following I consider the examples of protectorate, concert, and collective security systems.

Quadrant III covers unipolar orders with little superordinate authority. Whatever influence preponderant power may yield, authority remains primarily horizontal/coordinate; the system is constructed around multiple independencies rather than hierarchy. With only one great power, successful balancing is problematic. Bandwagoning and resentful resistance of varying degrees of effectiveness are common, even for powerful second-tier states. If the immediate post-Cold War international order was unipolar, it fell into this quadrant.

Quadrant IV encompasses unipolar orders with considerable superordinate authority. Following I distinguish hegemony, dominion, and empire.

Mainstream approaches focus on the diagonal running from the top left to bottom right of Figure 3.1. By failing to distinguish polarity (which typically yields influence) from authority and coordinate from superordinate authority this obscures the great variety of forms of (in)equality, authority, and hierarchy in international relations. It also misleads to suggest thinking of all forms of hierarchy and inequality as steps in the direction of empire.

Here I stress the other diagonal. Quadrant II draws attention to the possibilities for superordinate authority in multipolar, multiple-independency international orders, which is the focus of the historical material examined in the next three sections. Quadrant III highlights the possibilities of coordinate forms of order and authority in unipolar systems. Unipolarity need not create significant superordinate authority, let alone empire, as I illustrate in the case of contemporary American power in the sections "Form Matters" and "Reading Iraq."

Sovereign Inequalities

Even realists, who emphasize inequalities of power and their informal political consequences—"international politics is mostly about inequalities"[15]—typically associate anarchy with sovereign equality. As Waltz puts it, "formally, each is the equal of all the others."[16] In fact, however, equality is not inherent in anarchic international orders. "The political and social structure of Europe in the Middle Ages ... completely excluded the very idea of equality among States or rulers."[17] Through most of the Westphalian era, numerous forms of "semi-sovereign"[18] inequality have been standard. Even among full Westphalian sovereigns, significant formal inequalities have been systematic and common.

Sovereign equality may be "the essence of our understanding of the Westfalian [sic] system."[19] This, however, is a contingent feature of the Westphalian order, not a universal consequence of anarchy. Sovereign equality may indeed have "attained an almost ontological status in the structure of the international legal system."[20] It did so, however, only very slowly and incompletely.

And sovereign equality has always coexisted with a great variety of formal sovereign inequalities.

Forms of Sovereign Inequality

Formal inequality can result from either reductions in or additions to the rights, liberties, privileges, or powers of some (but not all) actors. This section briefly reviews the more common formal restrictions on sovereignty in Europe between Westphalia and San Francisco. The following sections consider the special rights and privileges of Great Powers and the unequal but non-imperial relations between European and non-European polities.

Sovereign inequality rests on the divisibility of sovereignty. As Henry Maine acidly noted, "indivisibility of Sovereignty, though it belongs to Austin's system, does not belong to International Law. The powers of sovereigns are a bundle or collection of powers, and they may be separated from one another,"[21] or as Lassa Oppenheim put it with understated reserve, "as there can be no doubt about the fact that there are semi-independent States in existence, it may well be maintained that sovereignty is divisible."[22] "Sovereignty is divisible both as a matter of principle and as a matter or experience."[23]

Treaties of protection and of guarantee[24] granted special rights to protecting/guaranteeing powers to assure that protected states act in a particular way or retain a particular internal status or international alignment—often with the less-than-enthusiastic agreement of the weaker party. Guarantees could be imposed even on great powers, most famously, the rights of guarantee granted by the Peace of Westphalia to France and Sweden in the Holy Roman Empire. Such restrictions range "from the relationship which imposes only slight limitations on the protected state to the so-called protectorate which has not international capacity at all."[25]

A few formal relations of protection exist today, such as India's right (acquired at independence from Britain) to control Bhutan's external relations. Syria's military and political presence in Lebanon following the civil war is a good example of an informal but widely recognized relation of protection that in 2005 largely reverted to the more ordinary influence of a powerful neighbor. U.S. participation in the Egyptian–Israeli peace process is a Cold War-era example of a semiformal guarantee.

Servitudes,[26] or legal obligations to permit or prohibit certain activities on the servient state's territory, have regularly restricted the sovereignty of strong and weak states alike, ranging from provisions for the use of rivers, canals, and inland waterways to requirements to allow a foreign army to march across a state's territory to the Treaty of Utrecht's specification that the Stuart pretender not be permitted on French territory. Leases of territory,[27] free cities (e.g., Krakow, Bremen, Hamburg, Lubeck, Danzig, Trieste),[28] and permanently neutralized states (e.g., Switzerland, Belgium, Luxemburg)[29] also fall into this class. Military basing agreements and various waterway regimes are common contemporary examples. The U.S. lease on Guantanamo is an example that has recently received considerable international attention.

Legitimate intervention, which is based not merely on superior power but also on some plausible claim of an internationally recognized right to intervene, has been another important source of inequality. "That intervention is, as a rule, forbidden by the Law of Nations which protects the International Personality of the States, there is no doubt. On the other hand, there is just as little doubt that this rule has exceptions, for there are interventions which take place by right, and there are others which, although they do not take place by right, are nevertheless admitted by the Law of Nations, and are excused."[30] Lists varied but usually included self-protection, preserving the balance of power, treaty rights, counterintervention, and protection of nationals.[31] The post–Cold War era has seen the development of a doctrine and practice of legitimate humanitarian intervention.

Imperfect unions,[32] in which the constituent parts retained some degree of international legal personality, regularly created sovereign inequalities in both the unions and the constituent parts. Leading examples include the Holy Roman Empire and its successor, the German Confederation of 1815/1820–1866, various Swiss confederations, and the early United States. Additional variants include dynastic "personal unions,"[33] British self-governing dominions,[34] relations of suzerainty and vassalage,[35] and condominia.[36]

The European Union (EU) is the obvious contemporary example of this class of inequalities. The members of the EU simply do not have the same rights to control their domestic law and politics as the United States, Japan, Brazil, or most other states. Nationals of EU member states have transnational legal rights. And the EU itself, even with the defeat of the constitution, seems well on the way to acquiring a recognized international personality, without being sovereign.

Minority rights regimes[37] have been another important source of sovereign inequalities. At Westphalia, in the new states created through the collapse of the Ottoman Empire, and in the League system after World War I, minority obligations applied, usually coercively, only to selected defeated and new states. Today, however, minority rights are handled within universalistic regional and global human rights regimes, making minority protection no longer a significant source of sovereign inequality.

Financial controls were common in the nineteenth and early twentieth centuries in the Americas, southeast Europe, and North Africa.[38] Common forms included supervision of customs houses and priority claims over state resources. In extreme cases, the state treasury operated under effective foreign control. Contemporary analogues include structural adjustment, creditor clubs, and other forms of coercive economic neoliberalism.

Although this section has been concerned primarily with relations between European states, the formal inequalities established by League of Nations mandates and United Nations trusteeships deserve brief mention. Although essentially imperial relationships, the mandatory trustee power was subject to (modest but real) international supervision. Bosnia and Kosovo have provoked a revival of discussions of international administration, sometimes under the label of "neotrusteeship."[39]

Most of the inequalities noted here were codified in unequal treaties between sovereign equals. *Unequal treaties* were a standard topic of seventeenth-, eighteenth-, and nineteenth-century international jurisprudence. The almost universally accepted view was that unequal treaties, including even treaties imposed by victors on the vanquished, were binding and fully compatible with sovereignty.[40]

Changing Conceptions of Sovereign Equality

The understanding of sovereign equality as a quasi-ontological principle is, at most, half a century old. The first two decades of the twentieth century "introduced conditions adding to the number of imperfectly independent states."[41] Even the United Nations charter enshrined fundamental inequalities, most notably the veto in the Security Council and the failure even to contemplate the breakup of colonial empires.

The 1960 Declaration on the Granting of Independence to Colonial Countries and Peoples (General Assembly [GA] Resolution 1514) marks a fundamental transformation in the rules for membership in the society of states.[42] The aftermath of decolonization led to the development of a very strict doctrine of sovereign equality, along with a parallel and comparably strict doctrine of nonintervention. As the 1970 Declaration on Principles of International Law Concerning Friendly Relations and Co-operation among States (GA Resolution 2625) put it, "No State or group of States has the right to intervene, directly or indirectly, for any reason whatever, in the internal or external affairs of any other State."

Most of us are children of these changes. Our values and historical experience lead us to reject formal inequalities among states. But sovereignty, whether equal or unequal, is a constructed legal relationship, not a material fact—or, rather, it becomes a material fact through historically variable and contingent social institutions, norms, and practices of recognition. Sovereign (in)equality rests on the decisions of states to recognize certain formal (in)equalities and then to participate in institutions that constitute and reproduce these (in)equalities.

I do not mean to suggest that new sovereign inequalities must, will, or should (re)emerge. Understanding the potential impact of American power, however, requires attending to the multiple possible forms of hierarchy and inequality.

That this survey of forms of inequality is no arcane historical exercise is suggested by a wide range of contemporary problems, principles, and practices, including failed states, neotrusteeship, structural adjustment, humanitarian intervention, the responsibility to protect, democracy promotion, international criminal tribunals, devolution, autonomy, the power of multinational corporations, private governance, and European integration (e.g., subsidiarity, more perfect union, enlargement). Although we are not likely to see a revival or, for example, treaties of protection and guarantee, less formal expressions of the practice—most prominently today in Iraq—are an important part of contemporary international reality. We need the conceptual resources to identify these practices accurately.

Great Powers

Special rights for some states constitute the other side of the story of sovereign inequality. Great Powers throughout the Westphalian era have set the shape of international order and have enjoyed rights—usually grudgingly conceded and often actively resisted—to supervise and manage international society. The Great Powers "possess a regulative authority and are deemed to speak for the whole body of European states."[43] "The leading powers of Europe undertook to settle concrete problems by meeting in groups apart and there taking decision which had the force of law."[44]

Great Powers have had unequal representation in and influence over peace- and lawmaking international congresses and conferences from Westphalia through San Francisco.[45] "At Vienna, sovereign equality remained, at best, a background claim ... The Great Powers made the law and the middle powers signed the resulting Treaty. The smaller powers, meanwhile, were erased from consideration."[46] The Great Powers have also been formally predominant in peace and security organizations, most notably the Concert of Europe, the League Council, and the Security Council.

Spheres of influence[47] are another example of at least semiformal mutual recognition of special rights. By the early twentieth century the Monroe Doctrine had obtained sufficient European acquiescence that it could plausibly be described as at least not illegal.[48] During the Cold War era there was an analogous quasiformal recognition of Soviet and American spheres, asserted most explicitly in the Johnson and Brezhnev doctrines.[49]

Not only the particular rights but also the very existence of great powers is socially constructed. Unsurpassed power resources are a necessary but insufficient condition for Great Power status, which is precisely that: a status, a rule-governed social relation. Great Powers play a particular role in international society. Mutual recognition of that role and its particular rights and responsibilities—a recognition that emerges out of varying mixtures of coercion, consent, and commitment—constitutes Great Powers and their authority.

The authority, rights, and status of Great Powers ultimately are given to them, however much they may encourage that grant. And this authority and status are in significant measure constituted in the giving. It is not a replacement for raw material power. It is not something that can be held without also having material power, but neither is the status and authority of Great Powers reducible to material resources.

The implications of this line of analysis for the understanding of contemporary American power are obvious and vital. The inability of the world's sole superpower to get its way in the Security Council, and the ensuing morass in Iraq, strikingly illustrate the centrality of recognized authority to the power—that is, capability to control outcomes—of even the greatest of Great Powers.

Outlaw States

A very different class of international inequalities involves what Gerry Simpson calls "outlaw states."[50] In early modern Europe, heretics were treated as outlaws. Westphalia in effect eliminated (certain Christian) heresies as international crimes. Following the defeat of Napoleon, the Holy Alliance[51] laid the foundations for a semiformal alliance of the Emperors of Russia, Austria, and Prussia to preserve sanctified monarchies against republican subversion or overthrow. Other examples include global protection regimes[52] outlawing piracy, the slave trade, and slavery; the effective prohibition of aggressive war under the charter regime on the use of force, as wars of conquest were in effect outlawed after World War II, much as Westphalia outlawed wars of religion; and the post-Cold War practice of legitimate humanitarian intervention, which has in effect outlawed genocide.

Here, however, I focus on outlaw conceptions applied to non-European peoples and polities, particularly non-European polities that had the power, allies, or good luck to avoid incorporation into a European empire. South and Southeast Asian polities generally were treated as (semi-)sovereign and were dealt with largely according to the same legal categories as their European counterparts until well into the eighteenth century.[53] The nineteenth century, however, saw international society become increasingly bifurcated into a European zone of sovereign toleration and an Afro-Asian zone of civilization-based domination.[54]

Even in the last third of the nineteenth century, however, inequality and subordination took many forms. In sub-Saharan Africa and Southeast Asia, formal imperial acquisition was the norm. Latin American states, however, although increasingly subject to intervention and even protection, remained sovereign. In North Africa and southeastern Europe, complex forms of divided sovereignty were common. And some important Asian states retained their sovereignty and considerable independence, despite being forced to accept special privileges and extraterritorial rights for western militaries, merchants, and missionaries.

The unequal treaties between China and the western powers[55]—as well as similar inequalities imposed on Japan,[56] the Ottoman Empire,[57] and

Siam[58]—were precisely that: unequal treaties. Such treaties, which as noted earlier were also common in Europe, recognized the sovereignty of China, Japan, Siam, and the Sublime Porte. In fact, China was initially forced to accept the idea of sovereign equality,[59] which was completely incompatible with the traditional conception of China as the Middle Kingdom.

Late nineteenth-century international law developed the idea of a standard of civilization for full membership in the family of nations.[60] And it was common to distinguish savages, seen as fit subjects for colonial rule, from barbarians, imperfectly civilized (rather than uncivilized)[61] and thus might reasonably be expected to change their ways and enter international society as fully equal participants—as Japan in fact did more or less successfully (although neither smoothly nor easily) in the 1890s and early twentieth century.[62]

The current war on terrorism, as has often been noted,[63] has revived the language of civilization versus savagery. The development of the global human rights regime also has certain parallels with the nineteenth-century standard of civilization,[64] as do recent efforts to establish an international right to democratic governance.

Nine Models of Hierarchical Security Systems

The preceding sections of this chapter focused on particular practices of sovereign inequality. In this section I turn to broader patterns of enduring unequal relationships. Table 3.1, based on Bruce Cronin's typology of international security systems,[65] summarizes nine hierarchical international orders that fall in varying places in the right hand column (superordinate authority) of Figure 3.1.

Protection, Concert, Collective Security

The first three models involve multipolar orders with a relatively strong commitment to the preservation of multiple independencies. Some security functions, however, are transferred to other states or international organizations.

Protection or guarantee, as revealed previously, involves special rights of intervention and control exercised by a protecting power. India in Bhutan and Syria in Lebanon (used already as contemporary examples) fall well toward the right edge of Quadrant II of Figure 3.1. Protectorates are distinguished from empire by the fact that the subordinated units remain fully separate rather than combined into a superordinate imperial polity. If spheres of influence become both extensive and intensive, however, the resulting relationships are probably better understood as falling in Quadrant IV, involving what I call hegemony or dominion in the following section.

Concerts[66] involve collective Great Power management of the international order. The Group of 8 is a contemporary analogy.[67] Some proposals for increasing the permanent membership of the Security Council can be seen as

Table 3.1 Systems of Hierarchy in Anarchy.

Security System	Dominant Identity	Constitutive Rules	Behavior Patterns	Primary Institutions
Multiple Independencies				
Protection/ Guarantee	State	Restricted Sovereignty Intervention	Protection, Guarantee, Intervention	
Concert	great power	Multilateral management	Consultation and joint action	Congresses and summits
Collective Security	Cosmopolitan	Indivisibility of peace collective action	International organization	
Hierarchical Domination				
Hegemony	Hegemon	Hegemonic leadership	Hegemonic leadership	Hegemonic alliance
Dominion	Empire	Semi-autonomy	Imperial subordination	Ritual subservience
Empire	Empire	Empire	Central decision making	Imperial government
Transnational Security Communities				
Pluralistic Security/Nonwar	Cognitive regionalism	No war	Demilitarization	Regional regimes
Common Security	Ideological community	Solidarity	Mutual support	Transnational association
Amalgamated Security	Pan-nationalism	Divided/pooled sovereignty	Political integration	Confederation

Source: Based on Bruce Cronin, *Community under Anarchy: Transnational Identity and the Evolution of Cooperation* (New York: Columbia University Press, 1999), p. 13.

an attempt to keep the council-as-concert abreast of changes in the international distribution of capabilities.

Collective security[68] is an ideal type model that has been implemented only incompletely in practice. An attack on any member is treated as an attack on all: the indivisibility of peace. The obvious post-Cold War example is the war to repel Iraqi aggression against Kuwait. Whether egalitarian or inegalitarian (which depends on the decision procedure within the collective security organization), collective security is hierarchical: Supreme authority with respect to the international use of force is transferred to the collective security organization (although in all other areas states remain sovereign).

Hegemony, Dominion, Empire

The next three models in Table 3.1 fall in Quadrant IV of Figure 3.1. A single preponderant state exercises hierarchical control over a group of states (rather than a single state, as in relations of protection or guarantee).

It is standard to distinguish empire and hegemony by the range of political control. Empires control both the internal and the external policy of the imperialized polity. Hegemons control only external policy, typically preserving both the formal independence and (within the limits of assuring a friendly regime) the internal autonomy of the hegemonized followers.[69] Classic examples of hegemony include Napoleonic France and the Spartan and Theban hegemonies that ruled ancient Greece in the fourth century BCE. Hegemony is defined by the interests of the dominant power rather than ideological solidarity and thus more like protection or guarantee than common security.

Between hegemony and empire lies what Adam Watson calls dominion, in which "an imperial authority to some extent determines the internal government of other communities, but they nevertheless retain their identity as separate states and some control over their own affairs."[70] Examples include the Soviet Union in Central and Eastern Europe and China at the turn of the twentieth century. Dominion, which often involves tribute or some other form of ritual subservience, is the unipolar analogue to highly restrictive forms of protection in multipolar orders.

Before moving on, it is perhaps worth noting that hegemony as a form of unipolar hierarchy has no special connection with the Gramscian conception of hegemony, which understands power as a function of combined control over the means of production, coercion, and persuasion; force and authority; and hard and soft power.[71] All of the orders in Quadrants II and IV are hegemonic in the Gramscian sense, involving superordinate authority, not just inequalities of power.

Pluralistic, Common, and Amalgamated Security Communities

The final three models in Table 3.1 do not fit readily into the typology of Figure 3.1. They involve instead inequalities based on particular types of transnational community.

Pluralistic security communities—or what Ole Waever calls nonwar communities[72]—are regional international societies with a reliable expectation that all conflicts between members will be solved peacefully. War within the community is unthinkable, not even planned for as a remote contingency. The Nordic States and North America are the standard examples. Nonwar communities are unequal in the sense that they create rights to peace not available outside the community.

What Bruce Cronin calls common security communities are defined by ideological solidarity. Classic examples include the Holy Alliance and the Cold War-era free world. Whether ideological solidarity is voluntary or imposed, community members have different rights and obligations from nonmembers.

What Cronin calls amalgamated security communities involve confederal political integration that still leaves the members a limited international legal personality. The Holy Roman Empire after Westphalia and the early United States are classic examples. Compared to pluralistic and common security communities, there is a much more substantial pooling of sovereignty, in the form of a superordinate polity with substantial international legal personality.

One might interpret the EU in terms of all three types of communities—or as the early stages in the process of the creation of a federal state of Europe.

Form Matters: Interpreting the American Colossus

Power in contemporary international relations is very unequally distributed. Formal and informal inequalities of rights, obligations, and opportunities are common. The United States is engaged in a wide range of activities that aim to restrict the rights of other states and to establish special rights, privileges, and exemptions for itself. All of this is true and of great practical and analytic importance. But little is new. Nothing is unprecedented. And none of it has any significant connection to empire.

Whether our purpose is to understand the world or to change it, we must appreciate the nature and variety of international (in)equalities. In this section I consider briefly the recent work of Niall Ferguson. Despite rightly insisting that we use empire as a neutral analytical category, Ferguson, like so many other contemporary analysts, ignores–even seeks to obliterate—the distinction between empire and other forms of hierarchy and inequality. Contemporary America is indeed something of a colossus. It is not, however, an empire. He asks, "What is this thing called hegemony? Is it merely a euphemism for empire, or does it describe the role of the primus inter pares, the leader of an alliance, rather than the ruler over subject peoples?"[73] Actually, as we have seen, hegemony is neither empire nor alliance. Although hegemonically subordinated allies have little choice about their continued participation in the alliance, they enjoy internal political autonomy (within the limits of, as the ancient Greeks put it, having the same friends and the same enemies). And the quality of political life of a hegemonized state that controls its internal policy is very different from that of an imperialized state that does not.

Empire, as Ferguson among many others emphasizes, may be informal or indirect. But not all informal or indirect influence, or even control, is empire. "The Victorians used their naval and financial power to open the markets of countries outside their colonial ambit."[74] True. But in some cases markets were opened by military coercion. In others, local elites perceived a mutual financial benefit, with little coercion from Britain. Even where markets were coercively opened, some states largely controlled their internal politics, but others did not. Some even exercised considerable foreign policy autonomy in other areas. Influence simply is not rule, which Ferguson rightly uses in his definitional comments about empire.[75]

It is certainly true that although Britain "did not formally govern Argentina ... the merchant banks of the City of London exerted such a powerful influence on its fiscal and monetary policy that Argentina's independence was heavily qualified."[76] But this makes Argentina no more a part of the informal British empire than, say, Portugal was an informal part of Britain's eighteenth-century empire; Portuguese wine had preferential access to British markets, and British interests dominated trade in, and even production of, Portuguese wine. Using *empire* in an extended sense to refer to states that comply with core state economic preferences and policies, at best, leaves us with the problem of developing another language by which to distinguish Argentina and Portugal from Singapore, Uganda, and India, or the General Agreement on Tariffs and Trade (GATT) from Japan's Greater East Asia Co-Prosperity Sphere.

Or consider Peter Winn's account of "informal British empire in Uruguay in the nineteenth century." In Winn's telling of the story, British interests were realized "without significant political or military interference."[77] With neither imposition nor even significant political interference, we have a convergence of interests in a relationship that is not imperial and, in this dimension at least, is not even hierarchical.

If powerful state A convinces weak state B to do X, without exercising (formal or informal) political rule over B, this is no more "informal imperialism" than hard work is "informal theft."[78] The fact that strong and weak or core and periphery cooperate tells us nothing about the terms, conditions, and modes of cooperation. How one obtains a particular result matters, sometimes even more than what is achieved.

Informal empire certainly is a worthy subject of inquiry, especially in a world where territorial control seems to be of declining importance. *Informal empire* may actually be the best term to describe relations involving what I called *dominion* previously. In this sense, the Soviet bloc during the Cold War era and U.S. relations with Central America were examples of informal empire. But U.S. relations with Canada and Mexico, as well as most of South America, were, at most, hegemonic. And however we conceptualize the relations of, say, Poland or the Czech Republic with Western Europe or the United States today, we must emphasize the huge difference made by the recovery of effective sovereignty—that is, the replacement of Soviet informal empire by other forms of (in)equality. Form matters, centrally, not only to the quality of political life but to the opportunities for and causally efficacious means of bringing about change.

Reading Iraq

The ongoing "war in Iraq," as it tends to be called in the United States, allows us to deploy a wide range of the analytical resources developed in this chapter—in sharp contrast to the common reading of "Bush's war" as crucial evidence of American empire.

Personally, I find the cause of the war to be a very loosely connected set of disparate and shifting interests and objectives. Both Congressional authorization and American public support, it seems to me, were cobbled together in a classic pluralistic process of log-rolling to construct a minimum winning coalition held together by nothing beyond a temporary convergence of interests. What follows, however, depends on no particular account of the true cause of the war. Rather, it focuses on the various justifications for the war in the lead-up to war, on the war itself, and on its aftermath. I focus on justifications because they point to ostensibly acceptable grounds of action, even when they are mere rationalizations. They also imply a vision of desired results and relationships.

Weapons of Mass Destruction

Weapons of mass destruction, especially in the now infamous claim by Tony Blair that Iraqi chemical weapons could be on the battlefield in forty-five minutes, provided a classic preemptive self-defense argument. Faced with a truly imminent threat of great magnitude, preemption is widely accepted as at least excusable and, if authorized by the United Nations Security Council, largely beyond legal reproach.

If the Bush administration perceived a genuinely imminent requiring exercise of a unilateral[79] right to self-defense, it was profoundly mistaken. The pattern of Iraqi facilities occupied in the immediate aftermath of hostilities suggests that this rationale was, at best, secondary and ineptly implemented. It thus seems plausible to suggest that an essential part of the American decision to act alone was a preference for unilateralism and a desire to foster an international security system based on U.S. predominance rather than even limited collective security.

But this is no evidence of imperial designs, unless we confuse unilateralism with empire. Powerful states have considerable freedom of unilateral action in a world structured around sovereignty, especially when power asymmetries impede the capacity of others to balance. But unilateral freedom of action simply is not an imperial right to rule. Ad hoc coalitions are alliances, not institutionalized hegemony.

American unilateralism in Iraq belongs squarely in Quadrant III, not Quadrant IV, with the collective security option in Quadrant II. We thus have an excellent example of the analytical value of the bottom left to top right diagonal in Figure 3.1 that I have emphasized. All of the actual options seriously pursued lie off the mainstream diagonal.

We should ask similar questions about negative reactions to the war. To what extent did the emphasis on UN authorization reflect a principled commitment to collective security? Was, for example, French opposition rooted in realist balancing against American primacy, support for a UN-based concert system, or simply the fact that France, along with many other countries, found none of the reasons offered for war provided adequate justification in this case?

Democratization

Especially after the surprisingly strong turnout for Iraq's January 2005 election, democratization has moved to the forefront of American justifications for the war. Although the armed spread of democracy certainly was a goal of many neoconservatives, initially democracy was a decidedly secondary theme in the administration's rationale for going to war—because it is a rationale for the use of force that has virtually no support in the society of states.

Although scholarly literature on an international right to democratic governance is growing, such a right is not part of positive international law. Virtually no serious commentator suggests that individual states, or even the international community acting collectively, may use force if that right is violated by even a long-standing and unusually brutal dictatorship. Not even the Bush administration has claimed such a right.

Current democratization justifications—to the extent that they reflect more than an opportunistic effort to provide an after-the-fact rationalization following the refutation of the primary before-the-fact justification—are perhaps best seen as an attempt to establish democracy as a new standard of civilization. Whether this succeeds or fails, it is no more a matter of empire than the Holy Alliance's attempt to outlaw the practice.

One might also see the wide range of democratization initiatives undertaken not just by the United States but by most other Organization of Economic Cooperation Development (OECD) countries as an attempt to foster common security. Again, though, this is very different from empire, or even hegemony.

Consider Latin America today. It would be absurd to say that the U.S.-supported spread of democracy—which has found local support some commentators on Latin political culture have found surprising—has created a new American empire precisely when U.S. intervention has been almost completely eliminated. Convergence of interests between core and periphery simply is no evidence of empire, especially when what we are talking about is the right of people to rule themselves. Even if we were to agree that democratization in contemporary Latin America is just a new, more subtle (and thus more effective) form of neoimperialism, how American control is exercised and for what purposes makes a huge analytical and practical difference.

One might argue that the United States is not serious about democratization, which it often understands in conveniently partisan terms. Consider, for example, American praise for announced electoral reforms in Egypt that would result in less free elections than those the United States rightly criticized in Iran. But under such a reading, the promotion of democracy simply is not at issue and thus cannot be a source of empire, or anything else. And it hardly need be emphasized that cynical abuse of ethical norms is no evidence of empire.

The War on Terror

As the war in Iraq drags on, it is increasingly associated with the global War on Terror. The Bush administration seems sufficiently committed to this goal even to permit legal action against a prominent anti-Castro terrorist. In sharp contrast to the Ronald Reagan administration's distinction of terrorists and freedom fighters, the Bush administration has fairly consistently condemned all forms of terrorism by nonstate actors. This campaign has received considerable international endorsement. But it has nothing to do with empire. If anything, it reflects and reinforces the logic of territorial sovereignty and the monopoly of states on the use of force in international relations.

The crusading tone often associated with antiterrorism may reflect efforts to establish it as a new standard of civilization. More likely it involves a narrower exercise in outlawry, along the lines of privateers, pirates, and mercenaries. It might even suggest an effort to establish a thin common security community. All of these visions, however, are fundamentally nonimperial, which does not make them unimportant. But we simply cannot adequately apprehend them in terms of empire.

Other Justifications

Were the Bush Doctrine of preventive war to be established in practice, even informally through a series of American wars in which no other major power fought on the other side, that would indeed be significant evidence of American hegemony (although not empire). In fact, however, the doctrine has run up against near universal international condemnation and substantial principled domestic opposition. Empire involves not simply announcing special rights for oneself but a pattern of practice that gives effect to such rights. There simply is no evidence for such a practice with respect to preventive war.

Much the same is true of regime change. Even the Bush administration has not tried to claim a right of the United States to determine the regime of another state simply on the grounds that it treats its people despicably. The principle of sovereignty—political independence and territorial integrity—has not been significantly weakened, let alone swept aside, by the war in Iraq.

Furthermore, there has been no significant spillover from the right of humanitarian intervention against genocide to humanitarian interventions in other instances of severe suffering. It is certainly a fine thing that Saddam Hussein no longer rules Iraq, however we evaluate the regime that has replaced Saddam's. But even the Bush administration deploys primarily as an excuse rather than a strong positive justification.

Guantanamo has appeared prominently in many arguments of American imperialism. In fact, it shows exactly the opposite. A state that cannot obtain widespread formal acquiescence to its preferred international norms is not an empire. Empires set the rules. They do not need to assert awkward, implausible, and widely rejected exceptions for themselves. More generally, American *exemptionalism,* to use the term from Ruggie's chapter in this volume, is a sign of Quadrant III unipolar unilateralism.

Turning to narrowly self-interested rationales, oil is probably at the top of most lists. But reliable access to strategic resources is a concern of all great powers. It says nothing about empire. Regional stability is another self-interested concern not restricted to empires. It is important to note that the United States has chosen to define and pursue this, like most other objectives, in unilateral terms. But, once more, unilateralism is not empire. We have here another struggle between policies rooted in Quadrants III and II.

Conclusion

Much of the talk about American empire reflects an understandable, even admirable, desire to comprehend the nature of contemporary international political changes. Some of the most important changes indeed involve deviations from absolute sovereign equality. But without an appreciation of the wide range of sovereign inequalities and multiple forms of hierarchy in anarchy we can understand neither change nor (in)equality. And our analytical impoverishment may have serious practical consequences.

As the multiple readings of Iraq in the previous section illustrate, simply having conceptual models is not enough. The central questions are ultimately empirical; their answers depend on actual states of affairs in the world. Without adequate conceptual resources, however, we cannot even ask the right questions.

The best brief description of Iraq today is "semisovereign." Whatever our normative problems with such a notion, it is essential to any accurate understanding of contemporary international relations. Whether the Iraqi protectorate proves to be more a matter of temporary trusteeship or an instance of more permanent American protection, it is neither empire nor full sovereign equality; instead, it is something else that needs to be understood in its own terms. And that something else is not necessarily just a transitional stage on the way to empire or equality.

Or consider the potential impact of American power and policy on emerging forms of transnational community. To what extent are we seeing the development of a world of concentric zones of peace, conflict, and instability—understood in either civilizational or more neutral political terms—reflecting differing degrees of physical, ideological, and political proximity to the OECD core? Are we seeing the development of broader nonwar communities? Are common security communities developing around either neoliberal economic models or what in some circles has been called the community of market democracies? If so, controversies over American empire divert attention from such much more interesting and important questions.

If the only categories we have are anarchy and hierarchy/empire, then either nothing changes, or change is complete. No less important, the only direction of possible change is away from or toward empire. This certainly is an inadequate basis for understanding modern international relations in the three centuries following Westphalia. And, I would suggest, it provides a no less impoverished understanding of contemporary international relations.

International relations today may not be more hierarchical than they were during the Cold War. Certainly from, say, the Polish point of view, hierarchy has declined dramatically. As neoconservative complaints about old Europe suggest, many Western Europeans also see the contemporary world as less, not more, hierarchical. The same might be said of the post-Cold War Americas.

But quality is no less important than quantity. American power is, both intentionally and unintentionally, pushing us toward new forms of hierarchy and reviving older practices of sovereign inequality. Whether we want to understand or influence American policy and its impact on international society, the concepts of hierarchy in anarchy and sovereign inequality—but not empire—are essential.

Notes

1. I thank Dave Forsythe for advice and helpful comments on several earlier drafts. I also thank Mariano Bertucci, Eric Fattor, and Jae Won Lee for their comments, and Eric and Jae for exemplary research assistance as well.
2. Although this concept is grossly underexplored and unappreciated given its importance, significant exceptions include Nicholas Onuf and Frank F. Klink, "Anarchy, Authority, Rule," *International Studies Quarterly* 33 no. 2 (1989), 149–73; Alexander Wendt and Daniel Friedheim, "Hierarchy under Anarchy: Informal Empire and the East German State," *International Organization* 49 no. 4 (1995), 689–721; David A. Lake, "Anarchy, Hierarchy, and the Variety of International Relations," *International Organization* 50 no. 1 (1996), 1–33; Katja Weber, "Hierarchy Amidst Anarchy: A Transaction Costs Approach to International Security Cooperation," *International Studies Quarterly* 41 no. 2 (1997), 321–40; Edward Keene, *Beyond the Anarchical Society: Grotius, Colonialism, and Order in World Politics* (Cambridge, UK: Cambridge University Press, 2002); Gerry Simpson, *Great Powers and Outlaw States: Unequal Sovereigns in the International Legal Order* (Cambridge, UK: Cambridge University Press, 2004); and John M. Hobson and J. C. Sharman, "The Enduring Place of Hierarchy in World Politics: Tracing the Social Logics of Hierarchy and Political Change," *European Journal of International Relations* 11 no. 1 (2005), 63–98.
3. The leading statements of the English School (ES) perspective are Hedley Bull, *The Anarchical Society: A Study of Order in World Politics* (New York: Columbia University Press, 1977); and Barry Buzan, *From International Society to World Society? English School Theory and the Social Structure of Globalization* (Cambridge, UK: Cambridge University Press, 2004). Andrew Linklater, "The English School," in *Theories of International Relations*, 3rd ed., ed. Scott Burchill and Andrew Linklater (London: Routledge, 2005) offers a good single-chapter introductory overview. Alex J. Bellamy, ed., *International Society and Its Critics* (Oxford: Oxford University Press, 2005) offers a wide-ranging critical assessment. For reasons of space, I offer only an application, not an exposition, of the English School's "international society" perspective.
4. Ellen Meiksins Wood, *Empire of Capital* (London: Verso, 2003), 32.
5. Richard Koebner, *Empire* (Cambridge, UK: Cambridge University Press, 1961).
6. J. S. Richardson, "Imperium Romanum: Empire and the Language of Power," *Journal of Roman Studies* 81 (1991), 1. Compare Koebner, *Empire*, 4–11.
7. *Oxford English Dictionary*.

8. Shmuel N. Eisenstadt, "Empires," in *International Encyclopedia of the Social Sciences*, ed. David L. Sills (New York: Free Press, 1968), 41; Michael W. Doyle, *Empires* (Ithaca, NY: Cornell University Press, 1986), 12, 36; Alexander J. Motyl, *Imperial Ends: The Decay, Collapse, and Revival of Empires* (New York: Columbia University Press, 2001), 4, 13; and Dominic Lieven, *Empire: The Russian Empire and Its Rivals* (New Haven, CT: Yale University Press, 2001), xi.
9. Michael Hardt and Antonio Negri, *Empire* (Cambridge, MA: Harvard University Press, 2000).
10. Raymond Aron, *Peace and War: A Theory of International Relations* (Garden City, NY: Doubleday, 1966), 152; Wood, *Empire of Capital*, 34.
11. The classic statement is Kenneth N. Waltz, *Theory of International Politics* (New York: Random House, 1979), 114–16.
12. See, for example, Stephen Peter Rosen, "An Empire, If You Can Keep It," *National Interest* (2003), 51–3.
13. Waltz, *Theory of International Politics*, 81.
14. Ibid., 88.
15. Waltz, *Theory of International Politics*, 94. Compare Robert W. Tucker, *The Inequality of Nations* (New York: Basic Books, 1977).
16. Ibid., 88.
17. J. H. W. Verzijl, *International Law in Historical Perspective: Volume I, General Subjects* (Leiden: A. W. Sijthoff, 1968), 305.
18. Georg Friedrich von Martens, *Summary of the Law of Nations, Founded on the Treaties and Customs of the Modern Nations of Europe* (Littleton: Fred B. Rothman & Co., 1986), book 1.1.1, 1.2.4; Henry Wheaton, *Elements of International Law*, 8th ed. (Boston: Little, Brown, and Company, 1866), 34–8; Johann Caspar Bluntschli, *Le Droit International Codifié*, trans. M. C. Lardy, 2nd ed. (Paris: Librairie de Guillaumin et cie., 1874), 92; and George B. Davis, *The Elements of International Law*, rev. ed. (New York: Harper & Brothers Publishers, 1900), 37. Other formulations include *part-sovereign*, T. J. Lawrence, *The Principles of International Law* (Boston: D. C. Heath & Co., 1895), 49, 71; *imperfectly independent*, William Edward Hall, *A Treatise on International Law*, 4th ed. (Oxford: Clarendon Press, 1895), 4; *not-full sovereign*, L. Oppenheim, ed. H. Lauterpacht, *International Law: A Treatise*, 8th ed. (New York: David McKay Company, 1955), 65; *half sovereign*, Arnold D. McNair, "Equality in International Law," *Michigan Law Review* 26 no. 2 (1927),131–52; Oppenheim, *International Law*, 8th ed., 126; and *conditionally independent*, Travers Twiss, *The Law of Nations Considered as Independent Political Communities* (Oxford: Oxford University Press, 1861), 24–6.
19. Allan Rosas, "State Sovereignty and Human Rights: Towards a Global Constitutional Project," *Political Studies* 43 no. 4 (1995), 63. The centrality of the principle of sovereign equality is almost universally accepted by the leading commentators. The standard monograph is Edwin DeWitt Dickinson, *The Equality of States in International Law* (Cambridge, MA: Harvard University Press, 1920). See also Gerry Simpson, *Great Powers and Outlaw States: Unequal Sovereigns in the International Legal Order* (Cambridge, UK: Cambridge University Press, 2004); Robert A. Klein, *Sovereign Equality among States: The History of an Idea* (Toronto: University of Toronto Press, 1974); Pieter Hendrik Kooijmans, *The Doctrine of the Legal Equality of States: An Inquiry into the Foundations of International Law* (Leiden: A. W. Sythoff, 1964); McNair, "Equality in International Law"; and Julius Goebel Jr., "The Equality of States I, II, III," *Columbia Law Review* 23 no. 1–3 (1923), 1–29, 113–41, 247–77.
20. Benedict Kingsbury, "Sovereignty and Inequality," *European Journal of International Law* 9 no. 4 (1998), 600.
21. Henry Sumner Maine, *International Law (the Whewell Lectures, 1887)*, 2nd ed. (London: John Murray, 1915), 58.
22. Lassa Oppenheim, *International Law: A Treatise*, 3rd ed., 2 vols. (London: Longmans, Green and Co., 1920), 70.
23. Ian Brownlie, *Principles of Public International Law*, 6th ed. (Oxford: Oxford University Press, 2003), 113.
24. Lord McNair, *The Law of Treaties* (Oxford: Clarendon Press, 1961), 239–54; Georg Ress, "Guarantee" and "Treaties of Guarantee," in *Encyclopedia of Public International Law*, vol. 7, ed. Rudolf Bernhardt (Amsterdam: North Holland, 1984); Gerhard Hoffmann, "Protectorates," in *Encyclopedia of Public International Law*, vol. 10, ed. Rudolf Bernhardt (Amsterdam: North Holland, 1987); J. W. Headlam-Morley, "Treaties of Guarantee," *Cambridge Historical*

Journal 2 no. 2 (1927), 151–70; Verzijl, *International Law in Historical Perspective: Part II, International Persons* (Leiden: A. W. Sitjhoff, 1968), 412–28, 457–9; Emerich de Vattel, *The Law of Nations or the Principles of Natural Law Applied to the Conduct of the Affairs of Nations and of Sovereigns* (Washington, D.C.: Carnegie Institution of Washington, 1916), book 1, 6, 192–9; Robert Phillimore, *Commentaries upon International Law* (Philadelphia: T. & J. W. Johnson, 1854), book 2, 56–63, 77–9; Hall, *A Treatise on International Law*, 4, 38; Dickinson, *Equality of States*, 240–52; and Oppenheim, *International Law*, 8th ed., 574–7.
25. Dickinson, *Equality of States*, 240–1.
26. Helen Dwight Reid, *International Servitudes in Law and Practice* (Chicago: University of Chicago Press, 1932); Pitman B. Potter, "The Doctrine of Servitudes in International Law," *American Journal of International Law* 9 no. 3 (1915), 627–41; Verzijl, *International Law in Historical Perspective: Part III, State Territory* (Leiden: A. W. Sitjhoff, 1970), 413–28; Dickinson, *Equality of States*, 264–9, 339–40, 343–4; Oppenheim *International Law*, 8th ed., 203–8; Ulrich Fastenrath, "Servitudes," in *Encyclopedia of Public International Law*, vol. 10; and Brownlie, *Principles of Public International Law*, 366–8.
27. Christian Rumpf, "Territory, Lease," in *Encyclopedia of Public International Law*, vol. 10; Verzijl, *State Territory*, 397–408.
28. Phillimore, *Commentaries*, 81, 82; Twiss, *Law of Nations*, 81, 82; Wheaton, *Elements of International Law*, 34; Verzijl, *International Persons*, 500–10; and Eckart Klein, "Free Cities," in *Encyclopedia of Public International Law*, vol. 10.
29. Dickinson, *Equality of States*, 252–5; McNair, *Law of Treaties*, 46–50; Oppenheim, *International Law*, 8th ed., 95–101; Verzijl, *International Law in Historical Perspective: Part IX-B, the Law of Neutrality* (Leiden: Sijthoff & Noordhoff, 1979), 21–8; Rodolf F. Bindschedler, "Permanent Neutrality of States," in *Encyclopedia of Public International Law*, vol. 7; and Stephan Verosta, "Neutralization," in *Encyclopedia of Public International Law*, vol. 4, ed. Rudolf Bernhardt (Amsterdam: North Holland, 1982).
30. Oppenheim, *International Law*, 3rd ed., 134.
31. Phillimore, *Commentaries*, 87–96; Theodore D. Woolsey, *Introduction to the Study of International Law*, 4th ed. (New York: Scribner, Armstrong, 1874), 43–6; Lawrence, *Principles of International Law*, 75–89; Hall, *A Treatise on International Law*, 4th ed., 88–95; Amos S. Hershey, *The Essentials of International Public Law* (New York: Macmillan Company, 1912), 148–54; Dickinson, *Equality of States*, 260–4; Ellery C. Stowell, *Intervention in International Law* (Washington, DC: John Byrne & Co., 1921); Charles Cheney Hyde, *International Law: Chiefly as Interpreted and Applied by the United States* (Boston: Little, Brown, and Company, 1922), 69–84; J. L. Brierly, *The Law of Nations: An Introduction to the International Law of Peace* (Oxford: Clarendon Press, 1949), 284–90; Oppenheim, *International Law*, 8th ed., 134–40; and Verzijl, *General Subjects*, 236–43.
32. Dickinson, *Equality of States*, 230–36; Felix Ermacora, "Confederations and Other Unions of States," in *Encyclopedia of Public International Law*, vol. 10; and Verzijl, *International Persons*, 132–98.
33. Bluntschli, *Le Droit International Codifié*, 70–8; and Wheaton, *Elements of International Law*, 39–48.
34. Arthur Berriedale Keith, *The Sovereignty of the British Dominions* (London: Macmillan and Co., 1929).
35. Verzijl, *International Persons*, 339–98; Phillimore, *Commentaries*, 87–101; Dickinson, *Equality of States*, 236–40; Oppenheim, *International Law*, 8th ed., 90–1; and Brownlie, *Principles of Public International Law*, 114.
36. Brownlie, *Principles of Public International Law*, 113–4; Peter Schneider, "Condominium," in *Encyclopedia of Public International Law*, vol. 10; and Verzijl, *State Territory*, 429–43.
37. Stephen D. Krasner, *Sovereignty: Organized Hypocrisy* (Princeton, NJ: Princeton University Press, 1999), ch. 3; Inis Claude Jr., *National Minorities: An International Problem* (Cambridge, MA: Harvard University Press, 1955); and Anthony Evelyn Alcock, *A History of the Protection of Regional Cultural Minorities in Europe: From the Edict of Nantes to the Present Day* (New York: St. Martin's Press, 2000).
38. Dickinson, *Equality of States*, 256–60; Krasner, *Sovereignty*, 131–43.
39. William Bain, *Between Anarchy and Society: Trusteeship and the Obligations of Power* (Oxford: Oxford University Press, 2003); Richard Caplan, "A New Trusteeship? The International Administration of War-Torn Territories," *Adelphi Papers* 42 no. 341 (2002); and

James D. Fearon and David D. Laitin, "Neotrusteeship and the Problem of Weak States," *International Security* 28 no. 4 (2004), 5–39.
40. Hugo Grotius, *De Jure Belli Ac Pacis Libri Tres* (Oxford: Clarendon Press, 1925), book I.3.21, II.25.7; Hyde, *International Law*, 493; Lawrence, *Principles of International Law*, 154; Stuart S. Malawer, *Imposed Treaties and International Law* (n.p.: William S. Hein & Co. Law Book Publishers, 1977); McNair, *Law of Treaties,* 206–11; Werner Morvay, "Unequal Treaties," in *Encyclopedia of Public International Law*, vol. 7; Oppenheim, *International Law*, 8th ed., 498–9; Phillimore, *Commentaries*, book 2, 49; and Georg Schwarzenberger, *Power Politics: A Study of International Society*, 2d ed. (London: Stevens, 1951), 92–3.
41. William Edward Hall, *A Treatise on International Law*, 8th ed. (Oxford: Clarendon Press, 1924), 30.
42. Daniel Philpott, *Revolutions in Sovereignty: How Ideas Shaped Modern International Relations* (Princeton, NJ: Princeton University Press, 2001), chs. 8–12.
43. Lawrence, *Principles of International Law*, 48.
44. Charles G. Fenwick, *International Law* (New York: Century Co., 1924), 135.
45. Oppenheim, *International Law*, 8th ed., 483–5; and Ernest Satow, *A Guide to Diplomatic Practice* (London: Longmans, Green and Co., 1917), 439–97.
46. Simpson, *Great Powers and Outlaw States*, 112.
47. Brierly, *Law of Nations*, 151–2; Hall, *Treatise on International Law*, 4th ed., p. 38; and Verzijl, *State Territory*, 494–500.
48. Hyde, *International Law*, 85–97. Compare Alejandro Alvarez, *The Monroe Doctrine: Its Importance in the International Life of the States of the New World* (New York: Oxford University Press, 1924); Peter Malanczuk, "Monroe Doctrine," in *Encyclopedia of Public International Law,* vol. 7; and Dexter Perkins, *A History of the Monroe Doctrine* (Boston: Little, Brown, 1963).
49. Thomas M. Franck and Edward Weisband, "The Johnson and Brezhnev Doctrines: The Law You Make Might Be Your Own," *Stanford Law Review* 22 no. 5 (1970), 979–1014.
50. Simpson, *Great Powers and Outlaw States.*
51. Maurice Bourquin, *Histoire De La Sainte Alliance* (Geneva: Georg, 1954); Bruce Cronin, *Community under Anarchy: Transnational Identity and the Evolution of Cooperation* (New York: Columbia University Press, 1999), 65–72; and Stephan Verosta, "Holy Alliance," in *Encyclopedia of Public International Law,* vol. 7.
52. Ethan A. Nadelman, "Global Prohibition Regimes: The Evolution of Norms in International Society," *International Organization* 44 no. 4 (1990), 479–526.
53. Edward Keene, *Beyond the Anarchical Society,* 44–52, 67–9, 75–7, 93–5, 105–8; and C. H. Alexandrowicz, *An Introduction to the History of the Law of Nations in the East Indies* (Oxford: Clarendon Press, 1967).
54. Keene, *Beyond the Anarchical Society,* ch. 4.
55. Gerrit W. Gong, *The Standard of "Civilisation" in International Society* (Oxford: Clarendon Press, 1984), ch. 5; G. W. Keeton, *The Development of Extraterritoriality in China* (London: Longmans, Green and Co., 1928); and Westel W. Willoughby, *Foreign Rights and Interests in China,* rev. ed., 2 vols. (Baltimore: Johns Hopkins Press, 1927).
56. Michael R. Auslin, *Negotiating with Imperialism: The Unequal Treaties and the Culture of Japanese Diplomacy* (Cambridge, MA: Harvard University Press, 2004); Gong, *Standard of "Civilisation,"* ch. 6; and F. C. Jones, *Extraterritoriality in Japan and the Diplomatic Relations Resulting in Its Abolition* (New Haven, CT: Yale University Press, 1931).
57. Gong, *Standard of "Civilisation,"* 106–19.
58. Ibid., ch. 7.
59. James L. Hevia, "Making China 'Perfectly Equal,'" *Journal of Historical Sociology* 3 (1990), 379–400.
60. Gong, *Standard of "Civilisation"*; Georg Schwarzenberger, "The Standard of Civilisation in International Law," *Current Legal Problems* 17 (1955); Dickinson, *Equality of States*, 223–9; B. V. A. Roling, *International Law in an Expanded World* (Amsterdam: Djambatan, 1960), ch. 4; Keene, *Beyond the Anarchical Society,* ch. 4; Martti Koskenniemi, *The Gentle Civilizer of Nations: The Rise and Fall of International Law, 1870–1960* (Cambridge, UK: Cambridge University Press, 2002), ch. 2; and Edward Keene, *International Political Thought: An Historical Introduction* (Cambridge, UK: Polity Press, 2005). For a much more critical take on this theme, see Mark B. Salter, *Barbarians and Civilization in International Relations* (London: Pluto Press, 2002).

61. Gong, *Standard of "Civilisation,"* 55–9; Salter, *Barbarians and Civilization*, 19–24.
62. Hidemi Suganami, "Japan's Entry into International Society," in *The Expansion of International Society*, ed. Hedley Bull and Adam Watson (Oxford: Clarendon Press, 1984); and Shogo Suzuki, "Japan's Socialization into Janus-Faced European International Society," *European Journal of International Relations* 11 no. 1 (2005), 137–64.
63. Robert L. Ivie, "Savagery in Democracy's Empire," *Third World Quarterly* 26 no. 1 (2005), 55–65; and Salter, *Barbarians and Civilization*, 163–7.
64. Jack Donnelly, "Human Rights: A New Standard of Civilization?" *International Affairs* 74 no. 1 (1998), 1–24.
65. Cronin, *Community under Anarchy*, 13.
66. Richard B. Elrod, "The Concert of Europe: A Fresh Look at an International System," *World Politics* 28 no. 2 (1976), 159–74; Robert Jervis, "From Balance to Concert: A Study of International Security Cooperation," *World Politics* 38 no. 1 (1985), 58–79; Cronin, *Community under Anarchy*, ch. 3.
67. R. E. J. Penttila, "The G8 as a Concert of Powers," *Adelphi Papers* 43 no. 355 (2003).
68. Claude, *Power and International Relations* (New York: Random House, 1962), ch. 4. Compare Charles A. Kupchan and Clifford A. Kupchan, "The Promise of Collective Security," *International Security* 20 (Summer 1995), 52–61; George Downs, ed., *Collective Security beyond the Cold War* (Ann Arbor: University of Michigan Press, 1994); Lynn H. Miller, "The Idea and Reality of Collective Security," *Global Governance* 5 no. 3 (1999), 303–32; and Schwarzenberger, *Power Politics*, ch. 27. The UN Security Council combines elements of collective security, concert (the veto), and balance of power (reserving a self-help right to individual and collective self-defense).
69. Doyle, *Empires*, 12, 40, 55–60; Motyl, *Imperial Ends*, 20; and Watson, *Evolution of International Society*, 15–6, 27–8, 122–8. Note that both imperial polities and regional hegemonies may be embedded in broader international orders that fall pretty much anywhere in the top row of Figure 3.1. For example, the British Empire operated in a "global" (European) concert system in 1830 (Quadrant II) but a more classic balance of power system in 1730 and 1930 (Quadrant I).
70. Watson, *Evolution of International Society*, 15–6.
71. Joseph V. Femia, *Gramsci's Political Thought: Hegemony, Consciousness, and the Revolutionary Process* (Oxford: Clarendon Press, 1981); and Stephen Gill, ed., *Gramsci, Historical Materialism, and International Relations* (Cambridge, UK: Cambridge University Press, 1993).
72. Ole Waever, "Insecurity, Security, and Asecurity in the West European Non-War Community," in *Security Communities*, ed. Emanuel Adler and Michael Barnett (Cambridge, UK: Cambridge University Press, 1998).
73. Niall Ferguson, *Colossus: The Price of America's Empire* (New York: Penguin Press, 2004), 8.
74. Ibid., 10.
75. "Ruler over subject peoples," "a polity that rules over wide territories and many peoples," "methods of rule," "imperial rule," "methods of informal rule." Ibid., 9, 10, 11, 12, 13.
76. Ibid., 10.
77. Peter Winn, "British Informal Empire in Uruguay in the Nineteenth Century," *Past and Present* no. 73 (1976), 126.
78. Sidney Morgenbesser, "Imperialism: Some Preliminary Distinctions," *Philosophy and Public Affairs* 3 no. 1 (1973), 25–6.
79. Ad hoc coalitions—alliances to pursue a particular war—are the antithesis of multilateralism, which involves recognition of the authority of multilateral institutions. John Gerard Ruggie, "Multilateralism: The Anatomy of an Institution," *International Organization* 46 no. 3 (1992), 561–98.
80. Gregory H. Fox and Brad R. Roth, eds., *Democratic Governance and International Law* (Cambridge, UK: Cambridge University Press, 2000) provides a good introduction.

4
American Security, the Use of Force, and the Limits of the Bush Doctrine

JON WESTERN

By almost any historic standard, the Bush Doctrine is the most ambitious and aggressive grand strategy the United States has ever had. To be sure, the quintessential Cold War containment document NSC-68 argued that the "free world" faced an existential threat from Soviet "slavery" and tyranny and that the United States needed to assume a "world leadership" role to ensure the eventual victory of liberalism over totalitarianism. But NSC-68 acknowledged that bipolarity in the nuclear age limited the utility of force in what was ultimately a global "conflict of ideas." The Bush Doctrine, by contrast, is the first time we have had a grand strategy that combines an ambitious vision to transform the world with unrivaled political and military power. This convergence of ambition and power is embodied in the Bush Doctrine's explicit declaration that the United States will use its power "to destroy global threats to liberty and freedom." Ultimately, as the doctrine proclaims, "The aim of this strategy is to help make the world not just safer but better."[1]

Although the broad goals of liberalism and democracy are certainly laudable, history and recent events suggest that we should be wary of the George W. Bush administration's bold and ambitious agenda. As the wars in Afghanistan and Iraq reveal, the administration has concluded that the strongest instrument in America's foreign policy arsenal is the use of its military force to meet the growing threats associated with the rise of international terrorism and the threat of illicit proliferation of weapons of mass destruction (WMD). Furthermore, not only does the Bush strategy rest on a profound belief and faith in the efficacy of force, the doctrine also represents a revolutionary change in American foreign policy with its calls for the United States to be willing and able to launch preventive wars and act unilaterally when it believes it needs to. Though the administration continues to give some lip service to multilateral institutions such as the North Atlantic Treaty Organization (NATO) and even the United Nations (UN) as key elements of American security, the Bush administration has opted for ad hoc coalitions rather than compromise within existing multilateral institutions in its actions since September 11, 2001.

This chapter critically examines how well the Bush Doctrine and the recent use of force in Afghanistan and Iraq have addressed American security concerns. I argue that even though the Bush administration has eliminated hostile regimes in Afghanistan and Iraq, the application of the Bush Doctrine has ignored some and sparked other threats that continue to pose significant dangers to the United States. Above all, America's ability to lead and influence others to participate in a comprehensive strategy to deal with the rise of international terrorism and the proliferation of WMD has been made more difficult by the dramatic rise of anti-Americanism around the globe since the promulgation of the Bush Doctrine and the beginning of the war in Iraq. I conclude that although several structural factors are likely to constrain the Untied States from launching new preventive wars in the near future, the United States will still face growing anti-American resentment to the American occupation of Iraq and to aggressive American unilateralism. Although the Bush administration has recognized the importance of controlling this widespread anti-Americanism, it will take significant policy corrections and a more concerted public diplomacy campaign to reverse the trends.

The Efficacy of Force

The Bush administration's view of the world and of its responsibilities for ensuring American and international security rests on a profound faith in the efficacy of force. No one in the Bush administration dismisses the need for diplomacy, economic trade and aid, and the host of other instruments of statecraft, but the Bush Doctrine as well as the wars in Afghanistan and Iraq reveal the central role of the use of force to win the war on terror, to control the proliferation of WMD, and ultimately, to promote democracy.

Much of this focus comes from the fundamental assumption that, in international politics, power begets respect, and weakness invites trouble. This assumption suggests that the projection of American military power can effectively ward off competitors and stabilize the international system because allies will bandwagon with the United States while potential adversaries will cower under American power. The Bush administration believes that the most dangerous episodes for the United States and international security have come when totalitarian regimes have gone unchecked and when the defenders of the free world have not adequately assembled and maintained their own power capabilities. Many in the Bush administration believe that the only instances in which American military power has failed have been those situations in which the military has been hindered by political indecision, vacillation, and naive moralism.

But exactly how effective is the use of force—and especially preventive war—in the war on terror or in the effort to stem the illicit proliferation of

WMD? American forces defeated the Taliban in Afghanistan and overthrew Saddam Hussein's regime in Iraq, and neither regime will pose a threat to the United States. American forces also destroyed Al-Qaeda training operations in Afghanistan and dispersed its leadership. But Bush's now infamous "Mission Accomplished" speech aboard the U.S.S. Abraham Lincoln in May 2003 illustrated the degree to which American leaders failed to anticipate and appreciate the complexity of modern warfare and, ultimately, the limits of the use of military. Although Bush warned that difficulties would still await American forces in Iraq, he triumphantly declared that "in the battle of Iraq, the United States and our allies have prevailed."[2]

War on Terror
It should be obvious that both military commanders and senior civilian leaders in the Bush administration underestimated the degree and magnitude of the insurgency in Iraq. Many have criticized the administration for its lack of planning and postwar implementation strategies, but the precipitous rise in insurgent attacks against both American and Iraqi civilians also illustrates the inherent limits in the use of force in general and the unintended consequences of the application of American military power done in a manner deemed inappropriate by much of the world. In the two years following the invasion, more than 1,500 American troops died in Iraq, and somewhere between 10,000 and 20,000 civilians were killed either by insurgent attacks or as a result of American military responses to the insurgency.[3]

Although the actual numbers of insurgents is unknown, the evidence suggests that the number of insurgents increased significantly in 2003 and 2004. Despite the repeated characterization of the insurgency by Bush and his advisers as nothing more than a few Baathist Party "dead enders" and Saddam loyalists, in early 2005 senior military commanders acknowledged a much larger insurgency and told members of Congress that some 15,000 suspected insurgents had been killed or captured in 2004.[4] Meanwhile, nearly two years after the beginning of the war, the Central Intelligence Agency (CIA) estimated that the insurgency was much stronger than anticipated and included former regime loyalists, foreign fighters linked to Al-Qaeda, Sunni Muslims and Iraqi nationalists, and many Shiite Muslims angered by the American occupation and the thousands of Iraqi civilian casualties. The CIA also concluded that Al-Qaeda and other terrorist organization have effectively exploited the war for on-the-ground training and in its recruiting efforts worldwide. In fact, even during the initial American military build-up in the Persian Gulf in the run-up to the war in late 2002 and early 2003, a United Nations report concluded that Al-Qaeda saw increases in recruiting in thirty to forty countries with volunteers reportedly "beating down their doors to join."[5]

Furthermore, American reliance on military power has been ineffective in controlling one of the key instruments of the insurgency: the use of suicide attacks. According to an extensive study by Scott Atran, professor of anthropology at the University of Michigan, suicide attacks have become more frequent, sophisticated, and deadly in Iraq. Thirty-three of the world's ninety-nine suicide attacks in 2003 occurred in Iraq; in 2004, 104 suicide attacks occurred there.[6] In February 2004 alone, more than 400 people were killed by suicide bombers in Iraq.

The evidence suggests that the use of force is not only ineffective in combating suicide attacks but also counterproductive. For example, the extensive military action by the United States in Fallujah in November 2004 resulted in a short-term tactical military success, but it also generated considerable anger throughout Iraq and elsewhere in the region and some sympathy for the insurgency. A study by the Pew Research Center for People and the Press in March 2005 revealed that nearly 70 percent of Jordanians believed that suicide attacks against the United States were justified.[7]

The psychological and sociological profile of suicide attackers suggest that they come from moderate, middle-class families who are more educated and economically advantaged than others in their countries and are drawn to the cause of martyrdom because of intense resentment of American policies. Surveys suggest that among Muslim populations who support suicide attacks against the United States, they are not motivated by some irrational hatred of freedom or democracy. Their anger is directed at American foreign policy, especially the history of American oil policy in the Middle East, its support for repressive political regimes, the seeming permanence of American military forces stationed there, and a widespread perception of American indifference to Arab and Muslim casualties and humiliation.[8] It is their education and privilege, in fact, that gives them the intellectual resources and experiences to critically interpret American foreign policy in the region. In this regard, a policy that focuses almost exclusively on the use of force may disrupt suicide networks, but it is unlikely to destroy them. Atran concluded in his report that the problem with relying on military force is that it "mutates suicide networks and cells to mean forms."[9]

To be successful, both in defeating the insurgency and in rebuilding the country, the United States needs the active cooperation of the civilian population. In March 2005, for example, American and Iraqi forces found and destroyed a training facility for foreign fighters after receiving a tip from local civilians.[10] The event was championed by U.S. military commanders as a major strike against the insurgency, and it demonstrated the need and effectiveness of civilian cooperation. Yet though most Iraqis were pleased that Hussein is no longer in power, many quickly became frustrated by and disgruntled with American occupation and indifferent to the fate of American troops.[11] This is in part inspired by the inherent tension between the means and ends of the American military occupation. The war and the violence of the insurgency has left thousands of Iraqis dead and wounded. And efforts to stem attacks on American troops, Iraqi police and security personnel, and Iraqi civilians have not been successful. In fact, many of these efforts have exacerbated the problems. In the first two years of the occupation, thousands of Iraqis were detained by American forces, suspected of collaboration with the insurgency; many were held without charge and ultimately were released. This, along with continued disruptions of electricity and gasoline and the unemployment rate hovering at 40 percent, has contributed to rising levels of anti-Americanism. Furthermore, the extensive looting in the days immediately following Hussein's collapse not only caused billions of dollars in damage to Iraq's infrastructure, most notably to many of the country's hospitals and clinics where medical equipment and medicine were stolen; the looting of almost all government ministries also demoralized Iraqi bureaucrats, intellectuals, and technicians—most of whom were, and are, needed to help rebuild the country.[12]

Ultimately, all of this resentment and indifference to the American occupation has had direct and tangible costs to the United States in both monetary and material casualties. Between Bush's formal declaration of the end of major combat operations in May 2003 and December 2005, more than 2,000 American troops were killed in Iraq, more the 150,000 are still stationed there, and taxpayers have paid more than $200 billion. General Richard B. Myers summed up the crux of the ongoing problem in his testimony before the Senate Armed Services Committee in February 2005. He noted that a critical problem in Iraq and in estimating and understanding the insurgency and its future success of failure is that "there are so many fence sitters" among the civilian population within Iraq.[13]

Proliferation

The application of American military power has shown little sign of winning the war on terror, and the assumptions of the Bush Doctrine on the proliferation of WMD are also suspect. The Bush administration has departed from its predecessors and has largely moved away from an emphasis on international treaties and institutions designed to deter and verify nonproliferation. Instead, the administration has relied heavily on brandishing the use of force to threaten and deter potential proliferators and, in the case of Iraq, on removing a regime.

The Bush Doctrine identifies that nuclear proliferation and the potential combination of radicalism and technology pose the greatest threat to the United States. The centerpiece of the doctrine is the administration's proclamation that the United States maintains the "right to respond with overwhelming force" to threats emanating from WMD. Because WMD are weapons that "can be easily concealed, delivered covertly, and used without warning," and because they are so catastrophic, the doctrine adapts "the concept of imminent threat to the capabilities and objectives of today's adversaries."[14] The administration argues that by declaring such a policy and by using force in Iraq and elsewhere, the United States sends an unambiguous signal to others of the dangers associated with nuclear proliferation. The administration, for example, was quick to highlight as an example Libyan President Muammar Qaddafi's decision to renounce his nuclear program.

Yet several recent studies suggest that the Bush Doctrine is insufficient to ensure nonproliferation. For example, a 2005 report by the Carnegie Endowment for International Peace warned that the world is at a nuclear tipping point on proliferation and that the Bush administration's almost singular focus on using force to stem proliferation is likely to be both costly and ineffective.[15] For countries that have been considering or developing nuclear weapons programs, the American war in Iraq may well create powerful incentives toward proliferation. Jack Snyder argued that "today, no combination of adversaries can hope to equal America's power under any circumstance. However, if they fear the unbridled use of America's power, they may well perceive overwhelming incentives to wield weapons of terror and mass destruction to deter" the United States.[16]

What is certain is that almost everyone recognizes weapons of mass destruction, and especially nuclear weapons, as great equalizers. Much of the prewar debate within the United States was that it was important to strike Iraq before it acquired such weapons because it would be much more difficult afterward. Even skeptics of the war, such as former ambassador Richard Holbrooke, for example, told the Senate Foreign Relations Committee in October 2002 that it would be far easier for the United States to defeat Saddam Hussein in 2003 than ten years later. The signal in this debate is that preventive war is more difficult and probably unlikely after a country develops nuclear weapons.

North Korea's open declaration of its development of nuclear weapons in early 2005 demonstrates that the war in Iraq did not stop proliferation. Arguably, North Korea was intent on developing nuclear weapons irrespective of the events in Iraq. Nonetheless, the war in Iraq did have opportunity costs for the United States by consuming American diplomatic and military resources that could have been employed to slow North Korea's proliferation.

Likewise in Iran, the implications of the war in Iraq might well be counterproductive. To date, Iran's nuclear ambitions remain unclear, and its ultimate decision to proceed or not to proceed with building nuclear weapons most likely will be wrapped up in a complex dynamic of internal Iranian politics. Iran has already sunk considerable costs into its nuclear research program, and issues of national (and Muslim) pride and domestic bureaucratic and interest group politics may well play a role in influencing Iran's course of actions. However, in the wake of the terrorist attacks of September 11, 2001, and the wars in Afghanistan and Iraq, Iran now finds itself surrounded by American forces to its east (in Afghanistan) and to its west (in Iraq). Furthermore, its geostrategic position coupled with the history of American involvement in the country and the Bush administration's rhetoric about Iran as a member of the axis of evil have not gone unnoticed among conservatives in Iran. Given the multiple motives underlying Iran's current position on nuclear proliferation and the American history in Iran, a deterrence model premised on explicit threats to use force to prevent Iranian proliferation may exacerbate the domestic pressures to proliferate.[17] At the very least, preventive American military action in Iran, such as limited airstrikes of suspected nuclear weapons sites, almost certainly would fuel anti-Americanism, Iranian nationalism, and very aggressive efforts to move toward the development of nuclear weapons program.[18]

Another concern with the Bush administration's extensive reliance on the use of force to eliminate regimes potentially proliferating WMD is that it may miss the more fundamental dangers of the WMD threat to American and international security. The weak American response to the case of Pakistani nuclear scientist A. Q. Khan and his transferring of secret nuclear technology and materials to a hidden network highlights the limits of the Bush Doctrine to this aspect of nuclear proliferation. Nuclear technology, fissile materials, and even nuclear weapons can easily be transferred covertly through these existing illicit networks once they are obtained by those who aspire to get them. The Bush administration quietly accepted Pakistani president-general Pervez Musharraf's pardoning of Khan, which has greatly limited the International Atomic Energy Agency investigation of Khan's activities. To date there is still no full accounting of these networks.[19]

And despite the rhetorical images of smoking guns in the form of mushroom clouds invoked by senior Bush administration officials in the run-up to the war in Iraq, the largest potential source for terrorists to acquire nuclear materials—including processed enriched uranium—resides in vulnerable facilities in Russia. The Carnegie Endowment for International Peace *Report on Nuclear Security* warned that the "gravest danger arises from terrorists' access to state stockpiles of nuclear weapons and fissile materials, because acquiring a supply of nuclear material (as opposed to making the weapon itself) remains the most difficult challenge for a terrorist group ... The most likely sources of nuclear weapons and materials for terrorists are storage areas in the former states of the Soviet Union and in Pakistan ... ."[20] The international community has repeatedly acknowledged the inadequacies of the storage facilities and the safeguard measures currently in place in Russia and has determined that some $30 billion is needed to protect these sites and to secure the materials. To date, however, the international community has pledged only $20 billion. For its part the Bush administration pledged $10 billion over the next ten years. Facing unprecedented budget deficits and the nearly $200 billion price tag for the war in Iraq, however, Bush reduced his budget request for fiscal year (FY) 2005 for the Nunn Lugar Cooperative Threat Reduction

Program to less than $1 billion. As a result, the stockpiles in Russia and elsewhere deemed to pose the greatest threat to American security will continue to be underprotected.[21]

Dominance, Unilateralism, and Ad Hoc Coalitions

Another component of the Bush strategy is the belief that American and international security are best enhanced with America dominance in global political and military power. According to the logic of the Bush doctrine, dominance allows the United States the greatest latitude to assume global leadership responsibilities and to protect the world against emerging threats. Dominance also allows the United States to act unilaterally and preventively if necessary.

The Bush administration argues that the new threats of WMD in the hands of terrorist organizations change the nature of international threats and require new approaches. They believe that terrorist groups are motivated by radical ideologies and that traditional deterrence or preemptive attacks may not be effective because these groups operate in clandestine networks and can attack with little or no warning. In this sense, their very existence, coupled with their intent to acquire WMD, constitutes a serious threat.

The problem with most multilateral institutions is that preventive war runs counter to established international norms and laws. As a result, the prevailing view in the Bush administration is that relying on multilateralism, with its deference to international institutions—and to the United Nations in particular—is an outmoded approach to protecting or advancing American interests.[22] These institutions may occasionally provide some benefit to the United States, but ultimately American security may be better served via ad hoc coalitions whereby each participant is there because it has tangible interests and values at stake in a particular crisis.

The logic of ad hoc coalitions is not new. A centerpiece of the now infamous 1992 Defense Planning Guidance, drafted by then deputy secretary of defense Paul Wolfowitz, suggested the need for the United States to seek to maintain global primacy in it military capabilities and to focus on "ad hoc assemblies, often not lasting beyond the crisis being confronted, and in many cases carrying only general agreement over the objectives to be accomplished."[23] Even though the Wolfowitz draft of the Defense Planning Guidance was widely ridiculed at the time, during much of the 1990s the ideas of American primacy and ad hoc coalitions gained considerable currency among conservative and neoconservative foreign policy elites. They noted, for example, that American consultations with the Europeans on Bosnia led to three years of international vacillation amid violent civil war. However, when Congress unilaterally lifted the arms embargo on Bosnia and the Clinton administration exerted explicit diplomatic pressure on the Europeans to allow NATO both to issue stern warnings to the Bosnian Serbs and to launch a series of air strikes, the war ended abruptly. Firm American leadership backed by military power ended the seemingly intractable Bosnian conflict.

Another formative lesson for the conservatives and neoconservatives came from the American and NATO experience during the Kosovo air war in 1999. Aside from a brief series of air strikes in Bosnia in 1995, the Kosovo air war was the first time a large NATO force was sent into combat. Although American commanders developed extensive war plans prior to the air campaign, they found themselves constrained on a daily basis by a process requiring extensive authorizations from the political leadership, especially among its European members. NATO's top commander, General Wesley Clark, recalled that this created enormous logistical constraints on military operations and targeting: "For each set of targets there were supporters and doubters. Positions shifted from day to day, and there was no clear authority for resolving the issues."[24] In addition, each participating member had its own view on when and how its forces should be used during the operations. For example, some countries demanded their forces and fighter aircraft be integrated into the air campaign, while others such as the Italians requested that Italian planes not be used until the Italian parliament met and formally approved their participation.[25]

The experiences of Kosovo reinforced the view held by many senior Bush administration officials that American leadership in the face of the new global challenges is better served with fewer multilateral constraints. For them, the debate in the run-up to the war in Iraq was only the latest example of how the United Nations is nothing more than a debating society while NATO still suffers from the fact that "postmodern" French and German elites want to slow or keep American power in check.[26]

The Bush administration's concerns are not without some merit. Multilateralism frequently experiences the basic constraints associated with collective action problems. These institutions are assemblies of member states, each with their own rationally calculated interests. As a result, they are slow and deliberative bodies where consensus is difficult to obtain, and there is a tendency by others to wait and allow others to take action.

Nonetheless, unilateralism and ad hoc coalitions also generate a number of problems. First, the costs of war are more difficult to distribute. In the recent wars in Afghanistan and Iraq, the United States gained more latitude for its objectives, but it also bore the costs of the war—both financially and militarily. The first two years of the Iraq War cost Americans roughly $200 billion for the war and the occupation and likely will cost another $5 billion for every month the United States projects to maintain a force level above 120,000 through the end of 2006. By contrast, in the first Persian Gulf War in 1991, the United States assembled a coalition that included most members of NATO and had the explicit authorization of the UN Security Council. Because of such widespread support, $54 billion of the total cost of $61 billion for the war was offset by coalition partners.[27]

A second problem with ad hoc coalitions is that they are often more short lived than needed. Because they are assembled from disparate community of states often not sharing much beyond a desire to meet a particular, short-term objective, once the initial objective is achieved the coalition dissolves quickly. There is no bureaucratic or organizational apparatus to provide the necessary momentum to keep the coalition in check. Despite the highly destabilized security situation following the collapse of Hussein's regime and the calls by the Bush administration for additional support, nine countries withdrew their forces from Iraq in 2004 and early 2005; at the time of writing, another four had announced plans to withdraw their forces by the end of 2006.[28] In fact, the three largest contributors of troops behind the United States and Great Britain—Italy, Poland, and Spain—are among those having withdrawn or in the process of withdrawing their forces.[29]

Third, because of claims by the United States that it is prepared to act unilaterally if necessary, coalition diplomacy is more difficult. There was perhaps no greater diplomatic failure in the run-up to the war in Iraq than the failure of the Bush administration to enlist the support of Turkey. As part of U.S. central command commander-general Tommy Franks' war plan, the United States planned to deploy the U.S. Army Fourth Infantry Division to Turkey to launch a ground offensive from the north simultaneously with U.S. forces invading Iraq from Kuwait. However, in late February, the Turkish government decided not to allow American forces staging rights from its territory. As a result, the Fourth Infantry Division was dispatched to the Persian Gulf and deployed through Kuwait. Much of its equipment, however, was delayed because of its initial deployment to the eastern Mediterranean waiting to be offloaded in Turkey. This created longer logistical networks and supply delays and disruptions during the initial assault on Baghdad in March and April 2003. Moreover, because the Fourth Infantry was not deployed from the north no major U.S. military force was on the ground in northern Iraq to prevent members of the Iraqi military and Baathist Party from dissolving into civilian population, from which they were able to quickly reconstitute as an insurgency force.[30]

Furthermore, while the Bush administration has criticized existing multilateral institutions for their extensive bureaucracies and excessive deliberations, these bureaucracies and institutional processes provide an added element of scrutiny to both strategic objectives and means. One of the central criticisms of the American war in Iraq was the failure of the American military to anticipate the security vacuum, the looting, and the rise of the insurgency. In part, this was because the U.S. military planning process and the postwar planning were developed by U.S. military and civilian planners outside of wider scrutiny with limited checks and balances on planning assumptions. For example, military planners did not develop extensive contingency plans to prevent looting or to prevent the Iraqi army and police from simply dissolving. Nor was their sufficient coordination between military commanders and civilian reconstruction authorities on the priorities immediately following the collapse of Hussein's regime. This was most evident by the public and chaotic feud between the American military commanders and the head of the civilian reconstruction team led by former general Jay Garner, who was not allowed into Iraq for several days following the fall of Baghdad.

By contrast, much of the NATO military planning bureaucracy, for example, has redundant structures that most certainly would have placed additional checks on many of the ambiguous "planning assumptions" in the U.S. plan. European military officials repeatedly noted their concerns about the possibility of significant looting and a destabilized security situation immediately following the collapse of Hussein's rule.[31] Had NATO been involved in the war, many of these concerns would have been worked and reworked through its planning and decision-making processes.

In fact, American military commanders and conservative and neoconservative politicians have long argued that America's European allies in NATO are much stronger on the postwar reconstruction and nation-building phase. In the debates over humanitarian intervention throughout the 1990s American officials routinely argued that even though U.S. forces were better at delivering decisive military blows, Europeans were much better suited for the long-term policing and security aspects of nation-building strategies.

Perhaps most significant, however, was that neither American commanders nor troops on the ground were prepared to secure the suspected WMD sites in Iraq. The UN and NATO bureaucracies may be burdensome, but both had experienced personnel, offices, and protocols for identifying and securing suspected WMD sites that exceeded the capabilities of the U.S. military and its disparate coalition partners. The International Atomic Energy Agency (IAEA) and the United Nations weapons inspection structure, UNSCOM throughout the 1990s and UNMOVIC since 1999, had extensive on-the-ground knowledge of Iraqi sites and had conducted repeated inspections of several installations, including potential bioweapons research laboratory facilities, the Tuwaitha nuclear complex, and other suspected WMD sites.[32] Ultimately, American forces secured the oil fields and the oil ministry in Baghdad, but none of them were sites of primary interest to the IAEA—the ones reportedly looted in the days following Hussein's defeat. Although much of Hussein's WMD program sites were either abandoned or atrophied under the strain of a decade of sanctions, these sites still may have contained remnants of high-precision machinery and other technology that could be helpful to others intent on developing nuclear weapons or other WMD.[33]

Finally, the decision by the Bush administration to forego the compromises necessary to generate greater international participation for the war in Iraq created added burdens on American military personnel. The unstable security environment in Iraq meant additional U.S. troop commitments, more call-ups of National Guard and reserve units, and extended tours for both reserve and active duty. This placed greater strain on the troops, their families, and their communities, and it has contributed in part to difficulties experienced by the Marine Corps and the Army in reaching its recruiting goals for the all-volunteer military. This also has led to additional indirect costs of the war, as Congress and the administration move to increase survivor benefits, to add more recruiting and reenlistment incentives, and to lower enlistment standards, which likely will mean new requirements for additional training for new troops.

In sum, a broader coalition, though slower and more difficult to mobilize, almost certainly would have provided more critical checks and balances on U.S. war plans. Certainly a UN-sanctioned military action would have integrated provisions for prioritizing and securing key weapons and research installations and for establishing an initial security force to limit the widespread looting. Additional troop contributions from other states most certainly would have lessoned the burden on both American troops and taxpayers.

Another fundamental problem with unilateralism and ad hoc coalitions is that they are seen as an affront to appropriate international behavior. The Bush administration generated considerable international ill will and outright resentment against the United States during its first year in office by rejecting several multilateral agreements. Among other things, the Bush administration withdrew the U.S. signature from the International Criminal Court, withdrew from the Kyoto Protocols, rejected new protocols on the biological weapons treaty, and abrogated the 1972 Anti-Ballistic Missile (ABM) Treaty. In response to these unilateral actions, several key Europeans withheld their support from the United States in summer 2001, and the United States subsequently lost its seat for the first time on the UN Commission on Human Rights.

However, it was the rejection of NATO support in Afghanistan and the war in Iraq that triggered the most anger toward American power. A poll conducted by the Pew Research Center for the People and the Press in 2004 found a precipitous decline in favorable attitudes toward the United States between 2002 and 2004 in many parts of the world. In March 2004, for example, only 37 and 38 percent of Germans and French, respectively, had a favorable perception of the United States.[34] Anti-American sentiment has spread throughout the world, raising concerns within the U.S. intelligence community and the diplomatic corps.

For most of Bush's first term, however, the administration dismissed the anti-Americanism as a short-lived response to the war in Iraq and without any real tangible significance to the United States. More recently however, the rising anti-Americanism has generated more concern even among supporters of the Bush administration. John Lewis Gaddis, a supporter of the Bush Doctrine, cautioned that the ability to sustain its global leadership requires greater sensitivity to America's image abroad. He noted that "influence, to be sustained, requires not just power but also the absence of resistance and, or, to use Clausewitz's term, 'friction.'"[35] Neoconservative commentator Robert Kagan similarly warned that anti-Americanism is a source of friction and that American power is not sustainable without legitimacy of its actions. The United States may be a dominant power; others may not be able to challenge the United States in the short run, but they can dramatically increase the costs to the country by resisting American actions and leadership.

This was demonstrated most clearly in Europe prior to the war in Iraq. The widespread perception and criticism of the United States as bullying the world raised the domestic political benefits to leaders critical of the United States and increased the domestic political costs to leaders who have endorsed the United States. The most telling example of this was the German national elections in fall 2002. Just six weeks before the elections, the popular Bavarian governor Edmund Stoiber and the Christian Democrats held a double-digit lead over German Chancellor Gerhard Schröder's Social Democrats. With unemployment at 9 percent and rising, Schröder shifted gears and campaigned heavily on an antiwar platform and publicly criticized the Bush administration's aggressive language toward the United Nations. The strategy led to a dramatic comeback win for the Social Democrats and swept Schröder back into office. U.S. National Security Advisor Condoleezza Rice complained that Schröder's campaign tactics were "poisoning" American–German relations, but the results not only catapulted Schröder into a leadership role in the European antiwar movement but also reinforced and hardened Germany's opposition in the United Nations and in NATO in the run-up to the war.

For example, five months later in February 2003, Germany, along with France and Belgium, blocked a request by the United States to have NATO provide assistance to Turkey in the event of war in Iraq. The request called for the deployment of NATO AWACs planes, Patriot missile batteries, and chemical and biological weapons protective gear. France, Germany, and Belgium concluded that the request was an effort by the United States to pressure the three NATO members into endorsing the war, and each balked at the request. The Belgian government's threat to exercise its veto was also motivated in large part by overwhelming public opposition to the war in Belgium and by the fact that national elections were scheduled for March. In the end, the United States used a procedural maneuver to move the decision to the NATO defense planning committee—of which France is not a member—and ultimately Belgium and Germany both backed down under intense pressure by the United States and other NATO members that saw this issue as a crucial test of the alliance.

Yet just one week after the fiasco at NATO, Turkey's parliament voted to deny the United States permission to use Turkey's territory as a staging ground for the Fourth Infantry Division's advance into Iraq. The parliament's vote was heavily influenced by widespread public opposition in Turkey to war. In its decision not to allow American troops to use its territory, the country lost a multibillion-dollar aid package from the United States and risked losing Washington's support from its strongest backer for European Union membership. In the end, however, Turkish public opinion outweighed the pledged benefit package offered by the United States.

The resentment to American policy is both an outgrowth of the policies themselves and a perception of American arrogance. Since the events of September 11, the United States has asserted its positions, proclaiming that even though it hopes others will follow American leadership, it is prepared to act with or without them. The internal NATO crisis over defensive aid to Turkey generated unprecedented ill will and even led to shouting matches among professional diplomatic corps at NATO. Secretary of Defense Donald Rumsfeld critically chastised the entrenched thinking in "old Europe" and called the Belgian, French, and German positions a "disgrace."[36]

Throughout all of this, American diplomatic efforts to patch up the tension were almost nonexistent. Despite the perception of then secretary of state Colin Powell as the most respected member of the Bush administration both at home and abroad, his diplomatic energy and record was remarkably weak. Perhaps the most telling illustration of this weakness can be found in a comparison between Powell in the run-up to the war in Iraq and James Baker, secretary of state during the first Bush administration, prior to the first Persian Gulf War in 1990 and 1991. In August 1990, much to the consternation of Europe, President George Bush proclaimed that he was drawing a line in the sand and declared that the Iraqi invasion of Kuwait would not stand. This initial proclamation was widely criticized both at home and abroad for its bellicose and unilateralist tone. At the time, no one anticipated the United States would ultimately assemble a massive international coalition backed by a UN Security Council resolution, launching a full-scale war to expel Iraq from Kuwait. Yet beginning on the day of the Iraqi invasion, Baker began an intense and sustained diplomatic effort. Over the next five-and-a-half months, Baker traveled to Europe six times and to Russia and the Middle East four times.[37] In the end, when no one thought possible, Baker cobbled together a twenty-eight-member coalition to oust Hussein from power.

By contrast, despite the catastrophic attacks of September 11, the proclamation of the most ambitious grand strategy in history by the United States, and two subsequent American wars, Powell was the least traveled of any secretary of state in thirty years. In the six-month run-up to the war in Iraq, Powell did not once alter his foreign travel schedule. He did not travel at all to the Middle East and made only two brief trips to Europe: to Prague for the previously scheduled NATO enlargement summit in November 2002 and to Davos, Switzerland, for two days in January 2003 for the World Economic Forum. Despite the intense disagreements with "old Europe," Powell did not travel to

Brussels, Paris, Berlin, or Moscow. In fact, Baker traveled to more foreign cities in the two weeks prior to the Persian Gulf War than Powell did in the six months prior to the war in Iraq.[38]

This is not to say that the Bush grand strategy would have been more acceptable to others simply with more travel by Powell. But throughout the first term, the Bush administration largely discounted the need for, and subsequently simply did not develop, a comprehensive diplomatic strategy to gain international support for its actions. This explains in part why the administration simply ignored the offer by NATO when the alliance invoked Article V of its charter for the first time in history on September 12, 2001, and offered full military and logistical support and participation for any action in Afghanistan. Instead, as it prepared its own military plans for the war in Afghanistan, the Bush administration opted for an alliance with, and support of, Afghan warlords rather than NATO partners.

The Way Forward

The Bush Doctrine has sparked an intense debate over the future of American empire. Twenty years ago the term *empire* was used only by various Marxist and other critics of American foreign policy. Now, almost all leading journals contain references and debates over American empire, and Paul Kennedy's 1987 thesis on the rise and fall of great powers is again a point of discussion.[39] Kennedy concluded that a traditional pitfall of empires is the over commitment of military force. The Bush Doctrine has many of the markings of leading the United States into a similar fate. Yet there is one major difference between the United States and other empires of the past. The United States, as a democracy may have self-correcting mechanisms.[40] Iraq may have been the perfect storm—coming after a decade of noncompliance by Iraq, a decade in which Saddam Hussein had become commonly portrayed as America's leading enemy, and two years after the catastrophic attacks on September 11, 2001. Even before the Bush administration began its massive effort to sell the Iraq war to the public, most Americans assumed that Hussein had some complicity in the terrorist attacks.[41] As a result, Americans by and large accepted the administration's claims that Iraq posed a grave and growing threat and that it was or would likely aid Al-Qaeda in its efforts to attack the United States. They also accepted the administration's proclamations that American troops would be greeted as liberators. Nonetheless, by the end of 2005, the United States maintained a force of 150,000 troops in Iraq and has endured more than 2,000 American deaths and more than 15,000 wounded. The costs continue to escalate, and there are no clear signs of an early or easy exit. This has left American troops exhausted and has left limited conventional force structure available for similar action elsewhere. The overselling of the war at home and abroad, combined with the failure to find WMD in Iraq, also has generated a credibility gap both at home and with the rest of the world. Barring another catastrophic attack against the American homeland, it is unlikely we will see a president successfully mobilize the necessary domestic and international resources to fight another preventive war in the near future.[42]

Furthermore, there are signs that the Bush administration will continue to face rising anti-Americanism generated by the war in Iraq and by the continuation of aggressive defense of the right and need for American unilateralism. The administration early in its second term acknowledged the importance of curtailing the global rise in anti-Americanism. Bush made a high-profile trip to Europe in February 2005 and held a bilateral working dinner with French President Jacques Chirac; Secretary of State Rice made two trips to Europe in the first two months of her tenure. Furthermore, Bush appointed one of his closest confidantes, Karen Hughes, as the undersecretary of state for Public Diplomacy and Public Affairs, suggesting that the issue of public diplomacy will command much greater attention in Bush's second term.

Nonetheless, Bush and his closest advisors continue to stress the core elements of the Bush Doctrine. And Bush's nominations of John Bolton as U.S. ambassador to the United Nations and Paul Wolfowitz as president of the World Bank—two of the Bush Doctrine's key proponents—suggest he has not shifted from his profound belief in the necessity and efficacy of American primacy and unilateralism. These actions, coupled with the ongoing war in Iraq and instability there, suggest that the United States will not likely see a significant decrease of international friction to American power and influence anytime soon.

Notes

1. "The National Security Strategy of the United States of America," http://www.whitehouse.gov/nsc/nssall.html (hereafter referred to as "The National Security Strategy") p. 1; NSC-68, http://www.fas.org/irp/offdocs/nst-hst/nsc-68.htm.
2. George W. Bush, "President announces major combat operations in Iraq have ended," news release, May 1, 2003. See http://www.whitehouse.gov/news/releases/2003/05/iraq/20030501-15.html.
3. Sabrina Tavernise, "Data Shows Faster Rising Death Toll among Iraqi Civilians," *New York Times*, July 14, 2005, A1.
4. Walter Pincus, "CIA Studies Provide Glimpse of Insurgents in Iraq," *Washington Post*, February 6, 2005, A19.
5. Scott Atran, "Mishandling Suicide Terrorism," *Washington Quarterly* 27 no. 3, 74.
6. Ibid., 72; and Atran, "Trends in Global Terrorism" (paper presented at annual meeting of the World Federation of Scientists, Sicily, Italy, May 3, 2005).
7. Pew Research Center for the People and the Press, "A Year after Iraq War: Mistrust of America in Europe Ever Higher, Muslim Anger Persists," March 16, 2004, http://people-press.org/reports/display.php3?ReportID=206 (hereafter referred to as Pew Research Center, "A Year after Iraq").
8. See Mark Tessler, "Do Islamic Orientations Influence Attitudes toward Democracy in the Arab World: Evidence from Egypt, Jordan, Morocco, and Algeria?" *International Journal of Comparative Sociology* 2 (Spring 2002), 229–49; and Tessler and Dan Corstange, "How Should Americans Understand Arab and Muslim Political Attitudes: Combating Stereotypes with Public Opinion Data from the Middle East," *Journal of Social Affairs* 19 (Winter 2002), 379–393.
9. Atran, "Mishandling Suicide Terrorism," 72.

10. Edward Wong, "At Least 80 Killed in Raid on Insurgent Camp in Iraq," *New York Times*, March 23, 2005, A1.
11. See, for example, Thomas E. Ricks, "80% in Iraq Distrust Occupation Authority," *Washington Post*, May 13, 2004, A10.
12. Peter W. Galbraith, "How to Get Out of Iraq," *New York Review of Books* 51 no. 8, May 13, 2004, 42–46.
13. Pincus, "CIA Studies Provide Glimpse," A19.
14. The National Security Strategy of the United States of America at http://www.whitehouse.gov/ nsc/nssall.html, accessed March 15, 2005.
15. George Perkovich and others, *Universal Compliance: A Strategy for Nuclear Security* (Washington, DC: Carnegie Endowment for International Peace, March 2005), 19.
16. Jack Snyder, "Imperial Temptations," *National Interest* 71 (Spring 2003), 40.
17. See, for example, the logic presented on this by Scott D. Sagan, "Why Do States Build Nuclear Weapons? Three Models in Search of a Bomb," *International Security* 21 no. 3 (Winter 1996–1997), 54–86.
18. Nasser Hadian, "Iran's Nuclear Program: Contexts and Debates," in *Iran's Bomb: American and Iranian Perspectives*, ed. Geoffrey Kemp and others (Washington, DC: The Nixon Center, March 2004), 63.
19. William Langewiesche, "The Wrath of Khan," *Atlantic Monthly* 296, (Nov. 2005), 4, 62–85.
20. Perkovich and others, *Universal Compliance,* 26–7.
21. Lawrence J. Korb, "Bush Failing at Nuclear Security," *Boston Globe*, January 2, 2005, C11.
22. See John R. Bolton, "Should We Take Global Governance Seriously?" *Chicago Journal of International Law* 1 no. 2 (Fall 2000), 205–21.
23. Patrick E. Tyler, "U.S. Strategy Plan Calls for Ensuring No Rivals Develop," *New York Times*, March 8, 1992, A1.
24. Wesley K. Clark, *Waging Modern War* (New York: Public Affairs, 2001), 249.
25. Ibid., 209.
26. Robert Kagan, *Of Power and Paradise: America and Europe and the New World Order* (New York: Knopf, 2003).
27. Office of the Secretary of Defense, *Final Report to Congress, Conduct of the Persian Gulf War* (Washington, DC: Office of the Secretary of Defense, April 1992) app. P.
28. "Iraq Coalition Troops" at http://www.globalsecurity.org/military/ops/iraq_orbat_coalition.htm, accessed Dec 15, 2005.
29. Ian Fisher, "Italy Planning to Start Pullout of Troops," *New York Times*, March 16, 2005, A1.
30. Pincus, "CIA Studies Provide Glimpse," A19.
31. NAME (senior official in NATO Joint Threat Assessment), interview by author, June 23, 2003.
32. Galbraith, "How to Get Out of Iraq," 46.
33. James Glanz and William J. Broad, "Looting at Weapons Plants Was Systemic, Iraqi Says," *New York Times*, March 13, 2005, A1.
34. Pew Research Center, "A Year after Iraq," 1. See note 7.
35. John Lewis Gaddis, "Grand Strategy in the Second Term," *Foreign Affairs* 84 (January–February 2005), 13.
36. Thomas DeFrank and Kenneth Bazinet, "Bush Blasts Rift in NATO," *New York Daily News*, Feb. 11, 2003, 7.
37. "Travels: James A. Baker, III" at www.state.gov/r/pa/ho/trvl/ls/13042.htm, accessed Dec. 15, 2005.
38. "Travels: Secretary of State Powell," at www.state.gov/secretary/former/powell/travels/index.htm, accessed Dec. 15, 2005.
39. Paul Kennedy, *The Rise and Fall of Great Powers: Economic Change and Military Conflict from 1500 to 2000* (New York: Vintage Books, 1987).
40. See argument by Snyder, *Myths of Empire: Domestic Politics and International Ambition* (Ithaca, NY: Cornell University Press, 1993).
41. Jon Western, *Selling Intervention and War: The Presidency, the Media, and the American Public* (Baltimore: Johns Hopkins University Press, 2005), ch. 6.
42. David E. Sanger and Scott Shane, "Panel's Report Assails CIA for Failure on Iraq Weapons," *New York Times*, March 29, 2005, A1.

5
The Bush Doctrine and Multilateral Institutions

KAREN A. MINGST

The past serves as a reference point for the present, but it is never a precise prologue for the future.[1] No place is this more evident than in the elucidation of American foreign policy goals and selection of means. With respect to goals, each generation has articulated goals suitable to its time and place, ranging from splendid isolationism of the founding years to containment during the Cold War era. Generally, those goals prioritized security of territory and defense of state sovereignty. With respect to means, the United States has displayed a shifting mix between acting unilaterally and acting multilaterally in concert with friends and allies. As David Malone, an astute Canadian scholar, observes, "U.S. impulses have been paradoxical, even when not strictly contradictory: On the one hand, throughout the twentieth century the United States sought to shape (when not actually creating) multilateral architecture on a broad range of issues; on the other, it often either stayed out of the ensuring organizations or worked, intentionally or unwittingly, to undermine them."[2] In this chapter, I examine continuities and discontinuities of American security policy over time and suggest how 9/11 dramatically changed U.S. security goals, while the means continued to be "mixed messages."[3]

Cold War Era

During the Cold War, U.S. security goals were clearly enunciated in terms of realist strategies of containment, deterrence, and balance of power. A number of postwar security alliances, including the North Atlantic Treaty Organization (NATO), were established to achieve these goals. Based on U.S. military strength, the alliances assured that each member retained the ability to make unilateral decisions about whether or not to act, while positioning troops for a greater probability that allies would come to each other's collective defense should an attack occur from the adversary, the Soviet Union. NATO represented a bargain struck: Both German rearmament and U.S. military might were acceptable as long as they were institutionalized in a constrained multilateral framework.

Occasionally the United States used military force independent of either the United Nations (UN) or NATO, as in Cuba (1962), the Dominican Republic (1964), Vietnam (1954–1975), Grenada (1983), and Panama (1988). In virtually every case, the justification was enmeshed in the goal of containing communism.

The UN, designed as the centerpiece of international security, was relegated to relative obscurity during the Cold War, reinvented only with the development of peacekeeping. Since the UN Security Council could not act on vital Cold War issues because of the Permanent Five (P-5) veto, under the peacekeeping initiative conflicts peripheral to the Cold War could be managed by neutral middle powers without mobilization of American forces. Consent of all the warring parties was necessary, and use of UN forces was limited to largely defensive actions. Thus, the UN and other multilateral agreements did serve useful purposes for both the United States and the international community, defusing security issues surrounding decolonization, preventing lesser conflicts from becoming a Cold War issue, and facilitating the 1968 Nuclear Non-Proliferation Treaty in effort to stop the spread of nuclear weapons to new states.

On other security issues the multilateral fora were largely irrelevant as the United States and the Soviet Union negotiated arms control agreements like the Strategic Arms Limitation Treaty I (SALT I) and the Intermediate Range Nuclear Forces (INF) Treaty bilaterally. Through it all, U.S. security goals were remarkably consistent—to prevent the spread of communism in all of its manifestations—and the means to achieve them were multilateral, bilateral, and occasionally unilateral. Generally, NATO served as the centerpiece of American multilateral security strategy. When the United Nations was convenient, it worked through that institution; when it was inconvenient due to the Security Council veto or when NATO members disagreed with American policy, the United States either bypassed or ignored multilateral organizations. Yet as John Ruggie reminds us in this volume, the United States helped to create clusters of multilateralism during the Cold War while effectively exempting itself from many of its outcomes.

Post-Cold War Era

The demise of the Soviet Union as superpower and American adversary in the Security Council meant that for a short period of time there might be a new world order as enunciated by President George Bush and that collective security could work as envisioned by UN founders. The 1991 Gulf War represented that new order—Iraq's aggression against a small defenseless neighbor could be met with military force led by the United States and its many allies with the overwhelming support of the international community. The position of the United States was reaffirmed not only with the ouster of Iraq from Kuwait but also in its ability to get others in the U.S.–UN coalition to pay the financial costs.

In general, there was widespread acceptance of the UN's legitimacy—in this case derived from its authorization of the successful use of force.

The new world order, however, turned rapidly to a new world disorder as the new threats proved more complex. The disintegration of the Yugoslav state and the Soviet empire resulted in regional instability, ethnic warfare, civil strife, and, by extension in Africa, in failed states. Having no overarching foreign policy goal, the United States responded to each new situation on an ad hoc basis.

For the first few years, the United States turned to use of limited force to restore order, to prop up failed states, and to respond to emerging complex humanitarian emergencies. Much of this action early in the decade was exercised under multilateral auspices, including NATO (Kosovo) and UN subcontracting to ad hoc coalitions (Iraq) or to the UN (Somalia and Haiti). The United States used its military forces in combat zones to achieve multiple ad hoc objectives, making more multilateral commitments than it had in the previous forty-five-year period.

Yet acting multilaterally did not always go as anticipated. The Somalia debacle magnified the problems of unclear, often multiple, and conflicting goals and insufficient means. The chains of command between the UN and the United States were unclear, and force structures were inappropriate to the tasks. The Kosovo action illustrated conflicting goals and means, as the multilateral action authorized by NATO proved more like an American operation. The multilateral imbroglio of Bosnia involving both UN and NATO dragged on without clear resolution. And in each case, multilateral troops were sent on too grandiose missions, with little advanced planning and coordination and thrust into civic and political responsibilities for which they were not trained. Acting multilaterally did not lower the costs in terms of U.S. commitments, and the anticipated positive military and policy outcomes did not materialize.

The American reevaluation of the situation was, in part, delineated in Presidential Directive (PDD) 25. Under PDD 25, the United States identified six conditions for participation in peacekeeping, including the necessity of U.S. participation to ensure success, an acceptable command and control relationship, clear specification of an end point, domestic (i.e., Congressional) support, and force availability without adversely effecting overall American military readiness. The United States became much more reluctant to participate in multilateral operations. Multilateralism became increasingly more selective and improbable.

The deteriorating relationship between the United States and the UN on security issues spilled over to the UN–U.S. relationship more generally. Congress refused to pay U.S. dues and arrears as long as specific reforms were not implemented. The United States delayed implementation of the 1993 Chemical Weapons Convention negotiated by the UN Conference on Disarmament with congressional exemptions ultimately weakening the agreement. And in July

2001, the United States rejected enforcement mechanisms to strengthen the 1972 Biological and Toxins Weapons Convention. In other multilateral fora, the United States was viewed as obstructionist, participating in negotiations for the Kyoto Treaty and the International Criminal Court and then at the last minute refusing to follow through. Furthermore, the U.S. decisions to pursue missile defense and space weaponization, to overturn prior commitments, and to withdraw from the Arab–Israeli negotiations were each interpreted by most of the rest of the world as the United States going it alone. The U.S.–UN relationship was not just troubled or indifferent but in crisis and even hostile, and the United States was seen as reneging on its multilateral commitments.[4]

NATO, once the centerpiece of U.S. security policy, was in disarray, its mission now undefined with the demise and dismemberment of the Soviet Union. In searching for a new role, NATO members issued the "New Strategic Concept" paper in November 1991, which recognized that instabilities caused by ethnic conflict outside of its core area could threaten NATO member security. In 1992, NATO endorsed its participation in UN peacekeeping, even under UN Security Council authority. Thus, NATO participated in the Yugoslavian crisis, monitoring the maritime embargo and implementing a UN safe-area policy. This in turn led to NATO deployment in Kosovo, this time without explicit Security Council authority. NATO's action led to a heated discussion of whether regional organizations needed authorization by the Security Council to use force.[5] The debate precipitated a broader discussion of UN Security Council legitimacy. Was the Security Council a body with a "pull toward compliance?" Do members of the international community believe that the body "operates in accordance with generally accepted principles of right process?"[6] The questioning of UN legitimacy was reignited in the aftermath of 9/11.

9/11 and All That

9/11 is a turning point in U.S. security policy. Several trends, each with a long-term genesis, congeal or collide (depending on one's perspective) in the aftermath of 9/11. The trends include (1) globalization—an unprecedented thickening of economic, political, and cultural independence; (2) the resurgence of the discourse of American exceptionalism—the closely held belief that the United States is special because of its successful experiments with democracy and liberal capitalism, making it uniquely positioned to both defend and spread those values in the world; and (3) the realization of unprecedented U.S. military capacity—the one and only superpower, the hyperpower in a unipolar world. Just as the seeming invulnerability of American superiority is recognized, the United States is brutally attacked—not by a state enemy but by an amorphous network called Al-Qaeda.

America's immediate response to the catastrophic events was an odd mixture of unilateralist and multilateralist actions and rhetoric. That very day the president declared, "Every nation, in very region, now has a decision to make.

Either you are with us or you are with the terrorists." When UN Resolution 1368 reiterating the right of states to defend themselves was passed a day later, the United States was silent. On September 20, the president spoke to Congress about the U.S. response, never mentioning the UN. And later in fall 2001, the United States, seeking to control the war theater, was reluctant to let even Great Britain provide relief in Afghanistan.[7]

Yet another side was also emerging, one that encouraged UN participation as an institution and multilateral participation more generally in responding to the global terror threat. On September 24, 2001, the U.S. House of Representatives released funds in arrears to the UN, acknowledging that its debtor status may be a hindrance to achieving cooperation for the war on terrorism. And a couple of weeks later, Secretary of State Colin Power affirmed, "Nobody's calling us unilateral any more. That's kind of gone away for the time being; we're so multilateral it keeps me up 24 hours a day checking on everybody."[8] Fareed Zakaria pronounced a similar sentiment: "For America, this is the end of unilateralism. For the first time, we need them as much as they need us."[9]

The ambivalent U.S.–UN relationship illustrated here can also be seen in NATO. Immediately after 9/11, the North Atlantic Council stated that the attack against the United States was covered under Article 5 of the Washington Treaty; in short, it represented an attack against all NATO members, a statement affirmed several weeks later. But the United States did not seek active involvement by NATO, preferring to act unilaterally in Afghanistan.

Selective or ambivalent multilateralism at this point is completely consistent with the post–World War II historical record: the United States choosing whether to be multilateral or unilateral or, as others have labeled it, multilateralism a la carte. What gradually changes in the aftermath of 9/11 are new goals and the decision to achieve those goals using unilateral military force if necessary.

From Afghanistan to Iraq: The Dance with the UN and NATO

UN Security Council Resolution 1368, passed within twenty-four hours of September 11, gave the United States multilateral authorization to defend itself. Although clearly the United States did not need that resolution—states have enjoyed that right since the Westphalian compromise—the resolution reaffirmed intangible multilateral support. One month later, following the placement of special operations officers on the country, the United States struck targets in Afghanistan to oust the Taliban from power; by mid-November, the Taliban was so ousted. The United States maintained very tight unilateral control over the operation. But in early 2003, the Bush administration made a midcourse correction in its policy "On Accelerating the Program in Afghanistan." That policy engaged participation by both coalition members and international institutions and worked with the Afghans to improve governance.[10]

In actuality, that policy only affirmed what already had been taking place on the ground.

Having a history of humanitarian work in Afghanistan, the UN became involved. Both Lakhdar Brahimi, UN special envoy for Afghanistan, and Kofi Annan, the secretary-general played key roles in supporting UN humanitarian efforts and in mobilizing the international financial community (e.g., United Nations Development Program [UNDP], World Bank, Asian Development Bank) for reconstruction efforts in a December 2001 meeting. In the same month, under UN auspices, Afghan political leaders met in Bonn to establish a provisional governmental arrangement, the Afghan Interim Authority. UN Security Council Resolution 1386 authorized an International Security Assistance Force (ISAF) under the mandate of Chapter VII to help the authority maintain security, with troops deployed under British control. With these new arrangements, the World Food Program could deliver food and the UN High Commissioner for Refugees (UNHCR) could service refugees. In 2002, the UN Assistance Mission in Afghanistan was established and was designed to coordinate the sixteen UN organizations, of which its most notable project was organizing the Loya Jirga process in June 2002. In the present day, the mission is deeply involved in helping to organize the elections to the Afghan parliament.

In August 2003, NATO took over IASF, and two months later its role was expanded to securing territory beyond Kabul, as authorized under UN Security Council Resolution 1510. In summer 2005, approximately 8,300 troops were in Afghanistan from thirty-six NATO and partner countries and two from nonpartner countries to assist the Afghan government in maintaining security, and another 3,000 were scheduled for deployment. They were engaged in diverse activities: both training and building future Afghan security forces; participating in the provincial reconstruction teams composed of both civilian and military personnel in nine northern provinces; conducting joint patrols in Kabul with the Kabul City Police and controlling Kabul International Airport; supporting the removal of heavy weapons to cantonment sites; and providing security for the presidential and parliamentary elections.[11]

The country still is 173rd out of 178 on the 2004 Human Development Index. It is not secure; corruption is rampant; a resurgence of the drug trade has occurred; and demobilization of the society remains incomplete. And ISAF has no mandate either to take on the drug trade or to intervene in factional fighting among militias.[12] Currently, infrastructure reconstruction has hardly begun, although some improvements have been noted in terms of economic growth (10 to 12 percent) and an increasing number of children in school (54 percent).[13] Currently, the United States has around 20,000 troops in the country. With multilateral involvement and better military integration, the United States hopes to decrease the number of troops deployed, yet that is not on the immediate horizon.

The Afghanistan story is one where multilateral agreement occurred on the goal of the operation—to overthrow the Taliban. The UN was involved from the outset, both providing multilateral approval and conducting operational activities. NATO was brought in and has continuously expanded its presence, including taking over security of the western region from the United States. Willing participation by NATO member countries gives that action multilateral legitimacy, even though ultimate effectiveness of the entire endeavor is not assured.

Compare that story with the story of Iraq, when the Bush administration chose to step out onto the dance floor alone. Since that story is better known, I only point to highlights. A unilateral approach and defiant tone dominated the discourse. Administration statements such as "Either you are with us or you are with the terrorists" became the tone of U.S. foreign policy. Any hint of criticizing American policy or any expression of concern about the direction of U.S. foreign policy was treated as hostility. The voices of European dissent were largely ignored.

Initially, the United States did make some effort to get Security Council approval, or, more accurately, the United States tried to demand council agreement and used the failure to get Security Council authorization to justify its own unilateral action. A cartoon published at the time said it all, with a picture of a tank emblazoned with "Iraq or Bust, My Way" and the U.S. president sitting in the tank ramming down the walls of the UN. The caption read, "The important thing is he went through the UN."[14] And when Congress authorized the president to use U.S. armed forced against Iraq on October 2, 2002, the unilateral trajectory was clear. In March 2003, the United States acknowledged its failure to get approval from the P-5 and stopped trying to fashion an amendment. On March 19, 2003, the decapitation attack was launched; on April 9, the fall of the Iraqi regime was announced.

Acting alone in war, now in the aftermath of the fall of the Iraqi regime, the United States returned to the UN to try to get others to support American actions, including occupation and postwar reconstruction. That change can be interpreted in different ways. One cartoon pictured Bush at the UN saying, "I need your help cleaning up the big success I've made."[15] Zakaria suggested, "With both its authority and its transition plans in jeopardy, the administration has decided the United Nations has some legitimacy after all."[16] One Bush administration official demurred, putting the onus on the UN: "This is as much a choice for the Council as it is for us. They can be multilateral and be part of it, or they can tell us to do it ourselves."[17]

On one level, the United States was successful. An October 2003 Security Council resolution formally authorized an American-led multinational force in Iraq and set up a timetable for return of the government to Iraqi hands. Although that act did end U.S. diplomatic isolation and gave the United States a UN-backed mandate, it was not an American victory. No new states promised military support, and significant concessions had been made to win support. This stands in sharp contrast to the 1991 Gulf War, when both Germany and Japan paid an overwhelming share of the financial costs and when the military units, large contingents from members of the diverse coalition, played a key military role.

On another level, the United States was less successful in convincing the international community to authorize and, hence, to legitimize U.S. unilateral actions. The UN and NATO's response to inconsistent U.S. behavior can only be described as ambivalent. In August 2003, the bombing of UN offices in Baghdad sent the UN out of the country. In October 2003, the United States conceded and agreed to a new agency, independent of American occupation and run by the World Bank and the UN, to have authority to operate the aid program for postwar Iraq. But with chaos in the country, reconstruction efforts lagged, and multilateral contributions only trickled in. In June 2004, the Security Council approved the U.S.–British timetable for the interim regime, elections, and adoption of the constitution.

The United States began to quietly push for a greater UN role, because they recognized that was the only way to ensure greater international participation in the process. At first the UN balked, fearing to participate in a process having only a democratic facade. But, again, Brahimi, special advisor to the secretary general, became a central element in U.S.–Iraq policy. He played a key role in consulting and engaging the informal power structures in Iraqi society.[18] The Electoral Assistance Division of the UN Department of Peacekeeping Affairs, under Carina Perelli, helped to establish the Iraqi Independent Electoral Commission to conduct the January 2005 elections. Despite the UN's role, NATO members continued reticent to play any major role, agreeing only to provide training to Iraqi security forces outside of the country and contributing only nominal funding.

What Changed: Goals and Means?

To explain the reluctance of the UN and international community to support U.S. action in Iraq, we must examine the subtle change in goals between Afghanistan and Iraq and even over the course of the Iraqi involvement itself. The war in Afghanistan was justified as the response of an attacked country against a perpetrator. Virtually all lamented the ghastliness of 9/11, and all acknowledged Al-Qaeda's responsibility, facilitated by Taliban-controlled Afghanistan. The classic self-defense argument resonated. With Iraq, the goal changed over time. Never convinced that Saddam Hussein had a direct link to 9/11, never assured that the regime had weapons of mass destruction that could fall into the hands of Al-Qaeda, never given proof that UN sanctions against Iraq and dismantling of weapons had really failed, most of the international community preferred not to pursue the military alternative.

Gradually, however, U.S. goals become clearer, as articulated in documents and speeches beginning in Bush's West Point address and in the National Security Strategy in September 2002. In the latter document, the United States announced its intention to "defend this just peace against threats from terrorists and tyrants," acting "against such emerging threats before are fully formed." Furthermore, the United States sought to take advantage of this opportunity "to bring the hope of democracy, development, free markets, and free trade to every corner of the world." The struggle may occur over a long time and the United States "will not hesitate to act alone, if necessary, to exercise our right of self-defense by acting preemptively ... Our forces will be strong enough to dissuade potential adversaries from pursuing a military build-up in hopes of surpassing, or equaling, the power of the United States."[19]

Similar language was repeated in Bush's September 2003 speech before the UN and in Bush's February 2004 State of the Union address when he stated, "We're all part of a great venture: To extend the promise of freedom in our country, to renew the values that sustain our liberty and to spread the peace that freedom brings."[20] The strategy is proactive and includes use of the military even without international support. As Jon Western concludes in this volume, "The Bush Doctrine ... is the first time we have had a grand strategy that combines an ambitious vision to transform the world with unrivaled political and military power." Lacking a vision in the decade after the demise of communism, after 9/11 the vision becomes increasingly clear, framed in terms of the moral imperative, the "responsibility" and "obligation" to conduct a "great struggle."[21] And who is the struggle against? David Frum and Richard Perle articulate the Bush administration's neoconservative view of the enemy in this way: "A radical strain of Islam has declared war on us ... All the available evidence suggests that militant Islam commands wide support, and even wider sympathy, among Muslims worldwide, including Muslim minorities in the West ... In militant Islam, we face an aggressive ideology of world domination."[22]

To fight the enemy, American military, economic, and ideological forces will be unleashed. While others have variously labeled the vision as *empire, neoimperial, imperial, hegemonic, empire lite,* or a *global liberal experiment,* I eschew a label and instead identify the goal by its core characteristics.

First, the enemy is anyone who targets the United States: a broad coalition of "religious extremists and security militants; Sunnis and Shiites; communists and fascists—in the Middle East these categories blend into one another. All gush from the same enormous reservoir of combustible rage. And all have the same target: the United States."[23] Using that definition, the number of potential enemies is huge; when all tyrants are included, likely enemies are found everywhere.

Second, whereas defeating the enemy on the battlefield may be necessary, the ultimate vision is the idealistic one, transforming the world into democracies, with attendant liberties and support of free markets. This pursuit of freedom and democracy worldwide, first espoused by Woodrow Wilson, is unequivocal. Democracies make better partners than other forms of government. They are drawn to the political center by their representative institutions; over time, they will prosper economically. Thus, as Walter Russell Mead concludes, "Wilsonian beliefs lead to the principle that the support of democracy abroad is not only a moral duty for the United States but a practical imperative as well."[24] Historically that has meant periodic interventions for humanitarian purposes. But in the post-9/11 revision, the Wilsonian vision becomes grander: intervention not only against terrorists, the perpetrators of 9/11, or would-be terrorists but also more generally against tyrants. So the vision of democracy is expanded from eliminating terrorists to transforming tyrants into democrats. Even though in Bush administration speeches the two are often used interchangeably, the latter is clearly a much broader goal, potentially threatening and targeting many states.

Third, the new goal is framed in terms of ensuring absolute security for the United States, not only for territorial security of the past but also for security to pursue America's democratic and liberal economic mission; no longer is relative security sufficient. This goal justifies the United States acting preemptively—when there is imminent danger, the traditional stand for preemption—as well as acting preventively, which suggests the United States will act against threats before they are firmly formed and act against threats before they arrive. In addition, the United States will prevent adversaries from equaling or surpassing the United States in military terms. In short, the United States seeks absolute security, acting preventively.

Fourth, to achieve these goals the United States requires an extensive period of high domestic mobilization. Though not as clearly articulated in the documents, the notion of a long struggle ahead is evident. The creation of a cabinet of Homeland Security (reminiscent of the discourse of totalitarian regimes), the mobilization of state and local jurisdictions as first responders, the expanding cooperation between the Federal Bureau of Investigation and the Central Intelligence Agency, the centralization of intelligence under a director of central intelligence, the massive growth in the military and intelligence budget, the strategy of utilizing emergency supplementary appropriations, and the national planning scenarios against universal adversaries all point to the domestic mobilization strategy. Periodic assessments of the threat level, often curiously timed with domestic political events, serve to further mobilize the domestic population. Not just a case of heightened rhetoric, U.S. security goals are changing, which has led to serious dilemmas.

The Dilemma of Goals

Four dilemmas emerge from the goals. First, although America has often framed its aspirations in grandiose terms ("making the world safe for democracy"), those aspirations were seldom translated into policy. What is different is that those goals—transforming ubiquitous enemies into democrats—are becoming policy, requiring an American omnipotence in both military and economic power. The United States may have the former; however, even if some military force may be impotent and unusable, it clearly does not have the latter.[25]

Second is the problem of how to achieve those goals. In addition to the Wilsonian vision of preferring to act in a democratic world was also the principle that war should be prevented at all costs. Wilsonians support various mechanisms to relieve the horrors of war through international humanitarian law, to the peace congress movement, to collective security through multilateral institutions. But can the Wilsonian vision be implanted through military force? Germany and Japan, though positive examples, represented societies whose populations already were educated, who had made the transition to economic development, and who, as completely defeated adversaries, were occupied by foreign military forces for long periods of time. In other places, there was success in reconstruction (e.g., Austria, South Korea, Kuwait), but in still others, reconstruction was a failure (e.g., Haiti, Nicaragua, Somalia, Vietnam). However, the verdict is still out on the efficacy of implanting democracy through force. Today in Bosnia the Office of the High Representative, presumed precursor to an emergent democracy, is often referred to as a British *raj,* and in Kosovo the same conclusion is reached: "In the last five years, we have seen not a single act that shows Kosovo what is democracy, what is rule of law, what is justice."[26]

After all, democratization represents a long process—it is not instantly achieved. It requires long processes of political socialization beginning in the schools; it involves development of a public sphere, a civil society based on voluntary groups, acceptance of minority rights, and the prerogative of majority rule. Elections are a first step, as shown in Iraq. But Zakaria offers a cautionary caveat: Democracy works "not only by free and fair elections but also by the rule of law, a separation of powers, and the protection of basic liberties of speech, assembly, religion, and property."[27] And Edward Rhodes goes one step further: "Governance based on consent rather than on force, amity between peoples, and the rule of reason and law cannot be meaningfully imposed or long sustained at gunpoint."[28]

Third is the dilemma of differential perceptions. Whereas the United States has elucidated these goals in the lofty language of democracy, has sold them to the American people in idealistic terms, and has compared them favorably with UN aspirations in hopes of enhancing their attractiveness, the perception held by others is often quite different. For others, U.S. actions may speak louder and with more potency than words. In an April 2004 speech Bush exclaimed, "We're not an imperial power as nations such as Japan and Germany can attest. We're a liberating power, as nations in Europe and Asia can attest as well."²⁹ Yet those words have to compete with remembrances of a different history, whether in Southeast Asia or in Latin America; they also have to compete with photographic images of the American GI guarding the oil derrick as Iraq national treasures are looted; or standing over dead Iraqi women and children; or running a U.S. flag up a pole; or images of prisoner abuse at Abu Ghraib. To still others, the lofty language of American goals does not represent an uncontested universal good but is rather a reflection of American national interest. The discourse of the European or Latin American political left still resonates in the Middle East, Africa, and Southeast Asia: Are these actions really to foster democracy? Or are the ultimate goals to guarantee a steady supply of oil? Or are they to ensure an international liberal economic order organized to strengthen U.S. economic power and prevent the rise of economic or political competitors?

Fourth is the problem of domestic mobilization. If achieving these goals requires sustaining a high level of domestic mobilization, then this could serve as a limiting factor. Will the U.S. public agree to stay engaged in emerging democracies over the long haul? Will they pay the costs in dollars and in manpower? Domestic political support is still salient in shaping American policy, and Ole Holsti's evidence presented in this volume suggests that domestic support is strongest when the United States has allies and international organizations behind it. The U.S. public is committed to an active international role, but responsibility must be shared. Using the military abroad is conditioned on this external support both to share the economic burden and to ensure legitimacy for the task. Executive leadership in promoting domestic mobilization is essential at the outset, yet the war footing or mobilization can only be continued by the willingness of Congress to finance mobilization over domestic priorities. And it can be sustained only by the acquiescence of a public who faces the burden. Absent another direct attack on U.S. territory, mobilization fever is apt to decline, becoming the limiting factor in achievement of the goals.

The Dilemmas of Means

Even though selective multilateralism has been the story of the past and will likely be the reality of the future, the United States dares to undermine its commitment to foundational multilateralism at its own peril. John Ikenberry's provocative argument is that the general American commitment to foundational multilateralism is solid and signals to others U.S. protection of its allies and U.S. constraint on its own actions. But if the United States chooses the unilateral path too often, its own legitimacy and the legitimacy of foundational multilateralism may be jeopardized.³⁰ After all, warns Ruggie in this volume, doctrinal unilateralism is hard to sustain.

The dilemma comes in the recognition that to preserve the viability of selective multilateralism in the eyes of other states and multilateral institutions, occasionally the United States must make itself specifically bound by the actions of others; only by it being bound will others acknowledge similar constraints. The unbroken record of doctrinal unilateralism during the late 1990s and early years of the new century has led others to question the foundational commitment to multilateralism. With unparalleled power by the United States comes the belief that it can go it alone, which is reinforced by American exceptionalist beliefs. This thought process is not just dangerous but actually tempts others to target number one in the short term. In the long term, it can undermine both the established order and the U.S. privileged role, in that order. Bruce Cronin explains the roots of the dilemma of means: "When a hegemon fails to act within the boundaries established by its role, the credibility of the institutions and rules it helped to establish weakens ... When these organizations are undermined, the legitimacy of the international order itself is threatened. If this persists over time, the hegemonic order declines."[31]

Multilateralism is often synonymous with acting through the United Nations; that pairing creates a second dilemma of means. The United Nations is one of the centerpieces of global governance and as such enjoys some comparative advantages in nation building. A Rand Corporation study compared UN and U.S. nation-building experiences on a number of dimensions. The UN advantages come in fielding smaller contingents both absolutely and relative to the size of the population. The organization remains in postconflict theaters a shorter period of time than U.S. forces and employs civilian police with greater effectiveness. In seven out of eight UN cases, peace was achieved, while only half of the U.S.-led cases were successful. The UN was advantaged by operating under highly negotiated, less grandiose mandates, utilizing a cadre of highly experienced international civil servants. As James Dobbins explained the findings, "The United Nations has an ability to compensate, to some degree at least, for its 'hard' power deficit with 'soft' power attributes of international legitimacy and local impartiality."[32]

As a result of these comparative advantages, the UN continues to engage in more complex peacekeeping emergencies even after the Iraq–UN fiasco and tensions in the Security Council. Expanded operations in Congo, Haiti, Liberia, and Côte d'Ivoire have mobilized 60,000 troops. They have benefited from the recommendations of the Brahimi Report by experiencing expedited deployment, creation of strategic stocks, and use of rapid deployment means.[33] Even the extensive UN response to the tsunami disaster in December 2004 illustrates unique multilateral comparative advantages. And a variety of other tasks pertinent to provision of security—intelligence sharing, anti-money laundering, infectious disease control, monitoring human rights, and humanitarian interventions—show the comparative advantage of multilateralism over unilateralism.

From another perspective, however, both the UN's capacity and hence its legitimacy are under intense scrutiny, the other side of the multilateral dilemma. With respect to capacity, the new UN emergencies represent highly complex operations with broad mandates similar to the 1990s. With western militaries playing virtually no role, there is clearly a lack of resources and capabilities. The December 2004 UN High Level Panel on Threats, Challenges, and Change points to these limitations and suggesting reforms on which have yet to be enacted.

With respect to legitimacy, both the inability of the UN members to agree on reform of the Security Council and the two major scandals weaken the institution. For all countries other than the P-5, the lack of Security Council reform to meet new economic and regional power realities delegitimizes the UN. As Edward C. Luck bluntly expressed, "For the UN, it's either reform or irrelevance."[34]

In addition, for all members of the international community, the Oil for Food scandal and the shocking abuses by UN peacekeepers in Central Africa undermine institutional authority and legitimacy at a critical time. Although persistent smuggling during the UN-mandated sanctions against Iraq was the responsibility of members of the Security Council who had operational capabilities to patrol the landscape, the corruption within the Oil for Food office and the inept oversight by the Department of Peacekeeping and by commanders on the ground over states sending troops to Central Africa leave a black mark on the UN as well as on unaccountable multilateral organizations in general. The danger is that these scandals may further undermine the basis of its legitimacy, irreparably undermining the institution. If that happens, the Bush administration's reluctance to pursue the multilateral alternative will be justified.

NATO represents another multilateral alternative for the United States and its allies. NATO stepped up to the task in Afghanistan, engaging in an unprecedented out of area operation, yet its outright refusal to supply combat troops in Iraq, giving only lackluster support for training, should serve as a warning to the United States. A newly empowered NATO, absent the direct threat of the Soviet Union and with many members emboldened by participation in a deepening and widening European Union (EU), will likely have increasingly divergent interests from the United States. Indeed, the major post-9/11 issues such as Iran or China are not even being discussed in NATO, leading Germany to propose a new transatlantic forum. And the new proposed European Constitution aggrandizes EU power at the expense of NATO, a fact the United States finds unacceptable.[35] Even though multiple fora do exist (e.g., the Association of South East Asian Nations [ASEAN], the African Union, the Organization of American States), in very few others is the United States able to exercise its hegemony. And the larger question remains as to how to adequately empower these regional bodies.

Means matter in a different way as well. Whether finally selecting unilateral or multilateral means, manners and language matter; after all, legitimacy emerges out of the ability to persuade. John Lewis Gaddis expressed it succinctly. As for manners, "It is always a bad idea to confuse power with wisdom: muscles are not brains. It is never a good idea to insult potential allies, however outrageous their behavior may have been. Nor is it wise to regard consultation as the endorsement of a course already set." As for language, Gaddis continues, "the president and his advisers preferred flaunting U.S. power to explaining its purpose. To boast that one possesses and plans to maintain 'strengths beyond challenge' may well be accurate, but it mixes arrogance with vagueness, an unsettling combination."[36] Not following manners and choosing acceptable and sensitive language carefully limits a state's options in the long run. The failure of the United States to persuade the rest of the world about the rightness of the Bush Doctrine and its application in Iraq has eroded any legitimacy the United States has left.

A Difficult Time Ahead

In sum, the choice of means to implement foreign policy goals is critical. In the past, the United States has always exercised selective multilateralism. Yet the rearticulation of goals post-9/11, coupled with readiness to use force unilaterally, comes at a potentially high cost. If doctrinal unilateralism is exercised too often in pursuit of those goals, then the post-WWII international system based on foundational multilateralism will be jeopardized, if not obliterated. Acting multilaterally through the UN has some advantages on specific security issues, as acting multilaterally through NATO in the past has had major advantages for the United States. Yet each institution is facing its own crises that may undermine its capacity to act and jeopardize its own legitimacy. The UN Security Council representation crisis and the troubling scandals and NATO's inability to discuss the major issues of the day and decreased power vis-à-vis the European Union power suggest difficult times ahead for those multilateral alternatives.

However, not to pursue the multilateral alternative is even more dangerous. American public support may wane, undermining the policy. Multilateralism can conceivably constrain and reshape the policy goals of the hegemonic United States. Multilateralism enmeshes that state in a series of commitments that are proving costly to break. Multilateral institutions, by slowing down the policy process, may prevent rash moves by states reacting under pressure. And multilateralism possibly can force a reexamination of goals. A new articulation of goals would suggest that threats to democracy and liberalism will come not just from terrorists and tyrants but also from states acting unilaterally and from weak and dispossessed peoples and states. The latter voices can be heard in multilateral institutions. Only through multilateral commitments will these human development disparities be resolved. So although traditionally the United States has pursued goals and has chosen either unilateral or multilateral means to achieve those goals, in this new era multilateral involvement may pressure the United States to redefine those goals in ways more acceptable to the international community.

Notes

1. My thinking on this subject was stimulated by Jeffrey Freyman, "Another Look at Pax Americana," speech, UN Association of the Bluegrass, Lexington, KY, February 5, 2005.
2. David A. Malone, "A Decade of U.S. Unilateralism?" in *U.S. Foreign Policy. International Perspectives*, ed. Malone and Khong (Boulder, CO: Lynne Rienner, 2003), 24.
3. Edward C. Luck, *Mixed Messages: American Politics and International Organization, 1919–1999* (Washington, DC: Brookings Institution Press, 1999).
4. Karen Mingst, "Troubled Waters: The United States–United Nations Relationship," *International Peacekeeping* 10 no. 4 (Winter 2003), 89–93.
5. See Dick A. Leurdijk, "The UN and NATO: The Logic of Primacy," in *The United Nations and Regional Security. Europe and Beyond*, ed. Michael Pugh and Waheguru Pal Singh Sidhu (Boulder, CO: Lynne Rienner Publishers, 2003), 57–74.
6. Definition of *legitimacy* taken from Thomas Franck, *The Power of Legitimacy among Nations* (New York: Oxford University Press, 1990), 24.
7. Mingst, 90–1.
8. Quoted in Patrick E. Tuter, "Russia and U.S. Optimistic on Defense Issues," *New York Times*, October 19, 2001, A1, B4.
9. Fareed Zakaria, "The End of the End of History," *Newsweek*, September 24, 2001, 70. Also available at http://www.fareedzakaria.com/articles/newsweek/092401.html.
10. S. Frederick Starr, "Silk Road to Success," *National Interest*, 78 (Winter 2004–05), 65–72.
11. See http://www.nato.int/issues/afghanistan.
12. Pankaj Mishra, "The Real Afghanistan," *New York Review of Books* 52 no. 4 (March 10, 2005), 44–48. Also available at http://www.nybooks.com/articles/17787.
13. Carlotta Gall, "Afghan Living Standards among the Lowest, UN Finds," *New York Times*, February 22, 2005, A3.
14. Cartoon drawn by Steve Sack, published in the *Star Tribune*.
15. Cartoon drawn by Mike Luckovich, published in the *Atlanta Journal-Constitution*.
16. Fareed Zakaria, "Bowing to the Mighty Ayatollah," *Newsweek*, January 26, 2004, 38.
17. Steven R. Weisman and Felicity Barringer, "U.S. May Drop Attempt at Vote on Iraq in UN," *New York Times*, October 8, 2003, A1.
18. Mats Berdal, "The UN after Iraq," *Survival* 46 no. 3 (Autumn 2004), 88.
19. "The National Security Strategy of the United States of America" (issued September 21, 2002), http://www.whitehouse.gov/nsc/nss.pdf.
20. President George W. Bush, "State of the Union Address," February 3, 2005. Available at http://www.whitehouse.gov/news/releases/2005/02/20050201-11.html.
21. Edward Rhodes, "The Imperial Logic of Bush's Liberal Agenda," *Survival* 45 no. 1 (Spring 2003), 139.
22. David Frum and Richard Perle, *An End to Evil: How to Win the War on Terror* (New York: Ballantine Books, 2004), 251.
23. Ibid., 50.
24. Walter Russell Mead, *Special Providence: American Foreign Policy and How It Changed the World* (New York: Routledge, 2002), 164.
25. Rhodes, "Imperial Logic," 141.
26. James Traub, "Making Sense of the Mission," *New York Times*, April 11, 2004, 32–42.
27. Fareed Zakaria, *The Future of Freedom: Illiberal Democracy at Home and Abroad* (New York: W.W. Norton and Co., 2003), 17.
28. Rhodes, " Imperial Logic," 142.
29. President George W. Bush, *President Bush's Press Conference at the White House, April 13, 2004*. Available at http://www.whitehouse.gov/news/releases/2004/04/20040413-20.html.
30. G. John Ikenberry, "Is American Multilateralism in Decline?" *Perspectives on Politics* 1 no. 3 (September 2003), 538–9.
31. Bruce Cronin, "The Paradox of Hegemony: America's Ambiguous Relationship with the United Nations," *European Journal of International Relations* 7 no. 1 (2001), 113.
32. James Dobbins, "The UN's Role in Nation-Building: From the Belgian Congo to Iraq," *Survival* 46 no. 4 (Winter 2004–05), 97.
33. Berdal, "The UN after Iraq," 89.

34. Luck, "Making the World Safe for Hypocrisy," *New York Times*, March 22, 2003, A11.
35. Jeffrey L. Cimbalo, "Saving NATO from Europe," *Foreign Affairs* 83 no. 6 (November–December 2004) 111–20.
36. John Lewis Gaddis, "Grand Strategy in the Second Term," *Foreign Affairs* 84 no. 1 (January–February 2005), 7.

6

American Public Opinion and Foreign Policy: Did the September 11 Attacks Change Everything?

OLE R. HOLSTI

The proper role of public opinion in the conduct of foreign affairs has been a source of controversy since the late eighteenth century, when the advent of democracies transformed the issue from a theoretical discussion among philosophers to a practical one that confronted, among others, the framers of the United States Constitution. Realists, including many of America's founding fathers, have typically agreed with Hans Morgenthau's dictum that policymakers would be unwise to count on the public for enlightened guidance.[1] French observer Alexis de Tocqueville, diplomat-historians E. H. Carr and George F. Kennan, and journalist Walter Lippmann were among other notable skeptics.[2] What is more, overwhelming evidence indicates that most members of the public have neither the time nor the inclination to satisfy the heroic demands of the well-informed and interested citizen who resides at the core of classical democratic theory.[3]

Nevertheless, extensive research in recent years has also provided quite compelling evidence that public opinion is neither as volatile nor as unstructured—called "non-attitudes" by Philip Converse, one of the pioneers of opinion research—as critics would have it and that, at least in some circumstances, public opinion can have a significant impact on policymaking. Although almost all presidents and other foreign policy officials routinely assert that their policy decisions are guided by what is best for the country rather than by polls or focus groups, at least since the Franklin Roosevelt era not only have virtually all administrations been consumers of poll data, but many have also conducted their own surveys.[4]

This chapter undertakes an examination of American public opinion on foreign policies issues during the years immediately preceding and following the September 11, 2001, terrorist attacks on New York City and Washington, D.C. Although the growing economic power of China, the expansion of the North Atlantic Treaty Organization (NATO) and the European Union (EU), continuing and unresolved Israeli–Palestinian and India–Pakistan conflicts, nuclear proliferation, unprecedented trade deficits, and compelling evidence of global warming are high on the agenda of important international developments, for many Americans the 9/11 attacks and the wars against Afghanistan and Iraq have been the dominant issues; thus, they take center stage here.

Two broad questions guide the analysis that follows. First, how has the American public reacted to the turbulent events of the past several years? Have they followed such visible critics as former presidential adviser, syndicated columnist, and presidential candidate Patrick Buchanan in linking the 9/11 attacks and ensuing events to feckless imperial American policies that have little bearing on vital national interests?[5] Alternatively, have they sustained the lament of another former presidential adviser, the distinguished historian Arthur Schlesinger, Jr., that America is abandoning a "magnificent half-century" of cooperative internationalism in favor of a new isolationism under the guise of unilateralism?[6]

The second question concerns the level of partisan agreement on the proper American role in the world, vital national interests, and the appropriate strategies and tactics to pursue those interests. During the approximately three decades between the Pearl Harbor attack that brought the United States into World War II and growing disillusionment with the Vietnam War, many Democrats and Republicans shared a number of core axioms about the broad outlines of an appropriate American foreign policy; electoral campaigns tended to center on which party and candidates could best implement that policy. Bipartisanship did not survive the bitter outcome of the conflict in Southeast Asia, and efforts to reconstruct a domestic consensus around such policies as détente (Richard Nixon), human rights (Jimmy Carter), and Cold War II (Ronald Reagan) did little to recreate a bipartisan basis for foreign policy. The question to be addressed here is this: Did the 9/11 terrorist attacks help to forge a new bipartisan foreign policy consensus, just as the Pearl Harbor attack in 1941 united an American public that was, even on the eve of the Japanese air strikes, sharply divided on how, if at all, the United States should react to the predatory policies of Nazi Germany in Europe and imperial Japan in the Far East?

In an effort to shed some light on these questions, this chapter initially examines public attitudes on several broad issues, including assessments of threats to vital American interests, the proper U.S. role in the world, the importance of various goals the United States might pursue in its foreign relations, and the appropriate circumstances for the use of American military power. The analysis then examines evidence about two specific issues involving the deployment of American armed forces abroad: the wars in Afghanistan and Iraq. Where available, the discussion examines evidence of partisan convergences or divergences on these issues.

Data

Extensive research during the 1970s and 1980s challenged the conventional wisdom that public opinion was volatile and unstructured but, in the final analysis, public views were largely irrelevant in formulation of foreign policy. As a consequence, the period witnessed the initiation of several major survey projects focused specifically on foreign affairs. Some of them also included for the first time systematic and continuing surveys of opinion leaders. Since 1974, the Chicago Council on Foreign Relations (CCFR) has undertaken ten surveys of the general public, each time also including smaller samples of leaders. These useful studies provide some of the data analyzed in this section.

The first Persian Gulf War, triggered by Iraq's invasion of Kuwait in 1990, stimulated an unprecedented number of surveys on the conflict. In his classic study of the period, John Mueller described the Gulf War as "the mother of all polling events."[7] That may well have been an apt description at the time, but subsequent events, starting with the September 11 terrorist attacks and continuing through the wars in Afghanistan and Iraq, have stimulated even more extensive polling of the American public. The Gallup Organization, CBS News/*New York Times*, ABC News/*Washington Post*, NBC News/*Wall Street Journal*, the *Los Angeles Times*, the Pew Research Center for the People and the Press, the Program on International Policy Attitudes, *Time*, *Newsweek*, and Fox News/Opinion Dynamics are among the organizations that have conducted repeated surveys touching on foreign and defense policy issues in the post–September 11 period. The analyses that follow draw extensively on data generated by these organizations.[8]

America and the World

Threats to Vital U.S. Interests

The Chicago Council on Foreign Relations conducted its surveys at four-year intervals between 1974 and 2002, but it broke that pattern by undertaking its tenth study only two years later in 2004. Among the many virtues of the CCFR surveys have been the repeated use of several clusters of key items, including assessments of threats to vital American interests. Table 6.1 summarizes threat appraisals in the three most recent surveys in 1998, 2002, and 2004. Because the first of these preceded the September 11 attacks, it provides something of a baseline against which to compare the two most recent studies.

Several points emerge from the data. Compared to opinion leaders, the general public has typically perceived a more threatening international environment. That was true across the board in 1998, with differences on the ten items averaging more than 18 percent. The gaps were especially pronounced on perceived threats arising from AIDS and other epidemics (38 percent), immigration (37 percent), and, interestingly in light of subsequent events, international terrorism (23 percent).

Table 6.1 Threats to Vital U.S. Interests: 1998, 2002, and 2004 Chicago Council on Foreign Relations Surveys[a]

	1998		2002		2004[b]	
	Public	Leaders	Public	Leaders	Public	Leaders
International Terrorism	84	61	91	83	81	—
Chemical and Biological Weapons	76	64	86	67	70	—
The Possibility of Unfriendly Countries Becoming Nuclear Powers	75	67	85	72	66	—
AIDS, the Ebola Virus, and Other Potential Epidemics	72	34	68	48	55	—
Large Numbers of Immigrants and Refugees Coming into the U.S.	55	18	60	14	51	—
Military Conflict between Israel and Its Arab Neighbors	—	—	67	73	43	—
Islamic Fundamentalism	38	31	61	61	38	—
Global Warming	43	27	46	28	37	—
Economic Competition from Low-Wage Countries	40	16	31	7	35	—
The Development of China as a World Power	57	46	56	56	40	—
World Population Growth	—	—	44	25	30	—
Tension between India and Pakistan	—	—	54	61	27	—
Economic Competition from Europe	24	16	13	9	20	—

[a] All numbers of critical assessments in percent.
[b] This survey did not include any questions on threats to vital U.S. interests.
Source: Chicago Council on Foreign Relations, Global View 2004: American Public Opinion and Foreign Policy: Topline Data from U.S. Public Survey and from U.S. Leaders Survey (Chicago: CCFR, 2004).

A very similar pattern emerged from the 2002 surveys, although two items that had not appeared four years earlier—the Arab–Israeli and India–Pakistan conflicts—gave rise to greater perceived threats on the part of leaders. The divergence between the two groups on threats arising from immigration and refugees expanded to 46 percent. The recession that began in 2001 no doubt led a number of respondents among the general public to blame rising unemployment on the influx of immigrants who might be willing to work for lower wages.

The 2004 CCFR survey unfortunately dropped the threats cluster of items from the survey of leaders, ruling out the possibility of additional comparisons with the general public. However, one striking pattern does emerge from the public responses. With only two exceptions, both of which deal with economic competition from abroad, respondents tended to perceive a less threatening international environment than they had two years earlier; the decline reached double-digit figures on nine of the threats. Indeed, in a number of instances there were fewer critical threat assessments in 2004 than had been reported in 1998, including appraisal of threats arising from terrorism, chemical and biological weapons, and nuclear proliferation. What could account for such counterintuitive results? The data do not yield clear answers, but one possibility is that the U.S. failure to find either weapons of mass destruction (WMD) in Iraq or links between the Saddam Hussein regime and the Al-Qaeda terrorist organization—the repeatedly asserted rationales for invading Iraq—may have contributed to a diminished sense of danger from such sources. Is this an example of the "cry wolf" phenomenon that when repeated warnings of danger prove to be invalid, there is a tendency to discount further warnings?

America's Role in the World

Within weeks after the United States was drawn into World War II, the Gallup Organization began asking whether the country should play an active role or stay out of world affairs. Some variant of that question has been posed quite regularly during the subsequent period of more than six decades. Although those years encompassed unprecedented changes in the international system, the threat of nuclear annihilation, American leadership in a long Cold War, several wars in Asia and the Middle East, and creation of a large number of international institutions, public preferences on the question have remained quite stable; in none of the more than sixty surveys did fewer than a 53 percent majority favor an active American role in the world.[9] This pattern of responses suggests that the fears often expressed during the decade following the end of World War II that a fickle and feckless public would drive the United States into replaying the withdrawal syndrome of the 1920s may have been overblown. Some critics have nevertheless raised the valid objection that responses to a question posing only two broad alternatives may not yield a sufficiently discriminating portrait of public sentiments. Moreover, an active role may encompass a wide variety of undertakings, ranging from foreign trade and development aid to forming alliances and engaging in military interventions abroad. Public support for an internationalist policy on one of these issues does not necessarily spill over into support for others.

More recently the Gallup Organization has posed the international role question with a wider set of response options: "In trying to solve international problems, do you think the United States should take the leading role, a major but not leading role, a minor role, or no role at all?" The results, summarized at the top of Table 6.2, yield further evidence of substantial stability of public attitudes, even though the four Gallup surveys bracket the September 11 attacks.

Table 6.2 America's Role in the World, Gallup Poll Surveys, 2001–2005[a]

"Think about the role the United States should play in trying to solve international problems. Do you think the United States should take …"

	The leading role	A major role but not the leading role	A minor role	No role at all
February 2001	16	57	21	4
February 2002	26	52	16	4
February 2003	26	53	16	3
February 2004	21	53	21	4
February 2005	19	53	21	5

"How satisfied are you with the position of the United States in the world today?"

	Satisfied	Unsatisfied
February 2001	67	30
February 2002	71	27
February 2003*	53	46
March 2003	69	29
April 2003	67	30
February 2004	47	51
February 2005	48	51

"How does the United States rate in the eyes of the world?"

	Favorably		Unfavorably	
	Very	Somewhat	Somewhat	Very
May 2000	20	53	22	4
February 2001	18	57	20	4
February 2002	20	59	17	3
March 2002	20	46	26	5
February 2003[b]	9	47	34	9
April 2003	12	49	28	9
February 2004	10	44	34	11
February 2005	7	41	39	12

[a] All numbers in percent. "No opinion" responses excluded.
[b] Average of two surveys.
Source: Gallup Organization surveys available at http://www.poll.gallup.com.

Solid, but not overwhelming, majorities favored a major but not leading role. These responses, combined with other evidence, indicate that the public is most likely to support international undertakings in which costs and responsibilities are shared. Although there were small variations in the number of respondents favoring the leading role, probably the most telling figures are those for a minor role and no role at all. Only about one-fifth to one-quarter of the respondents favored a substantial reduction in the U.S. position. Even the September 11 attacks do not appear to have had much impact in this respect; indeed, the differences between the 2001 and 2004 responses are within the margin of error of such surveys.

That said, further probes on the question do in fact indicate changes on some aspects of the manner in which the public appraises the U.S. global position. A sense of considerable satisfaction during the two years prior to the capture of Baghdad in April 2003 has eroded so sharply that less than a year later a majority of respondents asserted they were unsatisfied. That pattern is mirrored in answers to a question about the ways publics abroad rate the United States. Through March 2002, majorities of better than two to one believed the United States rated favorably in the eyes of the world, but subsequent surveys revealed a sharp decline in such ratings.[10]

The data in Table 6.2 thus reveal a stable majority most comfortable with a major but not leading U.S. role in world affairs. Most Americans are in no rush to play the role of the world's policeman, but there is also not much indication that a greatly reduced role is perceived as an attractive alternative. The clear signs of growing dissatisfaction with America's global position are almost surely a response to the turbulence accompanying the U.S. occupation of Iraq since ousting the Hussein regime in April 2003. Questions related to the Iraq war and its aftermath will be revisited later.

Goals for American Foreign Policy

Since their inception in 1974, the CCFR surveys have asked both the general public and opinion leaders to assess the importance of a broad range of possible goals for American foreign policy. This cluster of questions has proved to be especially useful because, unlike the "active role or stay out" question, it provides respondents with the opportunity to be selective about the more specific undertakings subsumed under an active role.

Table 6.3 reports responses to the three most recent CCFR surveys, providing the opportunity to compare those of the general public and opinion leaders.[11] The six-year span of three surveys also offers the possibility of at least an approximate judgment of how important events may have affected responses. The 1998 study preceded the 9/11 terrorist attacks, and the 2002 surveys took place less than a year after those tragic events. The survey in 2004 was undertaken at a time when the optimistic Bush administration scenario for a peaceful occupation and regime change in post-Hussein Iraq was being challenged daily on the ground by insurgents in Fallujah and many other major cities.

Several major patterns emerge from responses to the three CCFR surveys. The conventional wisdom that compared to the general public opinion leaders are invariably more international minded is not sustained, at least when measured by the importance attached to foreign policy goals. Indeed, in both 1998 and 2002 members of the general public were more inclined to attribute greater importance to most goals, albeit by narrow margins in some cases.

Table 6.3 The Importance of American Foreign Policy Goals: Assessments by the General Public and Leaders in the 1998, 2002, and 2004 Chicago Council on Foreign Relations Surveys[a]

"For each (foreign policy goal), please say whether you think that it should be a very important foreign policy goal of the United States, a somewhat important foreign policy goal, or not an important goal at all."

	1998		2002[b]		2004	
	General Public	Leaders	General Public	Leaders	General Public	Leaders
World-order security issues						
Preventing the spread of nuclear weapons	82	85	86	89	73	87
Combating international terrorism	79	74	83	87	71	84
Strengthening the United Nations	45	32	55	28	38	40
Protecting weaker nations against aggression	32	29	35	27	18	33
Strengthening international law and institutions	—	49	43	49	—	—
World-order economic and environmental issues						
Combating world hunger	62	56	54	59	43	67
Improving the global environment	53	46	55	43	47	61
Helping to improve the standard of living in less developed countries	29	36	28	42	18	64
Safeguarding against global financial instability	—	49	54	49	—	—
U.S. economic interest issues						
Stopping the flow of illegal drugs into the United States	81	57	72	45	63	46
Protecting the jobs of American workers	80	45	81	35	78	41
Securing adequate supplies of energy	64	55	69	51	69	57
Controlling and reducing illegal immigration	55	21	70	22	59	21
Reducing the U.S. trade deficit with foreign countries	50	34	51	21	—	—
Protecting the interests of American business abroad	—	—	51	23	32	22

U.S. values and institutional issues						
Promoting and defending human rights in other countries	39	41	41	46	—	—
Promoting market economics abroad	34	36	36	27	—	—
Helping to bring a democratic form of government to other nations	29	27	24	33	14	29
Cold war and security issues						
Maintaining superior military power worldwide	59	58	67	52	50	37
Defending our allies' security	44	58	57	55	—	—

[a] All numbers are percent of "very important" ratings.
[b] Figures are from the Internet rather than telephone survey.

Sources: John E. Reilly, ed., *American Public Opinion and U.S. Foreign Policy, 1999* (Chicago: CCFR, 1999); Bouton and Page 2002; and Chicago Council on Foreign Relations, *Global Views: American Public Opinion and Foreign Policy, 2004* (Chicago: CCFR, 2004).

The differences were especially pronounced on goals involving such U.S. economic interests as protecting the jobs of American workers, controlling illegal immigration and drugs, and reducing the U.S. trade deficit. In all cases the gaps reached double figures. Other differences between these two groups are also worth noting. In 2002, as the debate over how best to deal with the Iraq issue was in its initial stages, public support for both a stronger United Nations (UN) and the maintenance of superior military power increased markedly from the survey four years earlier. In contrast, ratings by opinion leaders for these two goals actually declined during the same interval. The remaining goals gave rise to smaller and often insignificant differences.

The 2002–2004 period between the two most recent CCFR surveys encompassed the invasion of Iraq, the overthrow of the Baathist regime in Baghdad, the capture of Hussein, and an increasingly violent insurgency against American occupation forces and those Iraqis perceived to be collaborating with the United States. Public responses to the fourteen goal items common to both surveys reveal a sharp drop in the importance attributed to thirteen of them; the steady judgment about "securing adequate supplies of energy" (69 percent said very important in both surveys) was the only exception to this pattern. The drop reached double-digit figures on ten of the goals, and the average decline was more than 11 percent. The conflict in Iraq and the war on terrorism notwithstanding, public appraisals of such goals as preventing nuclear proliferation, combating terrorism, protecting weaker nations, and maintaining military superiority in 2004 were viewed as somewhat less important than was the case two years earlier. The absence of any evidence supporting the administration's rationale for invading Iraq, followed by a violent insurgency that gave lie to the premise American forces would be viewed as liberators rather than conquerors, almost certainly contributed to these results. Even the goal of strengthening the United Nations, which was viewed as very important in 2002, did not escape the general pattern of declining support for almost all foreign policy goals. The deadlock in the Security Council during the months preceding the invasion of Iraq no doubt contributed to disillusionment with that organization.

In contrast to the declining importance attached to most foreign policy goals by the public in 2004 when compared to their responses two years earlier, opinion leaders attributed somewhat greater importance to a majority of them, although in most cases the changes during the interval between the CCFR surveys were quite small: in six of the fourteen cases 4 percent or less, thus within the margin of error for such surveys. The only changes reaching double-digit percentages were higher ratings assigned to strengthening the United Nations, to improving the global environment, and to improving the standard of living in less developed countries and declining importance attributed to democracy promotion abroad and maintaining superior military power worldwide. Responses to the latter two questions thus run directly counter to two pillars of Bush administration policies. The National Security Strategy of 2002 articulated the goal of maintaining U.S. military superiority against any possible combination of other countries, and the president and other top administration leaders have repeatedly asserted that creation of a democratic Iraq promotes vital U.S. interests by creating a model that will, by the power of example, inexorably force democratic reforms throughout the Middle East.[12]

In summary, even though the general public has shown few inclinations to retreat into a new phase of isolationism, its enthusiasm for a wide range of foreign policy goals declined during the two year period encompassing three phases of the war in Iraq: the controversies surrounding the run-up to the war; the predictably swift victory over Hussein's poorly armed, abysmally led military; and the turbulent postwar occupation. The long-term erosion of support for world-order economic issues—sometimes described as *compassion fatigue*—continued. With the exception of energy security, even the cluster of economic goals that have traditionally ranked at or near the top of public concerns seemed a little less important in 2004 than had been the case two years earlier.

The figures alone in Table 6.3 do not provide solid support for Schlesinger's lament that the age of cooperative internationalism died with the end of the Cold War. They do suggest, however, that superpower status notwithstanding, the public seems somewhat less sanguine and supportive than previously about the desirability and feasibility of pursuing an ambitious foreign policy agenda. Those doubts are less widely shared among opinion leaders.

Uses of Armed Forces Abroad

American armed forces have been deployed abroad since almost the birth of the republic—but rarely without controversy. The Japanese attack on Pearl Harbor catapulted a united country into World War II, yet in this respect it was almost unique. The War of 1812, the Mexican War, the Spanish–American War, and America's entry into World War I engendered often bitter debates in Congress about the wisdom and justice of going to war. Had public opinion surveys on declarations of war been available at those times, they almost surely would have revealed sharp divisions in the country at large. Since World War II, declarations of war have gone out of style, in part because the Constitution stipulates that war-making prerogatives are shared between the executive and legislative branches. Despite efforts to redress the balance between the two branches—for example, through the War Powers Act of 1973—in practice expansive presidential interpretations of prerogatives arising from the constitutional role of commander-in-chief of the armed forces have generally trumped calls for an active congressional role in decisions about war.

The CCFR surveys posed a cluster of items about circumstances that would justify the use of American armed forces abroad. Some of them concern situations

Table 6.4 Support for the Use of Troops in Various Circumstances: Chicago Council on Foreign Relations Surveys[a]

	1990		1994		1998		2002		2004	
	Public	Leaders	Public	Leaders	Public	Leaders	Public	Leaders	Public	Leaders
To stop a government from committing genocide and killing a large number of its own people	—	—	—	—	—	—	77	85	75	86
To deal with humanitarian crises	—	—	—	—	—	—	—	—	72	—
To be part of international peacekeeping force in Afghanistan	—	—	—	—	—	—	76	88	60	92
To ensure the supply of oil	—	—	—	—	—	—	—	—	54	36
To be part of an international peacekeeping to enforce a peace agreement between Israel and the Palestinians	—	—	—	—	—	—	65	79	52	81
If the government of Pakistan requested our help against a radical Islamic revolution	—	—	—	—	—	—	61	61	51	51
To be part of a UN-sponsored force to help keep peace between India and Pakistan	—	—	—	—	—	—	—	—	51	75
To fight drug lords in Colombia	26	57	39	82	30	74	66	31	51	27
If North Korea invaded South Korea	45	70	42	72	38	69	36	82	43	82
If Arab forces invaded Israel	—	—	—	—	27	51	48	77	43	64
If China invaded Taiwan	—	—	—	—	—	—	32	52	33	51
To install democratic governments in states where dictators rule	—	—	—	—	—	—	—	—	30	—

[a] All numbers are percent in favor.
Source: Chicago Council on Foreign Relations, *Global Views 2004: American Public Opinion and Foreign Policy* (Chicago: CCFR, 2004).

covered by such alliance commitments as the U.S.–South Korea pact, whereas others pose hypothetical scenarios that might give rise to demands the United States intervene with its armed forces. Responses to these questions in the five most recent CCFR surveys are summarized in Table 6.4.

Prior to the 9/11 terrorist attacks, opinion leaders were clearly more willing than members of the general public to use American troops abroad, whether to defend South Korea, Israel, or Taiwan. The differences were very large, ranging upward of 20 percent in each case. The 9/11 attacks did little to narrow the gap between the two groups in connection with defending these three potential targets of their neighbors; continuity rather than dramatic change characterized the responses of both the public and opinion leaders. Although the 2002 and 2004 CCFR surveys revealed the public was marginally more willing to come to the aid of South Korea, those who expressed this view still fell well short of the majority.

The two post-9/11 CCFR surveys introduced a number of new items to the use of troops cluster of questions. The pattern of greater willingness on the part of opinion leaders to deploy American forces abroad persisted with respect to situations involving genocide, as well as peacekeeping in Afghanistan, the Middle East, and South Asia. There were also two notable exceptions, as the public was significantly more inclined to use troops to ensure the supply of oil and to fight drug lords in Colombia.

The rather skimpy agenda of items on troop use abroad in the 1990, 1994, and 1998 CCFR surveys limits pre- and post-9/11 comparisons, but the data do suggest a greater degree of continuity than dramatic change in views among both the general public and opinion leaders as a result of the 2001 terrorist attacks.[13]

Iraq

Iraq has clearly been the dominant American foreign policy issue since Bush announced in his 2002 State of the Union address that Iraq, Iran, and North Korea constituted an axis of evil posing a threat to U.S. security.[14] As the issue unfolded in Washington, the UN Security Council, Iraq, and elsewhere, an unprecedented number of surveys provided almost weekly snapshots of assessments, opinions, and preferences on the issue. The analysis that follows focuses on four questions:

Did the United States do the right thing in taking military action against Iraq (see Fig. 6.1)?
How well are military operations in Iraq going (see Fig. 6.2)?
Has the campaign against Iraq enhanced American national security, especially from terrorism (see Fig. 6.3)?
Has the military campaign in Iraq been worth its costs (see Fig. 6.4), specifically in the casualty levels among the military (see Fig. 6.5)?

Table 6.5 Chronology of Key Events Concerning the Iraq War, 2002–2005

January 29	2002	Bush's State of the Union Address identifies Iraq as part of the "axis of evil"
June 1	2002	Bush's address at West Point justifies possible preventive action against those who may harbor aggressive designs against the United States (i.e., Bush doctrine)
September 4	2002	Bush administration begins campaign to gain congressional and allied support for the use of force against Iraq
September 27	2002	Secretary of Defense Donald Rumsfeld claims that the United States has solid evidence of links between Al-Qaeda and Iraq
October 10–11	2002	Congress backs the use of military force against Iraq
November 8	2002	UN Security Council passes Resolution 1441 demanding that Iraq readmit UN inspectors to determine whether Iraq is in compliance with the 1991 agreements to dispose of weapons of mass destruction (WMD)
February 5	2003	Secretary of State Colin Powell addresses UN Security Council, reporting the United States is in possession of incontrovertible evidence that Iraq is in violation of prohibition against WMD
February	2003	Army chief of staff Eric Shinseki tells Congress that "several hundred thousand troops" would be needed in postwar Iraq. Deputy Defense Secretary Paul Wolfowitz dismisses this estimate as "wildly off the mark" within days
March	2003	United States fails to get a Security Council resolution approving the use of force against Iraq when it becomes clear that it will not gain the approval of at least nine members
March 19	2003	U.S.-led invasion of Iraq begins, with support of some troops from Great Britain
April 9	2003	Baghdad falls to U.S. forces, but Saddam Hussein eludes capture
May 1	2003	Bush declares successful end of hostilities in Iraq ("mission accomplished")
July 2	2003	When asked about insurgents opposing U.S. occupation, Bush replies, "Bring them on"
August 20	2003	UN headquarters in Baghdad bombed with heavy loss of life
October 2	2003	David Kay, in preliminary report to Congress, states that his inspection team failed to find WMD in Iraq
November 6	2003	Bush declares that the spread of democracy to the Middle East is a vital American interest and that success in Iraq is a key part of achieving that goal
December 15	2003	Hussein captured
January 19	2004	Following his resignation, Kay tells Congress, "We were almost all wrong" because there is no evidence that Iraq stockpiled WMD prior to U.S.-led invasion

(Continued)

Table 6.5 (Continued)

April	2004	Insurgents inflict 147 deaths on the U.S. military during the month
Late April	2004	*60 Minutes II* and the *New Yorker* reveal photographic evidence of abuse of Iraqi prisoners by American military personnel
June 28	2004	United States hands over power to interim Iraqi government
September 30	2004	Report of the Iraq survey group, headed by Charles Duelfer, confirms Kay Report findings and states that Iraq's efforts to gain WMD were aimed at Iran
November	2004	U.S.-led counterinsurgency operation takes control of Fallujah, but most insurgency leaders escape
November	2004	Insurgents inflict 140 deaths on the U.S. military during the month
December 20	2004	Bush acknowledges that insurgents are having a significant effect but vows that planned January 2005 elections will be conducted as scheduled
January 13	2005	Iraq survey group formally calls off its two-year search for WMD
January 30	2005	Election turnout in Iraq is quite impressive at almost 60 percent, exceeding that figure in Kurdish and Shiite areas
August 15	2005	Iraqi constitutional negotiators, after failing to reach agreement on a charter to be presented to voters in October, given an additional week to settle such contentious issues as the role of Islam in Iraqi law, the rights of women, the division of oil wealth, and the degree of provincial autonomy

These figures report results from the polling organizations that posed the questions most frequently during the 2003–2005 period. Because even minor variations in question wording can have a significant impact on responses, they are reported in each table. Table 6.5, a chronology of some key events concerning the Iraq issue, provides the background against which the survey results can be appraised.

The Baathist regime in Iraq received massive material and intelligence aid from the Reagan and first Bush administrations during the 1980s and early 1990s, but following its invasion of Kuwait in 1990 and the Gulf War in 1991, Iraq and Hussein became the enemy everyone could love to hate. Even after the forcible expulsion of Iraqi forces from Kuwait and the agreement ending hostilities that left Hussein in power, every survey during the dozen years prior to the 2003 invasion of Iraq revealed that most Americans supported taking action to remove the Iraqi dictator from power. However, approval for doing so was consistently conditioned on obtaining support from allies. In the thirteen surveys posing the question, those in favor of taking military action to end Hussein's rule ranged between 52 and 74 percent; those who did so even if allies would not join reached a high of only 38 percent on the eve of the March 2003 invasion, whereas respondents who would take such action only if allies agreed ranged between 16 percent and 37 percent.[15]

Did the United States Do the Right Thing?

The March 2003 invasion of Iraq stimulated many polling organizations to ask the public to appraise the propriety of the action of the United States. Strong public approval of the successful military operations, culminating in the capture of Baghdad, reached a peak of 74 percent following Bush's declaration in early May that hostilities in Iraq had come to an end and that the mission had successfully been accomplished. Judgments that the United States had done the right thing in Iraq declined somewhat during the remainder of the year as insurgents—those dismissed as "dead enders" by Secretary of Defense Donald Rumsfeld—continued to resist American forces, but as late as December 2003, following the capture of Hussein, those approving of the invasion generally outnumbered the nay-sayers by margins of about two to one.

The Iraqi insurgency, especially in the Sunni triangle area that includes Baghdad and Fallujah, showed little sign of abating in 2004. A record 147 American military personnel were killed or reported killed by insurgents in April, a toll almost matched in November when U.S. forces recaptured the city of Fallujah.[16] Favorable public judgments of the Iraq undertaking declined slowly rather than precipitously throughout 2004; they fell to just below 50 percent in some surveys, whereas others revealed small majorities of well under 60 percent who judged the United States had done the right thing when it used military force against Iraq. By mid-2005, respondents who approved of the military action had fallen below 50 percent (see Fig. 6.1).

Is the War Going Well?

American actions in Iraq have been based on two elements of worst-case scenarios: (1) Iraq possesses weapons of mass destruction and (2) had intimate links to Al-Qaeda. Both of these assumptions have subsequently been disproved. The United States also acted on two elements of best-case scenarios: (1) U.S. troops would be viewed as liberators, and (2) for many Iraqis the opportunity to engineer a democratic regime change would trump any disagreements among Sunnis, Shiites, and Kurds about the future of the country.

Rarely has any government been provided with more substantial warnings than those provided to the Bush administration about its optimistic scenario for postwar Iraq. A State Department study involving scores of experts on Iraq offered ample evidence that should have caused at least some second thoughts among top administration officials, but it was largely disregarded by those responsible for the invasion of Iraq. Army chief of staff Eric Shinseki told a congressional committee that "several hundred thousand" troops would be required to administer postwar Iraq. He was promptly and publicly ridiculed

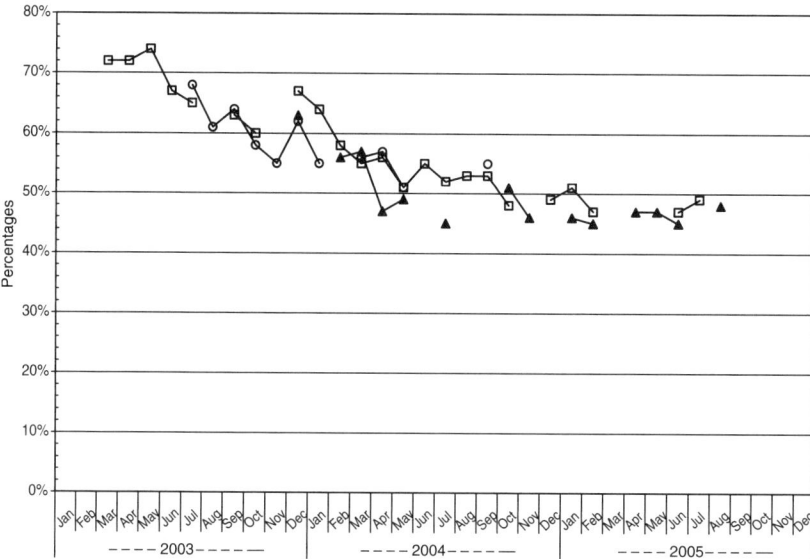

Fig. 6.1 Assessments of the war in Iraq: Did the United States do the right thing in taking military action against Iraq?
a. Pew (square):"Do you think the U.S. made the right decision or the wrong decision in using military force against Iraq?" [% "right decision"]
b. CBS/*New York Times* (triangle): "Looking back, do you think the U.S. did the right thing in taking military action against Iraq, or should the U.S. have stayed out?" [% "right thing"]
c. *Newsweek* (circle): "From what you know, do you think the United States did the right thing in taking military action against Iraq, or not?" [% "right thing"]

by top Defense Department officials Paul Wolfowitz and Rumsfeld and soon thereafter was subject to further public humiliation at his retirement ceremony. Amazingly, Wolfowitz asserted that Shinseki's numbers were wrong because there was no history of ethnic conflict in Iraq, as there was in Bosnia and Kosovo. He also asserted that an estimated $95 billion for costs of the war was much too high because Iraq's oil resources would cover most of the reconstruction costs.[17]

These warnings notwithstanding, shortly after U.S. forces routed the poorly equipped and poorly led Iraqi armed forces in March and April 2003, large majorities of 70 percent or more judged that the military effort in Iraq was going well; however, the onset of the insurgency during the months following the capture of Baghdad resulted in growing public skepticism on that score. As revealed in Figure 6.2, although the questions posed by Pew, Gallup, and CBS News/*New York Times* surveys were quite similar, they yielded some sharply different responses. For example, in November 2003 about two-thirds of Pew respondents judged that U.S. efforts were going well, but fewer than 40 percent of those polled by Gallup responded similarly. The capture of Hussein in

158 • Ole R. Holsti

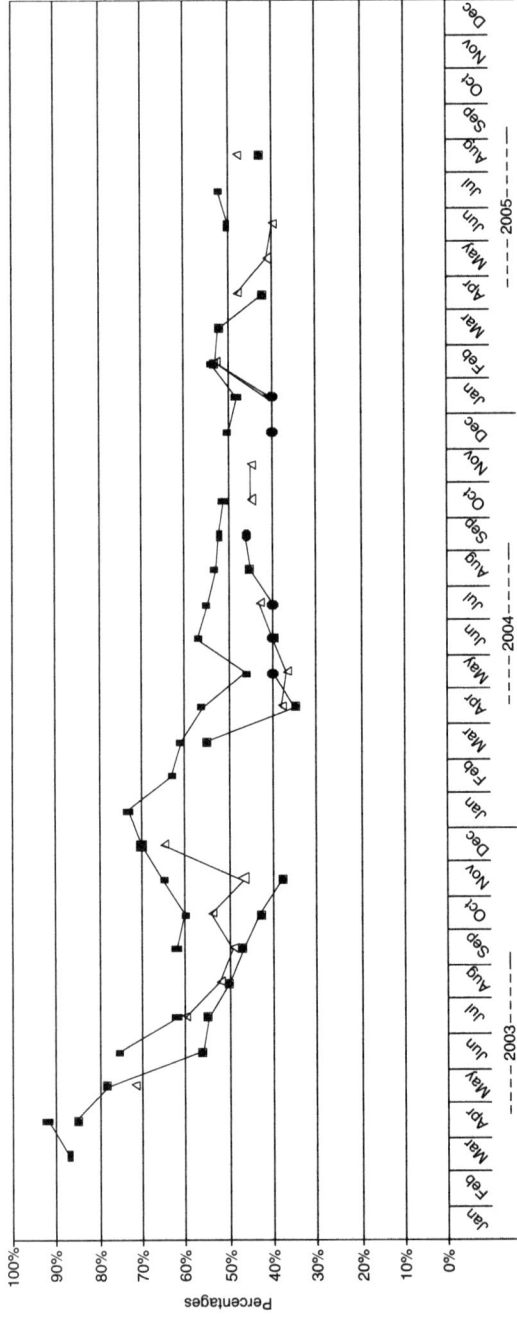

Fig. 6.2 Assessments of the war in Iraq: Is the war going well?
a. Pew (square): "How well is the U.S. military effort in Iraq going: very well, fairly well, not very well, or not well at all?" [% "very well" plus "fairly well"]
b. Gallup (circle): "In general, how would you say things are going for the U.S. in Iraq: very well, moderately well, moderately badly, or very badly?" [% "very well" plus "moderately well"]
c. CBS/*New York Times* (triangle): "How would you say things are going for the U.S. in its efforts to bring stability and order to Iraq? Would you say things are going very well, somewhat well, somewhat badly or very badly?" [% "very well" plus "somewhat well"]

December 2003 gave rise to increased optimism about the Iraq undertaking, which proved to be rather short lived. After repeated failures to locate the alleged Iraqi weapons of mass destruction serving as the *casus belli* and after a bloody insurgency had revealed how poorly the United States had planned for a post-Saddam regime in Baghdad, favorable assessments of American policy dropped steadily. By mid-2005 each of the three surveys yielded similar trends of growing public pessimism (see Fig. 6.2). The disparities in judgments among the 2003 surveys about how well things were going in Iraq gave way to a growing sense among respondents in each of the three surveys that things were in fact going badly.

Has the War Made the United States Safer?
Bush administration officials asserted repeatedly that the Hussein regime in Iraq presented an imminent threat to American security because of its weapons of mass destruction and its intimate links to terrorist organizations, including Osama bin Laden's Al-Qaeda, which perpetrated the September 11 terrorist attacks on New York and Washington. In the absence of compelling evidence either proving or disproving the validity of Washington's claims, during the months immediately following Hussein's ousting, modest majorities among respondents to surveys by ABC News/*Washington Post,* Pew, and CNN/*USA Today*/Gallup agreed that the United States had indeed become safer (see Fig. 6.3).

Failure to uncover WMD in Iraq, despite the best efforts of expert inspection groups headed by Americans David Kay and Charles A. Duelfer, may have contributed to growing doubts about whether the United States is indeed safer as a result of the war in Iraq.[18] Compelling evidence about the rather improbable ties between Hussein's secular regime in Iraq and such hard-core fundamentalist Islamic groups as Al-Qaeda have also eluded Bush administration officials, although Vice President Dick Cheney continues to claim he is in possession of such information. Barring some unlikely new revelations about WMD and ties to terrorist organizations, the evidence in Figure 6.3 suggests that increasingly skeptical public appraisals of triumphalist administration claims about the consequences of the war for American security are likely to persist. A Gallup poll in August 2005 revealed that only about one respondent in three believed that the Iraq war has made the United States safer from terrorism.

Was the War Worth It?
The most frequently asked question about the war in Iraq was about the bottom line: Was it worth it or not? Even before the March 2003 invasion of Iraq, the Gallup Organization began asking whether the current situation in Iraq was worth going to war or not. Since the invasion, the question has been posed repeatedly by several survey organizations, most frequently by Gallup

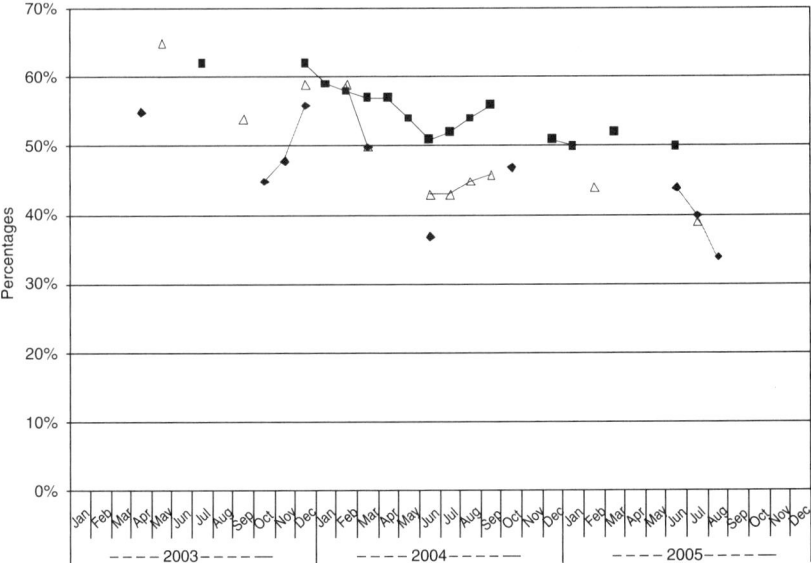

Fig. 6.3 Assessments of the war in Iraq: Has the war made the U.S. safer?
a. ABC/*Washington Post* (square): "Do you think the war with Iraq has or has not contributed to the long-term security of the United States?" [% "has"]
b. Pew (triangle): "Do you think the war in Iraq has helped the war on terrorism, or has it hurt the war on terrorism?" [% "helped"]
C: CNN/*USA Today*/Gallup (trapezoid): "Do you think the war with Iraq has made the U.S. safer or less safe from terrorism?" [% "safer"]

and the ABC News/*Washington Post* polls. The results are summarized in Figure 6.4.

In the immediate aftermath of the capture of Baghdad and the overthrow of the Baathist regime, about 70 percent of the public judged the invasion to have been worth its costs. The speed with which American forces overwhelmed Iraq's—combined with relatively few U.S. casualties—no doubt contributed to this judgment.

Although Bush recognized that the fall of Baghdad did not bring a complete end to low-level skirmishes, he seemed to welcome the opportunity to rout remaining insurgents: "Bring them on," he famously asserted.[19] But the following months brought growing evidence that the U.S. military faced more than just a few dead enders. The impact on public judgments about the war was felt almost immediately as those answering the question of whether it was worth it affirmatively fell below 60 percent, except for a brief upward turn following the capture of the despised Hussein in December 2003. Members of the public who believed the Iraq invasion was worth it constituted a gradually shrinking majority throughout the first half of 2004, and it was reduced further to a minority in many polls undertaken during the second half of the year.

American Public Opinion and Foreign Policy • 161

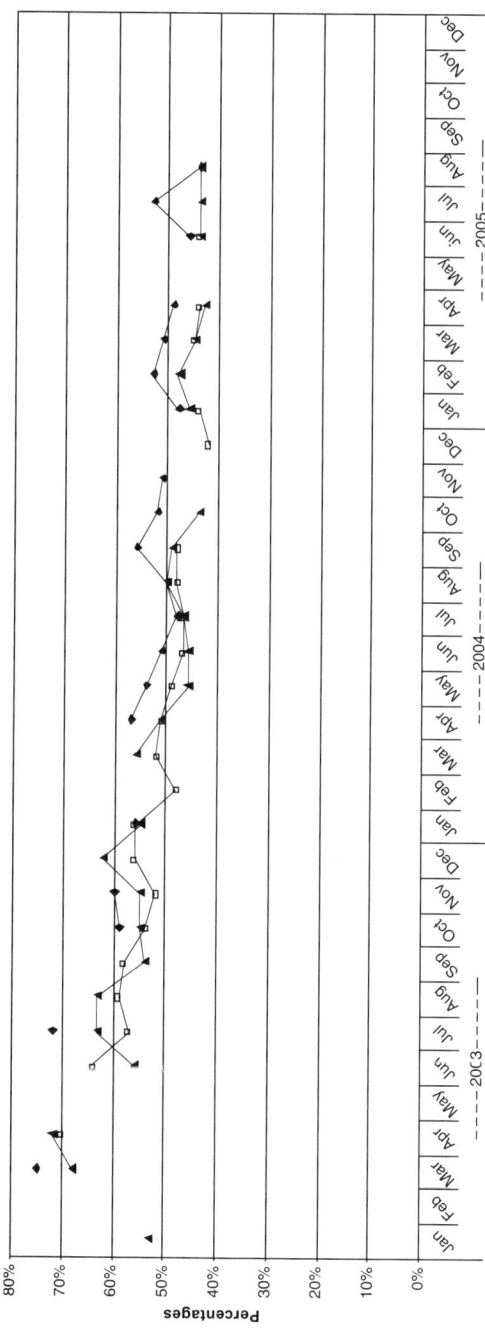

Fig. 6.4 Assessments of the war in Iraq: Was the situation in Iraq worth going to war?
a. Gallup (triangle): "All in all, do you think the situation in Iraq was worth going to war, or not?" Through mid-April 2003, wording was, "All in all, do you think the current situation in Iraq is worth going to war or not?" [% "yes"]
b. Gallup (trapezoid): "In view of developments since we first sent troops to Iraq, do you think the United States made a mistake in sending troops to Iraq, or not?" [% "no, not a mistake"]
c. ABC/Washington Post (square): "All in all, considering the costs to the United States versus the benefits to the United States, do you think the war with Iraq was worth fighting or not?" [% "worth fighting"]

The overall pattern of responses reveals a public sharply divided in its judgment about whether the Iraq war was worthwhile. As recently as August 2005, a Gallup Poll following the elections and formation of a government in Iraq revealed that people who thought the war was worth it were outnumbered by those in disagreement by a margin of 53 to 45 percent.

The ways in which the public reacts to wartime casualties and the impact of those opinions have long been controversial issues. On balance, the evidence indicates that casualty aversion has not been a powerful constraint on American foreign policy as long as the public believes the incurred undertakings are costs that are both desirable and feasible. There is also reason to suspect, however, that questions specifically mentioning casualties, as did those summarized in Figure 6.4, may evoke somewhat different responses than those reported in Figure 6.5 not mentioning such costs.

A comparison of Figures 6.4 and 6.5 does not provide overwhelming evidence casualty aversion is a powerful factor with respect to Iraq, but it does suggest that respondents are likely to express somewhat more sober enthusiasm for interventions abroad when confronted with the issue of costs. When compared to the wars in Korea and Vietnam, for which public support fell as casualties mounted,[20] combat deaths in Iraq have been relatively light

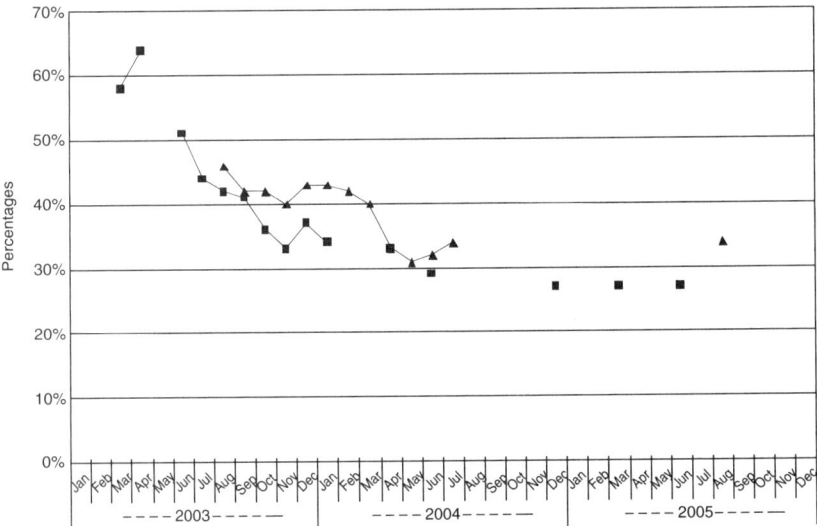

Fig. 6.5 Assessments of the war in Iraq: Was the war worth the loss of American lives?
a. CBS/*New York Times* (triangle): "Do you think the result of the war with Iraq was worth the loss of American life and other costs of attacking Iraq, or not worth it?" [% "worth it"]
b. ABC/*Washington Post* (square): "Again thinking about the goals versus the costs of the war, so far in your opinion have there been an acceptable or unacceptable number of U.S. military casualties in Iraq?" [% "acceptable number of casualties"]

(fewer than 2,200 in late-2005). That said, the data in Figure 6.5 seem to provide a partial explanation for growing public disenchantment with the war in Iraq, but they are probably not as important as other considerations, such as the purposes (desirability) and prospects for success (feasibility) of the war. Had the United States discovered weapons of mass destruction in Iraq or evidence of ties between Baghdad and Al-Qaeda—the repeatedly stated rationales for the invasion—would public judgments about whether the war was worth it have been more favorable than those summarized in Figures 6.4 and 6.5? Probably, but we cannot be sure.

In the absence of any evidence supporting the original reason for the war, the administration's goals have been transformed into democracy promotion in the Middle East, with Iraq as the keystone of the effort.[21] Yet long-standing evidence exists that the public has never attributed great importance to that goal,[22] a point Bush and his advisers seem to have recognized during the 2000 campaign when they derided the Clinton administration for placing the expansion of democracy at the core of its foreign policy agenda. The admirable goal of creating democracy in a country that has never enjoyed such institutions sets the standard for success in Iraq rather high; as a result, future public appraisals of the Iraq war are likely to depend at least in part on whether that goal can be achieved.

Partisanship

Despite efforts by some members of the Bush administration to equate questions about the conduct of the Iraq campaign with giving aid and comfort to the enemy in time of war (i.e., treason), American history in fact reveals that strong wartime criticism, often rooted in partisanship, is fairly common, as illustrated by the War of 1812, the Mexican War, the Spanish–American War, and the later stages of the conflicts in Korea and Vietnam. Optimism about a quick military victory followed by peaceful regime change in Baghdad eroded in the light of events on the ground in Iraq and coincided with the 2004 presidential election. Although many Democrats in Congress supported the October 2002 resolutions authorizing the use of force against Iraq, the war in fact has served to divide the country along partisan lines.

Table 6.6 summarizes responses to some of the central questions about the war: (1) Was going to war the right thing? (2) How well is the war effort going? (3) Was the Iraq situation worth going to war over? The partisan gaps on all of these questions are huge: in the range of 46 to 62 percent, with independents falling in between—though a bit closer to Democrats than to Republicans. Even if these results are discounted a bit because the presidential campaign may have heightened partisan sensibilities to all issues, the figures in Table 6.6 are startling; they almost suggest that Republicans and Democrats were appraising two quite different sets of events.

Table 6.6 Partisanship and Assessments of the War in Iraq, 2004–2005

Survey	Date	All	Republicans	Democrats	Independents
Did the United States do the right thing to go to war against Iraq? (percentage yes, the right thing)					
Time magazine	May 2004	48	75	29	48
CBS/*NY Times*	July 2004	45	78	22	42
CBS/*NY Times*	October 2004	52	89	21	47
Did the United States make a mistake in sending troops to Iraq, or not? (percentage no, not a mistake)					
Gallup	January 2005	48	82	21	40
How well is the U.S. effort in Iraq going? (percentage very well or somewhat well)					
CBS/*NY Times*	July 2004	43	71	25	40
Gallup	January 2005	40	68	18	33
CBS/*NY Times*	June 2005	40	69	20	36
Gallup	August 2005	43	72	19	38
Do you favor or oppose the war with Iraq?					
Gallup	March 2005	47	81	15	40
Gallup	June 2005	39	70	17	32
Was the situation in Iraq worth going to war over? (percentage yes, it was worth the cost)					
L.A. *Times*	July 2004	44	80	18	42
Gallup	January 2005	46	82	16	35
Gallup	April 2005	45	79	17	36
Do you think the results of the war in Iraq were worth the loss of American life and other costs of attacking Iraq, or not worth it? (percent yes, worth it)					
CBS/*NY Times*	July 2005	34	69	13	26

Source: http://www.PollingReport.com. Exact wording of the questions may be found in Figures 6.1, 6.2, 6.4 and 6.5 of this chapter.

Conclusion

The central question addressed in this chapter is whether the turbulent period since September 11 terrorist attacks witnessed an important watershed, dramatically transforming public opinion about foreign affairs on a scale similar to the impact of the Pearl Harbor bombing raid six decades earlier. The evidence reviewed here indicates that despite the terrorist attacks, two wars in the Middle East, and an incompetently managed occupation of postwar Iraq, most Americans remain committed to an active international role, with the added stipulation that responsibilities for coping with a complex agenda of challenges and opportunities should be shared with allies and international institutions.

More specifically, the evidence presented in Tables 6.1–6.4, spanning the years before and after the 9/11 attacks, provides little solace for those who would follow Buchanan in a program of retrenchment from what he believes is a disastrously overextended imperial position undermining rather than promoting vital national interests. Buchanan's attacks on trade liberalization and increasing immigration find support among the public, but that does not represent a recent change; surveys during the past three decades have shown consistent public unease about trade and support for restricting the number of immigrants, especially those crossing the border illegally.

Nor does the evidence lend much support to the previously cited fears expressed by Schlesinger that, since the disintegration of the Soviet Union, internationalist and multilateralist impulses among the American public have receded and have been overtaken by a growing tide of isolationism and unilateralism. A consistently strong majority of Americans accept an active American role across a broad spectrum of issues, but not without some important reservations. Public enthusiasm for efforts to remake the world in America's image—through promotion of democratic institutions, human rights, market economies, and the like—has consistently been quite limited, especially if such endeavors are undertaken by means of military interventions. When there is support for using armed forces abroad, it is generally on the condition that support of allies or international organizations must be gained as a way of demonstrating legitimacy for the undertaking and, probably more importantly, as a way of sharing the burdens of such undertakings. Although the United States took the lead in the campaign to oust Iraqi forces from Kuwait in the 1991 Gulf War, the Bush administration's successful diplomatic campaign to gain Security Council support, as well as military and financial contributions from many other countries, contributed to strong public support for the war.

What about the future impact of the Iraq war on public opinion? The invasion of Iraq in 2003 was undertaken without a supporting vote by the Security Council and in the face of widespread opposition from even traditional allies. The administration instead relied on what might be called *multilateralism a la carte,* wherein it established its own goals and then invited others to join a coalition of the willing. Some did so, sending mostly token forces to Iraq. Others were subjected to various kinds of penalties, ranging from ridicule to exclusion from bidding on Iraq reconstruction contracts.

Pre-invasion surveys consistently revealed that the public favored using force to remove Saddam Hussein but preferred doing so in conjunction with support from allies. Even in the absence of such external support, the successful military strike into Iraq generated a good deal of public approval for the invasion during the weeks following the capture of Baghdad. In the face of a bloody insurgency that persisted well into the third year of the American occupation of Iraq, surveys have uncovered a gradual erosion of public support for and optimism about the war.

The data have also revealed a partisan divide—perhaps partisan chasm would be a more accurate description—of almost unprecedented dimensions. Clichés that "politics stops at the water's edge" notwithstanding, bipartisanship is not the natural state on foreign affairs, as George Washington, James Madison, Woodrow Wilson, and many otherwise able leaders have learned; it can only be achieved by skilled presidential leadership. Appointments to key foreign policy positions are among the tools available to presidents. In selecting the American delegation to the Versailles Conference following World War I, Wilson could have included any of several distinguished Republicans on record as favoring the creation of international organization as part of the peace settlement, such as former president William Howard Taft. By failing to do so, Wilson went a long way toward framing American membership in the League of Nations as a partisan issue, thus materially reducing the chances the Versailles Treaty would gain approval of the Republican-dominated Senate.

Some of Wilson's successors have demonstrated greater political acumen. After the collapse of the French army in 1940, anticipating that the United States would be drawn into World War II, Franklin Roosevelt fired his isolationist secretaries of war and navy and replaced them with Frank Knox, 1936 Republican vice presidential candidate, and Henry L. Stimson, among the most distinguished Republican foreign policy officials of the twentieth century (who served as secretary of war and state in the cabinets of Taft and Herbert Hoover). When faced with negotiating a peace treaty with all of the countries that had been at war with Japan and then guiding it through the U.S. Senate, Truman turned to Republican stalwart John Foster Dulles, who would soon thereafter serve as Dwight Eisenhower's secretary of state. And, after winning a close election in 1960, John F. Kennedy appointed Republicans Douglas Dillon and Robert McNamara to head the Treasury and Defense Departments. These appointments certainly did not ensure Republican support for all administration foreign policies, but they represented significant steps in eliciting bipartisan cooperation on some important issues during World War II and the ensuing Cold War.

Whether the current partisan divide on Iraq and other foreign policy issues can be bridged probably depends on how events play out on the ground in Iraq and also on whether the second Bush administration makes even token efforts to reach out to Democrats to establish some semblance of bipartisan foundations for American foreign policy. Early signs on the latter point are not especially auspicious, as the official who might have worked most effectively with the opposition party, Secretary of State Colin Powell, was fired within days of the president's reelection. In general, members of the president's team who have questioned any aspects of his policies, including Army Chief of Staff Shinseki, Chair of the Foreign Intelligence Advisory Board Brent Scowcroft (who publicly opposed the invasion of Iraq), Treasury Secretary Paul O'Neill (who was not sufficiently enthusiastic about impending tax cuts because they would result in huge budget deficits), and Director of the National Economic Council Lawrence Lindsey (who had the temerity to state that the impending war against Iraq would cost $100 to $200 billion rather than the administration's figure of $50 to $60 billion), have quickly been shown the door. O'Neill and Lindsay fared better than Shinseki, as both received "lukewarm thanks" for their services.[23] Thus, it would take a major change of mind-set for the president to reach out to those who may not always have been vocal cheerleaders. However, the president made it clear in a long interview that his victory in the 2004 election essentially settled all issues relating to the Iraq war, including accountability for any mistakes and misjudgments.[24]

Openings at the World Bank and the American delegation to the United Nations provided Bush an opportunity for at least a couple of minor gestures toward bipartisanship, especially as neither the World Bank nor the UN play a central role in the administration's foreign calculations. Instead of grasping this chance, the president appointed two of the most partisan and ideological officials of his first administration—Wolfowitz and John R. Bolton—to serve as president of the World Bank and U.S. ambassador to the UN.

The longer-run impact of the war in Iraq is also likely to depend on the end game in the American intervention. The data presented in this chapter depict an American public that since the euphoria engendered by the rapid overthrow of the Hussein regime has become increasingly skeptical of the Iraq campaign. Yet there is no evidence of a groundswell of demands that American forces be withdrawn. There appears to be an appreciation of the "Pottery Barn rule"—break it and you own it—which precludes a precipitous withdrawal at a time when there is strong reason to fear that such action might transform a bloody insurgency in the Sunni triangle into a full-scale civil war. As indicated in Table 6.7, even though the United States has thus far been unable to quell the insurgency in Iraq, by a steady majority of about three to two the public has preferred keeping troops in Iraq to stabilize the country rather than withdrawing them immediately.

The 58 percent turnout in Iraqi elections in January 2005 met at least moderate standards of legitimacy both inside and outside Iraq. The new Iraqi government that will draft a new constitution was introduced three months later following intensive bargaining among the majority Shiite and minority Kurdish and Sunni factions. Hopes that formation of an elected government in Iraq would bring a concomitant diminution in the level of violence have, however, been disappointed. The weeks prior to introduction of the new government witnessed increased rather than diminished insurgent activity, seemingly aimed at undermining its credibility. Moreover, negotiations

Table 6.7 U.S. Opinion of Whether Troops Should Stay in Iraq, 2003–2005[a]

Do you think the United States should keep military troops in Iraq until the situation has stabilized, or do you think the United States should bring its troops home as soon as possible?[b]

	Keep Troops in Iraq (%)	Bring Troops Home (%)
2003		
September	64	32
October	58	39
2004		
January	63	32
Early April	50	44
Late April	53	40
May	53	42
June	51	44
July 8–18	53	43
August 5–10	54	42
September 8–13	54	40
October 15–19	57	36
December 1–16	56	40
2005		
January 5–9	54	41
February 16–21	55	42
June 8–12	50	46
July 13–17	52	43

[a] "Unsure" responses excluded.
[b] Wording in June 2004 and earlier surveys: "Do you think the United States should keep military troops in Iraq until a stable government is established there, or do you think the United States should bring its troops home as soon as possible?"
Source: Pew Research Center for the People and the Press surveys.

aimed at drafting a new constitution failed to break deadlocks on several key issues prior to the initial August 15 deadline. These events suggest that the crucial goal of creating well-trained Iraqi police and military units that can restore and maintain order appears unlikely to be achieved in the short run—that is, before the 2006 American congressional campaign moves into high gear.

But even achievement of the best-case scenario (i.e., establishing a stable democratic government in Iraq, permitting the gradual withdrawal of American forces) is not likely to resolve longer-term debates about the wisdom of the so-called Bush Doctrine—undertaking unilateral preemptive military action against countries suspected of posing future evil designs.

For many Americans, the discredited intelligence on which the United States based its invasion, the doubtful premises about how American occupation forces would be received and about how best to administer the post-Saddam occupation, and the inability to persuade America's oldest allies—save Great Britain—to support U.S. policy are likely to sustain some doubts about such undertakings in the future. A July 2005 Gallup poll revealed that 51 percent of respondents believed the Bush administration deliberately misled the American public about whether Iraq has weapons of mass destruction. For them, the war may well live on as cautionary lessons of Iraq.

For others, including the surprisingly large minority who continue to believe that Iraq had WMD as well as ties to Al-Qaeda, the Iraq War may well serve as a fount of quite different lessons including, perhaps, about the uses of military force in the pursuit of vital national interests.[25] Consequently, it appears likely that future debates about foreign policy will focus less on the appropriate American role in the world (i.e., internationalism versus isolationism) and more on the means by which the country pursues its vital interests (i.e., multilateralism versus unilateralism).

How the debate about the appropriate goals, strategies, and tactics of American engagement abroad—most notably when armed intervention, as in Iraq, is one of the options—of course will depend on the essential features of each situation. The evidence cited here reveals no groundswell in support of major retrenchment from an active international role. That said, the fact the administration led the country into war in Iraq on the basis of faulty arguments and flawed intelligence may well color how the United States is able to respond to future situations in which the alleged threat to vital national interests lacks the clarity of a Pearl Harbor or September 11 type of attack. Leaving aside constraints arising from evidence that American armed forces are stretched very thin, unmet military recruitment quotas, and the gigantic budget deficits of the past several years, the willingness of the American public to "rally 'round the president'" in support of military interventions is unlikely to be limitless.[26] Significant numbers of the public and opinion leaders may well recall the story of the boy who cried wolf too often. Although that may restrain unwise interventions, one of the long-term costs of the Iraq invasion may be that it also serves as a constraint when the threats are in fact real.

Notes

1. Hans J. Morgenthau, *Politics among Nations*, 5th ed. (New York: Knopf, 1978).
2. Alexis de Tocqueville, *Democracy in America*, vol. 1 (New York: Vantage, 1958); George F. Kennan, *American Diplomacy, 1900–1950* (Chicago: University of Chicago Press, 1951); and Walter Lippmann, *Essays in the Public Philosophy* (Boston: Little, Brown, 1955).
3. For a fuller discussion, see Ole R. Holsti, *Public Opinion and American Foreign Policy* (Ann Arbor: University of Michigan Press, 2004), ch. 1.
4. See, for example, the many studies on specific American administrations by Lawrence R. Jacobs and Robert Y. Shapiro, as well as their *Politicians Don't Pander* (Chicago: University of Chicago Press, 2000).
5. Patrick J. Buchanan, *The Great Betrayal: How American Sovereignty and Social Justice Are Being Sacrificed to the Gods of the Global Economy* (Boston: Little, Brown, 1998).

6. Arthur M. Schlesinger, Jr., "Back to the Womb?" *Foreign Affairs* vol. 74 no. 4 (July–August 1995), 2–8.
7. John Mueller, *Policy and Opinion in the Gulf War* (Chicago: University of Chicago Press, 1994).
8. Virtually all survey organizations asked some variant of a question about the president's handling of the Iraq issue—for example, "Do you approve or disapprove of the way George W. Bush is handling the situation with Iraq?" The tables and discussion that follow have excluded them, as mention of the president by name may distort the results, especially during the run-up to a highly contentious election. It may be unclear whether respondents are expressing views of the president or the policy.
9. See Holsti, *Public Opinion*, figure 3.1.
10. Numerous surveys reveal that favorable assessments of the United States and its policies have declined sharply in most countries since the Iraq issue took center stage in world affairs. For a summary of some evidence, see Holsti, "To See Ourselves as Others See Us: How Publics Abroad View the United States in the Post-9/11 Era" (paper presented at the annual meeting of the American Political Science Association, Chicago, IL, September 2004); and Holsti and Natasha C. Roetter, "How Publics Abroad View the United States" (paper presented at the annual meeting of the American Political Science Association, Washington, D.C., September 2005).
11. For an overview of public and leadership responses to the "goals" cluster of items, 1974–2002, see Holsti, *Public Opinion*, tables 3.3a, 5.5, 6.6.
12. George W. Bush, "Graduation Address at West Point Military Academy" (NY: June 1, 2002) available at www.whitehouse.gov/news/releases/2002/06/print/20020601-3.html; White House, *National Security Strategy of the United States* (September 20, 2002) available at www.globalsecurity.org/military/library/policy/national/nss-020920.htm; and George W. Bush, "President Bush on Freedom in Iraq and the Middle East" (speech to the National Endowment of Democracy, November 6, 2003) available at www.whitehouse.gov/news/releases/2003/11/print/20031106-2.html.
13. The earlier CCFR surveys included a number of other items (e.g., a hypothetical Soviet invasion of Europe, an Iranian invasion of Saudi Arabia) that have been dropped in the most recent survey and thus do not appear in table 6.4. The data are summarized in Holsti, *Public Opinion*, table 4.4.
14. George W. Bush, "State of the Union Address" (January 29, 2002) available at www.whitehouse.gov/news/releases/2002/01/print/20020129-11.html.
15. These surveys are summarized in Holsti, *Public Opinion*, table 6.8.
16. The precise numbers were 135 killed and twelve reported dead in April and 137 killed and three reported dead in November. Total battle deaths during March and April 2003—the period including the invasion of Iraq—were 138.
17. Eric Schmitt, "Pentagon Contradicts General on Iraq Occupation Force's Size, *New York Times*, February 28, 2003, A1.
18. David Kay, "Statement by David Kay on the Interim Progress Report on the Activities of the Iraq Survey Group before the House Permanent Committee on Intelligence" (October 2, 2003) available at www.cnn.com/2003/ALLPOLITICS/10/02/kay.report/; "Kay: No Evidence Iraq Stockpiled WMDs" available at http://www.cnn.com/2004/WORLD/meast/01/25/sprj.nirq.kay/ (January 26, 2004); and Charles Duelfer, *Comprehensive Report of the Special Adviser to Director of Central Intelligence on Iraq's Weapons of Mass Destruction*, 3 volumes (September 30, 2004) available at www.cia.gov/cia/reports/iraq_wmd_2004/.
19. "Bring Them On, Bush Says of Iraq Attacks" (Reuters, July 2, 2003) available at www.cbsnews.com/stories/2003/07/03/Iraq/printable561567.shtml. Also available at www.usatoday.com/news/washington/2003-07-02-bush-speech-text_x.htm.
20. John Mueller, *War, Presidents, and Public Opinion*. (New York: Wiley, 1973).
21. George W. Bush (speech, National Endowment of Democracy, November 6, 2003) available at www.whitehouse.gov/news/releases/2003/11/print/20031106-2.html.
22. Holsti, "Public Opinion and Human Rights in American Foreign Policy," in *The United States and Human Rights: Looking Inward and Outward*, ed. David P. Forsythe (Lincoln: University of Nebraska Press, 2000), 131–174; Holsti, "Democracy Promotion as Popular Demand?" in *American Democracy Promotion: Impulses, Strategies, and Impacts*, ed. Michael Cox, G. John Ikenberry, and Takashi Inogushi (New York: Oxford University Press, 2000), 151–180; Bruce W. Jentleson, "The Pretty Prudent Public: Post-Vietnam American Opinion

on the Use of Military Force," *International Studies Quarterly* 36 (1992), 49–73; and Jentleson and Rebecca L. Britton, "Still Pretty Prudent: Post-Cold War American Public Opinion on the Use of Military Force," *Journal of Conflict Resolution* 42 (1998), 395–417.
23. Edmund L. Andrews, "Upheaval in the Treasury: The Treasury Secretary; Bush, Shakeup of Cabinet, Ousts Treasury Leader," *New York Times*, December 7, 2002, A1; Elizabeth Bumiller, "Threats and Responses: The Costs; While White House Cuts Estimates of Costs of War with Iraq," *New York Times*, December 31, 2002, A1.
24. Jim VandeHei and Michael Fletcher, "Bush Says Election Ratified Iraq Policy," *Washington Post*, January 15, 2005. The full transcript of the interview appears in the same issue of that newspaper.
25. Steven Kull, *Misperception, the Media, and the Iraq War* (PIPA/Knowledge Networks Poll, October 2, 2003), A01. This study revealed that those who rely primarily on television for news (especially FOX television) were most likely to believe these counterfactuals.
26. A classified report from the Pentagon to Congress acknowledged that commitments in Afghanistan and Iraq have strained Pentagon resources. Thom Shanker, "Pentagon Says Iraq Effort Limits Ability to Fight Other Conflicts: Chairman of Joint Chiefs Tells Congress of Risks," *New York Times*, May 3, 2005, A1.

7

Supervising America's Secret Foreign Policy: A Shock Theory of Congressional Oversight for Intelligence

LOCH K. JOHNSON

> You see, the way a free government works,
> there's got to be a housecleaning every now and then … .[1]
>
> Harry S. Truman

The framers of the Constitution established a government for the United States based on the notion of sharing powers among the three branches of government: the executive, the legislative, and the judiciary. The idea was to prevent any one branch from becoming too powerful and, as a consequence, dangerous to citizens through an abuse of authority—a core principle of American government that applies to both foreign and domestic policymaking.[2]

This principle is put to a rigorous test in times of national emergency, when there is a tendency to concentrate power in the hands of the president and other officials in the executive branch. The nation's most egregious abuses of power have occurred under such circumstances. Examples in the modern era include the following:

- The confinement of Japanese Americans to guarded camps as a result of an executive order from President Franklin D. Roosevelt (FDR) during the Second World War
- Roosevelt's sweeping use of executive agreements to move the United States toward entry into that war
- The expansive use of war powers by Presidents Harry S. Truman and Dwight D. Eisenhower in the early stages of the Cold War
- President Lyndon B. Johnson's misleading of the American people about the poor progress of the war in Vietnam
- The Nixon Administration's preparation of a master spy plan (the Huston Plan) against student protesters

- Widespread domestic espionage by the Central Intelligence Agency (CIA) and the Federal Bureau of Investigation (FBI) against Vietnam War dissenters
- The violation of federal statutes during the Iran-Contra scandal, driven by a secret arms deal with Iran and an overzealous response to a left-leaning government in Nicaragua, opposed by the Contras.[3]

The constitutional principle of sharing power is undergoing another severe test now, as the nation focuses much of its foreign policy energies and resources on a struggle against global terrorism. This took on a special sense of urgency when Al-Qaeda terrorists struck the American homeland on September 11, 2001. Following this tragedy, Congress granted President George W. Bush wide discretionary powers to conduct war against Al-Qaeda and other terrorists around the globe. Lawmakers also provided the president with the Patriot Act permitting the CIA, the FBI, and military intelligence agencies wider scope to carry out investigations and interrogations against suspected terrorists. Moreover, the Congress granted the president open-ended authority to invade Iraq, out of a concern that Baghdad might have weapons of mass destruction and ties with Al-Qaeda. (Both hypotheses were soon found to be incorrect, but only after the war had been launched, even over the objections of the United Nations [UN].)

Added to this climate of fear about terrorism that led to the broad grants of authority to the second Bush administration came a series of electoral results magnifying the concentration of power into the hands of the administration, namely, a sweep of House and Senate elections that gave Republicans control over both the executive and legislative branches. The administration enjoyed the additional advantage of a conservative-leaning Supreme Court and the likelihood that the president would soon be able to augment its ideological tilt with two or more appointments to the high court. All of these events summed to a situation in which the Bush administration has enjoyed great leeway in its conduct of foreign affairs, far beyond what the founders would have considered prudent.

In light of these circumstances of a rising executive dominance over foreign policy, this chapter examines the efforts of Congress to maintain some semblance of constitutional balance in the domain of strategic intelligence. The guiding research question is this: How well have lawmakers responded to the challenge of supervising the programs and budgets of the Central Intelligence Agency (CIA) and America's fourteen other secret agencies, providing appropriate checks against their misuse?

The Sharing of Secret Power

The duty of maintaining a check on the abuse of power within the invisible side of America's government is especially difficult for lawmakers, since intelligence operations are highly secretive and often quite fragile; if exposed, the consequences can entail danger and even death for U.S. intelligence officers and their foreign agents in the field. Moreover, in this hidden realm, Congress has few interest groups on which to rely for information about executive branch plans, policy options, and mistakes. And when it comes to intelligence, the media is not a consistent and reliable source of information for lawmakers about questionable agency objectives and activities—unlike other more porous government entities where beat reporters routinely walk the halls and interview program managers and their aides. To an unusual degree, Congress must rely on its own devices for tracking the secret foreign policy of the United States.

On the general subject of oversight, Mathew D. McCubbins and Thomas Schwartz suggest a vivid police patrolling versus firefighting metaphor.[4] As patrollers, lawmakers *qua* overseers regularly review executive branch programs, just as a police officer might walk the streets, check the locks on doors, and shine a flashlight into dark corners—all to be vigilant against potential criminal acts. In contrast, firefighters classically respond to alarms after a fire has broken out. In a similar fashion, lawmakers can carry out routine but careful patrols in executive branch programs, or they can wait and then rush to the scene after an alarm sounds that a program has run afoul of the law or other societal expectations.

The research on intelligence oversight on Capitol Hill indicates that the efforts of lawmakers to patrol secret agencies have been "sporadic, spotty, and essentially uncritical."[5] The chief cause of this inattentiveness derives from the nature of Congress: lawmakers seek reelection and usually conclude that passing bills and raising campaign money is a better use of their time than the often tedious review of executive programs. Intelligence review is especially monotonous because it must take place for the most part in committee meetings outside of public view. Absent public awareness, credit-claiming, which is vital to reelection prospects, becomes difficult.[6]

A recent analysis of intelligence accountability suggests a pattern in recent decades: a major intelligence scandal or failure—a shock—converts perfunctory patrolling into a burst of intense firefighting, followed by a period of more dedicated patrolling that yields remedial legislation or other reforms designed to curb inappropriate intelligence activities in the future. Sometimes the high-intensity patrolling can last for months or, if the shock was particularly strong, even years. Once the firestorm has subsided and reforms are in place, however, lawmakers return to a state of relative inattention to intelligence issues.[7] Schematically, this pattern is depicted in Figure 7.1. The present chapter takes the analysis a step further by more closely exploring this sequence. First, though, it is important to place contemporary efforts at intelligence oversight into historical context.

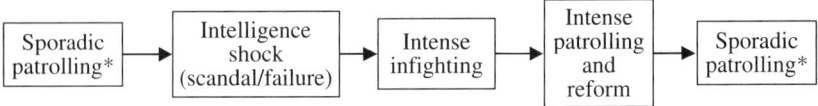

Fig. 7.1 The dominant pattern of intelligence oversight by lawmakers, 1975–2004.
*a result of insufficient opportunities for credit-claiming and the enhancement of reelection prospects, which in turn produce an inattentiveness to oversight duties and a concomitant ripening of conditions for scandal or failure.

The Philosophical Wellsprings of Congressional Oversight

The founders of the government of the United States were inspired by a core value: a fear of concentrated power.[8] "Power, lodged as it must be in human hands, is ever liable to abuse," warned James Madison, the Constitution's main author. In *The Federalist,* no. 51, he offered the celebrated counsel, "Ambition must be made to counter ambition."[9] The greatest gift of governance given to the new nation by the founders was the set of constitutional safeguards they established to keep power dispersed. Others at the time and down through the years have similarly extolled the virtues of a separation of powers, coupled with other checks and balances—perhaps the most popular phrase in school civics courses.

The focus of the nation's founders was not on government efficiency; had it been, they would have placed stronger authority in the office of the presidency or perhaps even have established a monarchy with the remarkable George Washington being first to wear the crown. Instead, they were most concerned about the question of liberty—freedom from the kind of repression that had visited the American colonies at the hand of King of England George III: taxation without representation, forceful quartering of British troops in the homes of the colonists, the yoke of unfair laws like the Stamp Act, and the impressment of sailors on the high seas. The brilliant Supreme Court justice Louis Brandeis restated Madison's argument for a modern audience in 1926 in *Myers vs. U.S.*, noting that the founders had sought "not to promote efficiency but to preclude the exercise of arbitrary power. The purpose was not to avoid friction, but, by means of the inevitable friction incident to the distribution of the governmental powers among three departments, to save the people from autocracy."[10]

The philosophy that the chances for liberty could be improved by guarding against the abuse of power is known today as government accountability or, less formally, by the awkward term oversight—in essence, the review of government programs and activities. Joel Aberbach provides a useful definition of oversight as a "review of the actions of federal departments, agencies, and commissions, and of the programs and policies they administer, including review that takes place during program and policy implementation as well as afterward."[11] A chair of the House Committee on Intelligence, Lee H. Hamilton

(D, Indiana) suggests that oversight "can help protect the country from the imperial presidency and from bureaucratic arrogance ... [and] help keep federal bureaucracies on their toes."[12] For another experienced oversight practitioner in the Senate, Wyche Fowler (D, Georgia), the objective of accountability is, simply put, "to prevent the bureaucrats from doing something stupid."[13]

Lawmakers have turned to a wide array of means to monitor events in the executive branch in an effort to ensure that the laws of the nation are honored by bureaucrats and their bosses, that the will of Congress—a 535-person surrogate for the American people—is respected, that scandals and mistakes are avoided, that taxpayer monies are properly expended, that efficiencies are encouraged, and, above all, that civil liberties are protected. Chief among the means of legislative review, according to a substantial body of research, are communications between the aides of lawmakers and program managers in the bureaucracy, as well as congressional hearings (open and executive session) designed to probe into government programs.[14] Hearings provide an important opportunity for lawmakers to practice accountability. In hearings they are able to pose questions that solicit information regarding the faithfulness of bureaucrats to the norms of lawful behavior, efficiency, attentiveness to congressional prerogatives, and congruence with the traditions and expectations of legislative review.

Of significance in the conduct of legislative review is the attitude of the committee chair. Like other members but with more authority to set the tone and direction for a committee, the chair can play the role of critic or advocate, or a combination of both. In Hamilton's view, properly conducted accountability relies on lawmakers behaving as both "partners and critics."[15] Criticism is warranted because bureaucrats are human and, therefore, fallible; so is advocacy because bureaucrats, like everyone else, need encouragement and praise. Advocacy occurs, too, because lawmakers often believe in the value of the programs they supervise and thus empathize with those in the executive branch who must carry out the policies established by Congress—sometimes in trying circumstances, such as gathering intelligence in hostile areas of the world.

At the heart of any discussion of accountability lies the question of how well it is performed. At one extreme, one can imagine (though based on conclusions in the research literature, it is difficult) a stalwart lawmaker fully devoted to a close inspection of executive branch programs that fall within the bailiwick of his or her oversight committee. This overseer would direct a well-qualified staff in day-to-day monitoring activities; would rarely miss an oversight hearing; would ask probing (i.e., hardball) questions, while at the same time offering praise when warranted; would introduce thoughtful legislation to correct and improve policy deficiencies; would require strict adherence to reporting requirements established to keep Congress informed; would tirelessly and skeptically investigate charges—even rumors—of power abuse; and would report regularly to home constituents and the broader public about the state of accountability within the specific policy domain, offering in public a critical eye or a pat on the back as the agency merited.

At the opposite extreme (more easily imagined) a slack overseer would view accountability as chiefly an annoying drain on a lawmaker's time and energy more profitably spent on less obscure activities that might aid reelection prospects, such as authoring legislation, championing interest group objectives, and raising campaign funds; would fill staff slots guided more by considerations of patronage than expertise; would seldom attend oversight hearings and, if in attendance, would float softball questions destined for the center field fence; would simply advocate an agency's point of view and lavishly fund its programs without serious evaluation; would turn the other way when bureaucrats ignored reporting deadlines; would rely on an agency's inspector general and managers to curb, or at least respond to, scandals and policy failures; and would see no need to keep the public informed about matters of accountability.

Research across the policy board, and certainly within the domain of intelligence, indicates that the slacker's approach has predominated. John Bibby referred to oversight as Congress's "neglected function."[16] Morris Ogul found oversight more intermittent than comprehensive and systematic.[17] And an intelligence scholar concluded recently that oversight was "an aptly chosen figure of speech."[18]

From Overlook to Oversight

The subject of intelligence provides an opportunity to explore in detail the dynamics of congressional oversight within an important policy domain. In this analysis, the term *intelligence* refers to America's fifteen major secret agencies and the myriad activities they carry out.[19] These activities are traditionally clustered into three prominent missions: collection and analysis, counterintelligence, and covert action.[20]

Collection and analysis is a phrase meant to capture, first, the modus operandi or tradecraft employed by intelligence officers and their agents (i.e., assets), as well as the use of machines (e.g., satellites, piloted and drone reconnaissance aircraft, listening and sensing devices), to gather information from around the world for the purpose of illuminating decision options available to policymakers; and, second, the insight brought to this raw information by trained experts or analysts. *Counterintelligence* refers to the methods used by intelligence agencies to protect their information and operations against hostile states and organizations. Examples of counterintelligence methods include using a polygraph test (i.e., fluttering) on CIA recruits to test their allegiance to the United States or the penetration of a foreign intelligence service with a mole to determine from the inside the extent of the other nation's spying against the United States. Covert action includes secret operations—propaganda, along with political, economic, and paramilitary activities—tailored to disrupt adversaries and, to the extent possible, to shape history in America's favor, say, by assassinating a foreign leader perceived as dangerous to the global interests and security of the United States or overthrowing the government of a hostile foreign regime.

For most of the nation's history, America's intelligence operations enjoyed an exceptional detachment from the normal strictures of legislative accountability.[21] In the prevailing view, intelligence activities demanded such tight secrecy that it was better to leave the hidden side of government to the supervision of the president and his national security team. Congress initiated a modicum of accountability in 1947 when lawmakers created the CIA and small congressional subcommittees to review intelligence budgets and programs, but these subcommittees met infrequently and were inclined to support whatever programs the director of central intelligence (DCI) recommended. An occasional intelligence flap, like the Bay of Pigs fiasco (1961) or dubious CIA ties to American student groups (1966), would stir calls in Congress for less desultory approaches to accountability, yet proposals for the establishment of full-blown oversight committees for intelligence continued to languish, unable to attract a majority vote in either chamber—that is, until the mid-1970s.

In the final months of 1974, the *New York Times* published a series of reports on alleged intelligence misconduct, most notably spying on American citizens—Vietnam war dissenters—and questionable covert action against the democratically elected regime of Salvador Allende in Chile, who was suspected of Marxist inclinations and worrisome ties to Moscow. It was one thing to have the Bay of Pigs operation blow up in Cuba and quite another to be caught spying at home, raising the fear of a Gestapo within the United States. Had the *Times* only revealed the covert action in Chile, the CIA might have slipped by again with only a few complaints from selected lawmakers and perhaps the reintroduction by Senator Mike Mansfield (D, Montana, who had risen to the position of majority leader) of his oft-proposed bill to create a standing committee on intelligence in the Senate. For most lawmakers, domestic espionage—spying on voters—was, however, a much more deeply troubling allegation, one that could not be easily dismissed. Here was a five-alarm fire, and, in January of 1975, the engines revved up on Capitol Hill, with most lawmakers clamoring aboard and hanging on as Congress sped off to put out the flames.

Shock as a Stimulus for Intelligence Oversight, 1975–2004

Thirty years have passed since Congress began taking intelligence accountability more seriously in 1975. Since then lawmakers have devoted approximately six years of time to intensive, retrospective, or firefighting investigations into intelligence controversies, as outlined in this section. The remaining twenty-four years, or 80 percent of the total, consisted of periods of patrolling characterized by varying degrees of intensity among overseers, with some of the patrolling highly intensive in the immediate aftermath of fires but mostly of low intensity. During this era, the domestic spy scandal revealed in late 1974 was the first intelligence alarm of sufficient shrillness to bring about a major congressional response. Several more alarms would follow in the coming decades.

When the first alarm sounded over the domestic spy scandal in 1974, Congress established House and Senate investigative committees, called the Pike and Church panels, respectively. They discovered extensive spying at home by the CIA, the FBI, the National Security Agency, and the Defense Intelligence Agency. The Church Committee issued massive reports critical of assassination plots and domestic intelligence operations, plus it recommended the creation of a permanent oversight committee in the Senate; the Pike Committee blasted the poor quality of intelligence analysis over the years.[22]

Alarm number 2, in 1987, was the Iran-Contra Scandal. In response to this, Congress established a joint investigating panel called the Inouye-Hamilton Committee, which exposed unlawful intelligence activities by the staff of the National Security Council (NSC) and the CIA, and issued a detailed report on executive branch intelligence violations of the law.[23]

In response to alarm number 3, the Ames counterintelligence failure in 1994, Congress insisted on a joint executive–legislative probe, the Aspin-Brown Commission, into the Aldrich H. Ames spy case, whereby the Soviet Union had proved able to recruit an American agent high within the CIA.[24]

The fourth alarm sounded with the September 11, 2001, attacks. The failure of the intelligence agencies to warn the nation about the most catastrophic foreign attack ever against the American homeland led Congress to form a joint committee of inquiry, the Graham-Porter Committee, and subsequently to urge the creation of a presidential investigative panel, the Kean Commission, in part comprised of former legislative intelligence overseers, to further examine the issue. The House Intelligence Oversight Committee also established a special inquiry into the inadequacies of CIA human intelligence, especially in the Middle East and southwest Asia.

When in 2003 it was revealed that no weapons of mass destruction (WMD) were found in Iraq, alarm number 5 sounded. In light of an erroneous national intelligence prediction in October 2002 about the likely presence of weapons of mass destruction in Iraq, Congress supported the creation of another presidential commission, the Silberman-Robb panel, to investigate the analytic failure. Moreover, the Senate Intelligence Oversight Committee undertook a special inquiry of its own into the faulty WMD estimate.

Table 7.1 Type of Stimulus and Intelligence Oversight and Response by U.S. Lawmakers, 1975–2005

Year	Stimulus	Oversight Response	Purpose of Response
1974	Fire alarm #1 (domestic spying)	Hughes-Ryan Act	Controls on covert action
1976–77	Fire alarm #1 (domestic spying)	Established oversight committees, critical reports	More robust oversight
1978	Fire alarm #1 (domestic spying)	FISA[a]	Warrants for electronic surveillance
1980	Fire alarm #1 (domestic spying)	Intelligence Oversight Act	Tighten oversight rules
1983	Patrolling	Intelligence Identities Act	Protect intelligence officers/agents
1989	Fire alarm #2 (Iran-Contra)	Inspector General Act	Improve internal CIA oversight
1991	Fire alarm #2 (Iran-Contra)	Intelligence Oversight Act	Further tighten oversight rules
1996	Fire alarm #3 (Ames)	Established director of central intelligence assistants, critical reports	Intelligence community management improvements
2001	Fire alarm #4 (9/11)	Patriot Act; authorization of war against Al-Qaeda and Taliban regime; increases in counterterrorism funding	Surveillance of suspected terrorists; paramilitary attacks against Al-Qaeda and Taliban
2004	Fire alarm #4 (9/11)	Critical reports	Improve human intelligence and analysis
2004	Fire alarm #4 (9/11) and fire alarm #5 (weapons of mass destruction in Iraq)	Intelligence Reform and Terrorism Prevention Act	Strengthen intelligence community coordination

[a]FISA = Foreign Intelligence Surveillance Act (P.L. 95-511; 92 Stat. 1783 [Oct. 25, 1978]).

As indicated by the findings in Table 7.1, Congress produced several key legislative proposals related to intelligence during this time span. Of the ten major initiatives shown in the table, only one occurred outside the context of a major fire-alarm response. That single exception, the Intelligence Identities Act of 1983, was the result of a conclusion reached by lawmakers (at the CIA's urging) that a law was necessary to provide stiff penalties against anyone who revealed without proper authorization the name of a U.S. intelligence officer or asset. The rest of the oversight initiatives were the result of inquiries and the stage of intense patrolling that followed fire alarms.

Some of the initiatives, such as the Intelligence Accountability Act of 1980, took a considerable amount of time for the Congress to craft—four years in this case. In this instance, some lawmakers originally hoped to pass an intelligence charter, over 270 pages long, designed to provide a broad legal framework for the secret agencies. Their intention was to construct an omnibus accountability law to replace the out-of-date language of the 1947 National Security Act. This sweeping measure attracted many dissenters, however, and the bold charter proposal ultimately gave way under the weight of effective CIA lobbying to a three-page bill. The much shorter law still had teeth, though, and required, among other provisions, the director of central intelligence to report to Congress in advance on all important intelligence activities.[25] The president could delay reporting in extraordinary circumstances, but only for a maximum of two days.

The Frequency of Intense Intelligence Accountability

The most important intelligence wake-up call for lawmakers in the period before the formal creation of the CIA and America's modern intelligence community in 1947 was the Japanese attack against Pearl Harbor on December 7, 1941. The intelligence portions of the National Security Act of 1947 were a delayed response to that intelligence failure, coupled with a growing concern about a new threat to the United States: the rise of the Soviet Union as a global rival, steered by a Marxist philosophy anathema to America's espousal of market-based democracies.[26]

Following the establishment of the intelligence community, several low-threshold fire alarms sounded during the early years of the Cold War. Among the most notable were the failure to predict the outbreak of war on the Korean peninsula (1950), the Bay of Pigs disaster (1961), the controversy over CIA ties to the National Student Association and other domestic groups (1966), and an alleged CIA connection to the Watergate burglars (1973).[27] None of these alarms was as shattering as the subsequent high-threshold shocks delivered by the domestic spy scandal, Iran-Contra affair, the Ames case, the 9/11 attacks, or the mistaken WMD report that helped fuel an American war in Iraq in 2003. With the possible exception of the Ames case, these fire alarms caught the attention of Americans across the nation, which in turn caused lawmakers to focus on the events; the Ames case certainly sounded an alarm among national security officials inside the D.C. Beltway.

Members of Congress may well have reacted sharply to the Iran-Contra scandal even if the public had not taken an interest, since it amounted to an insulting disregard for the congressional appropriations process. Prior to the scandal, a Democratic-led Congress rebuffed the efforts of the Reagan administration to fund covert action in Nicaragua; as a result, the NSC staff resorted to raising private funds as a means for carrying out covert action in Nicaragua, despite the Boland Amendments,[28] which strictly prohibited such operations against the ruling Sandinista regime. Lawmakers reacted strongly as well to the Ames counterintelligence case, since a Soviet penetration at the highest levels of the CIA—the worst counterintelligence failure in American history—was difficult to disregard, striking as it did at the heart of the Agency's mandate in the 1947 National Security Act to protect "sources and methods."[29]

In contrast to these high-threshold alarms, Korea in 1950 and the Bay of Pigs in 1961—though obviously disconcerting—dealt with matters outside the United States. The CIA–student and CIA–Watergate flaps occurred at home, but the former came across as a fairly narrow issue involving agency support for U.S. students attending international conferences, and the latter proved to have little substance. One of the men implicated in the Watergate burglary, E. Howard Hunt, was a former CIA officer who had requested a wig and other disguise paraphernalia from the agency's directorate of science and technology for the infamous break-in. But investigations showed that the CIA had not realized the purpose of Hunt's request and had no prior knowledge of the plot.

An examination of the frequency of both low- and high-threshold alarms (see Fig. 7.2) discloses the periodicity of intelligence scandals in the modern era.[30] Eliminating the CIA–Watergate scandal, in reality an insignificant

Year	**1941**	1950	1961	1966	1973	**1974**	**1987**	1994	2001	2003
Alarm	F	F	F	S	S	S	S	F	F	F
Interval/Yrs. Ave.: 7.6*		9	11	5	7	1	13	7	7	2

The Events: The Thresholds:

1941—Pearl Harbor attack   High
1950—Outbreak of war on Korean peninsula   Low
1961—Bay of Pigs   Low
1966—CIA–National Student Association scandal   Low
1973—CIA–Watergate scandal   Low
1974—Domestic spying scandal   High
1987—Iran-Contra scandal   High
1994—Ames counterintelligence failure   High
2001—9/11 attacks   High
2003—Faulty WMD analysis (Iraq)   High

*excluding the CIA–Watergate case (see text)

Fig. 7.2 The frequency of low- and high-threshold intelligence alarms, 1941–2004. (with high-threshold in bold). Abbreviations: F = failure of collection and/or analysis; S = scandal or impropriety; WMD = weapons of mass destruction.

matter, an intelligence alarm sounded roughly every seven and one-half years, on average. The longest gap—twice the average—occurred between the domestic spying scandal exposed in 1974 and the Iran-Contra Affair exposed in 1987: a total of thirteen years. The domestic spying scandal and the ensuing investigations were especially traumatic to the intelligence agencies; intelligence officers still remember 1975 as the Year of the Intelligence Wars: *annus horribilis*. The investigations established a new standard of ethics for the intelligence agencies that may have reduced the incidence of improper behavior by intelligence officers over the next decade. This good record came to an end as the Reagan administration's obsession with Nicaragua led the NSC staff to misuse the government's secret agencies and even to develop their own new secret agency, the "enterprise," in an attempt to destroy the Sandinista regime.

The briefest interlude between alarms occurred from 2001 to 2003, with the Iraqi WMD error coming quickly on the heels of the 9/11 failure—a double blow to the reputation of the CIA and the reason for its dramatic decline in 2004–05 as America's premier intelligence agency. Now the CIA is just one of the fifteen agencies in the intelligence community and no longer as central—a job given by the Intelligence Reform and Terrorism Prevention Act of 2004 to the new director of national intelligence. In June 2005, the White House informed the director of the CIA he no longer would be a regular attendee at NSC meetings.[31]

The conclusions presented here about the periodic inattentiveness of lawmakers as patrollers should not overshadow the fact that intelligence oversight since 1975 has been vastly more robust than "in the good old days," as some mossback intelligence professionals recall the years from 1947–74 when Congress left the secret agencies largely to their own devices. Intelligence overseers since 1975 have benefited greatly from two standing intelligence oversight committees, the Senate Select Committee on Intelligence (SSCI) and the House Permanent Select Committee on Intelligence (HPSCI), along with budget and subpoena powers. The authority of these two panels goes far beyond the powers enjoyed by any other legislative chamber in the world, today or in the past. Moreover, whereas lawmakers have been less than fully engaged in patrolling, they have been dedicated—even aggressive—firefighters.

Even during the more quotidian periods since 1975, the staffs of the intelligence committees, consisting of some fifty to seventy individuals who are often well educated and experienced, have regularly queried intelligence professionals about their activities, have pored over annual budget requests line by line, have visited intelligence installations at home and abroad, and have prepared detailed briefing books for the use of committee members during hearings. Very little of this kind of persistent staff work was carried out before 1975, underscoring the profound effect of the domestic spying scandal of 1974 and the sixteen-month-long Church and Pike Committee investigations, which were the most extensive probes into the operations of the intelligence agencies, even more comprehensive than the Aspin-Brown or Kean inquiries in 1995 and 2004, respectively.

Intelligence Failures and Scandals

A salient aspect of the findings presented here is the contrast between intelligence failures and scandals. Intelligence failures are frequently inadvertent, resulting from the lack of a well-placed agent, a surveillance satellite in the wrong orbit, an intercepted telephone conversation not translated quickly enough into English, or an analyst who makes an honest and well-intended but faulty judgment, perhaps because of inexperience. Of course, a CIA officer might also be lazy, an agent might be doubled, or an analyst might be poorly trained. Often as not, though, failures happen as a result of human fallibility. Mistakes in the prediction of world events are, in a word, inevitable.[32] This condition can be mitigated to some degree by improving a nation's capacity to gather reliable information from around the globe, say, by building more sophisticated spy satellites or reconnaissance airplanes; however, the chances of failure can never be eliminated. The future is an unknown place, shrouded in fog.

Through the expenditure of over $40 billion a year on intelligence, the United States attempts to pierce as much of the fog as possible; nevertheless, the world will never be fully transparent. The planet is too large, and adversaries are too cunning at hiding their activities, whether planning attacks against the United States from remote caves in Afghanistan or constructing atomic bombs in deep underground caverns in North Korea. Further, some things are simply unknowable in advance: mysteries, as opposed to secrets that might be stolen from a safe. An example of a mystery is the question of who will follow Vladimir Putin as the next Russian president. When failures to find out secrets occur, as with the war in Korea in 1950 and WMD in Iraq in 2003, the United States inevitably takes measures to improve its collection and analysis; still, new and unexpected threats are bound to rise somewhere in the world.

Scandals and improprieties, in contrast to failures, are usually intentional. Someone breaks a law, a regulation, or a standard operating procedure to achieve a goal. The violator hopes not to be discovered and may be convinced anyway that the importance of the goal trumps all other considerations. When called on to explain why they had broken the law during the Iran-Contra affair, NSC staffers from the Reagan administration said they were responding to a "higher law" requiring them to fight communism in Central America, even if Congress had foolishly passed the Boland Amendments.[33]

In theory at least, intelligence scandals could be eliminated by recruiting only virtuous people for high office: men and women who would never succumb to illegal spying on U.S. citizens, flaunting laws like the Boland Amendments, infiltrating and subsidizing student groups and other organizations in American society, providing disguises to former intelligence officers without checking on the purpose, or lying to congressional overseers, as happened during the Iran-Contra affair.[34] Yet scandals are as much an existential inevitability as collection and analytic failures. Indeed, the entire rationale for accountability presented by Madison in *Federalist Paper 51* rests on the supposition—confirmed every day—that humans are not angels. They will make mistakes and they will sin. So with respect to failures and scandals within the intelligence—or any other government—domain, one can anticipate more of both.

At the same time, though, a nation can take steps to decrease the odds of mistakes and wrongdoing by improving its intelligence collection-and-analysis capabilities, by carefully recruiting men and women of high integrity, and by steadfastly patrolling the secret agencies in search of incipient gaps in performance and signs of flaws in the human character, such as Ames's abuse of alcohol and luxury spending beyond a CIA officer's government salary. That is why oversight patrolling is so important: ideally, one would like to nip trouble in the bud, whether failure or scandal. Implicit in the notion of accountability is the hope that a few more elected eyes available to examine policy initiatives from the vantage point of Capitol Hill, not just the White House, will help discover perhaps—there is no guarantee—problems before they lead to catastrophes.

After the 9/11 terrorist attacks, lawmakers lamented their inattention to intelligence oversight duties. "We didn't understand ... the need for human intelligence," conceded SSCI overseer Mike DeWine (R, Ohio). "We simply did not provide the resources."[35] Bob Graham (D, Florida), SSCI chair and cochair of the joint committee investigation into the 9/11 intelligence failure, said, "We probably didn't shake the [intelligence] agencies hard enough after the end of the Berlin Wall to say: 'Hey, look, the world is changing and you need to change the way in which you operate ... new strategies, new personnel, new culture.' We should have been more demanding of these intelligence agencies."[36] The HPSCI chair at the time, Porter Goss (R, Florida), who served as the other cochair of the joint committee inquiry, issued a separate report by the House Committee in 2004 that was scathing in its criticism of CIA human intelligence.

What if these lawmakers and their colleagues had been sufficiently exercised about such intelligence deficiencies in the years preceding September 11, 2001? The attacks might have been discovered in advance with better human intelligence, faster translation of communications intercepts from Al-Qaeda plotters, and sharper analysis.

In 1995, a top-secret memo that is now partially declassified came from the CIA's Counterterrorism Center (CTC) to the Aspin-Brown Commission. It warned that "aerial terrorism seems likely at some point—filling an airplane with explosives and dive-bombing a target."[37] This warning appeared in the *President's Daily Brief*, delivered by the CIA to President Bill Clinton and his top national security advisers, and the agency briefed members of SSCI and

HPSCI about this hair-raising possibility as well.[38] Yet six years before the prediction became a reality, none of these policymakers took any significant steps to alert U.S. commercial pilots to the danger, to urge the FBI to watch flight training schools, or to tighten airport security.[39]

When Bush replaced Clinton as president, the White House counterterrorism expert Richard A. Clarke, as well as the Counterterrorism Center, provided fresh warnings to the new national security adviser, Condoleezza Rice (as well as, again, to members of SSCI and HPSCI), that Al-Qaeda might resort to aerial terrorism and other methods of attacking the United States. The Bush administration temporized from January to September 2001, and the congressional oversight committees also did little to improve America's defenses against an aerial attack by terrorists.[40] The 9/11 tragedy was an intelligence failure to be sure. But it was a policy failure as well, in the White House during both Democratic and Republican administrations, and it was a failure of accountability on Capitol Hill.

A Congressional Oversight Agenda for Intelligence

To lessen the chance of failure and scandal (however impossible the ideal of completely eliminating both), contemporary congressional overseers and their aides on SSCI and HIPSCI face a demanding agenda. Of foremost importance is greater devotion to police patrolling instead of waiting for fire alarms to sound, which in the closed world of intelligence are unlikely to erupt until a major scandal or disaster strikes. Lawmakers need to pay closer attention to an administration's threat assessments, as the mistakes related to the Iraq threat in 2003 attest; to its balance between human and technical collection; to its data-mining capabilities; to the perspicacity of its analytic reports; to charges of politicization; and to efforts to achieve institutional and computer integration to enhance the sharing of intelligence from all sources at the federal level of government (i.e., horizontal), as well as down to the state and local levels (i.e., vertical).

Truly meaningful oversight would also give closer scrutiny to covert action, especially with respect to the beguiling assassination option, and to questionable efforts by the Department of Defense to develop its own capabilities in this area. One would expect to see, too, a renewed focus on counterintelligence: appraising the merits of an MI5-like unit in the United States, reviewing the effectiveness of barriers against another Ames, and building protections against hostile electronic penetrations of new interagency computer-integration systems.

Among other issues needing a closer examination are the merits of providing the director of national intelligence with greater authority so as to overcome the powerful centrifugal forces that exist in the U.S. intelligence community. On the civil liberties side, lawmakers must also revisit the flawed Patriot Act, the procedures of the Foreign Intelligence Surveillance Court—which failed in the months preceding the 9/11 attacks—and the rights of law-abiding Muslim Americans. The latter face the danger of being lumped together, by virtue of religion and skin color, with suspected Al-Qaeda operatives.

Continuing Barriers to Effective Intelligence Oversight
Success in addressing the intelligence oversight agenda in Congress will depend above all on the motivation of SSCI and HPSCI members. Since the creation of these committees in 1976 and 1977, respectively, their members have already outperformed their marginally engaged predecessors from 1947–74, and their staffs are larger by a factor of thirty or so. Even so, the efforts of the two panels fall short of full engagement at the member level, and even the best of staffs cannot compensate for lawmakers who treat their oversight responsibilities as a secondary concern, although a few lawmakers over the years have been deeply committed to effective oversight.[41] Neither SSCI nor HPSCI managed to sniff out the Iran-Contra operation, the weakened counterintelligence posture that allowed the acts of treason by Ames and others,[42] the poor human intelligence prior to the 9/11 attacks, or the misleading WMD analysis that provided a rationale for the war against Iraq in 2003. Eternal vigilance is the price of liberty, according to Irish attorney John Philpot Curran's enduring counsel.[43] Similarly, eternal vigilance by SSCI and HPSCI members is the price of successful intelligence accountability.

Lawmakers must really want to be effective overseers, or else the safeguards extolled by the founders are doomed to failure. This will require building into the congressional culture better incentives to encourage attention to the duties of intelligence accountability. Incentives could include prestigious awards presented by the congressional leadership and civic groups to leading overseers, Capitol Hill perks dispensed by the leadership based on the devotion of lawmakers to oversight duties, and publicity in national and hometown newspapers underscoring admirable oversight accomplishments by individual members.

Membership motivation is, however, only half of the equation for success. The other half is executive branch cooperation in the quest for improved intelligence accountability. A common term of derision among intelligence professionals and White House officials toward SSCI and HPSCI members is *micromanagers*—the accusation that lawmakers and their staffs are meddlers likely to harm sensitive intelligence operations. Former president George Bush recently referred in the *Los Angeles Times* to the members and staff of the Church and Pike Committees of 1975 as "untutored little jerks."[44] A series of *Wall Street Journal* op-ed pieces in 2003 placed the blame for the 9/11 and WMD intelligence failures on legislative overseers and the damage they have caused by their probes into the operations of the intelligence agencies. These critics evidently wish to turn the clock back to the pre-1975 era, when oversight was weak and the intelligence agencies slipped into domestic spying and other questionable, and often illegal, activities.

If the executive branch insists on viewing lawmakers as "an outside interference," as the nation's national security adviser, Vice Admiral John M. Poindexter referred to Congress during the planning of the Iran-Contra operations,[45] then overseers will be cut off from the information they need to properly evaluate intelligence programs. The end result will be an intelligence community more and more isolated from any semblance of checks and balances and increasingly likely to present the nation with its next major intelligence scandal or failure. When Congress attempted to investigate the 9/11 failure, the White House, the director of central intelligence, and various intelligence officers sought to delay and obstruct the work of the joint committee.[46] Stonewalling and slow-rolling are prime enemies of accountability and the form of government envisioned by Madison and the other founders. The essence of genuine oversight is an attitude of comity between the branches, as executive officials and lawmakers join together to weed out inept and improper government activities.

Over and above strengthening its intelligence oversight agenda and developing an interbranch consensus about the value of cooperative accountability, the Congress must also put its own house in order with respect to a sensible division of labor for intelligence oversight. Presently, the tangled jurisdictional lines for accountability over the secret agencies make the Gordian knot look like a simple bowline. In addition to SSCI and HPSCI, the Committees on Armed Services, Judiciary, and Appropriations all have a claim on intelligence review. This list needs to be reduced to SSCI, HPSCI, and the appropriations committees, with the latter closely adhering to the budget ceilings and priorities of the authorizing committees rather than ignoring the work of the two intelligence committees, as is frequently the case today.[47] Along with the creation of attractive oversight incentives for lawmakers, nothing is more vital for improved intelligence accountability on Capitol Hill than the correction of this current jurisdictional chaos.

Conclusion

Intelligence accountability since 1975 has been infinitely more serious than before that watershed year; still, it is nowhere near as effective as it can and should be if the United States hopes to reduce the odds of another major intelligence scandal or failure in the future. In place of the sporadic patrolling and ad hoc responses to fire alarms, lawmakers and their staffs need to redouble their commitment to a continuous, week-in/week-out scrutiny of intelligence activities, praising meritorious operations, suggesting ways to improve new or faltering programs, and rooting out improper initiatives and miscreant officials before they lead to full-blown disasters that harm the nation's security and good reputation. For this to work, the public will need to acquire a better understanding and appreciation of accountability. Scholars, journalists, and public officials must engage in more effective public diplomacy to educate Americans about the value of oversight carried out by members of Congress.

None of this will be easy. Yet as America's founders understood, the virtue of democracy lies not in its ease but in its promise to protect the people against the abuse of power—perhaps most especially secret power.

Notes

1. Merle Miller, *Plain Speaking: An Oral Biography of Harry S. Truman* (New York: Berkley, 973), 420.
2. See Alexander Hamilton, John Jay, and James Madison, *The Federalist*, (New York: Modern Library, 1941), no. 10, 53–62, no. 51, 335–37; and Thomas Jefferson, "Draft of the Kentucky Resolutions" (October 1978), in *Jefferson* ed. A. Koch and W. Peden (New York: Library of America, 1984), 455. For classic modern statements of the framers' views, see *Myers v. United States*, 272 U.S. 52 293 (1926); and Richard E. Neustadt, *Presidential Power* (New York: Wiley, 1960).
3. Edward S. Corwin, *The President: Office and Powers* (New York: New York University Press, 1957); Louis Fisher, *Constitutional Conflicts between Congress and the President* (Princeton, NJ: Princeton University Press, 1985); Michael J. Glennon, *Constitutional Democracy* (Princeton, NJ: Princeton University Press, 1990); Louis Henkin, *Foreign Affairs and the Constitution* (New York: Norton, 1972); Loch K. Johnson, *America's Secret Power: The CIA in a Democratic Society* (New York: Oxford University Press, 1989); Harold Hongju Koh, *The National Security Constitution: Sharing Power after the Iran-Contra Affair* (New Haven, CT: Yale University Press, 1990); Daniel S. Papp, Loch K. Johnson, and John E. Endicott, *American Foreign Policy: History, Politics, and Policy* (New York: Pearson Longman, 2005).
4. M. D. McCubbins and T. Schwartz, "Congressional Oversight Overlooked: Police Patrols and Fire Alarms," *American Journal of Political Science* 28 (1984), 165–79.
5. Harry H. Ransom, "Secret Intelligence Agencies and Congress," *Society* 123 (1975), 33–8.
6. Donald Mayhew, *The Electoral Connection* (New Haven, CT: Yale University Press, 1974).
7. Loch K. Johnson, "Accountability and America's Secret Foreign Policy: Keeping a Legislative Eye on the Central Intelligence Agency," *Foreign Policy Analysis* 1 (2005), 99–120.
8. James Sterling Young, *The Washington Community, 1800–1828* (New York: Columbia University Press, 1966).
9. Hamilton, Jay, and Madison, *The Federalist*, no. 10.
10. *Myers v. United States*, 272, U.S. 52 293.
11. Joel D. Aberbach, *Keeping a Watchful Eye: The Politics of Congressional Oversight* (Washington, DC: Brookings Institution, 1990), 2.
12. Lee H. Hamilton and Jordan Tama, *A Creative Tension: The Foreign Policy Roles of the President and Congress* (Washington, DC: Woodrow Wilson Center Press, 2002), 56.
13. Wyche Fowler (senator, Georgia), interview by author, May 9, 2003, Washington, D.C.
14. See, for example, Aberbach, *Keeping a Watchful Eye*.
15. Quoted by F. Davies, "GOP-Controlled Senate Expected to Give Less Scrutiny to War on Terror," *Miami Herald*, November 7, 2002, A1.
16. John F. Bibby, "Congress' Neglected Function," in *The Republican Papers*, ed. Melvin R. Laird (New York: Anchor, 1968), 477–88.
17. Morris S. Ogul, *Congress Oversees the Bureaucracy: Studies in Legislative Supervision* (Pittsburgh: University of Pittsburgh Press, 1976).
18. William H. Jackson, Jr., "Book Review," *Intelligence and National Security* 5 (1990), 254.
19. See Mark M. Lowenthal, *U.S. Intelligence: Evolution and Anatomy*, 2nd ed. (Westport, CT: Praeger, 2003).
20. Johnson, *Secret Agencies: U.S. Intelligence in a Hostile World* (New Haven, CT: Yale University Press, 1996).
21. Gregory F. Treverton, "Intelligence: Welcome to the American Government," in *A Question of Balance: The President, the Congress, and Foreign Policy*, ed. Thomas E. Mann (Washington, DC: Brookings Institution, 1990), 70–108.
22. For the Church Committee Report, see Select Committee to Study Governmental Operations with Respect to Intelligence Activities, *Final Report*, 94th Cong., 2nd Sess., Sen. Rept.

No. 94-755, 6 vols (Washington, DC: Government Printing Office, March 1976). The Pike Committee Report was leaked and published as "The CIA Report the President Doesn't Want You to Read: The Pike Papers," *Village Voice*, February 16 and 23, 1976, 69–92. For an overview of these investigations, see Loch K. Johnson, *A Season of Inquiry: The Senate Intelligence Investigation* (Lexington: University Press of Kentucky, 1985); and Frank J. Smist, Jr., *Congress Oversees the United States Intelligence Community, 1947–1989* (Knoxville: University of Tennessee Press, 1991).

23. U.S. Congress, Report on the Iran-Contra Affair, Senate Select Committee on Secret Military Assistance to Iran and the Nicaraguan Opposition and House Select Committee to Investigate Covert Arms Transactions with Iran, Sen. Rept. 100-216 and House Rept. 100-433 (November 1987). For an overview, see William S. Cohen and George J. Mitchell, *Men of Zeal: A Candid Inside Story of the Iran-Contra Hearings* (New York: Viking, 1988).

24. Loch K. Johnson, "The Aspin-Brown Intelligence Inquiry: Behind the Closed Doors of a Blue Ribbon Commission," *Studies in Intelligence* 48 (Winter 2004), 1–20. On the specifics of the Ames case, see David Wise, *Nightmover* (New York: Harper Collins, 1995).

25. Intelligence Oversight Act, 94 Stat. 1981, Title IV, Sec. 501, 50 U.S.C. 413.

26. Rhodri Jeffreys-Jones, "Why Was the CIA Established in 1947?" in *Eternal Vigilance? 50 Years of the CIA*, ed. Jeffreys-Jones and Christopher Andrew (London: Cass, 1997), 20–41; and Loch K. Johnson, "A Central Intelligence System: Truman's Dream Deferred," *American Journal of Intelligence* 21 (Winter 2005), 16–36.

27. Johnson, *America's Secret Power*, op. cit., 4, 94, 102.

28. Sections 106 and 107 of Public Law 99-569 (Intelligence Authorization Act for Fiscal Year 1987); see Permanent Select Committee on Intelligence, *Compilation of Intelligence Laws and Related Laws and Executive Orders of Interest to the National Intelligence Community*, U.S. House of Representatives, 104th Cong., 1st Sess. (July 1995), 739–41.

29. PL 235-61 Stat. 496; USC 402.

30. This analysis does not attempt to include every intelligence failure—that list is much longer (see Johnson, *Secret Agencies*, XX)—but it does include the most significant. Not everyone will agree with the choices. For example, some believe the CIA's failure to predict the fall of the USSR represents its most significant analytic error. I believe this set the bar too high: none could, or did, predict that epic event with any accuracy. The CIA's Soviet analysts (SOVA), however, did a remarkable job of tracking the decline of the Soviet economy during the 1980s and suggesting that this could lead to marked political upheaval in Russia and beyond (Johnson, *Secret Agencies*, XX). The excellence of this tracking is why the surprise of the Soviet fall is not included here.

31. Timothy J. Burger, "A New White House Memo Excludes CIA Director," *Time*, June 5, 2005, 21.

32. See Richard K. Betts, "Analysis, War, and Decision: Why Intelligence Failures Are Inevitable," *World Politics* 31 (October 1978), 61–89.

33. See Cohen and Mitchell, *Men of Zeal*, 136.

34. Cohen and Mitchell, *Men of Zeal*, 137.

35. Senator Mike DeWine (R, Ohio), interviewed by Wolf Blitzer, *CNN News*, CNN, October 14, 2002; see, also, Kevin Whitelaw and David E. Kaplan, "Don't Ask, Don't Tell," *U.S. News & World Report* 137, September 13, 2004, 36.

36. Senator Bob Graham (D, Florida), interviewed by Jim Lehrer, *Lehrer News Hour*, PBS, October 17, 2002.

37. Johnson, "The Aspin-Brown Intelligence Inquiry," 12.

38. Seven senior officials in the Clinton Administration and four members of SSCI and HPSCI, interviewed by author (with assurances of anonymity) March 1995, Washington, D.C.

39. The 9/11 Commission Report, *Final Report of the National Commission on Terrorist Attacks upon the United States* (New York: W.W. Norton, 2004).

40. Richard A. Clark, *Against All Enemies* (New York: Free Press, 2004).

41. Johnson, *America's Secret Power*, 207–33.

42. In addition to Wise, *Nightmover*, see John Barron, *Breaking the Ring* (Boston: Houghton Mifflin, 1987); and David Wise, *Spy: The Inside Story of How the FBI's Robert Hanssen Betrayed America* (New York: Random House, 2002).

43. "Speech upon the Right of Election," 1790, John Bartlett, *Familiar Quotations*, 10th ed. (Boston: Little, Brown, 1919), 10431.

44. Quoted in Bob Drogin, "Spy Agencies Fear Some Applicants Are Terrorists," *Los Angeles Times,* March 8, 2005, A1.
45. U.S. Congress, vol. 8, 159.
46. U.S. Congress, Joint Inquiry into the September 11 Terrorist Attacks, *Final Report* (2003).
47. Whitelaw and Kaplan, "Don't Ask, Don't Tell," *U.S. News & World Report* 137, 36.

8

American Policy toward Enemy Detainees in the War on Terrorism

DAVID P. FORSYTHE[1]

The United States has long identified itself as a champion of human rights and the rule of law. The founding fathers, children of the enlightenment and believers in the rights of man, articulated a commitment to certain inalienable rights that would form the basis of a new politics. To early Americans, the new United States was to be a city on a hill, a beacon to others about how to respect individual freedom and dignity within the U.S. polity. The expanding United States was to represent an empire of liberty. American exceptionalism, a sense of an exceptionally good people devising an exceptionally good polity based on personal rights, was born along with the republic and has been carefully nurtured ever since.[2]

With growing American power came a growing activism to supposedly promote human rights and democracy abroad, not just by the more passive and isolationist example of perfecting American society at home. This became, at least in theory, the U.S. central mission in the world.[3] And so in the Spanish–American war William McKinley identified the United States with liberation against imperialism. U.S. involvement in World War I was justified by Woodrow Wilson in terms of advancing global democracy. World War II was presented by Franklin D. Roosevelt (FDR) at home in terms of four freedoms and abroad as the nations united for freedom against European fascism and Asian militarism. Cold War presidents stressed the free world containing, if not rolling back, oppressive communism.

The semantics of both foreign and domestic policy have often stressed commitment to human freedom based on civil and political rights under law as the very definition of what it means to be American. This abstract, theoretical, or semantic identification has the status of secular religion within the United States.

American exceptionalism, centered on civil and political rights, has always been as much rhetoric as reality. Many, if not most, of the founding fathers owned slaves, and many, if not most, of them were slow to abandon slavery as an institution. The United States was one of the last nations in the Western

Hemisphere to give up the practice, along the way contesting particularly the British attempt to end first the African slave trade and then slavery itself. Blatant and pervasive discrimination against African Americans continued into the 1960s, especially in the south.

The American idea of manifest destiny in North America was built on the practice of, at the very least, ethnic cleansing, if not genocide, for Native Americans. Women were discriminated against politically until the 1920s and in other ways after that. Advocates for labor rights were vigorously opposed and sometimes bloodily repressed. There was much bias and discrimination against immigrants from various places (southern Europe, Asia, Central America) at different times in different ways. Catholics and Jews were often the targets of Protestant abuse, presaging discrimination against many Muslims in modern times. The racist Ku Klux Klan had a national, mass membership well into the twentieth century, directing their hate speech and hate crimes not only at African Americans but also Jews and Catholics. The Cold War brought McCarthyism and its major attacks on civil liberties and political tolerance. Gays are the current targets of much bias, especially from religious conservatives.

To some, to compare the American rhetoric on law and rights with the reality of various repressive and oppressive American policies suggests a hypocritical streak rarely matched by other countries. To others, given the real rights and freedoms the government has supported, this comparison suggests a striving to overcome blemishes to move toward an ideal rarely approximated by other countries.[4]

Moreover, especially in times of perceived insecurity, human rights usually suffer.[5] If truth is the first casualty of war, violation of civil rights runs a close second. During the American civil war habeas corpus was suspended. During the First World War, Americans of German descent, German-speaking schools, and German language newspapers all were victimized to varying degrees. Many who were not of German ancestry also suffered when they dissented from Wilson's policies.[6] During the Second World War the official repression of Japanese Americans, some of them with relatives serving in the U.S. military, is well known. We have already noted McCarthyism during the Cold War. Hard feelings over dissent during the Vietnam War are also well known: The 2004 presidential race featuring John Kerry showed that intolerance of dissent, even from failed policies, remains widespread.

The contrast between the rhetoric and reality of American nationalism, and the point that American nationalism usually manifests a dark side during times of perceived insecurity, sets the frame for a discussion of U.S. foreign policy after the terrorist attacks of September 11, 2001. This study focuses on U.S. policy toward enemy detainees. The subject has been of great concern particularly in the Islamic world and for human rights advocates in the United States, even if the public and much of the Congress have been largely—but not entirely—quiescent on the matter, at least until Fall 2005.

To what extent has the U.S. rhetorical commitment to human rights under law impacted U.S. policy toward supposed enemy prisoners in places like Guantanamo Bay, Afghanistan, Iraq, secret detention centers, and various countries to which U.S.-held prisoners have been rendered? To what extent have the 1949 Geneva Conventions for Victims of War and the UN Convention Against Torture and Degrading Treatment been respected by U.S. authorities? On this subject do we find anything but the usual gap between rhetoric and reality in U.S. policy? Do we find anything but the usual assault on human rights during times of national insecurity? Given, as will be shown, that intentional prisoner abuse did occur, could the George W. Bush administration sustain this policy in the face of considerable criticism?

The Relevance of History: The French Case

Many Americans—some in high positions in government—with their ahistorical tendencies have seen the world as beginning a new age after September 11, 2001: the age of terrorism. The Al-Qaeda terrorist attacks supposedly ushered in a new, all-consuming struggle between those civilized and those otherwise. But just as the contemporary U.S. talk about imposing democracy and human rights by force was reminiscent of past rationales for European imperialism,[7] so U.S. counterterrorism policies were reminiscent of particularly French policies in Algeria.

Ernest Renan wrote that "historical error [is] an essential factor in the formation of a nation ..."; even more to the point is Eric Hobsbawm's paraphrasing: "Nationalism requires too much belief in what is patently not so."[8] This point is relevant not just to those American ultranationalists who sincerely believe in American exceptionalism. It is also relevant to the fact that most Americans have forgotten, if they ever knew, the pertinent history of the nationalism of others when fighting terrorism. On the subject of enemy detainees it is particularly French history that merits brief address—specifically French torture in the Algerian war. One searches in vain for U.S. policymakers and leading media personalities who refer to this history in the U.S. war on terrorism. But Bush policy is very similar to French policy from 1954 to 1962, for similar reasons and with similar, though not identical, results.

Relevant historians know the French–Algerian war was one of terror and torture, with atrocities committed on both sides. As for the French, struggling to hold their colony and rationalizing their role under their global civilizing mission, they did what they thought necessary to defend noble national interest. For General Paul Aussaresses, his role was clear, and he had no regrets.[9]

> What I did in Algeria was undertaken for my country in good faith, even though I didn't enjoy it. One must never regret anything accomplished in the line of duty one believes in ... [O]nce a county demands that its army fight an enemy who is using terror ... it becomes impossible

for that army to avoid using extreme measures. "Just think for a moment that you are personally opposed to torture as a matter of principle and that you have arrested a suspect who is clearly involved in preparing a violent attack. The suspect refuses to talk. You choose not to insist. Then the attack takes place and it's extremely bloody. What explanation will you give to the victim's parents, the parents of a child, for instance, whose body was torn to pieces by the bomb, to justify the fact that you didn't use every method available to force the suspect into talking.

Some important results of this position are poignantly captured by Jean-Paul Sartre:[10]

> But now when we raise our heads and look into the mirror we see an unfamiliar and hideous reflection: ourselves. Appalled, the French are discovering this terrible truth: that if nothing can protect a nation against itself, neither its traditions nor its loyalties nor its laws ... then its behaviour is not more than a matter of opportunity and occasion ... Happy are those who died without ever having to ask themselves: 'If they tear out my fingernails, will I talk?' But even happier are others, barely out of their childhood, who have not had to ask themselves that other question: 'If my friends, fellow soldiers, and leaders tear out an enemy's fingernails in my presence, what will I do?"
>
> Suddenly, stupor turns to despair: if patriotism has to precipitate us into dishonour, if there is no precipice of inhumanity over which nations and men will not throw themselves, then, why, in fact, do we go to so much trouble to become, or to remain, men? Inhumanity is what we really want. But if this really is the truth, if we must either terrorise or die ourselves by terror, why do we go to such lengths to live and to be patriots?"

So the democratic French, who had greatly contributed to the theory and practice of human rights, used torture. And because they had tortured, they could not put their enemies on trial, so they summarily executed them. And because they tried to sweep all this under the rug for many years, they lost much of their self-respect, as well as the respect of many others, starting with the Arab–Islamic world. Torture may have helped the French win the battle of Algiers, but they lost much in many other respects.

Bush policy replicates much of this French experience.

The Reality of Bush Policy

There are two schools of thought about the usefulness of torture and mistreatment of enemy prisoners.[11] It is impossible for an outside analyst to know which is correct. The first view holds that abuse can lead to valuable information, citing such things as the French in the battle of Algiers. The second view holds that abuse is unreliable and counterproductive, inferior to establishing rapport between interrogator and prisoner leading to valuable information over time. The first view has many adherents in the Central Intelligence Agency (CIA) and the military special operations units, among other circles. The second view is officially supported by the uniformed military and their military manuals. If the second view is correct, then there would be no use for the first one, even if on occasion it worked.

On this question, from the beginning of the U.S. war on terrorism, President Bush and his closest advisors (and their lawyers) Vice President Dick Cheney, Secretary of Defense Donald Rumsfeld, and Legal Counsel Alberto Gonzales opted for abusive over humane interrogation. They were backstopped by lawyers principally in the Justice Department. State Department officials and those from the National Security Council (NSC), including even NSC Advisor Condoleezza Rice, were apparently shunted aside early in deliberations. So were many uniformed lawyers in the Department of Defense. All of the lawyers centrally involved were civilian political appointees,[12] and they may have engaged in the unethical practice of advising their clients how to violate the law.[13]

The Bush administration, declaring a metaphorical *war* implying that the usual legal restraints and checks and balances did not apply, abused many enemy detainees. This was presaged by Cheney's statement on September 12, 2001: "We also have to work, though, sort of the dark side, if you wish. We've got to spend time in the shadows ... so it's going to be vital for us to use any means at our disposal, basically, to achieve our objectives."[14] Cofer Black, formerly of the CIA, told Congress, "After 9/11, the gloves came off."[15]

Like General Aussaresses, this inner circle deemed coercive interrogation necessary to the national interest—to prevent another attack on the homeland and later to get actionable intelligence for places like Afghanistan and Iraq. Partly driving the process was a righteous indignation that the virtuous United States had been attacked by terrorists with no morals who fought a total war involving attacks on innocent civilians.[16]

Vitiating Legal Restraint

The first step in the process was to vitiate law that might interfere with coercive interrogation, as well as to give legal cover to U.S. officials engaged in abuse.[17] This involved first the assertion that international humanitarian law (IHL), principally the 1949 Geneva Conventions for Victims of War (GCs), did not pertain to anyone held at the U.S. naval base at Guantanamo Bay, Cuba. The base was chosen as a holding and interrogation center in the hopes that U.S. courts would not assert jurisdiction over events there—it being leased from Cuba in perpetuity.[18] This assertion sought to deny those fighting for the Taliban government of Afghanistan, as well as any others detained by reason of the multifaceted armed conflict in that country, the legal protections of IHL.[19] This U.S. view clearly contradicts the plain meaning of the GCs, which apply to all situations of armed conflict. The widespread nonrecognition of the Taliban government makes no difference. Particularly, GCs 3 and 4 apply in whole or in part after U.S. attacks commenced, with GC 3 pertaining to combatants and GC 4 to civilians. The issue is not simply who is a prisoner of war (POW) under GC 3, for even those who do not qualify as a POW or privileged combatant but who are detained in connection to armed conflict retain various degrees of protected status under IHL.[20] Even illegal or irregular combatants merit certain minimal protections. The Bush administration also refused to allow an independent court to make determinations about such legal status, as called for by GC 3.[21]

Second, the Bush team sought to redefine provisions of the UN Convention Against Torture and Degrading Treatment so as to make that treaty, which is legally applicable in both peace and war, meaningless. For example, the prohibition on intentional infliction of severe pain, whether physical or mental, was said to mean that short of something like organ failure, torture did not exist. Or, as a second example, that same wording was held to mean that if an interrogator did not intend to cause severe pain, the existence of such pain would not block the abuse.[22] Though eventually these erroneous positions were rescinded when made public and criticized, the original objective was patently clear. The official attitude toward this treaty against torture and degrading treatment was that it had no intrinsic meaning: it only meant whatever the government said.[23]

Third, memos were written arguing that in times of war the president had unlimited authority to protect the nation and that even national laws did not necessarily always apply.[24]

Fourth, the decision was taken to "disappear" certain persons. That is, U.S. authorities held them in secret places but did not acknowledge detaining them, thus preventing in a practical sense any law applying to them. The Bush team displayed exceptional control over the information pertaining to such persons.[25]

Fifth, certain persons were rendered to foreign jurisdictions like Egypt, which is known for harsh interrogation practices, under the fig leaf that assurances had been obtained regarding prohibition of improper interrogation.[26] Apparently the Bush administration accelerated, rather than initiated, this policy, which prevented U.S. courts from exercising any jurisdiction under U.S. law.[27]

Various changes or additions to some of these early positions occurred over time. In Iraq after the invasion of March 2003, the Bush administration agreed that an international armed conflict and then occupation existed, to which IHL applied.

Still, consistent with the view permeating the Bush administration that international law and organization had no intrinsic value, and moreover were often used to restrain a virtuous United States,[28] there was a determined effort to minimize obligations under IHL, international human rights law, and U.S. law. The emphasis was on the unrestricted exercise of executive branch power, which by definition was seen as good. For many Bush officials—excepting parts of the State Department and the Judge Advocate General (JAG) division of the Pentagon—reference to law was to construct a certain image and to provide lower officials a certain legal defense,[29] while getting on with the violation of international standards protecting human dignity.

Instituting Coercive Interrogation

The initial flow of information from Gitmo under Brigadier General Rick Baccus and Major General Michael Dunleavey was deemed by Rumsfeld to be insufficient, so Major General Geoffrey Miller was dispatched to change things. Even though Rumsfeld issued, modified, and reissued a list of different categories of interrogation techniques that pertained to U.S. military personnel,[30] other instructions were no doubt issued by the CIA, and still others by the Federal Bureau of Investigation (FBI). There were reports that intelligence agents from certain foreign governments were also part of Gitmo interrogations. For the United States, Gitmo's primary use was for intelligence gathering and secondarily as a holding facility. Initially the question of legal prosecutions was marginal to Washington, until U.S. courts began to enter the fray.

Regardless of what exactly Rumsfeld may have intended, which was probably highly coercive interrogation for a limited group of prisoners with supposedly high intelligence value, certainly during 2002–04 at Gitmo a number of prisoners were abused. This we know from an International Committee of the Red Cross (ICRC) report leaked probably by dissidents within the U.S. executive branch, from released FBI memos obtained under the Freedom of Information Act, and from a U.S. interrogator who wrote a book about his experiences there.[31] Eventually there were also the claims of released prisoners.[32]

Some prisoners were sexually and religiously taunted and humiliated. They were restrained in painful positions. They were subjected to extremes of heat and cold. They were subjected to loud music or other noises, as well as to flashing lights. They were kept in isolation for long periods. They were force fed liquids and then made to urinate on themselves. They were also made to defecate on themselves. They were intimidated by military police dogs. In short, they were given the torture-lite treatment, which more or less the Israelis had practiced against Palestinian detainees for a considerable time in the Middle East and which the British had used for a time against members of the Irish Provisional Authority in Northern Ireland.[33] The process was such that both FBI and CIA agents sought to distance themselves from it, lest they be held legally responsible. The CIA might have been doing something similar in other places, but the agency did not want to be tagged for the abuses at

Gitmo.³⁴ In addition, some prisoners were physically beaten and otherwise abused by U.S. military police in actions that did not seem to be approved by military intelligence or higher authorities.³⁵

In Iraq from spring 2003, the U.S. invading forces found themselves with large numbers of detainees and also a persistent and violent insurgency against their presence. The poor management of prisoner affairs was part of a bungled occupation.³⁶ In that situation General Miller was transferred from Gitmo to Iraq in August to systematize and improve the quest for intelligence. One U.S. report said the U.S. treatment of Iraqi prisoners "migrated" from Gitmo; another such report said it did not.³⁷ Either way, certain prisoners were hidden from the visits of the ICRC and were kept in darkened isolation in an effort to break them into giving more information. As usual, abuse also occurred by troops in the field at the point of capture, especially by U.S. special operations forces trained to act outside the bounds of conventional warfare. This abuse was such that the CIA distanced itself from it.³⁸ The U.S. central command for Iraq, headed by Lieutenant-General Ricardo Sanchez, was never staffed and organized properly, which allowed the egregious abuses of Iraqi detainees to occur that became infamous in 2004 with the release of unauthorized photographs of improper treatment. Sanchez also explicitly authorized certain abusive techniques, as well as pressing subordinates for more actionable intelligence from prisoners.³⁹ In Iraq some of the prisoner abuse proved fatal, unlike Gitmo—as far as we know.

In Afghanistan from 2001, there were persistent reports of prisoner abuse.⁴⁰ As in Iraq, in Afghanistan some of the abuse proved fatal. Eventually the U.S. military reported investigations into some thirty deaths while in U.S. custody in both Iraq and Afghanistan. A lower-ranking reservist who admitted to fatal abuse and was convicted for it claimed he had been trained to do it and that supervising officers did not object to it.⁴¹ Released prisoners articulated the usual complaints—namely, about the same sorts of confinement in painful positions and other techniques used at Gitmo.⁴²

All of this coercive interrogation constituted a violation of IHL and also of the UN Convention Against Torture—the latter as well as the former prohibiting degrading treatment, or torture lite, as well as torture heavy. It violated the Uniform Code of Military Justice, based as that was on IHL. And it probably violated various tenets of U.S. constitutional law, particularly the 8th Amendment prohibiting cruel and unusual punishment, although U.S. courts have yet to so rule.⁴³

Covering Rhetoric, Reactive Policies
Early on, Bush sought to provide reassuring rhetoric about treatment of enemy detainees, but this was patently meaningless. He said that such prisoners would be treated humanely, in keeping with the principles of the GCs, but only insofar as "military necessity" permitted.⁴⁴ So obviously humane

treatment could be overridden on the basis of what U.S. leaders might deem military necessity.[45]

Other administration statements over time reiterated the theme of humane treatment that ruled out torture. But aside from withdrawing the more extreme assertions about the definition of torture,[46] the administration refused to say exactly what constituted torture or that torture lite was off limits.[47] Bush officials simply refused to address the fact that torture lite in the form of degrading treatment was also prohibited by international law. At times administration spokespersons simply avoided the truth, as when the Pentagon denied abuse at Gitmo, saying detainees were treated humanely and properly even when the reliable ICRC and other overwhelming evidence clearly indicated otherwise.[48] When in 2005 it became clear that abuse was part of the interrogation of the presumed twentieth hijacker, Mohamed al-Kahtani of Saudi Arabia, Rumsfeld did not deny the nature of the process but rather said that the process was closely monitored by specialists.[49] So the argument was that the process of coercive interrogation existed but was limited and controlled. Since it was presumably torture lite instead of torture heavy, then presumably it was legitimate. It was also presumably legitimate because it was yielding lifesaving information, or so it was said. Such arguments were more about political legitimacy than legality.

Still further, the process of disappearing persons or turning them into ghost detainees continued, as well as the policy of rendering persons to interrogators in places like Uzbekistan and Egypt, inter alia. One can understand the nature of interrogation in such places by looking at the State Department's annual human rights reports, which find repeatedly that torture and other abuse of prisoners is systematic in those states. There would be no point in having such policies if prisoners were to be treated humanely, in conformity with legal obligations. A legal and fully humane approach would not require disappearance or rendition. It is in the context of disappearances that there have been reports of water boarding, of making a prisoner think he will drown for his refusal to say what interrogators want. This certainly would qualify as torture heavy.[50]

At Gitmo and in Afghanistan and Iraq, the U.S. military brought criminal proceedings against a variety of individuals. Most of those charged were distinctly toward the bottom of the military hierarchy. There were some administrative sanctions, including of some higher officers. One brigadier general in the reserves, Janis Karpinski, nominally in charge of the infamous Abu Ghraib prison in Iraq, was demoted. Also sanctioned was Colonel Thomas Papas, despite his statement that he was pressured by superiors to get tougher with detainees in Iraq.[51] When the policy of coercive interrogation went out of bounds, then the United States brought charges or levied sanctions against its own military personnel. The role and fate of private interrogators under contract, or agents of the CIA and FBI, is not known for sure.

At the same time, the administration made sure the spotlight of inquiry did not proceed very far up the chain of command. After the photos surfaced regarding abuse at Abu Ghraib, several investigations were commissioned, mostly about Iraq. The military inquiries were carefully structured to fragment foci and to avoid review of the Office of the Secretary of Defense, and of course of the White House. The one so-called independent panel, made up of former members of the national security establishment like James Schlesinger, former secretary of defense, did find personal and institutional responsibility for prisoner abuse at high levels but refused to name names.[52] The follow-on report by Vice Admiral Albert Church III remained classified. A released summary cleared all high-ranking military officials in Iraq of any responsibility for abuse of prisoners.[53] Members of the Schlesinger panel did not vigorously protest.

No one beyond General Karpinski and Colonel Thomas Papas was held responsible for any sins of omission or neglect regarding Iraq. No high officer was held responsible for the conscious hiding of prisoners or for keeping them in inhumane conditions. General Miller, a major player regarding both Gitmo and prisons in Iraq, was cleared of any responsibility for events by Admiral Church. Lieutenant-General Sanchez, head of all military operations in Iraq, under the doctrine of command responsibility should have known what was occurring by way of unauthorized brutality and humiliation. At one point authorized harsh interrogation including the use of dogs to intimidate. He was said to be under consideration for further promotion.[54]

Others key in developing U.S. policy toward enemy detainees were advanced by Bush. Gonzales was nominated for attorney general. Jay B. Bybee, a Justice Department lawyer who had written some of the early, permissive memos, was nominated as a federal judge for the important Ninth Circuit Court of Appeals. William J. Haynes II, a Pentagon lawyer who had approved some of the early, permissive memos, was nominated to the Fourth Circuit Court of Appeals. Rumsfeld's two letters of resignation were not accepted.

Domestic Reaction

By and large, American society and the Republican majority in both houses of Congress did not want to delve deeply into the Bush policy toward enemy detainees until 2005. As Sartre noted back in the 1950s, it is disturbing to face the question of what to do when co-nationals are in favor of pulling out fingernails or something similar to it. It is painful to directly confront how much abuse of individuals is justified by attempts to protect the nation.

No sizable grassroots public movement arose in protest, which is not surprising. Even in the face of genocide, the American public has not roused itself to demand a proper response for its foreign policy officials.[55] After all, the country—including civilians—had been attacked. A free society has a dark side: the public is preoccupied with individual things such as family, jobs, schools, health care, and pensions.[56]

Congressional Republicans, likewise caught up in the nationalistic reaction to 9/11, were also reluctant to provide critical oversight of a Republican president. A few hearings were held, but military officials dissembled, tough questions were not asked, and issues were swept under the congressional rug.[57] Gonzales was confirmed as attorney general, despite his efforts to undermine much law. Because of the damage he had done to IHL, he was opposed by a number of high-ranking military officials. He said in his confirmation hearings that U.S. law against torture did not cover U.S. officials when interrogating foreign detainees outside the United States. Bybee was confirmed to sit on the ninth circuit appellate bench.

As time passed and American support for the war in Iraq waned, as American enthusiasm for the occupation there declined, and as the president's approval ratings on several issues fell, some members of Congress—including a few Republicans—began to speak about closing Gitmo and about other prisoner issues. There was thus some unease about detention policies among some Republicans as well as Democrats. But without divided government, and given Republican party loyalty, congressional review of the treatment of enemy detainees was anything but muscular. By 2005, enough Republicans joined Democrats to write a prohibition on coercive interrogation into the defense spending bill.[58] The Bush administration, having fought successfully a similar provision earlier,[59] yielded this time around. But when Senator Richard Durbin (D, Indiana), author of this legislation, said publicly that U.S. treatment of enemy detainees was similar to Nazi practice, he was so vigorously attacked by the administration and congressional Republicans that he was forced to apologize.[60] When certain Republican senators sought to ensure humane interrogation via further legislation, they were strongly opposed by the administration, with Cheney playing a leading role.[61]

Some members of Congress visited Gitmo, as if a short, scheduled visit would prove anything. Moreover, one interpreter claimed that some interrogations had been staged in the past when members of Congress were visiting.[62]

The *New York Times,* the one element of the national media that did the most to try to keep a critical focus on the issue, ran several prominent stories, not to mention editorializing against the relevant Bush policies. But the newspaper has little clout with the Bush administration or Republicans in Congress. It was also important that the *Wall Street Journal* and the *Financial Times,* two conservative papers, published leaked prison reports and ran stories on the ICRC and prisoner issues. But much of this was supportive of the Bush policies and critical of those interested in the human dignity and rights of enemy detainees.[63]

Liberal interest groups, like the American Civil Liberties Union (ACLU), played important roles by using the Freedom of Information Act to get important documents into the public domain, such as the FBI memos expressing concern about harsh military interrogation at Gitmo.⁶⁴ But, again, the ACLU has little influence in Republican policymaking circles or in that sizable part of public opinion that is conservative and highly nationalistic. It was also important that certain JAG lawyers, concerned about disrespect for IHL, which after all is supposed to protect U.S. military personnel when detained by others, expressed their concerns to Scott Horton, head of the New York City Bar Association, Committee on International Human Rights, who then directed several trenchant studies,⁶⁵ as well as engaging in public commentary in important media outlets such as the *Jim Lehrer News Hour* on PBS.

The problem for critics, especially in the Democratic Party, was that they did not control the congressional oversight and budgetary process. Moreover, in elections, particularly the 2004 presidential campaign, they did not want to appear soft on national security issues or to have to articulate an alternative policy to the one put in place by the Bush administration. So in that presidential race, Democrats did not raise the topic of treatment of enemy detainees in any central way.

Within the nation, a full and open debate only took place about U.S. policy and enemy detainees beginning in 2005. The subject was politically dangerous in an era of virulent nationalism, as Durbin found out. And even when members of Congress did focus on Gitmo, they did not usually discuss disappearances or renditions.

In this political context, U.S. courts slowly and gingerly stepped into the controversy, holding first that they did have jurisdiction over events at Gitmo, then that habeas corpus did obtain. In this legal climate the administration stalled, fighting on every legal point. The Bush team also slowly moved toward the use of military commissions to try "enemy combatants" in highly controversial procedures. Vigorous defense of prisoners by their lawyers again caused the process to move slowly, in fits and starts. Like in the federal courts, the military commissions had resolved very little at the time of this writing.⁶⁶

International Reaction and the ICRC

Needless to say, Bush policy toward enemy detainees contributed to a highly negative reaction in the Arab–Islamic world, among virtually all European publics, and in other circles already alarmed by the prospect of unchecked U.S. power.⁶⁷ Certain insurgents in Iraq were carrying reproductions of the Abu Ghraib pictures of abuse when they were apprehended, which is clear evidence that widespread knowledge of prisoner mistreatment made the U.S. role in the world more difficult.⁶⁸

At the same time, the British, Swedish, and certain other governments also engaged in rendition,⁶⁹ probably allowed secret prisons and may have cooperated in abusive interrogation at Gitmo. So there was a certain governmental sympathy for U.S. policy, whatever publics might think.

The UN system reacted in various ways on this topic, especially through its independent or nongovernmental or uninstructed personnel, but without much impact on the Bush administration, predisposed as it was to dismiss most UN initiatives that interfered with desired policies.[70] As a general rule, UN criticism of Washington is taken less seriously than congressional criticism or U.S. court action.

The UN high commissioner for human rights made a number of statements about U.S. treatment of enemy detainees, whether via Mary Robinson, Bertie Ramcharan, or Louise Arbour. None of these statements seemed to have any impact on Washington.

A group of UN human rights experts, related either to monitoring bodies of particular treaties or to the UN Human Rights Commission or to its subcommission, expressed concern about the reports of abuse at Gitmo, Afghanistan, and Iraq. From 2004 they requested that certain UN human rights experts be allowed to visit especially Gitmo. Washington refused to allow a serious visit that included prisoner interviews.[71]

International human rights group played important roles in keeping the issue alive. It is impossible to track all nongovernmental organization activity related to this subject, but some examples can be given. Particularly important as a thorough record was a long and detailed report by Amnesty International in November 2004.[72] Amnesty's 2005 annual report led to much controversy, stemming in part from its use of the word *gulag* to refer to Gitmo. These semantics both brought publicity to the issue but also allowed the Bush administration and its friends to deflect the debate away from its policies and toward Amnesty's judgment and reliability.

Human Rights Watch (HRW) also produced many reports on U.S. policy, including a major report about U.S. command responsibility for prisoner mistreatment.[73] The group repeatedly called for an independent inquiry into the subject, given the limits and weaknesses of both DOD reports and congressional oversight. Although congressional commentary picked up by 2005, at the time of writing no truly independent study had been allowed by the Bush team.

The Center for Constitutional Rights teamed with some former detainees at Gitmo to bring charges in a German court under the principle of universal jurisdiction. The defendants were Secretary of Defense Rumsfeld and others. German authorities dismissed the suit.

All of this nongovernmental organization activity, when linked to media reports and congressional actions, may have generated some pressure on the Bush administration to restrict the scope of coercive interrogation at U.S. military facilities.[74] However, disappearances and renditions continued, and by 2005 perhaps 150 persons were targeted in the latter program.

The one organization outside the U.S. government that knows in detail what is occurring at Gitmo and in Afghanistan and Iraq, but not in the U.S. secret detention centers, is the ICRC.[75] This founding agency of the International Red Cross and Red Crescent Movement focuses exclusively on armed conflict and internal unrest. It has a mandate to engage in humanitarian protection, which includes protecting the human dignity of prisoners in war and unrest. Under GCs 3 and 4, it has a right to visit detainees in international armed conflict, in order to observe and comment on whether IHL is being properly implemented. It has a right to offer its services in civil wars and domestic unrest, in which case the visitation process can be almost the same as in international wars.

Exactly what it is doing, how, and with what success is difficult to say. In its humanitarian work since 1863, ICRC prides itself on its independence, neutrality, and impartiality. These guiding standards do not preclude public comment, but discretion is its preferred mode of operation. Its basic approach to violations of human dignity is not covered in IHL but is spelled out in one of its doctrines, or general policy statements, no. 15, first articulated in 1981 and refined in 2005.[76] It normally does not make public comment about the details of what its delegates observe, since in its view this confidentially promotes access and trust and leads over time to positive developments. It may share detailed information confidentially with certain third parties in the quest for humanitarian improvements. It may make public statements and even public denunciations if discreet diplomacy does not yield significant progress over time and if such publicity is judged to be in the interest of the victims themselves. Other doctrines, such as no. 58, allow ICRC to make public comment for other reasons, such as to correct partial or inaccurate reports about its role.

The Bush administration, though resisting the application of IHL to Gitmo, did nevertheless allow an essentially permanent presence there by the ICRC from early 2002. Why this happened is not at all clear, because also during 2002 the Bush team began implementing a policy of abusive interrogation that violated the relevant international standards. It may be that Washington wanted to give a humanitarian gloss to an inhumane policy, anticipating that under the preferred confidentiality of the organization it could safely ignore any inconvenient comments. After all, ICRC has been present in Israel and the occupied territories since 1967, yet a certain Israeli abuse of Palestinian detainees is well known, at least until the 1999 Israeli Supreme Court ruling that prohibited what that same court had allowed—namely, "moderate" physical and psychological pressure, or torture lite.[77] Or it may be that Washington wanted ICRC to serve as an independent auditor for its policy of limited and controlled abuse, telling Washington when things were going out of control but not seriously interfering with the interrogation of high-value prisoners. After all, if the administration got good marks on most issues, would not the organization stay silent about a few rough edges? Or it may be that Washington only progressively moved toward systematic prisoner abuse at Gitmo during the course of 2002, not having fully decided on that policy when the first permission to visit was granted to ICRC.[78]

The ICRC did not agree that IHL was inapplicable to at least some of the Gitmo detainees,[79] but consistent with its preferred policies it did not engage in protracted and acerbic legal debate in public, especially since it was active on the ground at Gitmo on practical matters of humanitarian protection.

In May 2003, the ICRC went public about the deleterious effect of indefinite detention without prospect of charge or trial at Gitmo. It did so in a fairly low-key way, which is typical of the organization, posting a statement on its Web site and allowing the head of its Washington office to eventually give an interview to the *New York Times* repeating what had been posted online. Over thirty Gitmo detainees had attempted suicide, given their despair. Despite the fact that the United States was the largest donor to the ICRC budget and had been for some time, providing about 28 percent of the wherewithal for ICRC operations around the world in 2004–05, this fact did not affect the policy of the organization on this issue. Nor had donor status affected ICRC support for the Ottawa Treaty banning antipersonal land mines, which the United States opposed.

We now know that during the period from 2002–04, the ICRC lodged numerous private protests about certain U.S. policies at Gitmo, involving such things as the treatment of detainees under the age of 18, the lack of prayer mats and Korans, the abuse of Korans by interrogators, the sexual humiliation of prisoners, the use of medical records by interrogation teams, which constituted a violation of medical ethics, and other U.S. actions that in some cases were tantamount to torture. At times the ICRC was prevented from seeing some detainees.[80] On some issues ICRC representatives on the scene judged the policies serious enough to warrant a temporary suspension of visits, although no public statement was made.[81]

We also know that ICRC president Jacob Kellenberger went to Washington several times and met with high Bush officials, as well as the president himself in February 2005, to discuss Gitmo (and Afghanistan and other subjects). Kellenberger also involved himself with Gitmo and other IHL issues with the U.S. diplomatic mission in Geneva. So high-level ICRC diplomacy was trying to effectuate change in keeping with international norms for human dignity.

What we do not know is the exact Gitmo balance sheet of improvements and remaining problems. And we do not know the details of the ICRC cost-benefit analysis about staying or leaving with a public protest. We think we know that reports about abuse of the Koran stopped as of mid-2003. We think we know that use of sexual humiliation by female interrogators, wearing provocative clothing and pretending to smear menstrual blood on prisoners, also stopped at some point—perhaps because it simply was not working. We think we know that by 2005 Gitmo was mostly a holding center, with very little new interrogation going on at all.

We certainly do not know if ICRC asked the Gitmo detainees if it should stay or go with a protest. The organization sometimes poses this question to prisoners. If they want ICRC to continue with confidential visits, which give the prisoner a sole contact with the outside world, the ICRC can hardly do otherwise—even if humanitarian progress is slight to nonexistent.

Contrary to the assumptions of some observers, some beneficial change has occurred at Gitmo over time, stimulated by ICRC quiet diplomacy. We just do not know exactly how much. Kellenberger said in a press conference in 2005 that at Gitmo the organization had achieved progress on some issues, although all of its requests had not been met by U.S. authorities.[82] This type of mixed record is usually enough for ICRC to continue with its discreet diplomacy, at least where it can see some important progress. It takes a lot to make ICRC lodge a public, specific protest and walk away. The organization is very cautious, following the advice of Nelson Mandela, who told the ICRC not to suspend its visits to Robben Island, because then the agency would not be in a position to prevent the bad that might occur if it left. And if ICRC does leave Gitmo, it has used up the last arrow in its quiver and has put itself on the sidelines, which also causes it to lose its comparative advantage over other human rights and humanitarian agencies—its direct contact with victims inside countries. Complicating matters is the global role of ICRC. Would speaking out about Gitmo jeopardize ICRC access to prisoners in other countries? ICRC headquarters takes this kind of calculation into account, but we do not know the details of the process.

In Iraq, where the United States accepted the application of IHL in general, the process of prison visits was not that different from Gitmo. ICRC headquarters in Baghdad, having been attacked in early fall 2003 and previously experiencing a staff member intentionally killed, brought in its visitation teams from Jordan for limited time spans. This created some problems, particularly delays in obtaining relevant information. Interestingly, Geneva decided that the progress achieved by late fall 2003 was greater than in either Gitmo or Afghanistan. This was partially because much of the abuse at Abu Ghraib was unauthorized by higher authorities, even if in reality they were negligent about proper planning and supervision. So U.S. authorities in Iraq did not resist some of the changes demanded by ICRC. But there were intentional policies of abuse also, such as the CIA disappearing persons, most of whom were abused in one way or the other and at least one of whom died in captivity.[83] Also, there was slow U.S. action at times in response to ICRC reports, and on at least one occasion a U.S. officer proposed that ICRC visits be announced in advance so as to not interfere with coercive interrogation.[84]

This being so, some ICRC officials in both Iraq and Geneva wanted more than quiet suspension of ongoing visits; they wanted a strong public protest. But once again Geneva, after much debate, decided in favor of discretion. A leaked ICRC report about Iraq, published in the *Wall Street Journal,* did not come from ICRC sources but probably from dissidents within the U.S. executive branch. And even a certain faulty follow-up to ICRC reports by U.S.

authorities in fall 2003 did not occasion a radical change of plan by Geneva.[85] By the time of Kellenberger's meetings with such officials as Bush, Rice, and Rumsfeld in February 2005, Gitmo and Afghanistan, rather than Iraq, were the top agenda items. Many of the changes in Iraq were of course produced by the infamous pictures that circulated about Abu Ghraib—and not because of ICRC confidential reports. Nevertheless, as at Gitmo, a certain progressive change took place over time, perhaps more so in Iraq than at Gitmo on these humanitarian questions. In both places, as the ICRC had reported privately, most of the detainees were non-political. Thus, eventually a number of releases occurred.

In Afghanistan, numerous credible reports surfaced of detainees being abused while in U.S. captivity, whether at the Bagram or Khandahar military bases or at regional bases or a smaller holding centers. Somewhere around twenty fatal cases of prisoner abuse were being investigated at the time of this writing. From the beginning, it was clear that ICRC did not have immediate access to all detainees in all detention facilities. U.S. prisoner policy in Afghanistan was a subject of high-level ICRC diplomacy with U.S. leaders on several occasions.

Summing Up

On the one hand, some U.S. policy after 9/11 toward enemy detainees was more humane than French policy in the Algerian war. At least in military installations, the United States authorized torture lite rather than torture heavy. It coerced and abused a sizable percentage of those prisoners, but it did not pull out fingernails as a matter of military policy and then use summary executions to dispose of the incriminating evidence. It is not clear what policies were applied to the disappeared in secret locales, and when prisoners were rendered to other states. Torture heavy was more likely there. The United States, like France in the past, was faced with what to do with abused prisoners; they could not be put on trial and be allowed to testify about their conditions of detention.

On the other hand, the United States gravely damaged its reputation as champion of human rights, humanitarian norms, and the rule of law, just as was true for the French 1954–62. The United States, just as France, has gravely undermined its own standing in global attempts to legally protect human dignity. The driving calculation was the same—namely, the "necessity" of protecting a superior nation.

The next time the U.S. government engages in quiet diplomacy toward another state about torture, it could possibly be similar to when a British diplomat talked to a Nazi official about the German concentration camps. The Nazi pulled off his shelf an account of the British concentration camps in the Boer War, in which almost 30,000 persons died, mainly women and children[86]—end of discussion.

But the American polity shows little inclination to do what HRW has called for: create a special prosecutor or special commission to examine the origins of prisoner abuse at highest levels, military and civilian, to correct the impunity now existing for such officials. This investigation of high policymakers, as Sartre noted long ago, is agonizing and requires great courage. The French were not up to it, and neither are the Americans most probably. As a perceptive journalist has concluded, the public and Congress have agreed, "The less we know as a people about secret counterterrorism struggles and strategies, [and] the less we contemplate the possibly ugly consequences, the easier it will be for those in authority to get on with the job of protecting us."[87]

The necessity of protecting the group trumps legal standards for protecting human dignity. At least it seems that high policymakers intended to limit the necessary abuse, although that policy was badly articulated and managed. The abuse spread widely. And at times it was torture heavy, with fatalities as proof.

American nationalism after 9/11 has been less intolerant than some periods in American history—the Wilson and McCarthy eras quickly come to mind. But perhaps that is because there has been little open, vigorous debate and dissent yet about Bush security policies. Given this lack of serious domestic debate, at least until late 2005, the Bush administration has been able to sustain its policy of torture lite, even if it has had to clean up detention practices in military facilities a bit. Official debate and review of disappearances and renditions remain mostly absent. International criticism has been much less important than domestic factors, although the role of ICRC is not without importance.

The situation is not totally new, not only by comparison to France in Algeria. During the Cold War, the United States then too spoke of freedom and human rights and the rule of law but acted in the shadows to overthrow elected governments and to back murderous allies in places like Chile (1973) and Guatemala (1954). But at some point the hypocrisy of it all will severely trouble when we look in the mirror. The French can tell us about that.

Notes

1. The author would like to thank the following for comments on earlier drafts: Richard Bilder, Mel Gurtov, Ole Holsti, Patrice McMahon, Andrew Wedeman, Karen Mingst, and Michael Schechter.
2. For the tip of the iceberg on this subject see Anatol Lieven, *America Right or Wrong: An Anatomy of American Nationalism* (Oxford: Oxford University Press, 2004); Seymour Martin Lipset, *American Exceptionalism: A Double Edge Sword* (New York: Replica Books, 1998); Charles Lockhart, *The Roots of American Exceptionalism: Institutions, Culture, and Policies* (New York: Palgrave Macmillan, 2003); and Michael Ignatieff, ed., *American Exceptionalism and Human Rights* (Princeton, NJ: Princeton University Press, 2005).
3. Tony Smith, *America's Mission: The United States and the Worldwide Struggle for Democracy in the Twentieth Century* (Princeton, NJ: Princeton University Press, 1995). On the triumph of the activist version of American exceptionalism and doubts about it, see Michael L. Hunt, *Ideology and U.S. Foreign Policy* (New Haven, CT: Yale University Press, 1987).
4. American exceptionalism is not entirely exceptional. See David P. Forsythe, ed., *Human Rights and Comparative Foreign Policy* (Tokyo: UNU Press, 2000); and Lieven, *America Right or Wrong*.

American Policy toward Enemy Detainees in the War on Terrorism • 211

5. See further, David Forsythe and Patrice McMahon, eds., *Human Rights and Diversity: Areas Studies Revisited* (Lincoln: University of Nebraska Press, 2003), ch. 1.
6. The repressive spirit of those Wilsonian times is well captured in John M. Barry, *The Great Influenza: The Epic Story of the Deadliest Plague in History* (London: Penguin, 2004), 205–7.
7. See especially Rashid Khalidi, *Resurrecting Empire: Western Footprints and America's Perilous Path in the Middle East* (Boston: Beacon, 2005); and Niall Ferguson, *Empire: The Rise and Demise of the British World Order and the Lessons for Global Power* (New York: Basic Books, 2002).
8. On both points see E. J. Hobsbawm, *Nations and Nationalism since 1780: Programme, Myth, Reality* (Cambridge, UK: Cambridge University Press 1990, 1999), 12.
9. Paul Aussaresses, *The Battle of the Casbah: Terrorism and Counter-terrorism in Algeria, 1955–1957* (New York: Enigma Books, 2002), xiii, 17.
10. Preface to Henri Alleg, *The Question* (London: John Calder, 1958), 12–14.
11. For a discussion of the two schools, see Joseph Lelyveld, "Interrogating Ourselves," *New York Times Magazine*, June 12, 2005, starting at 36; Seymour Hersh, *Chain of Command: The Road from 9/11 to Abu Ghraib* (New York: Harper Collins, 2004); Mark Bowden, "The Dark Art of Interrogation," *Atlantic Monthly*, October 2003, starting at 51; Chris Mackey and Greg Miller, *The Interrogators: Inside the Secret War against Al Qaeda* (Boston: Little, Brown & Co., 2004); Sanford Levinson, *Torture: A Collection* (Oxford: Oxford University Press, 2004); Warren Richey, "Making Them Talk: The Moral Debate," *Christian Science Monitor*, May 26, 2004; Michael Ignatieff, *The Lesser Evil: Political Ethics in an Age of Terror* (Princeton, NJ: Princeton University Press, 2004).
12. See especially Tim Golden, "After Terror, A Secret Rewriting of Military Law," *New York Times*, October 24, 2004; and John Barry, Michael Hirsh, and Michael Isikoff, "The Roots of Torture," *Newsweek*, May 24, 2004.
13. This was suggested diplomatically in establishment circles. Richard B. Bilder and Detlev F. Vagts, "Speaking Law to Power: Lawyers and Torture," *American Journal of International Law* 98 no. 4 (October 2004), 689–95
14. Quoted in Human Rights Watch (HRW), "Getting Away with Torture?" April 2005, 9.
15. Ibid.
16. James Mann, *Rise of the Vulcans: The History of Bush's War Cabinet* (London: Penguin, 2004), 297 and passim.
17. See especially Karen J. Greenberg, Joshua L. Dratel, eds., and Anthony Lewis, *The Torture Papers: The Road to Abu Ghraib* (Cambridge, UK: Cambridge University Press, 2005); and Mark Danner, *Torture and Truth: America, Abu Ghraib, and the War on Terror* (New York: New York Review Books, 2004).
18. For a short and readable overview see Jordan Paust, "The Common Plan to Violate the Geneva Conventions," *Jurist*, May 25, 2004, http://jurist.law.pitt.edu/forum/paust2.php.
19. It is reasonable to characterize Afghanistan during 2001 and 2002 as manifesting an internal armed conflict between the Taliban government and the Northern Alliance, over which was imposed an international armed conflict between the United States and the Taliban government.
20. For a short and readable review of this issue, plus notation of its importance, see Adam Roberts, "Keeping the Unlawful Combatants out of Legal Limbo," *Washington Post*, February 3, 2002, Outlook.
21. Some detainees at Gitmo were of various nationalities, seized in Bosnia or Macedonia or Pakistan or some other place outside of Afghanistan and whose legal status was clearly different especially from Afghanistan nationals.
22. The relevant documents are presented in Greenberg et al., *Torture Papers*. See for example pp. 176–180.
23. There is no clear scientific or legal distinction between torture and lesser forms of mistreatment. Case law over time might clarify the difference, as per the European Court of Human Rights or the Israeli Supreme Court. But given that the international legal definition of *torture* hinges on the intentional infliction of intense physical or mental pain, the dividing line is largely subjective.
24. Greenberg, *op. cit.*, for example, pp. 202–207.
25. Douglas Jehl, "White House Has Tightly Restricted Oversight of CIA Detentions, Officials Say," *New York Times*, April 6, 2005, 19.
26. For a particularly good analysis of U.S. ties with Uzbekistan on this matter, with confirmation from British diplomatic circles, see Don Van Natta, Jr., "U.S. Recruits a Rough Ally to be a Jailer," *New York Times*, May 1, 2005, 1, 12. Also, an Australian security official confirmed

that another person was picked up in Pakistan, was then transferred to Egypt, and then was sent to Gitmo. *New York Times,* February 16, 2005, A9. U.S. officials had previously denied all this. See also Jane Mayer, "Outsourcing Torture," *New Yorker,* February 14 and 21, 2005, starting at 106.
27. Michael Scheuer, "A Fine Rendition," *New York Times,* March 11, 2005, A23. The author is a former CIA official.
28. In addition to Mann, *Rise of the Vulcans,* see Robert Kagan, *Of Paradise and Power: American and Europe in the New World Order* (New York: Vintage, 2003, 2004); and John F. Murphy, *The United States and the Rule of Law in International Affairs* (Cambridge, UK: Cambridge University Press, 2004). The author, a former State Department lawyer, sees the United States as now failing to fashion foreign policy with respect for international law.
29. See especially Elizabeth Holtzman, "U.S. Detention: Torture and Accountability," *Nation,* June 28, 2005.
30. Presented in Greenberg et al., *Torture Papers.*
31. The FBI memos were obtained and published by the American Civil Liberties Union (ACLU) on its Web site. The book is Erik Saar with Viveca Novak, *Inside the Wire* (New York: Penguin, 2005).
32. Amnesty International, Human Dignity Denied, passim, found at www.amnesty.org. For another summary see HRW, "Timeline of Detainee Abuse Allegations and Responses," May 7, 2004. For yet another reliable report, See Bob Herbert, "Stories from the Inside," *New York Times,* February 7, 2005, 27.
33. See Lelyveld, "Interrogating Ourselves"; Ignatieff, *American Exceptionalism and Human Rights.*
34. Douglas Jehl, David Johnston, and Neil A Lewis, "CIA Is Seen as Seeking New Role on Detainees," *New York Times,* February 16, 2005, 16. Porter Goss, new head of the agency, told Congress he could not confirm that all past CIA practices had been in keeping with federal laws prohibiting torture. Jehl, "Questions Left by CIA Chief on Torture Use," *New York Times,* March 18, 2005, 1.
35. Saar, *Inside the Wire.* His account on this point was later confirmed by other sources.
36. James Fallows, "Blind into Baghdad," *Atlantic Monthly,* January–February 2004, starting at 53; and Michael R. Gordon, "How the Postwar Situation in Iraq Went Awry," *International Herald Tribune,* from the *New York Times,* October 29, 2004.
37. The first was the Schlesinger report, reprinted in Greensberg et al., *Torture Papers,* and elsewhere. The second comment was from the report by Admiral Church, which has not been fully released.
38. Jehl, "CIA Order on Detainees Shows Its Role Was Curbed," *New York Times,* December 14, 2004, 13.
39. Reuters, "Harsh Tactics Were Allowed, General Told Jailers in Iraq," *New York Times,* May 30, 2005, 8.
40. A UN rapporteur on Afghanistan for the Human Rights Commission, M. Cherif Bassiouni who teaches at Depaul University in the United States, compiled a damaging report on prisoner treatment in Afghanistan, whereupon his tenure was not renewed by his parent body. Warren Hoge, "Lawyer Who Told of U.S. Abuses at Afghan Bases Loses UN Post," *New York Times,* April 30, 2005, 6.
41. For a journalistic account regarding Private First-Class Willie Brand, see Tim Golden, "GI Says He Was Trained in Blows That Killed Detainees," *New York Times,* August 9, 2005, A3.
42. See the reports of HRW.
43. It is relevant to recall that given the tenor of the times, American citizens seen as lending support to the enemy were treated badly when detained. James Yee, an Islamic chaplain at Gitmo, was given harsh detention conditions, including prolonged isolation, before all charges were dropped. John Lindh, captured while fighting for the Taliban in Afghanistan, was treated illegally and coercively before legal proceedings and plea bargaining led to his twenty-year jail term. For receiving a shorter sentence than the law allowed, he dropped his charges about mistreatment.
44. Pertinent memos are reproduced in Greensberg et al., *Torture Papers.* See pp. xxv–xxviii for a timeline and list. U.S. policy was similar to Israeli policy in occupied territory at least up to 1999: rejection of the formal application of the international humanitarian law (IHL) and promise to treat humanely but actual abuse of prisoners.
45. Amnesty International, "Human Dignity Denied."

46. Neil A. Lewis, "U.S. Spells Out New Definition Curbing Torture," *New York Times*, January 1, 2005, 1.
47. Various sorts of semantic games by governmental spokespersons tried to convey that "sleep management" and "stress positions" did not add up to abuse, humiliating treatment, degrading treatment, ill treatment, or, in combination, torture. See Adam Hochschild, "What's in a Word? Torture," *New York Times*, May 23, 2004, Op-Ed, 11.
48. Josh White and John Mintz, "Red Cross Cites 'Inhumane' Treatment at Guantanamo," *Washington Post*, December 1, 2004, 10. See also Anthony Lewis, "Guantanamo's Long Shadow," *New York Times*, June 21, 2005, 23, reacting to a statement by Vice President Cheney. See also the statement by Secretary of Defense Rumsfeld, denying that any abuse at Abu Ghraib was related to interrogation. Eric Schmitt, "Rumsfeld Denies Details of Abuses at Interrogations," *New York Times*, August 28, 2004, 1.
49. Johnston and Thom Shanker, "Pentagon Approved Intense Interrogation Techniques for Sept. 11 Suspect at Guantanamo," *New York Times*, May 21, 2004, 10; and Agence France Press, "Pentagon Gives No Excuses for Suspect Treatment: Senators Aghast," Yahoo news, June 13, 2005. Lexis-Nexis: m = 42f7724C8a90336bd.
50. A German national was seized by the United States in the Balkans and then was transferred to Afghanistan where he was abused. It was a case of mistaken identity, and NSC advisor Rice intervened after some months to get him released, with involvement by the German government. "Ghost detainees" could be "rendered" almost anywhere in this secret, unaccountable process. Apparently the prisoner was bound in painful positions, was beaten, and was injected with drugs. Johnston, "Rice Ordered Release of German Sent to Afghan Prison in Error," *New York Times*, April 23, 2005, 3.
51. See Jehl, "Officers Say U.S. Colonel at Abu Ghraib Prison Felt Intense Pressure to Get Inmates to Talk," *New York Times*, May 19, 2004, 21.
52. In addition to other sources, one can look at Steven Strasser, ed., *The Abu Ghraib Investigations: The Official Reports of the Independent Panel and Pentagon on the Shocking Prisoner Abuse in Iraq* (New York: Public Affairs, 2004).
53. The Church Report was widely seen as a whitewash of the issues. Among many typical press reports, see Tom Squitieri, "Pentagon Report on Prisoner Abuse Met with Skepticism; Probe to Go On," *USA Today*, March 11, 2005. Lexis-Nexis: m = c9e957d9dfab3b5ed.
54. Among many sources see Holtzman, "U.S. Detention"; and UPI, "Report: general urged dogs for Abu Ghraib," *Washington Times*, May 26, 2004. Lexis-Nexis: m= ccb8d10f4eb75a7b6.
55. Samantha Power, *"A Problem from Hell:" America and the Age of Genocide* (New York: Perennial, 2002).
56. See Michael Mandelbaum, *The Ideas That Conquered the World: Peace, Democracy, and Free Markets in the Twenty-First Century* (New York: Public Affairs, 2003), 93.
57. John Tierney, "Hot Seat Grows Lukewarm under Capital's Fog of War," *New York Times*, May 20, 2004, 14.
58. Eric Lichtblau, "Congress Adopts Restriction on Treatment of Detainees," *New York Times*, May 11, 2005, 14.
59. Jehl and Johnston, "White House Fought New Curbs on Interrogations, Officials Say," *New York Times*, January 13, 2005, 1.
60. Sheryl Gay Stolberg, "Leading Democrat Aplogizes for Prisoner Abuse Remark," *New York Times*, June 22, 2005, 14.
61. Schmitt, "Cheney Working to Block Legislation on Detainees," *New York Times*, July 24, 2005.
62. Saar, *Inside the Wire*.
63. Repeated efforts were made to discredit the ICRC. Editorials, op-ed pieces, and one Republican so-called study attacked the organization, using false statements and misrepresentations. Given some of the allegations, it was probable that some executive officials were involved behind the scenes. See, for example, Republican Policy Committee, "Are American Interests Being Disserved by the International Committee of the Red Cross?" June 13, 2005. See further, Sonni Efron, "GOP Committee Targets International Red Cross," *Los Angeles Times*, June 15, 2005, A3.
64. See their Web site.
65. Greensberg et al., *Torture Papers*, 558–629.
66. See the review of the Hamdi and Rasul cases, as well as the matter of military commissions, in the *American Journal of International Law* 99, 1 (January 2005), 261–2.

67. In 2005, a poll of citizens found that in Britain and France, China rated more favorably than the United States. Favorable views of the United States were 38 percent in Indonesia, 23 percent in Pakistan, and 23 percent in Turkey. Will Lester (for the Associated Press), *Lincoln Journal Star*, June 24, 2005, 4.
68. Neil MacFarquhar, "Lebanese Would-Be Suicide Bomber Tells How Volunteers Are Waging Jihad in Iraq," *New York Times*, November 2, 2004, 10.
69. See HRW, "UK: Promises on Torture Don't Work," hrw-news@topica.email-publisher.com.
70. See, for example, John H. Cushman, Jr., "UN Condemns Harsh Methods in Campaign against Terror," *New York Times*, October 28, 2004, 10. This refers to comments by Theo van Boven, UN rapporteur on torture.
71. UN Press Release, "United Nations Human Rights Experts Express Continued Concern About Situation of Guantanamo Bay Detainees," February 7, 2005; Bradley S. Klapper (for the Associated Press), "UN experts urge U.S. to allow inspections at Guantanamo," *Lincoln Journal Star*, June 24, 2005, 2.
72. "Human Dignity Denied." The report, not terribly well organized, consisted of 118 pages, with 771 reference notes.
73. HRW, "Getting Away with Torture? Command Responsibility for the U.S. Abuse of Detainees," April 2005. It consisted of 93 pages with 374 reference notes.
74. See Lelyveld, "Interrogating Ourselves," covering a new U.S. military manual on interrogation, and a U.S. report to the UN Committee against Torture.
75. The ICRC is a private Swiss association, part of Swiss civic society. But it is recognized in public international law and given certain rights in IHL. It is treated by the Swiss government now, and by most governments, as if it were a public international organization or intergovernmental organization. See further David P. Forsythe, *The Humanitarians: The ICRC* (Cambridge, UK: Cambridge University Press, 2005).
76. "Actions by the ICRC ... ," *International Review of the Red Cross*, 87, 858 (June 2005), 393–400.
77. See Lelyveld, "Interrogating Ourselves."
78. The flurry of memos by U.S. civilian and military authorities about what types and categories of interrogation techniques were permitted for use on enemy detainees did not occur until fall 2002. Also, it was in the second half of 2002 when FBI agents complained about military interrogation at Gitmo. General Miller took charge of Gitmo in October of that year. See Greenberg et al., *Torture Papers*, 223–238. See also Kate Zernike, "Newly Released Reports Show Early Concern on Prison Abuse," *New York Times*, January 6, 2005, 1.
79. ICRC press release, February 9, 2002. Some of the Gitmo detainees had no connection with Afghanistan and the armed conflict there but rather were seized in places like Bosnia and Macedonia.
80. GC #4, Article 143 stipulates that ICRC visits may be delayed for "military necessity," but this is supposed to be temporary. In some cases at Gitmo the ICRC was denied visits to certain individuals for months.
81. In general see Michael Ratner and Ellen Ray, *Guantanamo: What the World Should Know* (White River Junction, VT: Chelsea Green, 2004); in particular, see Neil A. Lewis, "Red Cross Finds Detainee Abuse in Guantanamo," *New York Times*, November 30, 2004, based on an ICRC report leaked by a U.S. source.
82. Agence France Press, June 17, 2005.
83. Amnesty International, "Human Dignity Denied," 8.
84. Ibid, 54.
85. The Fay report said that U.S. military authorities did not always take ICRC reports seriously or investigate the allegations properly. AR 15-6 Investigation, www.defenselink.mil/news/Aug 2004/d20040824fay.pdf, 64.
86. Ferguson, *Empire*, 232–3. The British tortured in Aden and Cyprus; Northern Ireland has already been mentioned. See further Kirsten Sellars, *The Rise and Rise of Human Rights* (Phoenix Mill, UK: Sutton, 2002).
87. Lelyveld, "Interrogating Ourselves," 39.

9

Democracy Promotion and American Foreign Policy: Afghanistan, Iraq, and the Future[1]

MARK PECENY

We are led, by events and common sense, to one conclusion: The survival of liberty in our land increasingly depends on the success of liberty in other lands. The best hope for peace in our world is the expansion of freedom in all the world ... So it is the policy of the United States to seek and support the growth of democratic movements and institutions in every nation and culture, with the ultimate goal of ending tyranny in our world.[2]

President George W. Bush

A president who expressed profound reservations about ambitious efforts to remake other societies in the image of the United States began his second term with a ringing declaration that the United States should make the promotion of liberty abroad a central guiding principle of U.S. foreign policy. Though President George W. Bush later went on to state, "This is not primarily the task of arms," listeners immediately placed this broad imperative in the context of the ongoing efforts to promote liberal democracy in Afghanistan and Iraq.[3] On November 27, 2001, thirty Afghans—representatives of the Northern Alliance, which had just routed Taliban forces throughout northern Afghanistan, and exile groups from Rome, Italy, Peshawar, Pakistan, and Cyprus—met in Bonn, Germany, under United Nations (UN) auspices to craft a post-Taliban government for Afghanistan. On December 5, 2001, they proclaimed,

> Acknowledging the right of the people of Afghanistan to freely determine their own political future in accordance with the principles of Islam, democracy, pluralism and social justice,

> Noting that these interim arrangements are intended as a first step toward the establishment of a broad-based, gender-sensitive, multi-ethnic and fully representative government,
>
> The Emergency Loya Jirga shall decide on a Transitional Authority, including a broad-based transitional administration, to lead Afghanistan until such time as a fully representative government can be elected through free and fair elections to be held no later than two years from the date of the convening of the Emergency Loya Jirga."⁴

Kandahari Pashtun Hamid Karzai was tapped to head an interim administration. Six months later, Afghanistan's deposed king, Zahir Shah, inaugurated an emergency *loya jirga*, or grand council of representatives from throughout the nation, to select a transitional authority. Eighteen months later, another *loya jirga* was called to draft a new constitution for Afghanistan. Afghans selected Karzai as their president in national elections in October 2004. Thus, since soon after the American intervention of 2001, Afghans have, with international support, worked toward the construction of liberal democratic institutions to govern their country.

On March 19, 2003, the Bush administration launched its war of liberation against the regime of Saddam Hussein in Iraq, announcing later to the people of Iraq that "we will end a brutal regime [and] help you build a peaceful and representative government that protects the rights of all citizens ... You deserve better than tyranny and corruption and torture chambers. You deserve to live as free people. And I assure every citizen of Iraq: your nation will soon be free."⁵ Within months of the inauguration of the American war in Iraq, the coalition provisional authority had set up a twenty-five-person Iraqi governing council. On March 8, 2004, the members of that council signed an interim constitution in preparation for the formal transfer of sovereignty to Iraqis by the end of June 2004. Elections for a national assembly were held on January 30, 2005.

Many analysts expect these democracy promotion efforts to fail. Afghanistan is about as unlikely a candidate for successful democratization as can be imagined. It does not possess the most basic of state institutions that are prerequisites for any stable political regime, let alone the representative institutions and rule of law necessary for successful democratization. It has been devastated by more than two decades of civil war. About the only functioning industry in the country is the drug trade. Afghanistan is one of the most poverty-stricken and destitute countries on Earth. It is divided by deep antagonisms among members of different ethnic, tribal and religious groups. Perhaps most crucially, the country is still dominated by local warlords who have little incentive to give up their power. It is no wonder, then, that many observers have labeled the effort to promote liberal democracy in Afghanistan an "impossible fantasy."⁶

Iraq is a richer and more developed country and therefore should have a greater chance of successful democratization than Afghanistan. Nevertheless, it is a country also devastated by two decades of interstate war, as well as domestic repression and international sanctions. Divisions between Kurds and Arabs, Shia and Sunni Muslims, and Baathists and anti-Baathists have already generated civil war among Iraqis and could easily thwart successful democratization. Finally, oil wealth can inhibit the consolidation of democracy because leaders can use patronage politics rather than effective governance to remain in power.[7]

Added to these roadblocks to democracy are the impediments to successful democratization imposed by the character of U.S. military interventions. By its nature, military intervention impinges on popular sovereignty. Furthermore, the United States intervened in both Afghanistan and Iraq to serve its material interests. The United States fought in Afghanistan to defeat the terrorist group that attacked the World Trade Centers and the Pentagon. It remains there to ensure the country will not reemerge as a sanctuary for anti-American terrorist groups. It invaded Iraq to thwart terrorism and the spread of weapons of mass destruction, to protect oil supplies from the Persian Gulf, and to assert American hegemony in the region and world. The most crucial nation-building task in those countries is to construct stable, capable states governed by leaders willing to serve the material interests of the United States. That task will be fully compatible with the successful democratization of Afghanistan and Iraq only if the peoples of those countries freely choose to elect leaders willing to serve the interests of the United States.

Why has the United States decided to promote democracy in these two countries if domestic impediments to democratization in both countries are substantial and if efforts to promote liberal institutions may compromise America's material interests? Can democracy promotion succeed in these inauspicious circumstances? This chapter argues that the United States often promotes democracy during its military interventions in an effort to legitimize those interventions to a domestic audience in the United States, to an international audience among America's liberal allies, or within the country in which the United States has intervened. Because domestic actors in the targeted country recognize this dynamic is a recurrent theme in U.S. policy, they often also push for democracy as a strategic policy designed to build alliances with the United States.

In Afghanistan, the Bush administration recognized it needed to create a strong, stable, and friendly Afghan government if it wanted to ensure that Al-Qaeda or similar anti-U.S. terrorist groups would not be able to use that country as a base of operations. It embraced democracy promotion as a tool to achieve this goal more as a response to an international audience and to the initiatives of Afghans than as a way to legitimate the intervention within the United States. The push for democracy flows from several sources in the

Iraqi case. Regime change was always a central component of Bush's strategy for transforming Iraq into an ally of the United States. Iraqi exiles had been pushing for a war of liberation for years, emphasizing the warm welcome American troops would likely receive and the ease with which democratic institutions could be constructed in Iraq. These forces inclined the Bush administration prior to the war to plan to promote democracy in Iraq in the wake of its liberation. In addition, as international, and especially domestic, opposition to the occupation of Iraq increased over time, the Bush administration responded in part by placing increasing emphasis on liberal themes in legitimating its war.

The opportunities and impediments to successful democratization in the two countries vary in interesting ways. In Afghanistan, the domestic structural impediments to democratization may be insurmountable. U.S. policymakers have been hopeful, however, because they believed the Afghan people would elect America's preferred candidate for the presidency of Afghanistan, Hamid Karzai—which did indeed occur in October 2004. Iraq is in some ways a mirror image of Afghanistan on these dimensions. The domestic structural impediments to democracy in Iraq are less profound than in Afghanistan, but the strategic dilemmas are more intractable. Policymakers have long been concerned that the candidates preferred by the United States would not win the January 2005 national elections, which also came to pass. The United States is still working out how it will manage a democratic process that has empowered Shia clerical parties. Thus, for somewhat different reasons, these democracy promotion efforts are likely to lead to some political liberalization and limited electoral competition but not to full-fledged consolidated democracies.

The logic of the argument for why the United States promotes democracy during its military interventions will be spelled out in the next section, followed by an in-depth examination of the Afghan case and a briefer discussion of the Iraqi case. Then the prospects for successful democratization will be briefly examined in each case.

Domestic Politics, Liberal Hegemony, and the Promotion of Democracy

The debate about U.S. efforts to promote democracy abroad tends to follow the contours of the liberalism versus realism debate in the international relations field. Among liberal arguments, some analysts emphasize the power of America's liberal ideals. In this approach, U.S. policymakers adopt pro-liberalization policies because they are compelled to do so by a universally shared cultural bias in favor of democracy.[8] Others have emphasized that institutional constraints imposed by Congress or interest groups have pushed the United States to promote democracy abroad.[9] Others, arguing more from realist or critical perspectives, have suggested that the promotion of democracy is fundamentally tied to America's security and economic interests. For some this means that presidents promote democracy to build more stable and friendly allied regimes.[10] Others look at the promotion of democracy in a broader sense as a central element of America's grand strategic vision.[11]

I offered a synthesis of these visions in a previous publication, arguing that there are two paths to the promotion of democracy during U.S. military interventions.[12] Arguments focused on security and economic interests provide the best explanation of the initial decisions of presidents. When presidents fail to adopt pro-democratic policies at the outset of an intervention, however, liberal ideological attacks from Congress often compel them to shift policies, despite the fact that they think pro-liberalization policies might harm U.S. security interests. Thus, the cultural and institutional components of the liberal argument must be integrated to understand why the United States does not pursue a consistent liberal policy. Liberal culture plays a crucial role in guiding policy, but only when political actors in important institutional positions in the democratic political process use liberal appeals in support of or opposition to policy. Furthermore, realist considerations are most important when decisions are lodged in the executive branch institutions most insulated from democratic politics.

More broadly, the promotion of democracy is one of the most important tools American leaders use to transcend the potential contradictions involved in being a liberal great power. America's liberal institutions do indeed constrain its ability to pursue a vigorous foreign policy abroad. In this context, the promotion of democracy has become a central theme in overcoming institutional inertia by forging a domestic consensus in favor of an active foreign policy. Internationally, America offers an appealing vision of a peaceful union of democratic states, under American leadership, that will bring liberty and prosperity to all like-minded states.

An element of strategic interaction also is built into this dynamic. Actors in the target country may embrace democracy in part because they are trying to forge alliances with international actors who care about democracy. By definition, external actors play a crucial role in deciding who will possess political power in the countries in which they have intervened. Embracing democracy is one way local actors can gain the favor of the external power.

Thus, U.S. efforts to promote democracy during military interventions can reflect efforts to overcome domestic pressure and to build a national consensus in favor of intervention. It can reflect a grand strategic vision designed to legitimate U.S. hegemony in the international system. It may be driven by a realistic assessment of local conditions and a belief that the promotion of democracy represents an effective strategy for creating a stable and friendly regime in the target state. Finally, the democratic project may be pushed forward by local actors seeking the support of the intervening power in their quest for local power. Each of these arguments will be applied first to the Afghan case and then more briefly to Iraq.

Congress and the Promotion of Democracy in Afghanistan

President Bush's policies toward Afghanistan may have been guided by his anticipation of the likely responses of Congress to a potentially long and difficult war, but it is difficult to find direct evidence that congressional pressure pushed the Bush administration to promote democracy in Afghanistan. Within a week of the terror attacks on New York and Washington, Congress had passed a broad authorization—with only one dissenting vote—allowing the president to use force to respond. Leadership from both parties in both houses of Congress released an unusual joint declaration of support in the immediate wake of Bush's attack on Afghanistan.[13] Democratic and Republican leaders engaged in an extraordinary level of bipartisan cooperation to support the president's agenda. Congressional support reflected Bush's 90 percent approval ratings in public opinion polls. A nascent opposition to the war did emerge from traditional peace activists, but public opposition to the war was limited and muted.

Concerns were voiced about the war effort. On October 3, 2001, Secretary of State Colin Powell met with the Senate Foreign Relations Committee to allay concerns that the war effort would set "the Islamic world afire" and create "Osama bin Ladens by what you will do," as suggested by the committee chair, Senator Joseph Biden.[14] Some raised concerns about the killing of innocent civilians in air strikes, but for the most part liberal themes were not prominent in the limited critical attention Congress accorded to the war effort. Instead, the most influential critiques from Congress came from senators like John McCain, John Kerry, and Max Cleland, who argued that the administration was not prosecuting the war in a sufficiently vigorous fashion.[15] Thus, direct congressional pressure does not provide an effective explanation for why the Bush administration supported nation building and democracy promotion in Afghanistan.

Grand Strategy

If support for free and fair elections in Afghanistan reflected the Bush administration's grand strategic vision, it seems as though the president and his principal advisors would have argued explicitly prior to the intervention that the promotion of liberal democracy should be a central focus of U.S. foreign policy. During the 2000 presidential campaign Bush at times expressed support for the kind of liberal grand strategy combining support for multilateral decision-making with U.S. support for liberal democracy and free trade.[16] In general, however, he and his foreign policy advisors emphasized their realism in contrast to the Bill Clinton administration's perceived embrace of Wilsonian idealism. As Condoleezza Rice, who would become Bush's national security advisor, noted early in 2000, when foreign policy is centered on Wilsonian ideals "the 'national interest' is replaced with 'humanitarian interests' or the interests of 'the international community.' The belief that the United States is exercising power legitimately only when it is doing so on behalf of someone or something else was deeply rooted in Wilsonian thought, and there are strong echoes of it in the Clinton administration. To be sure, there is nothing wrong with doing something that benefits all humanity, but that is, in a sense, a second-order effect."[17]

Indeed, attacks on the Clinton administration's participation in a variety of comprehensive multilateral peacekeeping operations became a central element of Bush's critique of Clinton's misplaced idealism. Clinton's nation-building efforts in Somalia, Haiti, and other peripheral states were harshly criticized by the Bush campaign. Rice even questioned whether the United States should retain its presence in Bosnia and Kosovo, noting that "we don't need to have the 82nd Airborne escorting kids to kindergarten" in Bosnia and Kosovo.[18] A discussion of the merits of nation building became the most serious foreign policy disagreement in the presidential debates between Bush and his Democratic opponent, Vice President Al Gore. This realistic strain in opposition to nation building was reinforced by the doctrine on military intervention created by new secretary of state Powell.[19] Powell argued consistently that the United States should not use force unless vital interests were at stake, it had clear objectives, the mission had the support of the American people, and it was prepared to use overwhelming and decisive force to achieve its objectives. Thus, the Bush administration entered office with an extreme aversion to the kind of open-ended long-term nation-building exercises it would later accept in Afghanistan.

Furthermore, when Bush declared the war on terror would become the new central mission of his administration, he framed the new strategy in terms reminiscent of the Cold War. In his September 20, 2001, speech to the nation, Bush proclaimed the war on terror a war between good and evil. States were either with the United States and a friend of freedom or against the country and an ally of terror:

> In Afghanistan, we see al Qaeda's vision for the world. Afghanistan's people have been brutalized—many are starving and many have fled. Women are not allowed to attend school. You can be jailed for owning a television. Religion can be practiced only as their leaders dictate. A man can be jailed in Afghanistan if his beard is not long enough ... Americans are asking, why do they hate us? They hate what we see right here in this chamber—a democratically elected government. Their leaders are self-appointed. They hate our freedoms—our freedom of religion, our freedom of speech, our freedom to vote and assemble and disagree with each other ... We are not deceived by their pretenses to piety. We have seen their kind before. They are the heirs of all the murderous ideologies of the 20th century. By sacrificing human life to serve their radical

visions—by abandoning every value except the will to power—they follow in the path of fascism, and Nazism, and totalitarianism. And they will follow that path all the way, to where it ends: in history's unmarked grave of discarded lies .... This is not, however, just America's fight. And what is at stake is not just America's freedom. This is the world's fight. This is civilization's fight. This is the fight of all who believe in progress and pluralism, tolerance and freedom.[20]

This rhetoric certainly suggested that the war in Afghanistan would be a war of liberation. As during the Cold War, however, this stark rhetoric also legitimated the embrace of a variety of autocratic regimes, like those of Pakistan or Uzbekistan, as allies on the side of freedom in the war against terror. The United States and its allies also instituted a wide range of new infringements on civil liberties and democratic political processes as part of the war on terror. Thus, to gain Russia's full support for U.S. military actions in Afghanistan, the United States and its Western European allies muted their criticism of Russia for its repressive policies in Chechnya. The United States removed sanctions against and increased aid to Pakistan's military government to gain its support. Saudi Arabia, Egypt, and other so-called moderate Middle Eastern allies of the United States insisted the United States not pursue a vigorous pro-democratic campaign that could make the autocratic nature of their governments more transparent. At the least, the promotion of democracy was not clearly a part of the new grand strategy being developed to win the war on terror.

Building a Stable Ally

In contrast to the congressional pressure and grand strategy arguments, there is some evidence that the Bush administration accepted a nation-building strategy in Afghanistan because it thought such a strategy might be necessary to construct a stable regime in Afghanistan. Bush was reluctant to admit that the United States should take on any kind of nation-building role in Afghanistan. On September 25, 2001, answering questions in the Oval Office, he said he was not interested in creating a government to replace the Taliban. "We're not into nation-building," he said. "We're focused on justice."[21] America's planned military action was "not designed to replace one regime with another regime," according to White House press secretary Ari Fleischer.[22] Deputy Secretary of State Richard L. Armitage summarized the feelings of the administration when he said, "We have said we don't want to run it; it's not ours."[23]

In the week following the start of the air war in Afghanistan, however, Bush's national security council met several times to have serious conversations about what should come after the successful expulsion of the Taliban from power.[24] As one official explained Bush's feelings on the subject, "He doesn't want a Vietnam, and he doesn't want to communicate to the Muslim world that we are another occupying force. He keeps saying, 'I don't want to leave American troops there,' but he knows that the only way to keep this powder keg from going up again is that the United States and its allies will have to make a long-term commitment of money and of people."[25] The Bush administration expressed its recognition that it would have to play a role in building a government Armitage and other administration officials labeled "broad based and representative of all Afghans."[26]

At this point, military necessity combined with a concern for the long-term stability of a friendly regime in Afghanistan to shape U.S. policy. The Northern Alliance possessed the only large, organized military resistance to the Taliban regime. If the Bush administration wanted to win the war without committing large numbers of U.S. combat troops, it would have to work with the Northern Alliance. Yet Bush's advisors also recognized that the Northern Alliance was a Tajik-dominated coalition of ethnic groups that represented a minority of Afghanistan's population. The phrase "broad based and representative coalition" was "code ... for the American determination that the Northern Alliance, which has long fought the Taliban, could not dominate a government."[27] Therefore, the Bush administration sought allies among the Pashtun tribes of southern Afghanistan and hoped to forge an alliance between the Tajik-dominated Northern Alliance and Pashtuns from the south. Without a southern alliance Bush officials feared that Pashtuns would coalesce around the Taliban against their ethnic adversaries from the north. Thus, building a multiethnic coalition was seen as necessary for victory as well as for long-term stability. U.S. officials did not emphasize building a liberal democratic regime. The nature of the coalition was considered more important than the nature of the institutional structures within which that coalition would operate. As Rice summarized the concerns of the administration, "This is not a country that is going to be ruled by ethnic populations that are 25, 30 percent of the country at best."[28] To understand how the Bush administration's decision to engage in a long-term project of nation building was tied to a liberal conception of that project, we must look at the responses of local actors and the international community.

A Fully Representative, Broad-Based, and Multiethnic Government

Within a month of the attacks on New York and Washington, calls for a fully representative, broad-based, and multiethnic government for Afghanistan had become a mantra for a variety of actors. U.S. policymakers, representatives of the United Nations, and spokespersons for at least two important Afghan factions—the Northern Alliance and a group of Pashtun expatriates surrounding Zahir Shah in Rome—began proclaiming their support for such a government at about the same time. It appears that UN officials and the Afghan factions began emphasizing this theme slightly before U.S. officials did, in the last days of September and the first week of October. U.S. officials did not begin emphasizing this theme in their public statements until a few days after the start of the air war in Afghanistan on October 7, 2001. This may suggest that the initiative for pursuing such a government emerged from the UN and Afghan groups. It could also reflect the Bush administration's desire to focus on one task at a time in its public diplomacy. Regardless, the UN, the Northern Alliance, and the Rome group coalesced around this formula relatively rapidly in the wake of the attacks. There is evidence that for at least some actors within this group, the formula meant more than just forging a multiethnic government; it meant embracing free and fair elections as well.

The alliance between the Northern Alliance and the Zahir Shah group was arranged in an October 1 meeting in Rome between the king and Yunus Qanooni of the Northern Alliance. At that meeting, the two groups agreed to set up a 120-person Supreme Council for the National Unity of Afghanistan with membership split between the Northern Alliance and representatives of the king.[29] That group would govern Afghanistan until a *loya jirga* could be convoked. Although the Northern Alliance never named its representatives to the supreme council, which therefore was superseded by the arrangements set out in the Bonn agreement, this meeting started to lay the groundwork for a fully representative, broad-based, and multiethnic government.

The Northern Alliance brought its military capabilities to this coalition, while the king brought the promise of international and domestic legitimacy for a new government.[30] Both groups emphasized the theme of a broad-based government in part because they thought it provided a reasonable framework for bringing peace to Afghanistan. They also sought to win the support of the United States and international community for their efforts to achieve power in a post-Taliban Afghanistan. Indeed, the parties invited a U.S. congressional delegation to witness the meeting in an effort to demonstrate to the United States that this coalition would be a useful ally to the United States in the war against terror.[31]

As the only opposition group with a reasonably well-organized and well-equipped army, the Northern Alliance could ingratiate itself to the United States by demonstrating their ability to help defeat the Taliban. By the end of October, U.S. air strikes were pummeling the Taliban's entrenched positions along several fronts. With the assistance of U.S. air power and timely defections by Taliban forces, the Northern Alliance was able to liberate most of northern Afghanistan by the last week of November. Indeed, it liberated Kabul by the end of the month despite its explicit promise to the United States that it would not do so.

Because the United States was concerned about the military and political consequences of allying itself solely with a coalition of ethnic minorities, the United States only consummated its pact with the Northern Alliance in the third week of the campaign, once it became clear that the Taliban would not collapse in response to U.S. bombing alone. Recognizing these concerns, a new generation of leaders of the Northern Alliance tried very hard to deemphasize the *mujahedin* Islamic insurgency of the alliance, positioning themselves as a modern, liberal, western force. No actors better represent this strategy than Abdullah Abdullah, who would become the foreign minister of the interim government, and Yunus Qanooni, the new interior minister. These actors emphasized their commitment to liberal norms both to win the support of the United States for the alliance and to win U.S. support in the internal struggle for power within the alliance in the wake of the assassination of alliance leader Ahmed Shah Massoud.

Thus, Abdullah consistently reassured everyone that the Northern Alliance favored a broad-based, multiethnic, representative government and that the alliance's military advances were a victory for freedom: "The victories and liberation of areas by our armed forces shouldn't affect our commitment to the formation of a fully representative, multiethnic broad-based government. It will rather encourage us to speed up our efforts with our national, regional and international partners in order to achieve that."[32] Qanooni reinforced this message in his opening remarks at the Bonn summit: "We are in a new era and we have the chance to become the champions of peace. It is not our intention to monopolize power. It will be our pride to work for a broad-based government based on the will of the people of Afghanistan. We want a system in which all Afghans, including women, participate in an equal manner in the structures of power."[33] So the Northern Alliance emphasized its commitment to liberal norms to convince U.S. policymakers and the international community more broadly that they would be worthy partners in the reconstruction of their country even after the war was completed.

The king controlled no military forces. Indeed, after nearly thirty years of exile, he also had few political allies within Afghanistan. He was a Pashtun, however, and could bring ethnic balance to a coalition that included the Northern Alliance. Many observers hoped his residual traditional authority as king and the fact that many Afghans remembered his reign as the last time of peace in Afghan history could bring some measure of domestic legitimacy to any government he might endorse. The Pashtun exiles surrounding the king also tended to be the most westernized and liberal of the potential Pashtun leaders that could join a post-Taliban government.

Because this group represented the possibility of ethnic balance, the promise of traditional legitimacy, and a commitment to western values it was a favored Afghan faction of many U.S. policymakers. The King's long-standing call for the inauguration of a *loya jirga* reflected this combination of themes nicely. Many Afghans were drawn to the traditional legitimacy of this institution, which has deep roots in Afghan history. To western audiences, the king's group emphasized how this illiberal institution could be tailored in ways that would generate a more broadly representative and democratic political process.

Since the king's group was also militarily and politically weak inside Afghanistan, it was an attractive ally for the Northern Alliance, which hoped to use the king's legitimacy and Pashtun heritage to mask a regime dominated militarily by the alliance. The most likely alternative Pashtun partner for a broad-based government was a group put together by Pir Sayed Ahmad Gailani, who had organized a *shura*, on council, attended by more than 700 tribal elders, Islamic scholars, politicians, and former guerrilla commanders in Peshawar, Pakistan.[35] Because this group was closely tied to the Pakistani government, possessed more potential political and military resources inside Afghanistan, and explicitly called for participation by elements of the Taliban in a new Afghan government, the Northern Alliance found this group to be a much less congenial potential ally. Because of the critical importance of maintaining strong ties with the Musharraf government, Secretary of State Powell supported the inclusion of the Peshawar group in the proposed broad-based, multiethnic government. Indeed, he even accepted Musharraf's contention that some Taliban leaders should be included in that government.[36] Connecting with the king's group provided the Northern Alliance an opportunity to marginalize the Peshawar group. It helped that U.S. suspicion made them reluctant to provide the Peshawar group much military assistance.[37]

One of the exiles linked to the king's group, Hamid Karzai—traditional leader of the Populzai Pashtun clan of Kandahar yet a thorough proponent of western liberal values—became the favorite of U.S. policymakers. Karzai had returned to his home province, heading a couple hundred armed supporters in an effort to push the Taliban out of Kandahar. Although Powell had apparently been reluctant to support Karzai because of the Pakistani government's concerns, by the beginning of November 2001 the United States began providing him substantial military assistance.[38] Indeed, U.S. forces probably saved Karzai's life when they evacuated him from a battle against the Taliban in early November. Furthermore, he was selected as the leader of the interim administration in Bonn, despite the delegation of the king's preference for another candidate, Abdul Sattar Sirat, a justice minister during Zahir Shah's rule.[39] He was selected in large part because he was the favored candidate of both the United States and the Northern Alliance. Indeed, Qanooni, Abdullah, and the Northern Alliance's military leader, Marshal Fahim, let the UN know before the Bonn conference that they would be happy to work with Karzai. "Karzai is a man who shares our vision of building a modern stable Afghanistan and creating a multi-ethnic government. We trust Karzai, he is a patriot who will put Afghanistan first rather than his clan, his tribe or his ethnic group."[40]

Thus, the new generation of leaders of the Northern Alliance, Karzai, and elements of the exile group surrounding Zahir Shah, coalesced around a project that combined elements of traditional Afghan politics, such as the *loya jirga*, with a liberal western project including free and fair elections. Each group even included women in their delegations at Bonn, because they realized western governments were concerned with the repression of women under Taliban rule. They embraced this liberal project in part because they believed this combination offered a reasonable strategy for ending nearly a quarter century of war and also because they suspected it would appeal to the United States and international community more broadly, realizing these external actors would play a crucial role in determining who would achieve power in a post-Taliban Afghanistan. Indeed, the link between the creation of a broad, multiethnic, and fully representative government and international support for the new government of Afghanistan was made very explicit at the opening ceremonies of the Bonn meeting. The world was prepared to provide billions of dollars to help rebuild Afghanistan after years of isolation, said German foreign minister Joschka Fischer, "but this readiness is linked with clear expectations to forge a truly historic compromise that holds out a better future for your torn country and its people."[41]

For Karzai and the king's faction, external sponsorship would compensate for military weakness. Indeed, Karzai's forces did not even represent the strongest anti-Taliban militia near Kandahar. That honor went to the troops of Gul Agha Shirzai, who would soon emerge as the new governor of the Kandahar region. For the Northern Alliance, this project would help legitimize their military domination of the new regime in Kabul. Abdullah, Qanooni, and Fahim would occupy the power ministries of foreign affairs, interior, and defense in the interim government. Support for elections also served another purpose for this trio. Alliance leaders were suspicious that the king's allies would use the Bonn meetings and the *loya jirga* process to empower Pashtun and royalist forces in Afghanistan. Support for national elections offered a way to limit this possibility. Furthermore, Qanooni went against the explicit instructions of the titular leader of the Northern Alliance, Berhanuddin Rabbani, in agreeing to set up an interim government at the Bonn meeting. By expressing a preference for Karzai as chief executive over the Northern Alliance leader Rabbani, who still held the formal title of president of Afghanistan, Qanooni illuminated an important fault line within the alliance. Rabbani had used liberal rhetoric to try to overturn the interim government crafted at Bonn, arguing that Afghanistan should be governed by an administration "based on the votes of the people."[42] Including elections in the final accord allowed the Northern Alliance's new guard to blunt this attack.

One additional element needs to be added to the explanation of how support for free and fair elections became an important part of the Bonn Agreement and the liberal reconstruction project for Afghanistan. This agreement was negotiated under the auspices of the United Nations. The United States was, of course, well represented at this meeting by Ambassador James Dobbins, who had been named special ambassador to the Afghan opposition and would later become ambassador to Afghanistan. Dobbins clearly worked toward the construction of the broad-based multiethnic government U.S. policymakers believed would help win the war and would bring some postwar stability. Dobbins did not mention elections prominently in any of his public comments on the Bonn negotiations.

Interestingly, Iranian representatives to the multilateral talks leading to Bonn took the lead in pushing for free and fair elections in Afghanistan and insisted this provision be included in the Bonn Agreement.[43] These diplomats represented the reform movement in Iran connected to President Khatami and realized that a democratic political order in Afghanistan might provide the best protection for the long-suffering Hazara Shia minority in Afghanistan. Support for elections also appears to have come more from UN representatives sponsoring the talks than from the United States, especially from Spanish diplomat Francesc Vendrell. Vendrell had been the UN secretary-general's special representative to Afghanistan at the beginning of the crisis and remained second in command of the mission after Kofi Annan brought back Lakhdar Brahimi—who had previously served in that role—as the new special representative. Though Brahimi emphasized the creation of a multiethnic coalition—rather than the creation of liberal institutions—in accord with Bush administration practice,[44] Vendrell emphasized the importance of democratic legitimacy for the new regime. In late September 2001, Vendrell expressed optimism that the crisis represented an opportunity for Afghans to achieve peace through the installation of democratic political processes. "This must be a truly Afghan solution, allowing the Afghans, without outside interference, to freely determine their future and to select a government that is committed to internationally recognized principles of pluralism, respect for human rights and minorities and friendly relations with all its neighbours."[45] On the eve of the Bonn meetings, Vendrell stated that "the root cause of the conflict in Afghanistan over the last 20 years is the lack of popular legitimacy of successive Afghan governments ... The lack of legitimacy raises challenges, which leads to conflict ... There should be enough incentives for the Afghans to move forward and not repeat the mistakes of the past ... If this is not enough, I don't know what it's going to take."[46]

The UN's support for free and fair elections and liberal social reconstruction as the preferred strategy for conflict resolution in societies experiencing civil wars has developed over the course of the past decade.[47] Indeed, today's framework of an interim government followed by a *loya jirga* and then by national elections is quite similar to the strategy pursued unsuccessfully by the UN a decade ago in Afghanistan. At that time, the UN never got over the first hurdle of crafting an interim government acceptable to all parties.[48] Whether this round of democracy promotion is likely to be more successful will be discussed in the following section.

Regime Change in Iraq

The Bush administration did not initiate democracy promotion efforts in Iraq in response to domestic or international pressure. Instead, Bush legitimated the war by emphasizing the threat of Iraqi weapons of mass destruction and Saddam Hussein's potential links to terrorist groups. The impetus for the promotion of democracy in Iraq initially reflected the Bush administration's strategic vision that the promotion of democracy in Iraq would lead to a stable, pro-American government in Iraq. The Bush administration also hoped the democratization of Iraq might lead to the spread of friendly liberal democratic regimes throughout the region. Iraqi exiles reinforced this strategy by persuading Bush officials that the Iraqi people would welcome liberation by the United States. The Iraqi case, therefore, represents a case of the presidential path to the promotion of democracy during U.S. military interventions. Nevertheless, the failure to find weapons of mass destruction or significant ties between Hussein's regime and Al-Qaeda, in the context of a deepening counterinsurgency war in Iraq, led the president to emphasize the promotion of democracy in Iraq as a central theme in his effort to legitimize the war to domestic and international audiences.

From the beginning of its push for war against Iraq, the Bush administration emphasized as the principal justification for war the threat posed to the United States and the world by Iraqi weapons of mass destruction. On January 29, 2002, Bush proclaimed in his state of the union address that "the Iraqi regime has plotted to develop anthrax and nerve gas and nuclear weapons for over a decade ... This is a regime that has already used poison gas to murder thousands of its own citizens, leaving the bodies of mothers huddled over their dead children. This is a regime that agreed to international inspections, then kicked out the inspectors. This is a regime that has something to hide from the civilized world ... States like these, and their terrorist allies, constitute an axis of evil, arming to threaten the peace of the world. By seeking weapons of mass destruction, these regimes pose a grave and growing danger."[49]

Nearly nine months later, on the day after the first anniversary of the attacks on the World Trade Centers and the Pentagon, Bush warned the United Nations, "Saddam Hussein's regime is a grave and gathering danger. To suggest otherwise is to hope against the evidence. To assume this regime's good faith is to bet the lives of millions and the peace of the world in a reckless gamble. And this is a risk we must not take ... Saddam Hussein ... continues to develop weapons of mass destruction. The first time we may be completely certain he has nuclear weapons is when, God forbid, he uses one."[50] A week later, the Bush administration released its *National Security Strategy Document*, which argued for the necessity of launching preemptive and preventive strikes against states that might threaten the United States with weapons of mass destruction.[51] As a secondary theme, the Bush administration emphasized the potential connections between the regime of Hussein and Al-Qaeda. The Bush administration linked the two issues by suggesting a nightmare scenario of a terrorist attack on the United States using weapons of mass destruction provided by Iraq.

Skeptics suggested that Bush was using the weapons of mass destruction issue to cover for other material interests. Some emphasized that the war with

Iraq was designed to protect access to the oil resources of the Persian Gulf. Others focused on the economic benefits that would flow to specific well-connected firms like Halliburton or Bechtel. The defeat of Hussein's Iraq could also make the region a safer place for America's Israeli ally. Finally, the invasion of Iraq would demonstrate the power of the United States and deepen U.S. hegemony in the region.

Most Bush administration officials believed the removal of Saddam Hussein would advance each one of these material interests. The same policy would reduce the threats of weapons of mass destruction and international terrorism, would guarantee U.S. oil supplies, would provide lucrative business opportunities for U.S. firms, would protect Israel, and would deepen U.S. hegemony in the region. They all agreed, as one State Department staffer put it, "It's the regime, stupid."[52] Iraq was dangerous because of the character of its regime; the destruction of that regime would serve a wide range of U.S. interests. Because of this, regime change in Iraq was a top priority of the Bush administration from its first days, long before the president had committed to invasion as the method to achieve this goal.[53] Indeed, pushing for regime change in Iraq had been one of the central themes of the Project for a New American Century, an organization including many individuals who would later become important players in the Bush administration.[54]

Regime change in Iraq need not involve a transition to democracy, however. The Bush administration certainly argued that Hussein's removal would advance the cause of freedom. It initially did not suggest, however, that the promotion of democracy was the central goal of the intervention. Neoconservative political appointees at the Department of Defense played an important role in insisting that the United States should make sure regime change involved a transition to democracy. Deputy Secretary of Defense Paul Wolfowitz believed strongly that only a democratic Iraq could provide the strong and stable U.S. ally needed to accomplish all of these objectives. Such a regime would serve as a powerful example in the region and could transform the Middle East. As Wolfowitz stated in September 2002, "I don't think it's unreasonable to think that Iraq, properly managed … really could turn out to be, I hesitate to say it, the first Arab democracy, or at least the first one except for Lebanon's brief history … I think the more we are committed to influencing the outcome, the more chance there could be that it would be something quite significant for Iraq. And I think if it's significant for Iraq, it's going to cast a very large shadow, starting with Syria and Iran, but across the whole Arab world."[55] Wolfowitz, and the civilians working closely with him in the Department of Defense believe that since the principal impediment to democratization in Iraq was Saddam Hussein, his removal from power could quickly lead to a democratic transition.

They were encouraged in this thinking by Iraqi exiles in groups like the Iraqi National Congress, which argued that the Iraqi people would welcome

U.S. troops as liberators and that a new Iraqi government would inherit a functioning state apparatus. It appears that at least some Defense Department planners envisioned a relatively quick transfer of a power to a provisional Iraqi government led by Iraqi National Congress leader Ahmed Chalabi. That provisional government would lay the groundwork for a constitutional convention and eventual transition to an elected government. Such plans fell victim to the State Department's opposition to Chalabi and the chaos and looting of the first weeks of the U.S. occupation. Despite the Defense Department's being forced to cede some of its power in Iraq to the State Department, as former State Department officer L. Paul Bremer took over as head of the occupation government, the broad goal of forging a democratic transition in Iraq was retained. Therefore, the initial impetus for democracy promotion reflected U.S. policymakers' assessment of the policies most likely to generate a strong and stable pro-American regime in Iraq; these assessments were shaped in part by Iraqi exile groups who hoped to ride to power on the back of a U.S. invasion.

In the years since the invasion, U.S. occupation forces have failed to discover any weapons of mass destruction. They have also failed to discover evidence of close ties between the regime of Saddam Hussein and Al-Qaeda. Furthermore, U.S. troops were clearly not welcomed with open arms in much of the country. Those troops continue to fight a low-intensity war against Iraqi insurgents. The failure to discover weapons of mass destruction has engendered increasingly sharp attacks against Bush policy within the United States. The presidential campaign of Democratic challenger John Kerry focused intently on these failures. Bush responded by placing increasing emphasis on the theme that the liberation of Iraq from the tyranny of Hussein and the installation of a liberal democratic regime in that country has always been a central goal of the intervention. The handover of sovereignty to an Iraqi government in June 2004 and the commitment to hold elections for a national assembly by the end of January 2005 were designed, in part, to send a positive message to the U.S. electorate prior to the November elections. Thus, as domestic opposition to the occupation rises in the United States, and as the presidential elections drew near, the need for domestic legitimation became an increasingly important force pushing the Bush administration to hasten the transition to democracy in Iraq. Bush has also sought out the United Nations as a partner in the democracy-building effort to send a signal to domestic audiences in the United States, to the international community, and to Iraqis that it is serious about its commitment to democracy. Although democracy promotion has played an increasingly important role in legitimating the intervention, this does not mean the initial strategic rationale for the democracy promotion enterprise in Iraq has been set aside. Today, the promotion of democracy in Iraq serves both strategic and domestic legitimation functions.

Strategic Interactions and the Prospects for Democracy in Afghanistan and Iraq

Both Afghanistan and Iraq face significant domestic impediments to successful democratization. The strategic dimension of democratization in both countries, however, illuminates some interesting contrasts. The United States would like to ensure that the Afghan and Iraqi peoples select its preferred candidates in free and fair elections. Only then will it have confidence that its efforts to promote democracy will be consistent with the material interests it intervened to protect. In Afghanistan it was confident its preferred candidate would win the presidential elections of October 2004. In Iraq the Bush administration struggled for some time in deciding who would be its preferred interlocutor in Iraq. It eventually decided that Ayad Allawi would best serve U.S. interests but could not be confident the Iraqi people would select him in free and fair elections. This has led to two very different dynamics in the two countries.

The United States decided early on that Hamid Karzai would be its preferred candidate to rule Afghanistan. From the beginning, it also appeared he would be acceptable to a broad range of Afghans. The United States supported his selection as interim leader at the Bonn Summit of 2001 but did not need to impose that choice on the delegates. When some groups in the first *loya jirga* pushed to select Zahir Shah as the new chief executive in 2002, U.S. envoy Zalmay Khalilzad intervened in the process and convinced the deposed king to decline the position, thus ensuring the success of the favored candidate of the United States—Karzai.[56] In retrospect, however, it appears that Karzai would have been the overwhelming choice of the *loya jirga*, even without Khalilzad's intervention.[57] Finally, during the constitutional *loya jirga*, the United States encouraged delegates to support a centralized unitary republic with a strong presidency, a system that would serve U.S. interests best if it could be assured its candidate would become president. The consensus within the U.S. government was that Karzai would easily win the national presidential elections.[58]

This confidence in Karzai's popularity has led the United States to work to dismantle the coalition it helped forge in 2001. Since the constitutional *loya jirga*, the United States has pushed Karzai to make every effort to weaken the power of regional warlords. Yet Karzai's power thus far has rested in part on alliances forged with those very same regional warlords. As the United States has pushed Karzai to challenge regional leaders, these alliances have been strained. In July 2004, Karzai broke with his allies in the Northern Alliance by removing Marshal Fahim as a vice presidential candidate on his ticket. The core commanders of the Northern Alliance then announced their support for Yunus Qanooni's candidacy for the presidency. The presence of Qanooni on the ballot ensured that Karzai would have some genuine competition. Nevertheless, Karzai won a clear majority of the vote, with 55 percent of the ballots.

Qanooni came in a distant second, with 16 percent of the vote. We will soon discover whether U.S. efforts to construct a strong unitary state centered on Karzai will lead to greater instability in Afghanistan or to the stable allied democracy for which U.S. policymakers hope. In either event, any limitations on Afghan democracy did not emerge from American attempts to manipulate Afghan elections to ensure Karzai's selection, because such manipulation was deemed unnecessary.

The Bush administration has faced more intractable strategic dilemmas in the movement toward free and fair elections in Iraq. The administration's strongest allies have been the Kurdish parties of Northern Iraq. The Kurds, however, represent less than a quarter of the national population. Therefore, it is unlikely that America's Kurdish allies could ever win a national majority in free and fair elections. Furthermore, a majority of Iraqi Kurds would vote to secede from Iraq if given the chance. Indeed, they did vote overwhelmingly for Kurdish independence in a parallel election held on January 30, 2005.[59]

Winning national elections depends on winning the support of Iraq's Shias, who represent perhaps 60 percent of the national population. The Bush administration therefore has searched for its preferred candidates among secular Shias who had passed most of the Saddam Hussein era in exile, because these leaders were the most likely simultaneously to appeal to a majority of the electorate and to embrace western values and American leadership. Bureaucratic actors within the Bush administration differed, however, on which secular Shia exile should be the principal ally of the United States. The Defense Department was close to Chalabi and his Iraqi National Congress. The State Department and CIA, however, favored Allawi and the Iraqi National Accord. Chalabi played an important role in the immediate postinvasion government but was pushed aside in 2004 amid allegations he had been spying for the Iranian government. Allawi came to the forefront as the first prime minister of an Iraq that had regained its sovereignty in summer 2004. Policymakers eventually discovered that Chalabi, like many of the exiles brought back to Iraq by the United States, was both unpopular and mistrusted. Although Allawi may have earned the respect of more Iraqis during his stint as prime minister, he is not a popular leader. The United States has not yet found its Iraqi Hamid Karzai.

Instead, Shia clerical parties, guided by Ayatollah Ali al-Sistani, soon became the principal champions of elections in Iraq, because they were convinced that they could mobilize the Shia majority behind their leadership and win any truly free and fair elections. The United States feared that, if elected, these clerical parties would pursue a set of domestic and international initiatives that run counter to the material interests of the United States. Because of this, the United States has been faced with significant temptations to manipulate Iraqi elections to avoid results that would threaten U.S. interests.

U.S. occupation authorities have tried to finesse this intractable strategic dilemma in a number of ways. First, it made sure the twenty-five-person governing council would have a Shia majority, but secular Shia exiles, like Chalabi, were overrepresented on this body, while clerical parties were underrepresented. Then, the United States crafted a complex caucus system for the selection of representatives for a constitutional assembly. It justified this system as necessary because of the dangerous security environment, yet such a system would also have allowed the Americans to limit the mandate of the Shia clerical parties and would have lengthened the rule of U.S.-selected prime minister Allawi. The postponement of national elections would push back the moment when the United States would have to address directly the dilemma of what to do if its preferred candidates did not win the elections. The United States had to abandon the caucus system in the face of opposition from Ayatollah al-Sistani, who argued that the creation of a caucus system would lead to an unacceptable delay in Iraq's progress toward genuinely democratic elections. Finally, the United States encouraged the drafters of the interim constitution to embrace two compromises that would limit the ability of Shia clerical parties to use their majority to push for policies that might conflict with U.S. interests or threaten America's allies in Iraq. First, the officers of the government emerging after the January vote would have to be elected by a two-thirds majority of the legislature. Second, any final constitution could be scuttled by a two-thirds vote in any three provinces. These provisions ensure that a Shia clerical majority cannot easily impose its will on others and also make it more likely the Kurds will gain sufficient autonomy to guarantee their continued participation in national Iraqi institutions.

These institutional mechanisms have worked as anticipated. The Shia list, a broad coalition implicitly sponsored by Ayatollah al-Sistani, won a small majority of the seats in the new legislature. They could neither select a president and prime minister nor govern, however, without the cooperation of either the Kurdish coalition, which won slightly more than a quarter of the seats in the legislature, or Ayad Allawi's list, which won approximately 15 percent of the seats. It took months for the new legislature to agree on a new government led by Prime Minister Ibrahim al-Jaafari. Serious negotiations on the shape of the new constitution had barely begun by early summer 2005, as the victorious Shia-Kurdish coalition sought in vain for effective ways to integrate Sunni Arabs into the drafting process. A new constitution, which is likely to take much longer than anticipated to draft, probably cannot be ratified without Kurdish support. Clearly, the Shia clerical parties will have to compromise with these other forces to break out of the gridlock that has dominated Iraqi politics since the January elections.

The checks placed on the Shia list give greater comfort to the Bush administration than would an unrestrained Shia-dominated Westminster system. Limiting the power of the Shia clerical parties, however, is a second-best solution for the United States in comparison to the election of clearly pro-U.S. candidates by the Iraqi people to run a strong authoritative central government. Navigating this difficult strategic arena will continue to challenge a Bush administration that may continue to be tempted to shape Iraqi democratic politics to suit its interests. Therefore, even though both countries face serious structural obstacles to successful democratization, the limited character of Iraq's democracy is likely to be reinforced by the strategic choices of U.S. policymakers.

Both countries, however, are likely to sustain at least limited electoral competition despite the numerous structural and strategic impediments that make the consolidation of full-fledged democracy unlikely. U.S. leaders will still have powerful incentives to use elections to legitimate their interventions to U.S., Afghan, Iraqi, and international audiences. Afghans and Iraqis will still possess equally strong incentives to legitimate their own rule to U.S., international, and local audiences by claiming electoral mandates. Thus, the need for legitimacy in a world with a developing global norm of democratic governance provides all actors with strong incentives to maintain the institutional forms of democracy in Afghanistan and Iraq, even if the quality of those democratic institutions may not reach the standards of full democratization.

Germany, Vietnam, or Cuba?

The success of the democracy promotion projects in Afghanistan and Iraq can have a huge impact on broad contours of American foreign policy. In its most fulsome vision, the Bush administration suggests that efforts to promote liberal democracy in Afghanistan and Iraq are analogous to the Harry Truman administration's democracy promotion efforts in Germany and Japan after World War II. As with the Axis powers, Bush believes a committed American effort can transform Afghanistan and Iraq into strong liberal democracies. Forging democracy in these two Muslim countries can transform the Islamic world, which, in turn, would make the world fundamentally more congenial for the United States. Such success could generate a broad elite foreign policy consensus behind an assertive liberal internationalism not unlike the Cold War consensus forged after World War II.

If nation building is doomed to failure in Afghanistan and Iraq, as many critics suggest, Vietnam may provide a more appropriate analogy. The extraordinary cost of the Vietnam War, combined with the failure to create any strong, stable, allied regime in South Vietnam and America's ultimate defeat in that conflict, shattered the Cold War consensus and made it difficult for future presidents to rally the American people around any assertive foreign policy. The longer the wars in Iraq and Afghanistan last, the more casualties they cause, and the more inept and undemocratic our local allies appear, the more likely it is that these interventions will generate political dynamics in the United States reminiscent of Vietnam.

The analysis presented here suggests that the outcome is more likely to resemble the situation in Cuba after the Spanish–American War than either Germany or Vietnam. In 1898, the United States proclaimed it was going to war to liberate Cuba from Spanish tyranny. Despite the U.S. government's doubts about whether Cubans were prepared for self-governance, pressure to live up to America's professed liberal ideals pushed it to hand over the office to the elected president of an independent Cuba in 1902. Cuba was a country with numerous structural impediments to successful democratization, which were exacerbated by efforts of the United States to limit the autonomy of Cuba's elected leaders. Indeed, the U.S. Senate enacted the Platt Amendment, spelling out the precise terms of the protectorate relationship the United States would forge with Cuba. The United States then insisted that Cubans enshrine these conditions in their new constitution.

Rather than total success as in Germany, or total failure as in Vietnam, Cuba experienced decades of intermittent partially democratic rule and chronic instability that brought about frequent low-level military interventions by the United States. Initially the outcome in Cuba was viewed as clearly superior to that in the Philippines, where the imposition of colonial rule generated a strong insurgent movement to which the United States responded with a vicious counterinsurgency war killing tens of thousands. Over time, however, Cuba left no clear message of success or failure around which elites could coalesce. If U.S. interventions in Afghanistan and Iraq generate partially democratic, partially friendly regimes requiring constant U.S. military support to compensate for chronic instability, as in Cuba at the turn of the century, this will neither cement a new foreign policy consensus nor shatter support for an activist foreign policy. Instead, it will probably mean that the wisdom of military intervention and the promotion of democracy will continue to be contested, and the quest for a new foreign policy consensus to rival that of the Cold War will remain unfulfilled.

Notes

1. Earlier versions of this chapter were presented at the International Studies Association Conferences in Montreal, Quebec, Canada, March 17–20, 2004, and Honolulu, Hawaii, March 1–5, 2005, and at the Standing Group in International Relations Conference, The Hague, Netherlands, September 9–11, 2004. I thank Emily Acevedo, Yuri Bossin, Ross Burkhart, Manus Midlarsky, James Scott, Reinhard Wolf, Richard Wood, the students in my graduate seminar on civil wars, the editors of this volume, and the participants in the 2005 Hendricks Conference at the University of Nebraska for comments on earlier drafts of this chapter. I also thank Eric Jepsen and Saraswati Khalsa for research assistance.
2. George W. Bush, "Inaugural Address," January 20, 2005, *Weekly Compilation of Presidential Documents* (Washington, DC: Government Printing Office, 2005), 74.
3. Ibid.
4. United Nations, *Agreement on Provisional Arrangements in Afghanistan Pending the Reestablishment of Permanent Government Institutions,* December 5, 2001, http://www.unama-afg.org/docs/_nonUN%20Docs/_Internation-Conferences&Forums/Bonn-Talks/bonn.htm.
5. George Bush, "President's Message to the Iraqi People," April 10, 2003, *Weekly Compilation of Presidential Documents* (Washington, DC: Government Printing Office, 2003), 424.

6. Marina Ottoway and Anatol Lieven, "Rebuilding Afghanistan: Fantasy versus Reality," *Policy Brief* 12, Carnegie Endowment for International Peace (January 2002), 5.
7. Terry Lynn Karl, *The Paradox of Plenty* (Berkeley: University of California Press, 1997).
8. Louis Hartz, *The Liberal Tradition in America* (New York: Harcourt, Brace, and Jovanovich, 1955); Samuel Huntington, *American Politics: The Promise of Disharmony* (Cambridge, MA: Belknapp Press of Harvard University, 1981); Robert Packenham, *Liberal America in the Third World* (Princeton:, NJ Princeton University Press, 1973); and George Quester, *American Politics: The Lost Consensus* (New York: Praeger Press, 1982).
9. Robert Pastor, *Whirlpool* (Princeton, NJ: Princeton University Press, 1992); Cynthia Arnson, *Crossroads: Congress, the President, and Central America, 1976–1993* (University Park: Pennsylvania State University Press, 1993); David Forsythe, *Human Rights and U.S. Foreign Policy: Congress Reconsidered* (Gainesville: University of Florida Press, 1988); and Lars Schoultz, *Human Rights and U.S. Policy toward Latin America* (Princeton, NJ: Princeton University Press, 1981).
10. Theodore Wright, *American Support for Free Elections Abroad* (Washington, DC: Public Affairs Press, 1964); Yale Ferguson, "The United States and Political Development in Latin America: A Retrospect and Prescription" in *Contemporary Inter-American Relations: A Reader in Theory and Issues*, ed. Yale Ferguson (Englewood Cliffs, NJ: Prentice-Hall, 1972), 348–91; Schoultz, *National Security and U.S. Foreign Policy toward Latin America* (Princeton, NJ: Princeton University Press, 1987); Pastor, *Condemned to Repetition* (Princeton, NJ: Princeton University Press, 1987); Michael D. Shafer, *Deadly Paradigms* (Princeton, NJ: Princeton University Press, 1988); Douglas MacDonald, *Adventures in Chaos* (Cambridge, MA: Harvard University Press, 1992); Sara Steinmetz, *Democratic Transition and Human Rights* (Albany: State University of New York Press, 1994); William Robinson, *Promoting Polyarchy* (New York: Cambridge University Press, 1996); and Barry Gills, "American Power, Neoliberal Economic Globalization and 'Low-Intensity Democracy': An Unstable Trinity" in *American Democracy Promotion: Impulses, Strategies, and Impacts,* ed. Michael Cox, G. John Ikenberry, and Takashi Inoguchi (New York: Oxford University Press, 2000), 326–44.
11. Tony Smith, *America's Mission: The United States and the Worldwide Struggle for Democracy in the Twentieth Century* (Princeton, NJ: Princeton University Press, 1994); Ikenberry, "America's Liberal Grand Strategy: Democracy and National Security in the Post-War Era," in Cox et al. (see note 9), 103–26.
12. Mark Peceny, *Democracy at the Point of Bayonets* (University Park: Pennsylvania State University Press, 1999).
13. David Rosenbaum, "Congressional Leaders Offer Strong Endorsement of Attack," *New York Times*, October 8, 2001, B11.
14. Jane Perlez, "Powell Tries to Allay Worry of Senators on Muslim Rage," *New York Times*, October 4, 2001, B3.
15. R. W. Apple, "Afghanistan as Vietnam," *New York Times*, October 31, 2001, B1.
16. George W. Bush, "A Distinctly American Internationalism: Speech at the Ronald Reagan Presidential Library, Simi Valley, CA," November 19, 1999, http://www.mtholyoke.edu/acad/intrel/bush/wspeech.htm; R.W. Apple, "Bush Questions Aid to Moscow in a Policy Talk," *New York Times,* November 20, 1999, A1.
17. Condoleezza Rice, "Promoting the National Interest," *Foreign Affairs* 79, 1 (2000), 47.
18. James Traub, "W's World," *New York Times Sunday Magazine*, January 14, 2001, SM30.
19. Colin Powell, "U.S. Forces: Challenges Ahead," *Foreign Affairs* 72 no. 1 (1992–93), 32–45.
20. George W. Bush, "Address Before a Joint Session of the Congress on the United States Response to the Terrorist Attacks of September 11," September 20, 2001, *Weekly Compilation of Presidential Documents* (Washington, DC: Government Printing Office, 2001), 1348–9.
21. David Sanger, "Bush, Who Denounced 'Nation-Building,' Must Look to the Future in Afghanistan," *New York Times*, October 12, 2001, A1.
22. Elisabeth Bumiller and Thom Shanker, "Bush Urges Afghans to Rid Their Country of Taliban," *New York Times*, September 26, 2001, A1.
23. Sanger, "Goals Include a Broad Coalition and Economic Development," *New York Times*, October 14, 2001, A1.
24. Ibid.
25. Sanger, "Bush, Who Denounced 'Nation-Building.'"
26. Sanger, "Goals Include a Broad Coalition."
27. Ibid.

28. David Rohde, "Afghan Victors Agree to Talks on Interim Rule," *New York Times*, November 19, 2001, A1.
29. Melinda Henneberger, "Ex-King and Rebels to Hold Special Council," *New York Times*, October 2, 2001, B2.
30. Ahmed Rashid, "Eurasia Insight: Formation of a New Afghan Government Overshadows Military Campaign," Eurasianet.org, October 17, 2001, http://www.eurasianet.org/departments/insight/articles/eav101701.shtml.
31. Melinda Henneberger, "Ex-King Meets Taliban Foes and 11 from U.S. Congress," *New York Times*, October 1, 2001, B2.
32. Rohde, "Afghan Victors Agree."
33. Steven Erlanger, "With Many Absent from Talks, a Kabul Meeting Is Suggested," *New York Times*, November 28, 2001, A1.
34. Rashid, "Eurasia Insight: The Risks and Benefits of War in Afghanistan," Eurasianet.org, September 24, 2001, http://www.eurasianet.org/departments/insight/articles/eav092401.shtml.
35. Barry Bearak, "Leaders of the Old Afghanistan Prepare for the New," *New York Times*, October 25, 2001, B4.
36. Patrick Tyler, "Powell Suggests Role for Taliban," *New York Times*, October 17, 2001, A1.
37. Rashid, "Eurasia Insight: Post-Taliban Order Is a Source of Concern for Pakistan," Eurasianet.org, October 19, 2001, http://www.eurasianet.org/departments/insight/articles/eav101901a.shtml; Rashid, "Eurasia Insight: U.S. Support for Northern Alliance Rankles Pakistan," Eurasianet.org, October 22, 2001, http://www.eurasianet.org/departments/insight/articles/eav102201a.shtml.
38. Rashid, "Eurasia Insight: Hamid Karzai Moves from Lightweight to Heavyweight in Afghan Politics," Eurasianet.org, December 10, 2001, http://www.eurasianet.org/departments/insight/articles/eav121001.shtml.
39. Alexandra Poolos, "Eurasia Insight: Bonn Talks See Some Progress on Interim Government," Eurasianet.org, December 3, 2001, http://www.eurasianet.org/departments/insight/articles/pp120301.shtml.
40. Rashid, "Hamid Karzai."
41. Erlanger, "With Many Absent from Talks."
42. Poolos, "Eurasia Insight: Talks in Bonn Seen as Stalling," Eurasianet.org, November 30, 2001, http://www.eurasianet.org/departments/insight/articles/pp113001.shtml.
43. Interview with author, Crystal City, VA, May 2003. All interviews were conducted in confidentiality, and the names of the interviewees are withheld by mutual agreement.
44. Lakhdar Brahimi, "Briefing to the United Nations Security Council by the Special Representative of the Secretary-General for Afghanistan," November 13, 2001, http://www.un.org/News/dh/latest/afghan/brahimi-sc-briefing.htm.
45. United Nations, "Current International Climate Could Spell Opportunity for Afghanistan, UN Envoy Says," September 27, 2001, http://www.un.org/apps/news/storyAr.asp?NewsID = 1646&Cr=Afghanistan&Cr1, paragraph 6.
46. Rohde, "Afghans Wait for Portents in Bonn Talks," *New York Times*, November 26, 2001, B1.
47. Roland Paris, "Peacebuilding and the Limits of Liberal Internationalism," *International Security* 22 no. 2 (1997), 54–89; Michael Barnett, "Bringing in the New World Order: Liberalism, Legitimacy, and the United Nations," *World Politics* 49 no. 4 (1997), 526–51; Krishna Kumar, ed., *Postconflict Elections, Democratization and International Assistance* (Boulder, CO: Lynne Rienner, 1998); Michael Doyle and Nicholas Sambanis, "International Peacebuilding: A Theoretical and Quantitative Analysis," *American Political Science Review* 94 no. 4 (2000), 779–803; and Peceny and William Stanley, "Liberal Social Reconstruction and the Resolution of Civil Wars in Central America," *International Organization* 55 no. 1 (2001), 149–82.
48. Barnett Rubin, *The Search for Peace in Afghanistan: From Buffer State to Failed State* (New Haven, CT: Yale University Press, 1995).
49. George W. Bush, "Address Before a Joint Session of the Congress on the State of the Union," January 29, 2002, *Weekly Compilation of Presidential Documents* (Washington, DC: Government Printing Office, 2002), 135.
50. George W. Bush, "Address to the United Nations General Assembly in New York City," September 12, 2002, *Weekly Compilation of Presidential Documents* (Washington, DC: Government Printing Office, 2002), 1531.

51. Bush, "The National Security Strategy of the United States of America," September 17, 2002, http://www.whitehouse.gov/nsc/nss.html.
52. Interview with author, Department of State, May 2003. All interviews were conducted in confidentiality, and the names of the interviewees are withheld by mutual agreement.
53. Bob Woodward, *Plan of Attack* (New York: Simon and Schuster 2004), 9–23.
54. Project for a New American Century, "Letter to President Clinton," January 26, 1998, http:// www.newamericancentury.org/iraqclintonletter.htm.
55. Bill Keller, "The Sunshine Warrior," *New York Times*, September 22, 2002, SM51.
56. Camelia Entekhabi-Fard, "Eurasia Insight: Former King Deflects Political Controversy as Afghan Vote Waits," Eurasianet.org, June 10, 2002, http://www.eurasianet.org/departments/insight/articles/eav061002a.shtml.
57. Interview with author, United Nations, October 2002. All interviews were conducted in confidentiality, and the names of the interviewees are withheld by mutual agreement.
58. Interviews with author, Department of Defense, Department of State, and Crystal City, VA, May 2003. All interviews were conducted in confidentiality, and the names of the interviewees are withheld by mutual agreement.
59. Nir Rosen, "In the Balance," *New York Times Sunday Magazine*, February 20, 2005, 30–37, 50, 56–58.

10
Draining Swamps and Transplanting Values: Nation Building and the American Military

CONRAD C. CRANE

State stabilization and reconstruction are missions the American military would rather not perform. A traditional institutional aversion to anything resembling nation building was reinforced by the disastrous experience in Vietnam.[1] Most everyone else supports this view of civilian responsibility for stabilization and reconstruction in some form as well, whether involving international organizations, such as the United Nations (UN), or other U.S. governmental agencies, such as the new Office of the Coordinator for Reconstruction and Stabilization in the State Department. But the harsh historical truth is that no international or governmental agency has been as successful as the U.S. military in twentieth-century stabilization and reconstruction, and the capabilities gap between them for such missions remains a yawning chasm. The global war on terror has highlighted the importance of such operations and has set a high bar for expected results, both of which have significant implications for the organization and employment of American military power.

The United States has had much experience with postconflict or transition operations since its founding. In the nineteenth century the army had such missions in Mexico, the post-Civil War South, and the American West. These experiences were generally extremely unpleasant and helped motivate military reformers at the end of the nineteenth century who focused on building an American military establishment worthy of a great power and designed to win major conventional wars. They agreed with the philosophy of the influential Prussian general and theorist Count Helmuth von Moltke the Elder, who believed the primary role of the modern military was simply to successfully conclude major combat operations once the diplomats had gotten the nation into war and then to quickly withdraw while the diplomats resolved the aftermath.

Since the beginning of the twentieth century, the United States has conducted generally successful efforts with reconstruction in Cuba, Puerto Rico, the Philippines, Germany, Italy, Japan, Austria, South Korea, Panama, and Kuwait. Some successes were the result of good planning, like in World War II; others came from adept scrambling, as after Desert Storm; and still others resulted from a combination of luck and patience. Notable failures occurred in Haiti, Nicaragua, Somalia, and Vietnam. Ongoing efforts continue in Bosnia, Kosovo, Afghanistan, and Iraq.

Twentieth-Century Postconflict Examples

Recent history provides a number of useful examples to illustrate the missions and challenges involved in postconflict operations. Though recent cases have more often involved restoring regimes than changing them, many valuable insights still can be gained from careful analysis.

Panama

Operations in Panama leading to the overthrow of the Noriega regime have been touted as a model use of quick and decisive American military force,[2] but postconflict activities did not go as smoothly. The crisis period was exceptionally long, beginning with public revelations about General Manuel Noriega's nefarious activities in June 1987 and culminating with the execution of Operation Just Cause in December 1989. Planning for military intervention began as early as February 1988.[3] When Noriega annulled the May 1989 election, sent his paramilitary thugs to assault opposition candidates, and increased his harassment of Americans, the United States executed Operation Nimrod Dancer. This show of force, executed by U.S. Southern Command, was designed to demonstrate further American resolve in the hope that it would pressure Noriega to modify his behavior. When there was no obvious modification, the president directed the execution of Operation Just Cause. A textbook example of the quality of the new armed forces and doctrine developed in the United States, it encompassed the simultaneous assault of twenty-seven targets at night.[4]

Due to a focus on conducting a decisive combat operation and not the complete campaign, the aftermath of this smaller-scale contingency did not go as smoothly, however. Planning for the postconflict phase, Operation Promote Liberty, was far from complete when the short period of hostilities began. Missions and responsibilities were vague, and planners failed to appreciate adequately the effects of combat operations and regime change.[5] Though guidance from Southern Command (SOUTHCOM) on post-hostility missions was fairly clear, tactically oriented planners at the 18th Airborne Corps in charge of the joint task force carrying out the operation gave postconflict tasks short shrift. For instance, the plan assigned the lone military police (MP) battalion the responsibility for running a detention facility, conducting security for all of the numerous convoys, and providing security for many key facilities, as well as for being prepared to restore law and order.[6] Though the battalion was mainly concerned with a relatively small geographic portion of the country, it was quickly overwhelmed by its responsibilities.

With the elimination of the Panamanian Defense Force, the task of restoring law and order became particularly demanding as looting and vandalism spread throughout the country. This is a common occurrence in situations where national security forces are removed, thus creating instability and a security vacuum. Chaos reigned as American forces scrambled to restore some semblance of order.[7] Military police trained in law-and-order missions did not perform well in unfamiliar combat operations and had inadequate numbers to deal with the problems they faced in the aftermath.[8] They also could not handle all the prisoners of war and refugees for which they were now responsible. Similarly, there were not enough civil affairs personnel or engineers for the rebuilding effort. This seems to be a common theme in American transition operations. Personnel deficiencies were exacerbated by slow and disorganized reserve call-ups relying on volunteers. Political–military interagency cooperation was also poor, as many agencies were excluded from Department of Defense planning and the embassy was severely understaffed.[9]

Senior commanders admitted afterward that they had done poorly in planning for postconflict operations and hoped the army would remedy that situation in the future.[10] Despite these deficiencies, the United States Military Support Group, activated in January 1990 to support the growth of independent Panamanian institutions, was able to be deactivated just one year later in a much more stable country, though whether it or Panamanian leaders deserved most credit for this success was unclear to observers.[11]

Haiti

Like Panama, this was another smaller-scale contingency in response to a long-festering crisis. It began with the military overthrow of President Jean-Bertrande Aristide by Lieutenant General Raoul Cedras in September 1991. On April 1, 1993, the Joint Chiefs of Staff sent the first alert order to the commander-in-chief, U.S. Atlantic Command (CINCUSACOM), to begin planning for contingency operations in Haiti. Planning for active intervention intensified in October of that year after armed protesters in Port-au-Prince turned away a ship loaded with UN peacekeepers. During the next year, international pressure on the military leaders of Haiti increased and was intensified even further by obvious American preparations for an invasion. The decision of the Haitian government in September 1994 to return Aristide to power was to a large extent because they knew army helicopters and 10th Mountain Division soldiers aboard the *USS Eisenhower*, along with elements of the 82nd Airborne Division deployed from Fort Bragg, were headed for Haiti.[12] In fact, Cedras did not begin to negotiate seriously with the American diplomatic delegation until he had confirmed that the 82nd Airborne contingent was in the air. The overwhelming force deployed in the initial occupation, along with the soldiers' professional and disciplined conduct and appearance in continuing operations, did much to deter and control the actions of potential troublemakers.[13] Generally it is always better to begin occupations with a very strong and pervasive ground presence to control and intimidate looters as well as potential resistance. This was not the case in Iraq in 2003, to a large extent because of rosy assumptions about how Iraqis would treat occupation forces.[14] Even Ambassador Paul Bremer has conceded that "we never had enough troops on the ground" there to adequately control the postwar environment.[15]

The long lead time between the beginning of the crisis and actual military intervention, combined with lessons learned from operations like those in Panama and Somalia, greatly facilitated planning for Operation Uphold Democracy.[16] USACOM prepared operational plans for both forced and unopposed entry, while the Department of Defense conducted extensive interagency coordination.[17] Its Haiti Planning Group, with the assistance of other government agencies, prepared a detailed "Interagency Checklist for Restoration of Essential Services." The lead agency for all major functional areas was the U.S. Agency for International Development (USAID), with Department of Defense support (mostly from army units) in reestablishing public administration, conducting elections, restoring information services, assisting the Department of Justice with setting up and training a police force, training for disaster preparedness and response, running airports, and caring for refugees. Military units did have primary responsibility for security measures, such as explosive ordinance disposal, for protecting foreign residents, and for demobilizing paramilitary groups. These were mostly army functions, and the service provided 96 percent of deployed military forces.[18]

These plans and their execution were affected by the desire of military leaders to avoid getting involved with nation-building missions like the ones leading to so much grief in Somalia. Army lawyers wrestled with interpreting humanitarian requests for reconstruction to classify them as related to the mission or as nation building. Requests that fell into the former category were approved, and ones interpreted as nation building were denied.[19] Medical units were told to focus on supporting the Joint Task Force and not humanitarian assistance, as leaders were concerned about not replacing the medical facilities of the host nation.[20] This reluctance to embrace peacekeeping or nation building had its most regrettable result on September 20, 1994, when restrictive rules of engagement prohibited American forces from intervening as Haitian police killed two demonstrators. The next day, American officials expanded the rules of engagement to allow more military involvement in restoring and maintaining law and order.[21]

Such "mission creep" should be expected and has been a part of virtually all American involvement with complex postconflict operations. Similar expansion of army roles and missions happened in most other areas of the restoration efforts in Haiti.²² The attorneys eventually rationalized that any action making Americans look good lessened security risks and could therefore be approved as mission related.²³ Other governmental agencies were slow to arrive or to build up resources, so the military picked up the slack. Generally, the other departments had not done the same detailed planning of the Department of Defense and often wanted more support than this department had expected to provide.²⁴ A typical example was when the ambassador to Haiti asked for military advisers to help set up new government ministries get established until efforts from USAID and the State Department could be established. The result was the hasty deployment of a ministerial advisor team from the 358th Civil Affairs Brigade, "the first large scale implementation of a civil administration effort since World War II."²⁵ The scope and pace of civil affairs missions increased so rapidly that they threatened to get out of control and raised fears that such actions would only heighten Haitian expectations that U.S. forces could fix all of the nation's problems; thus, the missions could set the people up for great disappointment later.²⁶

These expanded missions caused many other problems, to some extent because civil affairs units are relatively small organically and require considerable support from other organizations. Engineer planning, equipment, and personnel were inadequate for their required civil affairs and reconstruction projects. Soldiers had to develop new policies and procedures to help set up internal security forces and expend funds. This often required working around U.S. Code, Title 10 restrictions. They assumed expanded roles in maintaining law and order, including manning and operating detention facilities and developing new crowd control techniques. Items like latrines and police uniforms were in short supply. Doctrine and personnel were not available to establish proper liaison with the myriad civilian organizations working in the country. Intelligence assets were severely taxed, and the force in Haiti had to rely heavily on theater and national intelligence assets to make up for deficiencies.²⁷

However, the military in general, and the army in particular, received much praise for its performance in Haiti. Nonetheless, once the last American troops left the island in April 1996, the situation there deteriorated to conditions approaching those in the early 1990s. Without long-term military involvement, most U.S. policy goals were frustrated. The civilian agencies that replaced military forces did not have the same resources available, and persistent flaws in the Haitian economy, judicial system, and political leadership obstructed reform. American officials decried the results of subsequent elections and admitted the failure of their policies. Even the secretary-general of the UN recommended against renewing the mission there.²⁸ One key lesson from that frustrating experience is that the redeployment of military forces should be predicated on the achievement of designated measures of effectiveness and not based on time limits. Another is that follow-on civilian agencies must be capable of maintaining those standards as well as achieving new ones.

The Balkans

The U.S. Army has picked up its usual predominant load of postconflict tasks requiring several thousand troops in Bosnia and Kosovo and seems resigned to a long-term commitment in the region. Rotational schedules have been prepared through 2005, and discussions have taken place in Washington about establishing a "permanent presence" there.[29]

Current American operations in the Balkans again reveal how force and mission requirements change during the postconflict phase. Two years after the signing of the agreement between the North Atlantic Treaty Organization (NATO) and the Yugoslav Army over Kosovo, U.S. Army troops there were still engaged in "peacekeeping with an iron fist." They were primarily focused on establishing a safe and secure environment under the rule of law, with patrols backed by armored vehicles and detention centers to control troublemakers. The UN–NATO justice system has been heavily criticized, and a Judge Advocate General Legal Assessment Team found the UN mission in Kosovo so severely short of facilities and personnel to establish the rule of law that it recommended teams of fifteen army lawyers be rotated through the country to reinforce the UN effort. Additionally, the resentment of impatient Kosovars has grown against a UN presence that seems to be making little progress toward a transition to local control.[30]

Efforts in Bosnia are more advanced, and the environment is more secure and peaceful. Deployed army task forces have become lighter with every rotation and have moved from immediate security concerns toward enhancing long-term stability. By late 1997 it became apparent to the Stabilization Force that a large disparity existed between the ability of military forces to achieve their initially assigned tasks of the General Framework Agreement for Peace (GFAP) and that of their less-capable civilian counterparts to meet their own implementation requirements. The Stabilization Force realized it could not disengage with such a large "GFAP Gap" remaining and expanded its mission to "assist international organizations to set the conditions for civilian implementation of the GFAP in order to transition the area of operations to a stable environment." U.S. military leaders on the scene recognized they were moving into the area of nation building but saw no alternative if the Stabilization Force was ever going to be able to withdraw or significantly reduce its commitment without risking the peace.[31]

As the nature of the stability operations and support operations in Bosnia evolved, so did the requirements of the peacekeeping force. It needed fewer combat troops and more engineers, military police, and civil affairs personnel. Intelligence requirements changed and expanded. After-action reports highlighted many shortfalls in the Balkans force structure and peacekeeping policies, many of them common to previous smaller scale contingencies (SSCs). Army lawyers again proved adept at "thinking outside traditional fiscal rules and applications" to support operational requirements.[32] The roles of military police expanded to include performing as maneuver battalion task forces and working with international law enforcement agencies.[33] Difficulties with tactical military police trying to perform law-and-order missions reappeared.[34]

There were problems again with shortages and recall procedures for reserve component engineer, military intelligence, and civil affairs augmentation.[35] The massive engineering requirements for Operations Joint Endeavor and Joint Guard especially highlighted branch deficiencies with command and control, construction unit allocations, and bridging.[36] A split-based logistics system trying to meet requirements in the Balkans and back in the central region of Europe required considerable augmentation but still strained combat support and combat service support assets considerably.[37] Liaison officers were in great demand, not just as Joint Commission observers with the Entity Armed Forces but also to coordinate with the myriad nongovernmental organizations and other civilian agencies.[38] There were shortages of linguists throughout the theater, which especially exacerbated problems with intelligence. Military intelligence doctrine was completely inadequate for supporting peace operations, and understaffed intelligence units had to adapt as best they could for the complex "multi-service, multi-agency, and multi-national" situation further complicated by a host of treaty requirements.[39]

A Defense Science Board study concluded that the Balkan operations revealed many shortcomings in psychological operations as well, especially in planning and resources to support engagement and postconflict activities for all the geographic combatant commanders.[40] Even with all these problems, army units in Bosnia have continued to compile a superlative record of accomplishments. However, the GFAP gap remains, with recurring UN problems coordinating and directing civilian agencies. Recent elections were dominated by continuing political divisiveness, reflecting the limited progress in changing peoples' attitudes.[41] Yet although American military leaders have complained about the troops remaining in the Balkans, the fact that decisions about their redeployment have been based on achieving measures of effectiveness and not on reaching a time limit has at least ensured stability in the region.

The world has changed a great deal since the massive occupation efforts following World War II, and wars and smaller-scale contingencies since the end of the Cold War are generally the best source for insights about contemporary postconflict operations. However, a number of important guidelines can also be obtained from analyzing the major American wars of the twentieth century.

The Philippines

In the aftermath of the Spanish–American War, the United States began a long occupation of the Philippine Islands that officially ended with their independence in 1946. This very lengthy transition to self-government is not typical of American experiences with occupation, and the most useful insights are to be gleaned from the early years, when American forces were trying to subdue resistance and establish control in the former Spanish colony.

The Philippines example reinforces the point that *postconflict* operations are a misnomer. To be successful, they need to begin before the shooting stops and will be conducted simultaneously with combat. Ideally, appropriate planning must be completed before the conflict begins so that military forces are prepared to begin immediately accomplishing transition tasks in newly controlled areas. All soldiers need to accept duties typically considered in the purview of civil affairs detachments. There will never be enough civil affairs troops to go around, and immediate needs must be met by whoever is on the scene. Even in the midst of combat, leaders and their soldiers must keep in mind the long-term goals of peace and stability and must conduct themselves accordingly.[42]

In the Philippines, both military and civilian officials recognized that the best agent for local pacification was the military leader on the spot. Considerable decentralization was required for a situation where village attitudes and characteristics varied widely. Officers had great discretion and were not closely supervised, though they also had clear directives from higher headquarters providing guidelines. The requirement for local familiarity meant that soldiers could not be rotated quickly. In village societies personal relationships are important and take considerable time and effort to establish. Even one-year tours in a tribal society like Iraq are probably too short. The army in the Philippines had to accept some decline in the combat efficiency of their units to keep them in lengthy occupation duties. Troops had to be aware of the cultures they were in and not try to force American values. Knowledge of the Koran and local customs were important for everyone. Even John J. Pershing could spend hours talking to local imams about religion. This does not lessen the requirement to achieve the right balance of force and restraint, but the long-term consequences must be considered for every action. General Leonard Wood's predilection for punitive forays in response to even minor incidents like theft did cow many Moro chiefs, but he also undermined many alliances and relationships painstakingly established by local commanders. Instead of quieting small disturbances, Wood's expeditions often created larger problems by driving pacified or neutral villages into joining more rebellious ones and made it more difficult for his subordinates to gain local trust.[43]

Germany

The United States has been involved in the occupation of Germany twice in the past century. At the conclusion of World War I, 200,000 American troops moved to positions around Coblenz, preparing for the possibility the Germans would not sign the peace treaty. When they agreed to the Versailles Treaty in summer 1919, the occupation force rapidly diminished, numbering only 16,000 a year later. By the end of 1922 that figure was down to 1,200, and all left the next year.[44] Though the bulk of responsibility for the details of the occupation and regime change fell on other Allied governments, occupying American troops did find themselves in charge of a million civilians. The U.S. Army and government had not really accepted the administration of civil government in occupied enemy territory as a legitimate military function after the Mexican War, Civil War, or Spanish–American War, and the officer in charge of civil affairs for the U.S. military government in the Rhineland after World War I lamented that the American army of occupation "lacked both training and organization" to perform its duties.[45]

As World War II approached, Army War College committees went back to the World War I reports and developed formal doctrine for military government. In spring 1942, a School of Military Government was established at the University of Virginia, and thinking began there about postwar reconstructions of Germany, Japan, and Italy.[46] By the time Germany surrendered in May 1945, detailed Allied planning for the occupation of that nation had been ongoing for two years. All staff sections at Supreme Headquarters Allied Expeditionary Forces and Army Group headquarters invested considerable resources in developing what became Operation Eclipse. The plan correctly predicted most of the tasks required of the units occupying the defeated country. Within three months, those formations had disarmed and demobilized German armed forces, had cared for and repatriated four million prisoners of war and refugees, had restored basic services to many devastated cities, had discovered and quashed a potential revolt, had created working local governments, and had reestablished police and the courts.[47]

Before any Allied armies entered Germany, planners designated specific military governance units to follow combat forces closely. The first civil affairs detachment in the country set up in Roetgen on September 15, 1944, only four days after U.S. troops entered Germany. Once the Third Reich surrendered, small mobile detachments were sent out immediately to every town in the U.S. occupation zone. Typically, unit commanders confronted mayors with a number of demands: a list of local soldiers and party members, the turn-in of all military and civilian firearms, and housing for American troops. Detachment leaders also imposed curfews after dark and immobilized the population. They also had the authority to replace uncooperative mayors.[48]

The regime in Germany was changed from the bottom up. Throughout history this has been the best approach to rebuilding states. Local elections and councils were allowed to function, and responsibility was shifted to local authorities as quickly as possible. State governments were next in priority, and only after they were working effectively were national elections considered.

At the same time, political life was strictly controlled to prevent any resurgence of radicalism, although public opinion polls were conducted on an almost weekly basis to monitor what the German people thought about occupation policies. The German legal profession was totally corrupted by the Nazis, and each occupying ally took a slightly different approach in reestablishing courts. The British used a lot of old Nazi lawyers and judges while the Americans tried to reform the whole system, which was a slow process. The best solution was probably the one the Soviets applied: they found educated and politically loyal people and gave them six weeks of legal training. Their system built around these lay judges got criminal and civil court systems working very quickly.[49]

One of the most vexing problems for occupation authorities was how to dismantle the Nazi Party and its security apparatus while retaining the skills of some members who performed important functions. This was accomplished by having every adult German fill out a detailed questionnaire about their associations. Heavy penalties applied for lying or failing to answer questions. A board of anti-Nazi Germans and Allied representatives reviewed the *fragebogen* (German for questionnaire) and determined which people had held leadership positions and deserved to have their political and economic activities curtailed for the occupation. By the time they were allowed to regain their rights, democratic Germans were so solidly established that a Nazi revival was impossible.[50] This approach also allowed occupation authorities to clear key administrators and technicians along with some security forces to remain at their posts to assist in the reconstruction efforts. Most commentators agree that the most critical mistake made in the occupation of Iraq was the total disbanding of the Iraqi Army and extensive purging of Baathists without any similar attempt at discriminatory screening.[51]

Japan

The occupation force for Japan, a country slightly smaller than Iraq, included almost twenty-three divisions amounting to more than 500,000 soldiers in 1945. Because of uncertainty about how occupation forces would be received, General Douglas MacArthur decided an overwhelming force was the best insurance against unrest. Most ground forces were American, though allies were used in some sensitive areas, such as British and Australian units in Hiroshima.[52] Although there had been ongoing interdepartmental deliberations in Washington about occupying Japan since the aftermath of Pearl Harbor, the actual planning in the Pacific for Operation Blacklist did not begin until May 1945.[53] Within two years, most Japanese soldiers had been disarmed and repatriated (except from Soviet-controlled areas), a purge list of persons restricted from political activity completed, basic services restored, police reform programs implemented, the economy restarted, land reform begun, and a new democratic constitution adopted that renounced war as an instrument of national policy.[54]

In October 2002, reports emerged that the George W. Bush administration was looking at the Japanese occupation as a model for achieving democratization and demilitarization in Iraq. The administration quickly withdrew from that position, and many experts have highlighted the important differences between the scenarios. The Japanese surrendered unconditionally after total defeat, and the whole world acknowledged the legality and necessity of Allied occupation. Millions were dead, cities were in ashes, and the populace was destitute and cowed. Their more homogeneous culture did not feature the ethnic, tribal, and religious divisions so evident in Iraq, and the Japanese were conditioned to obey the command of the emperor to accept defeat and submit to their conquerors. They also had some experience with limited democracy, though it can be argued that Iraq had similar experiences during their earlier history this past century. Another major difference is that Iraq is much richer in natural resources than Japan, providing another set of opportunities for occupying powers.[55] However, Operation Blacklist does provide useful insights about purging undesirable political elements and how to design the insertion of military forces into a situation where the possibility of armed resistance remains ambiguous. Similarities also can be found between the way Americans viewed the Japanese in 1945 and the way they perceive Iraq today—as a totally foreign and non-Western culture. Historian John Dower, who wrote the seminal work on the American occupation of Japan, argues strongly that it does not provide a useful model for Iraq, with the important caveat that it should give a clear warning to current policymakers, "even under circumstances that turned out to be favorable, demilitarization and democratization were awesome challenges."[56]

These historical examples show a consistent pattern of military effectiveness in stabilization and reconstruction when properly motivated and resourced. But even though armed intervention can provide stability, it cannot force values on a society. And because of the lack of capability for civilian agencies to assume the myriad burdens required for successful occupation, the length of military deployment is going to depend on how ambitious goals are for the endstate. If the establishment of real democracy in failed or rogue states is going to be a key component of the American National Security Strategy, then the U.S. military will have to resign itself to a future filled with long commitments to stabilization and reconstruction. This has major implications for doctrine, force structure, and organizational attitudes.

The Dilemma of Endstates

Many critics of the George W. Bush administration's foreign military excursions forgot that it came into office vowing to cut back on such involvements. The great escalation in American military contingencies abroad was a product of the end of the Cold War and the foreign policy of the Bill Clinton administration. The Defense Department was under great strain before the events of September 11, 2001.[57] The Bush administration wanted to reduce commitments overseas to focus on transforming military forces and preparing to confront China, which was seen as the long-term threat to U.S. security. The concept of *engagement,* an important part of the Clinton National Security Strategy, was no longer acceptable to the Bush administration. It replaced that term in its National Military Strategy with *security cooperation,* which it saw as a more limited mission that did not siphon away as many resources.[58] At the beginning of the Bush administration's first term, nation building was even more to be avoided.

But 9/11 changed all that. At the core of the Bush administration's revised National Security Strategy was a realization of a new American vulnerability. The United States was no longer shielded from harm by two oceans or nuclear deterrence. In fact, a key assumption of their National Security Strategy was that no deterrent would stop the current enemies of the United States, and they would particularly like to inflict the country with mass casualties. Accordingly, these enemies must be killed before they can strike the United States, and all possible efforts must be made to deny them access to weapons of mass destruction. In the short term, this leads to a preference for preemptive actions. But security cannot be gained just by killing alligators; the swamp must also be drained—hence the new emphasis on democracy and freedom and the end to sermons about misguided efforts at nation building.[59]

One of the continuing problems with the conduct of operations to stabilize and rebuild states after decisive combat operations evident from the cases just mentioned is that civilian agencies lack the capabilities and resources to take responsibility from deployed military forces in a timely or effective manner.[60] As part of the effort to create a more robust American interagency capacity for such operations, in 2005 the U.S. State Department created the Office of the Coordinator for Reconstruction and Stabilization. The stated mission for this organization is to "Lead, coordinate, and institutionalize US Government civilian capacity to prevent or prepare for post-conflict situations, and to help stabilize and reconstruct societies in transition from conflict or civil strife so they can reach a sustainable path toward peace, democracy and a market economy."[61] That closing vision is a laudable one, but the history of past American experiences with such operations suggests that proclaimed goals for endstates are best kept vague or modest. Rarely can the course of reconstruction be predicted, and the ultimate success or failure of such efforts is often predicated on the management of public expectations for their result.

The United States can gain many sobering and relevant insights from its experience with Reconstruction after the American Civil War. Radical Republicans in Congress, supported by army leaders like Ulysses S. Grant, championed a vision of a South transformed socially, politically, and economically, but local resistance frustrated their lofty objectives. Despite early advances in expanding civil and political rights, by 1870 papers like the *New York Tribune* were proclaiming that the nation was "tired and sick" of Reconstruction and were pleading for its end. James McPherson's writings on the ensuing decade have titles like "The Retreat from Reconstruction" and "Reconstruction Unravels," reflecting the disappointing course of reform efforts. A true two-party system did not reemerge in the South until the last third of the twentieth century, and it took a hundred years for African Americans there to gain the civil rights and status promised them in the 1860s.[62]

The nation's next experience with rebuilding states came as a result of the Spanish–American War. America was really not prepared for its first excursion into empire, and President William McKinley's initial stated vision for end-states of conquered territories remained understandably vague. Goals for the Philippines evolved over time, and an independent democracy of sorts was finally established after almost fifty years. The experience with Cuba is particularly revealing as to how flexible strategic goals can facilitate perceived success in occupation. The president's first instructions to his occupation forces emphasized security for the populace, along with protection of their personal rights, and though implying a future "new order of things," were overall very cautious about major changes. In his annual message to Congress in December 1898, McKinley stated that military occupation would continue until "complete tranquility and a stable government" had been achieved in Cuba. He added, "It should be our duty to assist in every proper way to form a government which shall be free and independent." Military governors, most notably General Leonard Wood, used this leeway to attempt to match their Progressive impulses with local realities and to establish "good government" in Cuba. Though contemporary critics pointed out that Wood's efforts brought into "sharp relief the danger involved in [attempting] to transplant institutions which are out of harmony with traditions of a people," he was successful in transferring formal political control back to Cuban authorities in May 1902. The occupation was touted as a great success because it apparently achieved public security and a stable indigenous government, demonstrated American beneficence, and ended fairly quickly. Since avowed occupation goals had been kept relatively modest, the public did not take much notice when American troops had to return to the island for brief periods to help quell insurrections in 1906, 1912, and 1917 or when Wood's electoral and humanitarian reforms were short lived. Though little real progress had been made, and coups and revolutions continued until the advent of Fidel Castro, generally Cuba attracted little public or international attention for many decades.[63]

Another reason the continuing troubles in Cuba garnered so little notice was because the world was distracted by the series of crises in Europe leading to World War I. Though President Woodrow Wilson initially tried to keep the United States out of the war, after the nation became an active belligerent he developed an ambitious postwar agenda known as the Fourteen Points. It emphasized liberal democratic values like free trade and self-determination for minorities, was generally a nonpunitive settlement, and relied upon the creation of a League of Nations to maintain international comity and to ensure political independence of all states. The difficulties Wilson faced in getting Allied approval for his idealistic agenda at the Versailles Conference in 1919 are well known. One observer called his failure "one of the major tragedies of modern history," as Wilson sacrificed most of his Fourteen Points to get Allied approval for his League of Nations—which failed to be ratified by the U.S. Senate due to Republican intransigence and his own stubbornness.[64]

Allied considerations also influenced the American vision for endstates after World War II. However, even though Franklin Roosevelt appeared to echo Wilson's desire for an international body that became the United Nations, Roosevelt's public pronouncements of his vision for the postwar world were much less specific than Wilson's, and behind the scenes he remained much more realistic about what he could achieve. The United States and its allies had an avowed goal of unconditional surrender in order to ensure that German and Japanese militarism would never again threaten the world. This vision allowed a lot of postwar leeway as to how it would be accomplished. Inter-Allied and interdepartmental disputes over how Germany should be treated during occupation continued right up to the actual surrender, and the actual occupation directive avoided difficult issues or delayed their resolution. Not until 1947 was a really constructive policy direction for German occupation completed, and the beginnings of the Cold War adjusted it even more. The desire to rearm Germany as a buffer against communism overwhelmed any vestiges of the Morgenthau Plan to make the former Nazi state an agrarian backwater.[65] American occupation policies in the rest of Europe at the end of the war were usually just as incoherent. A recent conference in Vienna on the postwar recovery of Austria concluded that the emergence of a free democracy there occurred despite Allied occupation policies, not because of them.[66]

The reconstruction of Japan did not face the same disputes between allies, but the vision for a specific endstate underwent the same sort of evolution. The crucial decision to keep the emperor was made only in August 1945 as the surrender was being finalized. By September, MacArthur had received a directive that expanded on the Potsdam Declaration and made clear he was to micromanage an accelerated program of demilitarization and democratization throughout all aspects of Japanese life. Dower called the agenda of almost seven years of American occupation "a remarkable display of arrogant idealism." In the end the Cold War again led to compromises with more conservative elements of Japanese society to establish another partner against communism in the Pacific, but the ideals of peace and democracy did indeed take root in Japan.[67]

Occupations in the rest of Japan's lost empire were not as successful, however. In Korea, for example, Americans again displayed a lack of cultural awareness and attention to detail contributing to the conditions that led to the outbreak of war there in 1950.[68] Desires for Cold War security trumped any motivation to support democratic reform, and the United States bolstered the authoritarian regimes of Syngman Rhee and Park Chung Hee. Only in the 1980s did real democracy begin to appear in South Korea. Lest American reconstruction efforts there be judged too harshly, it must be noted that South Korea's northern counterpart is today as far away from demilitarization and democracy as any state on earth.

In part to gain French support for the postwar rearming of Germany, the United States had to commit to supporting French efforts to retain its empire in Indochina, eventually drawing this nation into another war in Asia after the French withdrew. National Security Memorandum 288 in March 1964 established the American aim of "an independent, non-communist South Vietnam" that could stand on its own, and this essential goal was emphasized continually throughout Lyndon Johnson's presidency.[69] That endstate vision appears to be an ideal model, being clear without imposing too many conditions or demonstrating arrogant idealism. However, that is not always a guarantee of success, and it proved unachievable in this case.

American efforts at stabilization and reconstruction have not always come as a result of major wars. As noted already, since the end of the Cold War, the United States has participated in numerous interventions to repair failed or failing states with infusions of liberal democratic principles. The best plan was the 1994 incursion into Haiti to restore Aristide to power and finally establish a functional democratic state. Extensive interagency coordination established a list of tasks and responsibilities to achieve that laudable goal, but again local realities and a lack of long-term will by occupying powers precluded success.[70] At a recent symposium on stability operations, attendees joked sarcastically about the repeated "successful reconstructions" of Haiti, highlighting the apparent intractability of the problems there.[71]

Parties involved in recent stability operations in the Balkans have shown more willingness to stay the course, but long-term success remains elusive. There is peace in Bosnia and Kosovo because of strong military forces deployed there; however, the ethnic tensions that spawned fratricidal warfare remain, and the pluralistic democracy the international community wishes to establish is still a dream. Kosovo experienced deadly ethnic rioting as recently as March 2004. After five years of international control, it elected as prime minister a former Albanian guerilla leader being investigated for war crimes against Serbs by the International Criminal Tribunal for the Former Yugoslavia.[72] A recent alarming report by the International Crisis Group on the lack of progress in achieving liberal democratic stability opens with "Time is running out in Kosovo. The status quo will not hold."[73]

According to Kimberly Zisk Marten, this result should not be surprising, because such recent failures to transplant democracy have much in common with similar efforts by colonial powers. The United States, Great Britain, and France have all repeated the aforementioned experience of Cuba in trying to relinquish control of colonial holdings while leaving lasting positive change behind. The record of international attempts to impose democracy is especially dismal during the wave of such interventions in the 1990s. Looking at operations such as those in Haiti, the Balkans, and East Timor, Marten concludes, "Nowhere have the liberal democratic military peacekeeping operations of the 1990s created liberal democratic societies. They did not even create much forward momentum in that direction, in any of the countries where they were deployed." Her study emphasizes that recent interventions, like the imperial era, demonstrate the continuing ability of disciplined soldiers to establish order but also shows that liberal democratic states rarely demonstrate the will, or coherent policy direction, to successfully transplant their values to other cultures.[74]

This dismal historical record suggests some guidelines for policymakers. They should avoid setting the bar too high, or being too specific, when proclaiming visions for postwar endstates. It is relatively easy to remove threats or restore order, but changing values and cultures takes much longer. The same liberal democratic system that seems so worth transplanting also hinders such states from conducting the long-term occupations necessary to make it stick. And even after extended reconstructions, the end result will still most likely be more a result of local realities than of imposed structures. The best course of action appears to be to recognize these trends and to aim for generic peace and stability with unique regional characteristics rather than more specific reforms. This leads to quicker withdrawals and fewer heartaches, even if the result will not be as ideologically satisfying. But if it is really true that democracy is the only way to drain the international swamp of terrorism, and lengthy western stewardship is required to create it in many areas, then the U.S. military will have to pay more attention to stability and reconstruction operations. That will mean new force structures, new doctrines, new training, and new attitudes. The army's new modularity reforms are a step in the right direction, and a whole generation of military leaders has now developed in Somalia, Haiti, the Balkans, Afghanistan, and Iraq who realize the importance of such missions in accomplishing policy goals. But the nation still has to grapple with the question of whether it really desires its military forces to focus on such roles. Recent problems with army and marine recruiting indicate that it may be difficult to sustain an all-volunteer structure involved in extensive stabilization and reconstruction operations.[75] That may become the ultimate limitation on using the military to help spread democracy and free markets.

Notes

1. Conrad C. Crane, *Avoiding Vietnam: The U.S. Army's Response to Defeat in Southeast Asia* (Carlisle Barracks, PA: Strategic Studies Institute, 2002).
2. Combat operations were conducted superbly and quickly in a complex situation (with difficult terrain, many civilians, and restrained rules of engagement) that required intricate joint planning and execution.
3. John T. Fishel, *The Fog of Peace: Planning and Executing the Restoration of Panama* (Carlisle: U.S. Army War College [USAWC] Strategic Studies Institute, 1992), 7.
4. Thomas Donnelly, Margaret Roth, and Caleb Baker, *Operation Just Cause: The Storming of Panama* (New York: Lexington Books, 1991).
5. Fishel, *Fog of Peace*, 29–63.
6. USAWC, *American War Plans Special Text, 2001* (Carlisle Barracks, PA: USAWC, 2000), 233–306.
7. John Fishel and Richard Downie, "Taking Responsibility for Our Actions? Establishing Order and Stability in Panama," *Military Review* (April 1992), 66, LXXII, 69–70.
8. Ibid., 70–5; Carmen Cavezza (former commanding general, 7th Infantry Division), interview by Larry Yates, Robert Wright, and Joe Huddleston, April 30, 1992, Fort Lewis, WA, oral history interview JCIT 097Z, Joint Task Force South in Operation Just Cause, http://www.army.mil/cmh-pg/documents/panama/jcit/JCIT97Z.htm.
9. Cavezza, interview; Fishel, *Fog of Peace*, 38, 58–9.
10. Cavezza interview. Cavezza expressed doubt, however, that he could have trained his unit adequately for the mission-essential tasks list required for war and for the complexities of the postconflict operations he faced.
11. Fishel, *Fog of Peace*, 63.
12. CINCUSACOM CD-ROM, *Operation UPHOLD DEMOCRACY: U.S. Forces in Haiti, 1997* (executive-level AAR [After Action Review] pamphlet), Norfolk, VA, 1–13.
13. Joint Universal Lessons Learned System entries 10451-37950 and 10754-92362, USACOM CD-ROM.
14. Michael R. Gordon, "Poor Intelligence Misled Troops about Risk of Drawn-Out War," *New York Times*, October 20, 2004, 1A.
15. CNN, "Bremer: More Troops Were Needed after Saddam's Ouster," October 5, 2004, http://www.cnn.com/2004/WORLD/meast/10/05/bremer.rumsfeld/index.html.
16. David Bentley and Robert Oakley, "Peace Operations: A Comparison of Somalia and Haiti," National Defense University Strategic Forum no. 30, (Washington, D.C.: NDU Press, May 1995).
17. CINCUSACOM, *Operation UPHOLD*, 2–9.
18. Haiti Planning Group, "Draft Interagency Checklist for Restoration of Essential Services," furnished to author by Mike Fitzgerald, CENTCOM J-5; U.S. Army Program Analysis and Evaluation Directorate, *America's Army ... into the 21st Century* (Washington, DC: HQDA, 1997), 5.
19. Karl Warner, interviewed by Dennis Mroczkowski, JTF-190 Operation Uphold Democracy AAR, 266-267, CINCUSACOM, *Operation UPHOLD*.
20. Gerald Palmer, interview by Christopher Clark, JTF-190 Operation Uphold Democracy AAR, 269, CINCUSACOM, *Operation UPHOLD*.
21. Chronology, Operation UPHOLD DEMOCRACY, CINCUSACOM, *Operation UPHOLD*.
22. This expansion of missions is evident from the Operation UPHOLD DEMOCRACY Logistics Support Operations briefing from the CINCUSACOM, *Operation UPHOLD*.
23. Warner, interview, 267.
24. JULLS entry 10829-67459, CINCUSACOM, *Operation UPHOLD*.
25. Memorandum, 358th Civil Affairs Brigade to Commanding General, U.S. Army Civil Affairs and Psychological Operations Command, "After Action Report, USACOM Operation Uphold/Maintain Democracy," May 26, 1995, CINCUSACOM, *Operation UPHOLD*, 3.
26. JULLS entry 11566-55234, CINCUSACOM, *Operation UPHOLD*.
27. JULLS entries 00676-58398, 00969-70100, 01040-06216, 02656-20553, 10355-63106, 10447-74360, 10758-27517, 11558-362234, 11640-05029, 11640-61760, 50257-20594, 50258-39326, 92638-89373 CINCUSACOM, *Operation UPHOLD*.
28. U.S. General Accounting Office (GAO), *Foreign Assistance: Any Further Aid to Haitian Justice System Should be Linked to Performance-Related Conditions*, GAO-01-24, October

2000; "Haiti Is Nightmare for U.S.," *Charleston Post and Courier*, October 5, 2000; "Haiti's Disappearing Democracy," *New York Times*, November 28, 2000, 28A; Ben Barber, "U.S. Officials See Failed Haiti Policy," *Washington Times*, November 29, 2000, 13A; "Annan Urges End to U.N. Mission in Haiti," *New York Times*, November 29, 2000.

29. "Army Has Begun Reviewing Options for Long-Term Balkan Presence," *Inside the Pentagon*, October 26, 2000, 1; Steven Lee Myers, "Army Will Give National Guard the Entire U.S. Role in Bosnia," *New York Times*, December 5, 2000, 8A.

30. Gregory Piatt, "A Good Bit Of Progress ... A Long Way to Go," *European Stars and Stripes*, September 17, 2000, 2; "UN-NATO Court Setup In Kosovo Faulted," *New York Times*, October 20, 2000, 4A; Donald G. McNeil, Jr., "GIs in Kosovo Are Judges, Jailers, and Much More," *New York Times*, November 22, 2000, 4A; Emily Kelly, "Peacekeeping with an Iron Fist," *Stars and Stripes Omnimedia*, November 29, 2000; Memorandum, by Donald Campbell, "Trip Report for Reserve Component (RC) Judge Advocate General (JAG) Legal Assessment Team for Kosovo Deployed between 26 May and 5 June 2000," June 9, 2000, copy furnished to author by Peter Menk; Yaroslav Trofimov, "U.N.'s Long Stay and Power in Kosovo Stir Resentment," *Wall Street Journal*, January 3, 2003, 1.

31. Headquarters, U.S. Army Europe, *After Action Report: Operation Joint Guard*, (HQ, USAREUR: Heidelberg, GE, Nov 1998), 3-2, 3-21–3-23 (hereafter referred to as *Operation Joint Guard*).

32. Ibid., 9–26.

33. Ibid., 9–36.

34. Headquarters, U.S. Army Europe, *Operation Joint Endeavor: After Action Report*, (HQ, USAREUR: Heidelberg, GE, May 1997), 2-35 (hereafter referred to as *Operation Joint Endeavor*).

35. *Operation Joint Guard*, 4-5, 5-18. Problems were so acute that the AAR asked for both the reserves and national guard to realign their units and specialties for peacekeeping missions.

36. David A. Kingston, *Towards a More Relevant Engineer Command* (Carlisle Barracks, PA: USAWC, 2000); *Operation Joint Endeavor*, 206, 210.

37. *Operation Joint Endeavor*, 130–1.

38. Center for Army Lessons Learned, *Joint Military Commissions: Lessons Learned from Operation JOINT ENDEAVOR*, May 1996. The large requirement for military liaison with the myriad agencies involved in such contingencies was a key point of discussion at Center for Strategic Leadership, "Postconflict Strategic Requirements Workshop" USAWC, Carlisle Barracks, PA, November 28–30, 2000.

39. *Operation Joint Endeavor*, 78–94; Melissa E. Patrick, *Intelligence in Support Operations: The Story of Task Force Eagle and Operation Joint Endeavor* (Carlisle Barracks, PA: USAWC, 2000).

40. "Outdated Equipment, Organizational Issues Hamper Effective PSYOPS," *Inside the Pentagon*, September 28, 2000, 1.

41. Leighton W. Smith, "NATO's IFOR in Action: Lessons from the Bosnian Peace Support Operations," National Defense University Strategic Forum no. 154, (Washington, D.C.: NDU Press, January 1999), R. Jeffrey Smith, "An Ethnic Hatred Permeates Bosnia's Bitter Peace," *Washington Post*, November 10, 2000, 30; Paul Watson, "Bosnian Vote Seen as a Setback," *Los Angeles Times*, November 14, 2000, 9. For a good summary of the lack of long-term progress in the Balkans, see Kimberly Marten, *Enforcing the Peace: Learning from the Imperial Past* (New York: Columbia University Press, 2004).

42. Most of the ideas in this section on the Philippines were developed in conjunction with Brian Linn's (Texas A&M University), discussion with the author on October 30 & 31, 2002. He is the author of *The U.S. Army and Counterinsurgency in the Philippine War, 1899–1902* (Chapel Hill, University of North Carolina Press, 1989) and *The Philippine War, 1899–1902* (Lawrence: University of Kansas Press, 2000).

43. Linn, discussions; Jack C. Lane, *Armed Progressive: General Leonard Wood* (San Rafael, CA: Presidio Press, 1978), 124–5.

44. Edward M. Coffman, *The War to End All Wars: The American Military Experience in World War I* (Lexington: University of Kentucky Press, 1986), 359–60.

45. Earl F. Ziemke, *The U.S. Army in the Occupation of Germany, 1944–1946* (Washington, DC: Center of Military History, 1975), 3.

46. Ibid., 6–8.

47. Kenneth O. McCreedy, *Planning the Peace: Operation Eclipse and the Occupation of Germany* (Fort Leavenworth, KS: School of Advanced Military Studies, 1995).
48. Wally Z. Walters, *The Doctrinal Challenge of Winning the Peace against Rogue States: How Lessons from Post-World War II Germany May Inform Operations against Saddam Hussein's Iraq* (Carlisle Barracks, PA: USAWC, 2002), 18.
49. The ideas in this paragraph were provided by James Corum (School of Advanced Airpower Studies, Maxwell AFB, AL) via e-mail on October 29 & 30, 2002.
50. Ibid.
51. Gordon, "Debate Lingering on Decision to Dissolve the Iraqi Military," *New York Times*, October 21, 2004, 1A.
52. John W. Dower, *Embracing Defeat: Japan in the Wake of World War II* (New York: W. W. Norton, 1999), 73; and Charles A. Willoughby, ed., *Reports of General MacArthur, Volume 1 Supplement, MacArthur in Japan: The Occupation: Military Phase* (Center for Military History: Washington, DC, 1966), 2, 16.
53. Dower, "Lessons from Japan about War's Aftermath," *New York Times*, October 27, 2002, A13; Willoughby, *Reports of General MacArthur*, 2.
54. For more complete descriptions of these reforms, see Dower, *Embracing Defeat*; and Willoughby, *Reports of General MacArthur*.
55. Dower, "Lessons"; Chalmers Johnson, "Rebuilding Iraq: Japan Is No Model," *Los Angeles Times*, October 17, 2002, 19B; James P. Pinkerton, "Iraq Is No Stage for MacArthur–Japan Sequel," *Long Island Newsday*, October 15, 2002, 33A; and Trudy Rubin, "Pre-Occupation Blues," *Philadelphia Inquirer*, October 16, 2002, 15A.
56. Dower, "Lessons."
57. Crane, *Landpower and Crises: Army Roles and Missions in Smaller-Scale Contingencies during the 1990s* (Carlisle Barracks, PA: Strategic Studies Institute, 2001).
58. Office of the Chairman of the Joint Chiefs of Staff, *National Military Strategy of the United States, 2004—A Strategy for Today: A Vision for Tomorrow* (Washington, DC: U.S. Government Printing Office (USGPO), 2004).
59. The White House, *The National Security Strategy of the United States* (Washington, DC: USGPO, 2002).
60. For more on this issue see Crane and W. Andrew Terrill, *Reconstructing Iraq: Insights, Challenges, and Missions for Military Forces in a Post-Conflict Scenario* (Carlisle Barracks, PA: Strategic Studies Institute, 2003), 3–11, 17, 43–47.
61. Carlos Pascual (keynote address, Stability Operations Symposium, U.S. Army Peacekeeping and Stability Operations Institute, Carlisle Barracks, PA, December 13, 2004).
62. James M. McPherson, *Ordeal by Fire: The Civil War and Reconstruction* (New York: Alfred A. Knopf, 1982), 493–619.
63. Lane, *Armed Progressive*, 55–113; Thomas G. Patterson, J. Garry Clifford, and Kenneth T. Hagan, *American Foreign Relations: Volume 2, A History since 1945* (New York: Houghton Mifflin, 2000), 41–3.
64. Patterson and others, *American Foreign Relations*, 89; Harold Nicolson, *Peacemaking 1919* (New York: Grosset and Dunlap, 1965), 195. For a recent excellent book on the Versailles Conference, see Margaret Macmillan, *Paris 1919: Six Months that Changed the World* (New York: Random House, 2002). Nicolson is the quoted observer.
65. Mark Stoler (visiting Harold K. Johnson, Professor of Military History, U.S. Army Military History Institute), discussion with author, Carlisle Barracks, PA, January 27, 2005; for a detailed discussion of the process that led to occupation policies in Germany, see Harold Stein, ed., *American Civil–Military Decisions: A Book of Case Studies* (Birmingham: University of Alabama Press, 1963), 311–464.
66. "Vom Krieg zum Frieden: Militarverwaltungen und Post-Conflict Nation Building," a symposium held at *Diplomatische Akademie*, Vienna, Austria, May 18–19, 2004.
67. Dower, *Embracing Defeat*.
68. Ronald Spector, "Failed Occupations: American, British, and Indian Soldiers and the End of Japan's Asian Empire" (lecture, Perspectives in Military History, Carlisle Barracks, PA, December 15, 2004).
69. Charles F. Brower IV, "American Strategy in the Vietnam War, 1965–68" (lecture, Naval War College Senior Course, Newport, RI, March 1992).
70. For more on the Haitian example, see Crane and Terrill, *Reconstructing Iraq*, 5–8.

71. Discussions at Stability Operations Symposium conducted by the U.S. Army Peacekeeping and Stability Operations Institute, Carlisle Barracks, PA, December 13, 2004.
72. "A Poor Choice in Kosovo," editorial, *New York Times*, December 24, 2004, 18A.
73. International Crisis Group, *Kosovo: Toward Final Status*, January 24, 2005, http://www.crisisgroup.org.
74. Marten, *Enforcing the Peace*, 13–7.
75. Eric Schmitt, "Marines Miss January Goals for Recruits," *New York Times*, February 3, 2005, 12A; Will Dunham, "U.S. Army Struggles to Coax Recruits amid Iraq War," originally published by Reuters, now available at http://www.commondreams.org/headlines 05/0306-4.htm.

11
The United States and Europe: Explaining the Transatlantic Bond[1]

ROBERT J. LIEBER

In recent years a narrative about European–American relations had become fashionable and even commonplace. It held that the rapidly developing European Union (EU) was well on the road to a fundamental transformation in its relationship to the United States. Having expanded to twenty-five countries with a population of 460 million people, in an area extending from the Atlantic to the Russian border and from the Arctic Circle to the Mediterranean, and with a common currency and aspirations for a common foreign and defense policy, Europe would soon emerge as a powerful competitor to the United States.

In this narrative, the half-century after World War II was often imagined as a kind of halcyon era of cooperation, understanding, and multilateral collaboration. But the end of the Cold War had removed the common threat posed by the Soviet Union. And a decade later, the George W. Bush administration, with its disregard for international law and institutions, and in the aftermath of the 9/11 terror attacks its unilateralist policies and resort to force against Iraq, was described as pushing transatlantic relations to the breaking point. On both sides of the Atlantic journalists, authors, and politicians offered strident criticism of American policy, and it appeared by no means excessive to ask whether the United States and Europe might now be on the verge of a divorce in which their alliance of more than a half-century collapsed or of even becoming great power rivals.

Yet although it is true that European resentment of American political, economic, and military predominance is real and that disputes have multiplied over a wide range of issues, it remains utterly premature to write the epitaph for the transatlantic bond. Not only does the deep structure of these relations rest on mutual security needs, shared economic interests, and common values, but recent events also have served to highlight just how exaggerated much of this narrative had become. On the European side, these events include dramatic election results in Germany, France, and the Netherlands. In the German case, the May 2005 regional election in North Rhine Westphalia, followed by federal elections in September showed that the Schroeder government had lost the confidence of many of its historically most loyal supporters. In the French and Dutch cases, in May and June 2005, decisive rejection of the proposed European constitutional treaty demonstrated that even among the populations of the EU's most loyal founding members, opposition to centralization in Brussels, resentment at the lack of democratic accountability, and concern about national priorities were now paramount. Moreover, the referendum result in France weakened President Jacques Chirac, who had envisaged Europe as "a means to struggle against American hegemony."[2]

In short, despite its historic expansion, the EU is not about to emerge as a formidable superpower, let alone take on the role of balancer against the United States. The enlarged EU lacks sufficient central authority and the military capacity for a truly effective common defense policy. In addition, a community of twenty-five countries now includes member states from Eastern Europe, whose history provides strong motivation for maintaining close ties with the United States. This perspective was evident in the support of the ten governments of the Vilnius group for American policy toward Iraq. Indeed, the intra-European divide over Iraq policy provided evidence that the member states of the EU will not reach a consensus on balancing against the United States. Moreover, domestic politics, economic problems, and the demographic profile of aging populations are much more likely to produce reductions in defense spending than the increases required to provide the EU with the military capability of a major world power.

Europe's lack of unanimity on foreign and security policy, the inability to provide for its own security, and shared interests in transatlantic economic cooperation and institutions require a continuing partnership with America. Moreover, despite what Freud called the narcissism of small differences, the legacy of common values remains fundamental. Europe has neither the will nor the capability for a real break, and the interests of the United States work against a divorce as well. Nonetheless, the sources of disagreement are deep-seated and have been increasing, and they deserve close attention.

Sources of Conflict

If, as Lord John Acton famously said, power corrupts, then lack of power may also do so. For today's Europe, and especially for countries once accustomed to a true international great power status, the disparity with the United States is especially painful. During the Cold War, sheltering under the American security umbrella was an unavoidable imperative, though under Charles de Gaulle and his successors the French quest for autonomy repeatedly pushed the Atlantic relationship to its limits.

These problems were not exclusively of Parisian origin. Virtually from the time of its inception in 1949, the Atlantic alliance weathered a wide range of disputes, concerning not only strategy but economics and politics as well.

One of the earliest crises erupted over German rearmament and the 1954 rejection of a proposed European Defense Community by the French National Assembly. The controversy was serious enough for Secretary of State John Foster Dulles to threaten an "agonizing reappraisal" of America's relationship with Europe. Two years later, in 1956, the Dwight Eisenhower administration found itself at loggerheads with France and Great Britain when it joined with Moscow to condemn the Anglo–French expedition to retake the Suez Canal from Egypt. A more subtle but far-reaching problem arose after the October 1957 Soviet launch of Sputnik, the world's first orbiting space satellite. With the American homeland potentially vulnerable to Soviet intercontinental ballistic missiles, how could an American president credibly sustain the commitment to Europe if defending Paris or West Berlin now meant exposing Chicago or New York to a potential Russian nuclear attack? Intra-alliance conflicts continued with the French withdrawal from the North Atlantic Treaty Organization's (NATO) integrated military command structure in 1966. Symptomatic of disputes at the time was the title of a book by Henry Kissinger, *The Troubled Partnership*.[3]

Out-of-area disagreements also developed over France's desperate and ultimately futile efforts to keep control in Indochina (1946–54) and Algeria (1954–62), and subsequently over U.S. intervention in Vietnam. A severe crisis erupted after the October 1973 Yom Kippur War, with the accompanying Arab oil embargo against the United States and the Netherlands and the French-led tilt toward the oil-producing countries in contrast to American support for Israel. Oil- and energy-related issues continued to reverberate in policies toward Iran after its 1979 revolution and in disputes over the construction of a pipeline to carry natural gas from Russia to the West. In the early 1980s, an intense crisis developed over the U.S. and NATO decision to deploy intermediate-range nuclear forces in Europe to counter Soviet SS-20 missiles. Multiple examples could be added to the list: trade frictions, economic competition, agricultural protectionism, cultural clashes, and disagreements about policy toward the Israeli–Palestinian conflict, among other issues.

Though these disputes were often intense, the underlying mutual security imperative caused Western Europe to remain closely allied with the United States to preserve an unambiguous American guarantee. In recent years, however, and without Cold War concerns, the possibilities for fragmentation have increased. Among the Europeans, France has become the most strident critic of American power and the most avid in seeking ways to increase its own autonomy and to steer the European Union toward an independent course. Near the end of his life, President François Mitterrand gave vent to a deep antagonism, declaring, "France does not know it, but we are at war with America. Yes, a permanent war, a vital war, an economic war, a war without death. Yes, they are very hard, the Americans, they are voracious, they want undivided power over the world."[4] Subsequently, then French foreign minister

Hubert Vedrine proclaimed, "We cannot accept ... the unilateralism of a single hyperpower," and President Jacques Chirac called for a "more balanced ... distribution of power in the world."[5]

Mitterrand, Vedrine, and Chirac expressed these resentments during the mid- and late 1990s, while the Bill Clinton administration guided American foreign policy and well before the 2000 election and the election of George W. Bush. Indeed, under Clinton tensions had emerged over Bosnia and Kosovo, the treaty to ban antipersonnel land mines, the Kyoto Treaty on global warming, the International Criminal Court, the Anti-Ballistic Missile Treaty, enforcement of United Nations (UN) sanctions against Iraq and Iran, and the Israeli–Palestinian conflict. This list serves as a reminder that serious disagreements, including complaints about American hegemony and unilateralism, have emerged under both Democratic and Republican administrations and under presidents with very different leadership styles and policies.

Reactions to the Bush Doctrine

With the start of the Bush presidency in January 2001, European–American relations became increasingly acrimonious. Two important reasons were the disputed outcome of the November 2000 election and because the Texas governor was largely unknown abroad. European political leaders as well as journalists, commentators, and foreign policy analysts displayed the anxiety that occurs when the White House suddenly is occupied by a chief executive unfamiliar to elites in Paris, Berlin, London, and Brussels. Many took cues from their American counterparts, most of whom had preferred Al Gore for president, and expressed strong antipathy to the new administration. European first impressions thus became lopsidedly negative, and there was not only an immediate uneasiness, but increasingly inflammatory press coverage, of the new president. Despite taking office with an experienced foreign policy team, Bush was frequently derided as a primitive, a Texas cowboy, and even, in the words of one prominent British columnist, a "global vandal" and "reckless brigand."[6]

In the wake of the September 11, 2001 terror attacks, European criticism of the Bush administration subsided, and political leaders, the media, and the public embraced the United States in the presence of what seemed a threat not only to America but also to the entire modern world and its values. Despite an undercurrent of smug satisfaction that even the seemingly omnipotent United States was not invulnerable or that America might somehow have deserved the attacks, solidarity was widespread. This was evident in public opinion polls and took the form of political support and active cooperation in intelligence and antiterrorism measures.

Indeed, just one day after the attack, on September 12, 2001, the nineteen members of NATO invoked Article V of the North Atlantic Treaty for the first time in the history of the alliance. Article V treats an attack on one member state as an attack on all and requires they take action under their respective constitutional procedures. Ultimately, sixteen of the nineteen member countries contributed personnel to the Afghan campaign. In the ensuing months, American air power and special forces, working with the Afghan opposition, quickly defeated the Taliban regime and its Al-Qaeda allies. The victory occurred far more rapidly and with far fewer casualties than many observers had expected,[7] but to retain tight control of the operation the Bush administration opted not to conduct the Afghan war as a NATO operation. The decision made sense militarily, but it contributed to European resentments about unilateralism.

These reactions increased in response to the president's January 2002 State of the Union address to the Congress, in which he spelled out what became known as the Bush Doctrine ("The United States of America will not permit the world's most dangerous regimes to threaten us with the world's most destructive weapons") and especially Bush's use of the phrase *axis of evil* to describe Iraq, Iran, and North Korea. During the following year, with the growing divide over the impending use of force against Iraq and the September 2002 release of the president's National Security Strategy document,[8] European criticisms of American policy intensified. The change in attitude marked a shift away from the solidarity expressed by the allies in the initial days after September 11, and it occurred for reasons specific not only to the United States but also to Europe.

First, American policymakers together with a substantial part of the public saw 9/11 as a watershed, and in their view the country now found itself in a war against terrorism. By contrast, with the passage of time Europeans were less inclined to share this understanding. For example, an opinion poll conducted by the German magazine *Der Spiegel* eight months after the attacks found that by a 3-to-1 margin Europeans saw 9/11 as an attack on America but not on Europe or the world.[9] Though the analogy was misplaced, they tended to equate 9/11 with their own experiences of domestic terrorism during prior decades. Indeed, in France a sizeable minority even saw the United States as a threat. In response to an April 2002 opinion poll asking respondents to choose from a list of France's principal adversaries in the world, 31 percent pointed to the United States, ranking it the third greatest threat after international terrorism (63 percent) and Islam (34 percent) and just ahead of small countries armed with nuclear weapons (30 percent).[10]

Second, there was a reaction against America's willingness and ability to employ its formidable power without the agreement of the UN Security Council or deference to the expressed views of European leaders, particularly those of France and Germany. In addition, foreign as well as domestic critics seized upon two features of the National Security Strategy: preemptive military action against hostile states and terrorist groups seeking to develop weapons of mass destruction; and the determination to maintain primacy by dissuading the rise of great power challengers. Some even expressed the view that the United States was becoming a rogue nation.

Third, much of the European reaction was directed against the American-led effort to disarm Iraq and to oust the regime of Saddam Hussein. Policy differences had existed before, but in this case the intensity of German and especially French opposition and the way in which more animus seemed directed against a democratic ally, the United States, than at the tyrannical regime in Iraq, with its record of aggressive wars against its neighbors and flagrant defiance of binding UN Security Council resolutions, suggested an entirely different attitude. Yet European governments were by no means unanimous in opposition, and the leaders of eight countries signed a letter by Prime Ministers Tony Blair of Great Britain and José Maria Aznar of Spain that supported the United States. The other signers represented the Czech Republic, Denmark, Hungary, Italy, Poland, and Portugal.[11] Shortly thereafter, ten countries of the Eastern European Vilnius group signed their own letter of support. On the eve of the Iraq War, the Bush administration could thus claim backing from the leaders of four of the six largest countries in Europe—Great Britain, Italy, Spain, and Poland—and from the leaders of at least eighteen European countries.

This official support masked the problem that by the time the war began on March 20, 2003, European public opinion, with the partial exception of Great Britain and a number of Eastern European states, had become increasingly opposed to the use of force against Iraq. Between July 2002 and March 2003, there was a strongly adverse shift in European attitudes toward the United States. In Germany, for example, where 61 percent of the public had held a favorable view of the United States versus 34 percent unfavorable, the numbers shifted to just 25 percent favorable and 71 percent unfavorable. In France a similar swing occurred, from a favorable 63 percent versus 34 percent unfavorable to an unfavorable 31 percent versus favorable 67 percent; during the war, one-fourth of the French public wanted Hussein to win.[12] Even in Poland and Great Britain where the public remained sympathetic to the United States, support began to erode. Great Britain dropped from 75 percent favorable versus 16 percent unfavorable to 48 percent versus 40 percent, and Poland from 79 percent versus 11 percent to 50 percent versus 44 percent.[13] These views reflected the heated political climate and often intense public opposition to the war, but even a year after the war, in March 2004, only 37 percent of the Germans and 38 percent of the French expressed a favorable view of the United States.[14]

European Attitudes and Structures

On both sides of the Atlantic, it has become commonplace to depict Europe as a single entity with shared attitudes and policy predispositions increasingly at odds with those of the United States. But Europe is not monolithic, as evident not only on controversial foreign policy issues but also on wider questions of European unity and whether an enlarged and increasingly institutionalized EU should plot its course as a counterweight to the United States or in partnership with it. Great Britain and France have frequently been at odds over these issues, but other cleavages exist as well. The smaller and medium-sized countries (Austria, Belgium, Denmark, Finland, Greece, Ireland, Luxembourg, the Netherlands, Spain, Sweden, Portugal) and many of the new member states of Eastern Europe have differed with the largest ones (Germany, France, Great Britain, Italy) over the extent to which decision-making authority within the EU should be based on the size of each state. And historically, disagreements have taken place between those who seek a truly federal United States of Europe versus those insisting on limiting the transfer of sovereignty. These internal differences limit the extent to which Europe can take on an adversarial role vis-à-vis America. Nonetheless, some commonalities transcend the EU's internal divisions.

Even countries that sided with the United States on the use of force in Iraq and that favor a close Atlantic partnership do see multilateral institutions in a more favorable light than does Washington. On support for the Kyoto Treaty, the International Criminal Court, the Comprehensive Test Ban Treaty, and the role of the United Nations as a fundamental source of international legitimacy, European policymakers and publics mostly agree. These shared views also exist on sensitive cultural and lifestyle issues. One in particular is the death penalty, where European governments now uniformly oppose capital punishment, though popular attitudes have been less uniform. Countries applying for EU membership are required to have abolished the death penalty, and the issue has become a source of friction with the United States.

Europe's receptivity to multilateralism and to international institutions has been shaped by experiences of the past half-century in which the continental countries have finally transcended centuries of conflict and war. Together they have achieved a substantial degree of cooperation and integration, the codification of agreed rules and procedures, and the transfer of previously sovereign state powers to the EU. As a consequence, Europeans tend to draw lessons from their specific regional experience and to transpose these to a global level.

This perspective can create tensions with the United States, as does a structural trait of the EU itself. As the EU's original institutions (the European Coal and Steel Community, followed by the Common Market and European Community) expanded from six member states (France, Germany, Italy, and the Benelux countries) to nine, then twelve, fifteen, and now twenty-five, agreement on European policies has become an ever more cumbersome task. Though provisions for decision by weighted majorities has increased, unanimity is still required on the most important issues, including foreign and defense policy. Thus, when the EU does manage to overcome coordination problems and to succeed in hammering out positions on specific issues, the policy stance often becomes inflexible. As a result, negotiations between Europe and the United States become fraught with difficulty since the opportunities for compromise and adjustment that would ordinarily exist between two large countries—each with its own central authority—are much less likely to be available on the European side.

Two other structural problems create obstacles to cooperation. One is reflected in a widely quoted comment attributed to Kissinger: "When I want to call Europe, whom do I call?"[15] In some instances, the EU does have a single individual empowered to negotiate on its behalf, and the draft constitutional treaty attempted to address this problem by providing for a president and a single representative for foreign policy. However, even if the constitution were to be ratified it is hard to imagine that countries such as France, Great Britain, or Germany will be content to abdicate their own foreign policy roles. Another difficulty is political as well as structural. In establishing their common identity, European states face a temptation to do so by defining their own position as distinct from that of the United States. This creates an incentive for disagreement almost regardless of the substance of the issue at hand.

Then there remains the disparity of power. The disproportion between the capacities of the United States and those of the individual European countries is so great that the latter often embrace multilateral institutions and rules as a means of limiting their superpower ally's freedom of maneuver. This impulse is intrinsic to disparities of size and influence, regardless of specific policies. Indeed, a former French foreign minister once observed that if France were to possess the kind of power the United States now enjoys, Paris would be even more cavalier in its exercise. The power disparity also contributes to a free-rider problem. Achievements such as security represent a form of collective or public goods for all the countries of the alliance in the sense that they are able to benefit from it whether or not the Europeans contribute. As Michael Mandelbaum noted, peace in Europe, nuclear nonproliferation, and access to Persian Gulf oil are examples of international public goods.[16] Not surprisingly, there is a temptation to evade responsibility because participants know the United States is likely to pay the cost of dealing with potential threats, including economic ones, whether or not they contribute.

Note, however, that this kind of tension has been a feature of long standing and that it existed well before the end of the Cold War and the emergence of the United States as the world's sole superpower. A graphic example of free riding—and of the accompanying buck passing—in which a costly or dangerous task is avoided, whether through inaction or deliberate evasion, was for many years evident in French policy toward terrorist groups operating in Europe. During much of the 1970s and 1980s, Paris applied the sanctuary doctrine in tolerating the presence of terrorist groups provided they did not carry out operations against French interests.[17] An egregious case of this behavior took place following the 1977 arrest in Paris of Daoud Oudeh, known as Abu Daoud, a founder of the Palestinian terrorist group Black September. His group was responsible for the Munich Olympic massacre of Israeli athletes in 1972 and for the murder of American ambassador to Sudan Cleo Noel in 1973. Ignoring extradition requests from Israel and Germany, the government of President Valery Giscard d'Estaing instead deported him to Algeria.[18] During the 1980s and 1990s, however, as the groups became more violent and in some instances took actions within France the policy began to break down, and intelligence cooperation with the United States and other European countries significantly improved.

Policy Conflicts

On issues large and small, European and American differences have multiplied, and they are by no means confined to foreign policy. In trade policy, for example, there have been continual frictions, for example over governmental subsidies to aircraft manufacturers Airbus and Boeing. In another case, the EU filed a complaint against the United States in the World Trade Organization (WTO), challenging a policy that allowed major American corporations to establish foreign subsidiaries in tax havens as a means of reducing taxes on exports. The WTO ruled against the American policy, and the judgment temporarily allowed the EU to impose punitive tariffs on $4 billion worth of U.S. exports until Congress passed legislation changing the law.

In a case that combined trade, culture, and politics the United States and twelve other countries, including Argentina, Canada, Egypt, Mexico, and Chile, filed suit against the EU for its five-year moratorium that had blocked exports of genetically modified agricultural products even though no scientific evidence of health risks had been found. American officials criticized European policies for causing unwarranted fears in famine-stricken African countries that have a pressing need for food aid as well as for the improved yields of these crops. In turn Europeans faulted the United States for refusing to join 100 other countries in ratifying the Convention on Biological Diversity, or the Cartagena Protocol on Biosafety, an agreement for importers and exporters of genetically modified crops.[19] However, the protocol was drafted in the face of U.S. objections about allowing importing countries to reject genetically modified crops even without scientific evidence of risk—a provision American negotiators saw as unduly restrictive.[20]

European critics of the United States sometimes convey the impression that the EU countries are far more altruistic and cooperative in their global relationships and in helping other countries to develop. However, the EU, along with America and Japan, shares a pattern of protecting domestic agriculture in ways harmful not only to consumers and taxpayers but also to agricultural exporters in the developing world who find it harder to compete against these subsidized products. Indeed, the EU's agricultural protectionism has been especially egregious (a tribute to the political effectiveness of French farmers), and the international aid organization Oxfam reports that the EU has higher barriers to imports from the developing world than any other large industrial economy.[21]

On many of these issues, the domestic structure of European economies and political systems makes cooperation harder not only with the United States but with other countries as well. Historically high levels of unemployment, demographic pressures from an aging population, and rising costs to maintain generous social services and pension benefits, coupled with relatively higher taxes and rigidities in the mobility of labor and in regulatory policies, tend to undercut Europe's competitiveness with America and Asia. These conditions foster restrictive economic and trade policies and thus greater friction with the United States and others. In addition, European parliamentary systems, with the exception of Great Britain, mostly produce coalition governments seriously constrained by the demands of their component groups.

The sources of transatlantic conflict are evident on the American side as well. The U.S. political system can complicate the efforts of administrations of either party to implement coherent foreign policy strategies and to bargain pragmatically with others. At times divided government, in which the opposition party controls one or both houses of Congress, has been a feature of contemporary political life, as for example was often the case between 1981 and 2002. Under those circumstances, a president may have to compromise on much of his foreign policy agenda, especially on appropriations, confirmation of appointees, treaty ratification, trade policy, and economic sanctions. For example, the Clinton administration, after its first two years in office, had to deal with a Senate Foreign Relations Committee chaired by the formidable Jesse Helms, who saw the world in very different terms. As a result, administration policies on such issues as arms control, trade, the environment, and multilateral institutions were less consistent with European preferences than might otherwise have been the case.

Even when the executive and legislative branches of government are controlled by the same party, as with Republican control during most of the George W. Bush presidency, serious problems in foreign policymaking often exist. For example, legislation in response to the WTO ruling on foreign sales corporations took a long time to pass because of partisan disputes among legislators. The structure of Congress also tends to magnify protectionist pressures, as evident for example in the web of subsidies and other nontariff barriers that shield domestic producers of steel, sugar, and cotton from foreign competition.

American Exceptionalism

American exceptionalism—the unique character of the ethos, society, and culture—also sets the United States apart from Europe. For nearly two centuries, observers of America, from Alexis de Tocqueville writing in the 1830s to contemporary social scientist Seymour Martin Lipset, have identified fundamental factors shaping the American character. These include the absence of a feudal past, a nonconformist religious tradition, and the manner in which, during the nineteenth century, the legacy of the American Revolution evolved into a liberalism emphasizing individualism and anti-statism. An early-twentieth-century American author, Mark Sullivan, provided a similar list of "distinctive characteristics," including individual freedom of opportunity, zeal for universal education, faith in representative democracy, adaptability, responsiveness to idealism, and "independence of spirit."[22] As Lipset later observed, Americans prefer a competitive, individualist society with equality of opportunity and effective but weak government.[23] In contemporary terms, these traits often take on a form almost guaranteed to antagonize European elites who, in the words of Walter Russell Mead, find American society "too unilateralist, too religious, too warlike, too laissez faire, too fond of guns and the death penalty, and too addicted to simple solutions for complex problems."[24]

American idealism also comes into play in ways that can influence foreign policy, as for example in the language of the Bush second inaugural in January 2005. The president's emphasis on freedom and liberty caused some uneasiness among Europeans, who feared an excess of crusading zeal to impose democracy by force. But the inaugural speech echoed themes with deep roots in American life, and precedents for it can be found in the language of Presidents Woodrow Wilson, Franklin Roosevelt, John Kennedy, and Ronald Reagan. The Bush language was tempered with assurances that this was "not primarily the task of arms" and that "America will not impose our style of government on the unwilling." Nonetheless, there remained transatlantic differences of emphasis and belief, as evident in contrasting U.S. and European approaches toward dealing with past and present leaders such as Saddam Hussein, the late Yasir Arafat, and the rulers of Iran and North Korea. That contrast was evident in the words of Condoleezza Rice to a British audience on her first trip as secretary of state: "There cannot be absence of moral content on American foreign policy. Europeans giggle at this, but we are not European, we are American, and we have different principles."[25]

Diverging attitudes also are reflected in differing understandings about modern society and world affairs. In foreign policy, the most salient of these competing notions concerns nationalism and the use of force. Robert Kagan, David Brooks, Walter Russel Mead, and others have written eloquently about the diverging twentieth-century experiences of Europeans and Americans.[26] For Europeans, nationalism brought repeated and catastrophic wars, and the use of force did not prevent most of their societies from being ravaged by war. By contrast, with the exception of the Civil War and the terrorist attacks of September 11, 2001, Americans have been largely insulated from such devastation, and twentieth-century military campaigns, with the exception of Vietnam, have been mostly successful and often laudable in moral terms.

Intervention against Germany in World War I, liberation of Western Europe from Nazi occupation in World War II, defense of Europe from Stalin and his successors during the Cold War, and liberation of Kuwait are among the major cases, but even a number of recent smaller scale interventions (e.g., Panama, Bosnia, Kosovo, Haiti) can be seen in a positive light.

World War II experiences also help to explain differences between Great Britain and the continental Europeans. Virtually all the European powers either were defeated and occupied by Nazi Germany in the early years of the war or, in the case of the Axis powers—Germany, Austria, Italy—were ultimately defeated and occupied by the allies. By contrast, England managed to stand alone after the fall of France in 1940 and ultimately emerged at the end of the war with America and the Soviet Union as one of the victorious Big Three allies. Great Britain did share the 1956 Suez debacle with France, but it did not suffer the kind of disastrous colonial wars Paris fought in Indochina and Algeria from 1946 to 1962. These experiences help to explain why Great Britain delayed so long in seeking Common Market entry and why it has typically been the least willing among EU member countries to relinquish sovereignty.[27]

Sources of Solidarity

Based on the previously mentioned wide-ranging causes for a parting of ways—the end of the Cold War and differences of structure, attitude, experience, and policy—it would seem logical to begin writing the epitaph for the European–American relationship. Indeed, not a few students of the subject have been doing exactly that. Nonetheless, that conclusion is almost certainly mistaken. Instead, practical experience not only of the Cold War decades but also of the years since 1989 suggests an entirely different lesson. The EU's capacity in the realm of foreign policy and defense remains limited, and on issues including proliferation, terrorism, international trade, financial stability, the environment, foreign aid, and disease, the evidence again and again is that there simply is no alternative to cooperation with the United States. Overall, the sources of Atlantic solidarity are grounded in the deep structure of the world in which Europe and America live, and they are at least as durable as the stubborn problems the Western world continues to face.

Europe in the International System

European aspirations to a certain high-mindedness are often evident in the rhetoric of its leaders. By addressing the outside world as though the European experience of the past half-century was somehow universal, they imply the Kantian categorical imperative, "Act as if the maxim from which you act were to become through your will a universal law."[28] But Latin America (*viz.* Cuba and Columbia), East Asia (North Korea), and South Asia (Kashmir, Pakistan, India) are not well understood through the EU lens, and even less is this optic useful in viewing the brutal realities of the Middle East (Iraq, Iran, terrorism, Al-Qaeda, the Israeli–Palestinian conflict), let alone Africa (Sudan, Congo, Liberia, Ivory Coast). In this sense the precepts and practices that now prevail on the European continent—especially peace, domestic stability, the rule of law, cooperation, the transcending of national sovereignty, and agreed means for nonviolent resolution of disputes—are noble as ideals but often are beleaguered or irrelevant in troubled parts of the world. Indeed, insofar as portions of the Balkans are concerned even Europe itself does not enjoy uniform cooperation, tranquility, and the rule of law.

At the international level, the basic reality remains that of anarchy, meaning the absence of effective and binding sovereign authority above the level of the state. In other words, there is no government of governments. This feature has been repeatedly cited by contemporary scholars as well as in the classic writing of Thucydides and later in the work of thinkers such as Niccolo Machiavelli and Thomas Hobbes. The anarchy problem gives rise to security anxieties. Realist scholars describe a self-help system, in which states fear for their security and are ultimately dependent on their own efforts. This in turn leads to a security dilemma, as states' efforts to provide for their own security tend to make other states feel insecure. This insecurity has been neatly expressed by John Mearsheimer, who has observed that "... because there is no higher authority to come to their rescue when they dial 911, states cannot depend on others for their own security."[29]

Of course, there exist important realms in which multilateral institutions and even international law do operate successfully. Examples abound in economics, trade, communications, air and sea travel, health, and other areas. But on the most urgent and lethal dangers, existing law and institutions as well as the United Nations are frequently without the capacity or political will to act. Evidence from recent decades provides numerous examples: Iraq's invasions of Iran in 1980 and Kuwait in 1990; Saddam Hussein's flagrant defiance of UN Security Council resolutions; genocide in Rwanda; ethnic cleansing in Bosnia and Kosovo; North Korea's violations of the Nuclear Non-Proliferation Treaty; Iran's pursuit of nuclear weapons (also in contradiction of the Nuclear Non-Proliferation Treaty); contraband trade by countries knowingly engaged in violating UN sanctions regimes; state complicity in drug-running, money laundering, and terrorism; and the desperate problems created for their own populations and their neighbors by failed states (e.g., the Congo, Liberia, Sudan).

In cases such as these, the use of state power and of military force by the United States or by other countries that have the ability to act is often the sine qua non. For example, in the Kuwait crisis of 1990–91, without American leadership UN Security Council Resolutions and sanctions would have been unable to prevent Iraq's incorporation of that UN member state as Iraq's nineteenth province. In the case of Bosnia, weapons embargoes, Security Council resolutions, the creation of UN-protected "safe areas," and European intervention under UN auspices proved ineffective in halting murderous ethnic violence. Only after three years and 200,000 dead did the United States finally take the lead in ending the killing.

Impressive as it is, the EU's experience of cooperation, law, and institution building as a means to end conflict and war does not by itself explain how Europe managed to reach its present state. Although the miracle of Franco-German rapprochement and European unity had multiple causes, the central factors in ending three centuries of balance of power rivalry in Western and Central Europe included World War II, the Cold War, and the role of the United States. Among these were the devastating military defeat of Germany and the Axis powers, which discredited fascism and aggressive nationalism; the occupation of Germany and Italy by U.S. and allied forces; the threat posed by the Soviet Union, which required a large American military presence for the purposes of deterrence and defense; and the need for states that had previously been rivals to cooperate within the American-led NATO alliance. World War II and the Cold War were critical factors in creating the conditions for European unity, and the American security umbrella had the effect of solving the anarchy problem on a regional basis. As a result, European states no longer needed to fear or balance against one another.

Beginning with Marshall Plan aid in the late 1940s, the United States also provided crucial support for the development of European economic and political integration. This was motivated by the desire to strengthen Europe in the face of Cold War challenges and to ward off the kind of economic and political instability that had afflicted much of Europe during the 1920s and 1930s. Of course the ideals, passions, energy, and institutions that went into creating the EU were necessary conditions, but by themselves they would not have been sufficient. The relevant comparison can be found a generation earlier in the aftermath of World War I. Then too, there was revulsion against the destruction and carnage of war, widespread expression of idealistic hopes for doing away with armed conflict, the creation of new institutions—most notably the League of Nations in 1919—as well as solemn international agreements such as the 1928 Kellogg-Briand Pact to outlaw war. But none of these prevented the downward spiral that saw Adolf Hitler and the Nazis take power in Germany and unleash the events leading to World War II and the Holocaust.

Europe's Foreign and Defense Policy Vacuum

With the enlargement and deepening of the EU, efforts to develop a truly European foreign and defense policy have intensified. This is not altogether new. Since at least the 1992 Maastricht Treaty, the EU countries have been formally committed to a common foreign policy and since 1999 to important elements of a shared defense policy. Yet Europe's quest has delivered limited results, and progress toward a European defense has proved elusive. This lack of achievement is no mere failure of policy or leadership. The obstacles are deep-seated and are unlikely to be overcome for the foreseeable future. They stem from two fundamental European deficits: the inability to reach internal political agreement, and the inability to mount a common defense even if such agreement did exist.

Foreign and defense policies exist in a sphere of high politics and national sovereignty in which states are reluctant to relinquish autonomy. Decisions about the use of force, with their life-and-death implications, are not readily delegated. Indeed, for all its insistence on a European identity separate from America, France has been the most assertive of its own foreign policy autonomy, even when this contradicts the positions of its European partners. French unilateralism has been evident in numerous cases ranging from the oil shocks of the 1970s to interventions in Africa and policies toward the former Yugoslavia and Iraq. British leaders, too, have long been outspoken on not ceding control of foreign policy, considering it a core prerogative of sovereignty.

Prior to the 2004 signing of the constitutional treaty, the EU had not just one but two senior foreign policy representatives empowered to speak on its behalf. One of these, Chris Patten, was a representative of the European Commission, and the other was Javier Solana, a spokesperson for the European Council, which brings together the leaders of the member governments. Yet in the immediate aftermath of 9/11, it was neither of these figures but the individual leaders of Great Britain, France, Spain, and Germany who flew to Washington to meet individually with Bush at a time of grave crisis.

Another serious obstacle to a common EU foreign policy is that differences among the member countries have sometimes been as great as those between Europe and the United States. Political differences, such as those on Iraq, are not new. For example, in 1991, responding to the increasing turmoil in Yugoslavia and the unwillingness of the United States to intervene in another crisis in the immediate aftermath of the Gulf War, the president of the European Council, Foreign Minister Jacques Poos of Luxembourg, proclaimed that "the age of Europe has dawned."[30] But a lack of political agreement and of capability left the EU unable to act, thus compounding Yugoslavia's tragedy. Kosovo was another case in point, with Great Britain more assertive than the United States in advocating the use of force; Greece, historically sympathetic to the Serbs, opposed the action.

The expansion of the EU widens these differences even as it adds to the number of countries supportive of close ties with the United States. The Czech Republic, Hungary, and especially Poland have painful historical memories of their treatment at the hands of their powerful neighbors Germany and Russia, and they have good reason to look to the United States for credible security guarantees. The Baltic states of Lithuania, Latvia, and Estonia have even stronger motivation. After signing a statement supporting the U.S. use of force against Iraq, these countries found themselves the target of intense pressure from France. Chirac uttered the condescending words, "Ce n'est pas très bien élève"[31] [This does not show good upbringing] and implied that East European dissent could adversely affect their pending EU membership. As another example, Lithuania complained that France had failed to consult it during delicate EU negotiations over Russian transit access to the territorial enclave of Kaliningrad.[32]

These incidents illustrate a larger point about the conduct not only of France but also of other leading member states of the EU. For all their rhetorical embrace of European solidarity, fidelity to multilateralism, and commitment to international institutions and laws, when they believe their national interests are at stake they are capable of acting unilaterally, regardless of these stated principles. France's protection of its agricultural interests, its refusal to allow the import of British beef despite EU clearance, its arm-twisting of the East Europeans, and its indulgent position on Iraqi sanctions in the years from 1992 to 2001 (not entirely unrelated to Iraq's large debts for purchases of French arms) are cases in point. But France is not alone, and whether in dealing with terrorism, national security, powerful domestic lobbies, or sensitive matters of national sovereignty Great Britain, Germany, Italy, Spain, and others have been capable of acting with lesser regard for lofty ideals.[33] As an example, Germany has sought a permanent UN Security Council seat without regard to EU priorities. Moreover, in the face of stubborn economic problems, including lagging growth rates and historically high levels of unemployment, France and Germany, as well as a number of other smaller countries, have defied the EU's limit on domestic budget deficits. These countries incurred deficits that broke the EU-imposed ceiling of 3 percent of gross domestic product (GDP). Indeed, Germany exceeded that limit in the years from 2002 through 2004, even though its own government had played a major role in writing the rules for the EU's "stability pact," created to coincide with adoption of the Euro.

Even if the countries of the EU were to find themselves in complete policy agreement and to relinquish sovereignty concerns, their weaknesses remain a stubborn obstacle to the emergence of a credible European defense. The United States devotes more than $400 billion annually to defense. In absolute terms this dwarfs the spending of all likely competitors combined, yet it amounts to just over 4 percent of the GDP, a figure well below the 6.6 percent peak during the Reagan build-up of the mid-1980s and much less than the double-digit levels of the early Cold War years. In contrast, the 25 counties of the EU spend just 55 percent of the U.S. figure,[34] but even that amount gives them far less capability because the effort is divided among separate national defense budgets—and much is wasted in duplication.

Europe has more men and women in uniform than the United States; however, its large forces—many of them reliant on conscripts—are mostly more suited to traditional land warfare than to the specialized foreign interventions and high-technology weaponry characteristic of twenty-first-century conflict. Until recently, the capabilities have remained remarkably limited. For example, in the Kosovo crisis of 1999, despite the Europeans having two million men and women in uniform, it took "an heroic effort" (in the words of the British Foreign Secretary) merely to deploy 2 percent of them as part of a peacekeeping force.[35]

In material terms, the EU does have the ability to organize a significant and effective defense. The creation of a new European Defense Agency (EDA) for the purpose of coordinating military research and spending reflects the aspiration to improve capabilities and prepare for global security threats. Nonetheless, the EDA is a very modest undertaking, and the structure of the EU's political institutions, differences among its twenty-five member countries, demographic and financial constraints, and the weight of competing budget priorities largely work against fundamental change.

As if these were not sufficient obstacles to Europe's going it alone, there remains the problem of fragmented European defense industries: the larger states seek to protect their own corporate champions while often excluding more efficient foreign producers. Even when Europeans have cooperated to acquire military equipment, they often face disproportionate costs or other limitations. For example, a consortium of European countries is building the Galileo system of space satellites for its own global positioning system. Though this gives them a capability of their own, it does so at a cost of more than three billion dollars and largely duplicates what is already available from the United States. As another example, seven European countries—Belgium, Great Britain, France, Germany, Luxembourg, Spain, and Turkey—finally agreed in May 2003 to purchase 180 large military transport planes from the European aerospace consortium Airbus at a cost of $24 billion. In opting for European manufacture rather than buying existing and less costly American models, they purchased an aircraft, the A400M, that does not yet exist and the initial delivery of which will not begin until the year 2009. As another example of added costs in buying European, the $3.6 billion contract to build the engines for this aircraft went to a French–British consortium, despite a bid by American manufacturer Pratt & Whitney for 20 percent less.[36]

Even with the new transport plane and the Meteor air-to-air missile system being developed by an Anglo–French consortium,[37] Europe will remain far behind the United States in air warfare capabilities. Though the quality of European weaponry in air-to-air and air-to-ground systems actually meets or exceeds that of the United States, air superiority requires the integration of the most modern high-performance aircraft and avionics, weapons systems, surveillance, satellites, real-time intelligence, communications, targeting information, sophisticated radar, and battle-management systems. In the absence of this complete package, the impact of any one component is limited.

The types of military systems required for Europe to achieve effective modern capabilities demand not only a much more rational use of existing funds but also a higher level of funding altogether. Although France spends 2.6 percent of its GDP on defense and Great Britain 2.4 percent, Germany, the European country with the largest population and economy, spends less than 1.5 percent.[38] Moreover, the imperatives of German economic modernization, high unemployment, budget deficits, an aging population, and the political dynamics of coalition government, as well as cultural and historical factors, create pressures for lower rather than higher defense spending.

Elsewhere in Europe, comparable political, economic, and societal constraints also tend to cause downward pressure on defense budgets. The consequences are evident in the difficulty Europe has encountered in creating an effective Rapid Reaction Force. The idea for such a body was conceived in 1999, in the aftermath of the American-led Kosovo action. European governments, led by France and Great Britain, sought to create by 2003 a force of 60,000 troops capable of being deployed within sixty days and sustained in action for up to one year. This force was to be available for action in cases where NATO opted not to intervene and to carry out the so-called Petersberg tasks, i.e., largely humanitarian missions. However, even this capacity, directed mainly at peacekeeping not the much more difficult requirement of peacemaking, remained at least temporarily out of reach. The Europeans lacked not only the overall number of 180,000 designated troops (required for training and rotation purposes to sustain the 60,000-member force in the field) but also the transportation, surveillance systems, precision-guided weapons, and other modern equipment that such a force would require.[39]

Given its population, modern technology, and wealth, the EU does possess certain kinds of military potential. Great Britain maintains well-trained forces available for deployment in combat outside Europe, and its military personnel played active roles in the 1991 war to oust Iraq from Kuwait and again in the 2003 campaign to defeat Hussein. British aircraft also took part in the Bosnia and Kosovo campaigns of 1995 and 1999 and in enforcing the no-fly zones in Northern and Southern Iraq (1991–2003). France has somewhat less capacity but has intervened periodically in Africa in times of chaos or civil war, as in Ivory Coast and the Congo, French generals took command of the NATO peacekeeping forces in Afghanistan in August 2004 and in Kosovo in September 2004.

EU countries did take a modest but tangible step forward in November 2004, with a commitment to create battle groups of 1,500 troops, each available for deployment within five days from a formal decision to undertake a crisis mission. In 2005, France and Great Britain created standby groups made up of their own personnel, and additional commitments were made for a multinational French–German–Spanish battle group and for a largely Scandinavian group composed of Swedes, Finns, Norwegians, and Estonians. The EU objective was to have a dozen of these groups available for deployment by 2008 for operations outside the NATO framework, for example in missions authorized by the UN. Nonetheless, even these arrangements have faced equipment shortfalls, especially in the airlift capacity necessary to deliver the troops quickly to crisis areas.[40]

American Capabilities and European Insecurity

Given its limitations in foreign and defense policy, Europe has fundamental reasons to rely upon America as a hedge against future threats. Though Russia appears considerably less chaotic than in the immediate aftermath of the breakup of the Soviet Union, its nascent democratic features have been seriously curtailed by President Vladimir Putin's government, and Russia's future behavior cannot be ensured. Important parts of the old USSR remain troubled, and the long-term stability of the central Asian republics Uzbekistan, Tajikistan, and Kazakhstan; the Caucasus Georgia, Armenia, and Azerbaijan; and the large East European Republics Ukraine and Belarus appears far from certain. Elsewhere, instability throughout parts of the former Yugoslavia, internal problems within the countries of the southern Mediterranean, and dangers stemming from the Middle East and Persian Gulf all represent potential risks. Upheaval along the European continent's eastern or southern periphery, whether from economic collapse, ethnic conflict, or interstate war, also could send waves of refugees flooding into Europe.

As evident in the cases of Pakistan, Iran, and North Korea, the actual or potential diffusion of weapons of mass destruction—including missile technology and nuclear, chemical, and biological weapons—poses significant dangers for Europe. Although these threats are more diffuse and conjectural than the Soviet threat during the Cold War, they are not negligible and provide a reason for European countries to retain their alliance with the United States as a form of insurance. Consistent with these concerns, the EU heads of state and government in December 2003 endorsed a European Security Strategy based on a proposal by Javier Solana, their high representative for common foreign and security policy, for facing five security threats: terrorism, proliferation of weapons of mass destruction, regional conflict, failed states, and organized crime. Although the European Council deleted a reference in the original Solana strategy paper implying support for the preemptive use of force, it did retain language referring to robust intervention, preventive engagement, and a crucial role for the United States: "Acting together, the EU and the U.S. can be a formidable force for good in the world."[41]

Closely connected to Europe's need for an American security partnership is the fact of U.S. primacy. Only the United States possesses the means to project power abroad in a decisive and compelling manner. Since the end of the Cold

War, American might has been apparent both when it was deployed (e.g., Kuwait and Bosnia in 1995, Kosovo in 1999, Afghanistan in 2002, Iraq in 2003) and when it was absent (e.g., Rwanda in 1994, Bosnia prior to 1995, presently in Darfur). With time, the relative margin of U.S. power vis-à-vis other actors appears to be increasing rather than decreasing. Not only does the United States possess the ability to move large forces by sea and air across great distances on a timely basis, but it also enjoys wide advantages in precision-guided munitions, stealth technology, satellite communication, command and control, and the whole panoply of forces and technologies needed to prevail in the air and on the modern battlefield.

Despite the unusually harsh and vindictive rhetoric leading up to the Iraq War in 2003, even governments most adamant in their criticisms of Washington still took pains to cite the overriding importance of the American security tie. Thus, Germany's foreign minister Joschka Fischer observed, "As anyone with any sense of history realizes, the transatlantic relationship is the crucial cornerstone of global security, of peace and stability not just in Europe, not just in the United States, but around the whole world. To call this cornerstone into question would be worse than folly."[42] Similarly, just one week after the start of the Iraq War, Dominique de Villepin, who was French foreign minister at the time and who had been the most strident critic of the United States, nonetheless proclaimed that "because they share common values, the U.S. and France will reestablish close cooperation in complete solidarity."[43] The German defense minister was even more direct in observing that there could be no security in and for Europe without America.[44] Despite continuing tensions after the Iraq War, Fischer was explicit in expressing a sense of the common threat to regional and global security from "destructive jihadist terrorism with its totalitarian ideology."[45] And in the aftermath of the Bush reelection, Chirac told British journalists that "constructing Europe in opposition to the United States makes no sense."[46]

In this context, the countries of the EU do have a security contribution to make, not only in intelligence and antiterrorism cooperation but also in peacekeeping, policing, and nation building—tasks for which U.S. forces have often been less well suited. Such activity mostly takes the form of cooperation with NATO, since the organization is by far the best suited for coordinating large-scale multinational engagements. As France's minister of defense has observed, the European defense capabilities are meant to work as part of NATO, in relief of NATO, and on their own without NATO.[47] The EU took a small practical step in March 2003, when it assumed command of what had been a NATO peacekeeping mission in Macedonia and deployed slightly more than 300 troops there in a noncombat role. Subsequently, the EU took over peacekeeping responsibilities in Bosnia in late 2004. European forces also have played leading roles in Kosovo, with the NATO-led international force responsible for establishing and maintaining security,[48] and in Afghanistan, where

NATO's International Security Assistance Force operates primarily in and around the capital of Kabul.

Shared Interests and Values

Security imperatives underpin the European–American connection, and despite disparaging words hurled across the Atlantic, so do shared interests and values. European–American economic relations are simultaneously cooperative and competitive. They are competitive in their rivalry for export markets and commercial advantage, but they remain cooperative insofar as all parties share a deep interest in preserving the successful functioning of existing arrangements for trade, investment, financial flows, and the international economic institutions that sustain them. Europe and the United States find themselves needing to cooperate through the International Monetary Fund, Group of Seven, WTO, and other groupings, not only to resolve mutual problems but also to cope with global financial and economic dangers. Europe and the United States are one another's top trading partners, and they have a huge stake in each other's economic health, as demonstrated by vast two-way flows of investment and transatlantic mergers in many industries.

Shared experiences and values complement these material interests. Although the western leaders who founded the great postwar institutions have long since passed from the scene and the events of the Cold War are a rapidly receding memory, other factors tend to sustain cooperation among policy elites, including easy familiarity with each other's culture and, in the case of most Europeans, a broad knowledge of American English. The information revolution, the Internet, and the media have also fostered increasing communication and contact across a wide range of activities. To be sure, not all these contacts are positive, as reflected in complaints about mass culture, "Disneyfied" entertainment, McDonald's, and the like. Resentment about American predominance in these spheres is very real, but complaints have been expressed in some form throughout the past half-century, often as much by cultural critics in America as those in Europe. Moreover, at the popular level (discussed in the following chapter) attraction to or at least fascination with American mass culture, clothing styles, music, entertainment, leisure, and language has spread throughout Europe, especially among younger generations.

Perhaps most important, however, is the fact that Europe and the United States continue to share basic values, including liberal democracy, open economies (albeit in different variations), the rule of law, the dignity of the individual, and western notions of morality and rationality. This underlying commonality remains fundamental, even—or especially—in an era of globalization. Regardless of highly publicized differences, Europe and America continue to have far more in common with each other than with any other regions of the world.

Radical Change?

Could Europe and the United States nonetheless one day come to an irreversible parting of the ways and even become great power antagonists? Momentous events often arrive by surprise, so the question deserves attention. In essence, a fundamental rupture would require the combination of two elements. One of these is capability—the capacity of Europe to act as a great power opponent of the United States. The other is will—whether Europeans or Americans desire this to happen and seek to bring it about. Despite the rhetoric of conflict, neither of these elements now exists nor seems likely, but under what conditions could they ultimately occur?

In terms of capability, the EU would need to achieve an unprecedented breakthrough in which member countries did not just talk about relinquishing fundamental political sovereignty but actually did so. But the existing ability of each of the twenty-five members to exercise a veto necessarily limits EU foreign policy. In contrast, a true European federation, a United States of Europe, would possess the institutional prerequisites for acting as a single great power in defense and foreign policy. Even then, the EU countries would also need to make the politically difficult decision to allocate scarce resources to build a powerful military and to choose competition rather than partnership with the United States. French leaders have tended to favor such a course of action, but theirs is not the prevailing view. Could these changes ever take place? Theoretically, yes, though the likelihood remains remote and has been further diminished by opposition to the constitutional treaty in key member countries. Some scholars of international relations and history argue that reaction to America's extraordinary predominance will lead to such an outcome, but for the combination of reasons cited here, there is little reason to anticipate such a transformation.

Motivation and will also are key factors. If the Europeans were to find themselves facing some unprecedented threat to their survival in circumstance where the United States was no longer able or willing to provide security, the political impetus for Europe to provide its own security could emerge. On the other hand, the alternative of EU political fragmentation or breakdown cannot be ruled out either. By itself, a growing European–American divergence in values and beliefs of the kind to which Kagan and others have pointed is unlikely to sustain this kind of change. Instead, a steadily worsening climate of political dispute finally reaching a breaking point on both sides of the Atlantic would have to occur, and with it a collapse either in the will or ability of the United States to sustain its own world role, for example in reaction to a military quagmire or some devastating series of attacks on a scale far greater than those of September 11.

Explaining the Lack of Balancing

Just as it has been said that Great Britain and America are two countries divided by a common language, so it is tempting to add that Europe and the United States are divided by their shared history, interests, and values. Though some European leaders, most notably those of France, have proclaimed the need for Europe to counterbalance American power and indeed had sought to do so over Iraq, it remains highly unlikely that any sustained balancing will take place. At the time, leaders such as Chirac and de Villepin seemed to become intoxicated with the accolades they received in heading the opposition to America's use of force in Iraq. Their efforts went well beyond the boundaries their predecessors de Gaulle, Georges Pompidou, Giscard, and Mitterrand observed, in that they were no longer acting as allies who disagreed with a policy but as leaders of a putative coalition of adversaries. Their efforts ultimately failed because the United States was not stopped from undertaking the Iraq campaign and because the controversy highlighted the deep divisions within Europe as well as the shortcomings of the UN and the limitations on the role of France.

For the foreseeable future, Europe does not have a viable alternative. The United States is too preponderant and the countries of the EU too divided. Europe lacks the means of its own defense, and there is no real alternative to the security tie with the United States. At the same time, Europe does possess a comparative advantage in postwar peacekeeping and nation building. Both Europe and the United States have a vital interest in the viability and institutions of the existing economic order, and only through their cooperation is there any possibility of addressing broader world problems. In addition, they share far more in common than appears from the cacophony of Atlantic debate. In sum, however ardently it may be predicted—or desired—by disgruntled critics, divorce is not on the horizon.

Notes

1. This chapter provides an updated and revised version of Robert Lieber, "Europe: Symbolic Reactions and Common Threats," in Lieber, *The American Era: Power and Strategy for the 21st Century* (Cambridge, UK: Cambridge University Press, 2006), ch. 3.
2. Quoted in *Economist*, April 26, 2003.
3. Henry A. Kissinger, *The Troubled Partnership: A Re-Appraisal of the Atlantic Alliance* (New York: McGraw-Hill, 1965).
4. Mitterrand died in 1996. The passage is from a biography by Georges-Marc Benamou, *Le dernier Mitterrand* (Paris: Plon, 1997), quoted in Conrad Black, "Britain's Atlantic Option and America's Stake," *National Interest* (Spring 1999) 22.
5. Charles Krauthammer, "Not for Moi, Thanks," *Washington Post*, November 26, 1999. Vedrine had used the word *hyperpuisance* to describe American power, though Chirac later disavowed the term. Chirac's more restrained language can be found in an interview with Craig R. Whitney, "With a Don't Be Vexed' Air, Chirac Assesses U.S.," *New York Times*, December 17, 1999.
6. Polly Toynbee, "Special Report: European Integration," *Guardian* (London), July 18, 2001.

7. For a pessimistic assessment of prospects for success in the battle for Afghanistan, written shortly before U.S. and Northern Alliance forces captured Kabul, see John Mearsheimer, "Guns Won't Win the Afghan War," *New York Times*, November 4, 2001.
8. The White House, "The National Security Strategy of the United States of America," September 20, 2002, http://www.whitehouse.gov/nsc/nss.html.
9. Cited in R. C. Longworth, "Allies Are Worlds Apart," *Chicago Tribune*, July 29, 2002.
10. "Sondage Ifop," *Le Figaro*, April 2, 2002.
11. The letter is reprinted in "Europe and America Must Stand United," *Times* (London), January 30, 2003.
12. *The Economist*, June 12, 2004.
13. Pew Research Center for the People and the Press, cited in "Sinking Views of the United States," *New York Times*, March 23, 2003.
14. Pew Research Center for People and the Press, "A Year after the Iraq War: Mistrust of America in Europe Ever Higher, Muslim Anger Persists," March 16, 2004, http://www.people-press.org.
15. According to a close associate of Henry Kissinger, Peter Rodman, neither he nor Kissinger has any recollection of the former secretary of state having written or said this. Peter Rodman, in discussion with the author.
16. Michael Mandelbaum, "The Inadequacy of American Power," *Foreign Affairs* 85 no. 5 (September–October 2002), 66.
17. Jonathan Stevenson, "How Europe and America Defend Themselves," *Foreign Affairs* 82 no. 2 (March–April 2003), 77.
18. *New York Times*, August 6, 1981.
19. Elizabeth Becker, "U.S. Contests Europe's Ban on Some Food," *New York Times*, May 14, 2003; and "Bush Decries Europe's Biotech Policies," *Washington Post*, May 22, 2003.
20. On the controversy surrounding early steps toward what became the Cartagena Protocol, see Robert Paarlberg, "The Eagle and the Global Environment," in Robert Lieber, *Eagle Rules? Foreign Policy and American Primacy in the 21st Century* (New York: Prentice-Hall and the Woodrow Wilson International Center for Scholars, 2002), 333–40.
21. "Oxfam Brands EU Bloc as Most Protectionist," *Financial Times*, April 10, 2002.
22. Mark Sullivan, *Our Times, 1900–1925* (New York: Scribners Sons, 1935), a six-volume survey of national life, quoted in Robert J. Samuelson, "The American Edge," *Washington Post*, January 9, 2003.
23. Seymour Martin Lipset, "Still the Exceptional Nation?" *Wilson Quarterly* 24 no. 1 (Winter 2000), 45.
24. Walter Russell Mead, "The Case against Europe," *Atlantic Monthly*, April 2002, 26.
25. "Condoleezza Rice Brings Morality to Realpolitik," *Daily Telegraph* (London), February 2, 2005.
26. See, for example, Robert Kagan, *Of Paradise and Power: America and Europe in the New World Order* (New York: Knopf, 2003); Brooks, "Among the Bourgeoisophobes," *Weekly Standard*, April 6, 2002; and Mead, "The Case against Europe."
27. For elaboration, see Lieber, *British Politics and European Unity: Parties, Elites and Pressure Groups* (Berkeley: University of California Press, 1970), 16–27.
28. Immanuel Kant, *Critique of Judgment* (1790).
29. John J. Mearsheimer, *The Tragedy of Great Power Politics* (New York: W. W. Norton & Company, 2001), 33.
30. Dusko Doder and Louise Branson, *Milosevic: Portrait of a Tyrant* (New York: Free Press, 1999), 109.
31. *New York Times*, February 23, 2003.
32. Radio Free Europe/Radio Liberty, "Lithuania: Officials Say Russia Stalling on Kaliningrad Transit Talks," March 31, 2003, http://www.rferl.org/nca/features/2003/03/31032003155817.asp. As a result of World War II, the Baltic port of Kaliningrad (formerly Breslau and part of Germany) became Russian territory. However, it lies between Lithuania and Poland, and Russian access requires transit through Lithuania.
33. Robert Jervis makes a similar point in Jervis, "The Compulsive Empire," *Foreign Policy* no. 137 (July–August 2003), 83–7.
34. Data from "The European Defense Agency: Will It Make a Difference?," *Strategic Comments*, International Institute for Strategic Studies 10 no. 5 (June 2004).

35. Robin Cook (British foreign secretary), Queen's speech debate, House of Commons, London, November 22, 1999, New York: British Information Service.
36. John Tagliabue, "Airbus's Military Jet Gets a Boost," *International Herald Tribune*, May 28, 2003.
37. Meteor is being developed by a consortium of the French company Matra and British Aerospace, in a collaborative venture with Germany, Italy, and Spain. The comparable American weapon, AMRAAM, is produced by Raytheon. See David Cracknell, "Cohen Begs Britain Not to Purchase Euro Missile," *Sunday Telegraph* (London), May 14, 2000; and British Embassy press release, "Defence Procurement: The Rt. Hon. Geoffrey Hoon, Secretary of State for Defence," May 16, 2000.
38. Data for 2003 from *The Military Balance, 2004–2005* (London: International Institute for Strategic Studies and Oxford University Press, October 2004).
39. "Ready, or Not: Europe's Not-So-Rapid-Reaction Force," *Economist*, May 24, 2003.
40. Reuters, "EU Boosts New Battle Groups," May 23, 2005, http://reuters.co.uk.
41. "A Secure Europe in a Better World: European Security Strategy" (Brussels: European Union, December 12, 2003), 13. See also Fraser Cameron, "The EU's Security Strategy," *Internationale Politik: Transatlantic Edition* 5 no. 1 (Spring 2004), 16–24. For analysis of the Solana paper, see John Van Oudenaren, "The Solana Security Paper," American Institute for Contemporary German Studies, June 2003, http://www.aicgs.org/c/solana.shtml.
42. Speech to the Bundestag, quoted in German Information Center, *The Week in Germany*, July 12, 2002, www.germany-info.org.
43. *New York Times*, March 28, 2003.
44. Peter Struck (German minister of defense), quoted in *The Week in Germany*, May 23, 2003, www.info-germany.org.
45. Joschka Fischer (federal minister for foreign affairs, speech, 40th Munich Conference on Security Policy, Munich, February 7, 2004).
46. *Economist*, November 20, 2004.
47. Michele Alliot-Marie (French defense minister), cited in Craig S. Smith, "For U.S. to Note, Europe Flexes Muscle in Afghanistan," *New York Times*, September 22, 2004.
48. The Kosovo Force entered Kosovo on June 12, 1999, under a UN mandate, two days after the adoption of UN Security Council Resolution 1244.

12
The Bush Doctrine in Asia

MEL GURTOV

As a result of the war in Iraq, the Bush Doctrine has come under heavy fire from both right and left. Many analysts have said the doctrine, with its emphasis on unilateral action, preemptive (or preventive) attack, and regime change, amounts to a quest for empire. If it is not quite "neo-imperialism," U.S. policy at the least seeks more than mere hegemony.[1] Others have argued that the Bush Doctrine has resulted in greatly diminished U.S. legitimacy in the world,[2] so much so that conservative critics like Clyde Prestowitz have said the United States has become a "rogue nation."[3] Whatever the appropriate label might be, one thing seems clear: In its quest for absolute security, the United States under George W. Bush has by its actions contributed to global insecurity. His administration's response to the 9/11 attacks has been disproportional and self-defeating. The United States has turned its back on international cooperation on the environment and arms control, has invaded another country under false pretenses, and has violated international law. It has favored threats and use of force when diplomatic alternatives, in particular preventive measures, were available. In this new, supposedly post-Cold War era, the Bush team remains mired in Cold-War thinking—the thinking of a "new American century" in which the United States dictates the rules and expects others—states and international organizations alike—to abide by them.[4] The difference between then and now is that both the domestic and international constraints on U.S. primacy are far weaker today than during the Cold War.

In this chapter I examine Asia policy in light of the Bush Doctrine and draw conclusions about what U.S. policy seeks to accomplish, what it ignores, and how well—particularly from the perspectives of human security and common security[5]—it is working. Each subregion of Asia casts the Bush policies in a somewhat different light, though all are affected by the U.S. emphasis on acting unilaterally, on giving top priority to strategic interests, and, in all, on strengthening American primacy. In Central Asia the United States has bedded down with autocratic regimes that provide military access for the war on terror and have significant oil and gas deposits. In Northeast Asia, where the main danger points are the Korean peninsula and the Taiwan Strait, a strategy of toughness has not served the Bush administration well. It has boxed itself into a corner by refusing to engage in direct dialogue with North Korea and has driven a wedge between South Korea and the United States. Disagreement over North Korea policy, as well as continuing differences over Taiwan, are also among the growing list of differences in China–U.S. relations, notwithstanding a supposedly common stance on the war on terror. At the top of that list is Japan's more active security partnership with the United States, which is feeding the Japan–China rivalry.

In Southeast Asia, some countries have to one degree or another bought into Bush's war on terror; but those same countries have spoken out against his notions of preemptive attack and limited sovereignty. Finally, in South Asia, the administration has relied on military cooperation to cement relations with India and Pakistan, but this has been of little help either in its pursuit of Osama bin Laden or in its efforts to hinder the proliferation of mass-destruction technologies. In all regions of Asia, the focus of U.S. assistance on the security of friendly regimes in the course of the war on terror has been detrimental to the professed interest in meeting human development needs and promoting democratic rule.

Origins

The Bush administration came to office on the heels of vigorous criticisms of Bill Clinton's "engagement and enlargement" strategy—his reliance on multilateral cooperation and "Wilsonian" values—and calls for reviving Ronald Reagan's toughness.[6] Both the criticisms and the calls for a Reaganite revival emanated most forcefully from the Project for a New American Century (PNAC), a neoconservative group founded in 1997. Its membership included conservative intellectuals, politicians, and former government officials, notably former defense department officials such as Dick Cheney, who had served under Ronald Reagan and the elder George Bush.[7] George W. Bush appointed numerous people—such as Donald Rumsfeld, Paul Wolfowitz, Elliot Abrams, Eliot Cohen, Richard Perle, and Zalmay Khalilzad—associated with the PNAC to senior policymaking positions. Regarding Asia policy, PNAC members argued for regime change in rogue states like North Korea and even China,[8] major increases in military spending, strong support of Taiwan's defense, unilateral action by the United States rather than reliance on multilateral institutions or coalition building, and infusion of moral clarity in foreign policy generally. Clearly, the principles of the PNAC significantly shaped Bush's post-9/11 September 2002 *National Security Strategy*.[9]

Members of the Bush team not associated with the PNAC, neorealists such as Colin Powell and Condoleezza Rice, nevertheless subscribe to several important elements of the PNAC platform.[10] They too reject engagement and multilateral cooperation as primary components of U.S. strategy—although, as argued later in this chapter, Powell stood out for his endorsement of engagement in some circumstances, notably on North Korea. Like the neoconservatives, the neorealists believe in the preeminence and universality of U.S. values, urge more military spending, eye China and Russia with suspicion, and regard rogue states as major threats to U.S. security interests. By contrast, the security import of global issues such as environmental degradation, energy and resource competition, and growing poverty receive virtually no consideration. Both groups have adopted James Baker's characterization of the U.S. security role in Asia when he served in the elder Bush administration: the hub of the wheel, consisting of forward-deployed forces and alliances with Japan, South Korea, Australia, the Philippines, and Thailand.[11] Groupings that have convened at Asian initiative, such as the Asia-Pacific Economic Cooperation forum, the Association of Southeast Asian Nations (ASEAN) Regional Forum (ARF), and the ASEAN+3 (China, South Korea, and Japan), receive only secondary attention. There are, of course, differences between the neorealists and the neoconservatives: less loose talk by the neorealists about regime change, for instance, and more about reforging ties with European allies. But the areas of agreement seem clearly to outweigh the areas of disagreement.

One might conclude that for all its unilateralist rhetoric, the Bush team's approach to foreign policy still closely resembles that of previous administrations. After all, like his predecessors Bush seeks to preserve primacy for the United States; his strategic view has no place for competitors or a true balance of power. The Bush administration emphasizes both power-political and liberal economic interests—both, for example, containment of rogue states and use of the global trading order to enmesh all comers in the Washington consensus. Thus, as Andrew Bacevich concludes, in Asia the essence of the Bush grand strategy holds to long-standing U.S. interests: "To open the world to American enterprise, to foster stability and adherence to norms of behavior essential to American prosperity, to maintain military preeminence with forces held in readiness to restore order where it breaks down—these remain the mainstays of U.S. grand strategy, both in Asia and around the world."[12]

But that is not the whole story. The 9/11 attacks not only pushed terrorism to the top of the administration's agenda; they also pushed to the fore the cardinal elements of the PNAC's agenda: unilateralism, preemptive attack, and regime change, which then became embedded in the Bush Doctrine. Though Asian affairs necessarily took a back seat to the Middle East, U.S. Asia policy was certainly affected. The stock of China, Russia, and the Central Asian states as security partners went up; Japan's alliance value increased; pressure on North Korea to give up its nuclear ambitions increased; and security relations with Southeast Asia gained emphasis. But what lost ground after 9/11 is equally if not more significant: the opportunity to join regional governments in creating a new set of incentives that might get North Korea to abandon weapons of mass destruction programs; in addressing growing poverty and environmental decline; in avoiding association with undemocratic, unstable regimes; and in encouraging Japan to reduce tensions with China and the two Koreas.

Central Asia

One of the least-noted aspects of the Bush national security policy is its expanded frontiers. The 9/11 attacks provided license for strategic deployments around the globe, from Djibouti to Colombia. No sooner did the war against the Taliban get under way than intensive preparations began for the war on Iraq. In Central Asia, new and expanded air bases provided jump-off points, not just to protect U.S. interests in the Middle East from terrorist attacks but also to protect new oil supplies.[13] About 60,000 U.S. military personnel moved into forward bases in the Middle East and surrounding areas.[14] In Central Asia, U.S. forces are currently encamped in two bases in Kyrgyzstan (about 1,000 soldiers) and one in Uzbekistan (about 2,000 soldiers), in addition to three air bases in use in Pakistan, four in Afghanistan, and—following the occupation—four in Iraq.

The bargain struck with virtually every former Soviet republic of Central Asia, regardless of its political complexion, is roughly the same: U.S. political and economic support, sometimes in the form of World Bank loans, in return for access to military facilities and energy resources. No serious account is taken of these governments' internal conditions, such as the obliviousness to human rights standards, departures from ordinary democratic practices, or political instability. Instead, just as was often true during the Cold War, absolutist regimes friendly to the United States are free to treat their citizens as they wish. This fool's bargain has the potential to embroil the United States in civil wars, to become an accomplice to state terror, and to risk confrontation with other countries, notably Russia and China, that have a strategic interest of their own in what happens next door.

Consider, for example, the situations in Azerbaijan, Kazakhstan, and Uzbekistan. The transfer of power from father to son in Azerbaijan in October 2002 ensured the continuity of dictatorship in recognition of the country's potential oil riches. While Washington congratulated the son, Ilham Aliyev, on his "strong showing" in winning a rigged election, protestors were arrested and killed, and the political opposition was kept under tight control.[15] Azerbaijan received $7 million in aid in fiscal year (FY) 2002 and $52.9 million in FY2003; $44.9 was allocated or promised in FY2004.[16] In Kazakhstan, which has enormous oil potential, top officials, including its president and former prime minister, are widely believed to have accepted bribes in return for oil contracts.[17] But the government allowed hundreds of U.S. overflights in the war on Iraq and protected private U.S. investments. For FY2002 and 2003, Kazakhstan received just under $100 million in U.S. military aid and was promised around $36 million more in FY2004. As for Uzbekistan, its leader, Islam Karimov, had been denied a visa to enter the United States in the early

1990s because of his government's human rights violations. Uzbeks, like their neighbors, suffer under intense poverty and stifling restrictions on travel, business, and civil liberties.[18] After 9/11, though, Uzbekistan became the jump-off point for the initial assault on Iraq. In return, the United States elevated Uzbekistan's importance. U.S. military aid to Uzbekistan from FY2001 through FY2003 amounted to over $170 million, with another $53 million promised in FY2004. Despite escalating violence in 2004 between government and antigovernment forces that Karimov blamed on Muslim terrorists, and despite around 7,000 political prisoners (according to human rights groups) in Uzbekistan's jails, that country's relationship with Washington remained solid.[19] Only in 2005, when Uzbek security forces went on a shooting spree following a prison revolt, killing at least a few hundred protesters, did the State Department express mild disapproval.

The interest of U.S. energy corporations works in tandem with the Pentagon's. For an administration determined to increase energy supplies rather than to invest in conservation, the Caspian Sea region's enormous untapped oil and gas reserves are again part of the great game in Central Asia. Under Bush as under Clinton, assisting U.S. energy corporations to compete for resources in Kazakhstan and the rest and running new energy pipelines through Afghanistan and Georgia (while avoiding Russia and Iran) are vital concerns.[20] The trouble is that the bargaining position of the Central Asian energy states increases as a result. The closer these governments get to Washington, the freer the hand their leaders evidently believe they have to jail opponents, to muzzle the press, to salt away aid money and corporate bribes in personal bank accounts—and to receive military aid and blessings from U.S. officials.[21]

China

On the surface, U.S.–China relations, thanks mainly to the war on terror and a huge volume of trade and investment, have the appearance of solidity. But just below the surface lurk many long-standing differences that neither the war on terror nor commercial ties will drive away. How to sensitively manage the relationship is always going to be a challenge. But in the Bush administration, creative management is at the mercy of State-Pentagon rivalry, which may account for the vacillation between treating China as a competitor or as a partner, depending on whether or not China changes in ways that please the United States.[22]

Colin Powell got the administration off to a good start with China. He made a deft response to the Bush administration's first foreign policy crisis when a U.S. spy plane collided with a Chinese jet fighter and then made a forced landing on Hainan Island in April 2001. Washington offered careful apologies, China returned the plane, and life went on. Thereafter, Powell followed the traditional course with China, protecting trade and investment interests, occasionally (and politely) chiding China on human rights, and consulting with China in efforts to defuse the long-running nuclear crisis with North Korea. Rumsfeld and company, on the other hand, clearly preferred a tougher stance. Viewing China as a strategic competitor, the Pentagon, evidently with support from Rice,[23] pressed the case for theater missile defense, for a larger security role for Japan in East Asia, and for the imposition of trade sanctions on Chinese companies believed to be involved in exporting dual-use technology and equipment, mainly to Iran and Pakistan).[24] The Pentagon is behind the push for sanctions and military pressure on North Korea, measures the Chinese consider likely to increase the chance of war. The militarization of U.S. foreign policy in the context of the war on terror also includes access to bases throughout Central Asia that make the Chinese military nervous. Beijing bridles at the expansion of the U.S. military presence in bordering countries, seeing it as evidence that "hegemonism, power politics and seeking for all-round military superiority" remain the core of U.S. foreign policy.[25]

On the central issue in U.S.–China relations, Taiwan, whereas the State Department under Powell sought to halt what it regarded as a dangerous drift toward an outright declaration of independence by the Taiwan government, the Pentagon, reflecting the pro-Taiwan views of the neoconservatives, sought to maintain a strong U.S. commitment to Taiwan's defense. The Defense Department's 2002 report on the People's Republic of China's (PRC) military capabilities dwelled on China's "coercive approach toward Taipei" and its objective of quickly bringing Taiwan to terms in the event of another crisis in relations.[26] The first clear sign of a difference in perspective came during and after the Hainan spy plane incident. Whereas Powell reportedly had conducted the U.S. response without Pentagon interference,[27] the neoconservatives got their way after the crisis when Bush announced a list of weapons Taiwan would be allowed to purchase.[28] It was the largest arms sale to Taiwan since the elder Bush sold Taiwan 150 F-16 fighter-bombers in 1992. The day after Bush's announcement he said the United States would provide "whatever it took to help Taiwan" defend itself. "And the Chinese must understand that," he added.[29] Although Bush also supported the one-China policy and warned Taiwan against declaring its independence, his remarks opened the door to renewed debate in the United States over the U.S. commitment to Taiwan and in Beijing over U.S. interference in Chinese affairs.

Since then, however, Bush has in one important respect moved back to the mainstream of U.S. China policy. When China's premier, Wen Jiabao, visited Washington in December 2003, Bush explicitly opposed any unilateral alteration of the status quo in China–Taiwan relations.[30] The president said nothing about China's missile build-up across the strait from Taiwan, which is generally considered to have doubled or even tripled since Bush took office.

He thus rebuffed efforts by Taiwan's President Chen Shui-bian to leverage U.S. support of a sovereign Taiwan. Bush later bowed to criticism from the PNAC about "appeasing" China by reiterating that the United States "would have to get involved if China tried to use coercion or force to unilaterally change the status of Taiwan." But in essence he had restored the policy of his predecessors: Don't rock the boat; this is sensible, since the status quo—marked by vigorous cross-strait trade, around $100 billion in Taiwan investments in mainland businesses, and numerous visits to China by relatives and professionals—is in the best interest of people and governments on both sides.[31]

The two missing ingredients in U.S. China policy are reducing arms sales to Taiwan and keeping Japan out of the Taiwan dispute. The Reagan administration promised to reduce arms sales but never did so; they consequently are a continuing irritant in relations with China. The United States delivered $4.5 billion in arms to Taiwan between 2000 and 2003, the third-highest amount of U.S. deliveries worldwide.[32] The latest PRC defense white paper, *China's National Defense in 2004*, calls the Taiwan situation "grim" because of Shui-bian's moves toward independence as well as U.S. arms sales to Taiwan.[33] If arms sales to Taiwan were reduced, China might respond with reduction of its missile deployments opposite Taiwan. As for Japan, of late its government has joined with the United States in declaring Taiwan's security a "common strategic objective"—just the sort of language certain to antagonize a Chinese leadership that is already aroused over several other "anti-Chinese" acts.[34] Public and Internet protests in China against Japan in spring 2005, including calls for a boycott of Japanese goods, show that Chinese nationalism is a volatile ingredient in inter-Asian politics.

Taiwan should not dominate the U.S.–China agenda the way it does. Nor should Sino–Japanese rivalry be downplayed; it is every bit as important as Sino–Japanese trade. We need to keep in mind, as Samuel S. Kim urged, that the China we see today is largely the one U.S. leaders have long wanted—a country that has embraced economic globalization rules and market forces, that is diplomatically engaged with all its neighbors, and that is far more concerned about internal than about external threats.[35] The larger U.S. policy agenda with China—the agenda that has the best opportunity to move relations in a cooperative direction—should be supportive of that direction. The agenda should include the improvement of China's environment (in particular, destructive land-use policies and a looming water crisis), reduction of China–Japan friction, a resolution of the North Korea nuclear weapons issue, and China's energy needs. U.S. policies and programs can play influential roles in each of these issue areas. Beyond that, they may also positively affect other areas of U.S. concern, such as China's respect for labor, ethnic, and religious rights; adherence to the rule of law; and nonproliferation of materials and equipment with potential use in weapons of mass destruction.[36]

The Korean Peninsula

Kim Dae-jung, president of South Korea, was one of the first official visitors to Washington after January 20, 2001. Bush startled his guest by making clear that his administration did not trust the North Koreans and would not support Kim's "sunshine" policy of diplomatic and economic engagement.[37] The rebuff also amounted to official discarding of Clinton's engagement policy based on the 1994 Agreed Framework with North Korea.[38] In its place, Bush decided to pursue a hard line, a position long advocated by the neoconservatives and just about everybody else except, it seems, Powell.[39] After Kim's visit, Bush made little effort to conceal his personal distaste for Kim Jong-il. In one supposedly off-the-record meeting, Bush called Kim a "pygmy" who was in charge of "a gulag half the size of Austin," and on another occasion Bush said, "I loathe Kim Jong-il."[40]

The sharp differences between the Clinton and Bush administrations when dealing with North Korea (the Democratic People's Republic of Korea, DPRK) can be summarized as follows:

- Clinton accepted that North Korea had legitimate security concerns,[41] whereas Bush considers North Korea, as he said in his January 2002 State of the Union address, part of an "axis of evil."[42]
- Clinton believed it was necessary to bargain with North Korea and to create a reliable agreement, whereas Bush seems to consider bargaining on a package deal the equivalent of appeasement.
- Clinton believed in the value of direct U.S.–DPRK talks—for example, the U.S.–DPRK joint communiqué (October 12, 2000)[43] in which the parties "stated that neither government would have hostile intent toward the other" and would work "to build a new relationship free from past enmity"—whereas Bush assigns such talks low priority, believing that North Korea can be pressured to dismantle its nuclear weapons facilities.[44]
- Clinton believed that the use of force should be a last resort, whereas Bush believes in the utility of military threat—hence, his "axis of evil" speech, the 2001 Nuclear Posture Review mentioning North Korea as a potential target of U.S. nuclear weapons, and North Korea's appearance in the National Security Strategy in connection with the doctrine of preemptive attack.

It is this last aspect of the Bush policy—coercive diplomacy—that bears a fair share of the responsibility for the current crisis in U.S.–DPRK relations, though North Korea's own behavior in playing the nuclear card certainly has provided the neoconservatives with ammunition (literally) for rationalizing coercion. In October 2002 U.S. Assistant Secretary of State James Kelly went to Pyongyang with evidence supposedly showing that the North Koreans were engaged in a clandestine bomb program based on highly enriched uranium. Washington regarded this development as a material breach of the Agreed Framework, whereas the North Koreans, contrary to Kelly's report of an admission, insisted they had a right to possess nuclear weapons to deter a U.S. threat. From that point on, U.S.–DPRK relations went into a tailspin. North Korea withdrew from the Nuclear Nonproliferation Treaty, removed the nuclear-fuel rods from their primary facility at Yongbyon, reactivated that facility, nullified the North–South Korea denuclearization accord of 1992, sent home International Atomic Energy Agency (IAEA) inspectors and removed their monitoring devices, and declared the Agreed Framework with the United States at an end. Thereafter, the DPRK threatened to reprocess all 8,000 of its spent nuclear-fuel rods, which it may now be doing. On February 10, 2005, the DPRK's foreign ministry announced that the North does indeed possess nuclear weapons, claiming they are needed to counter U.S. threats of regime change and unwillingness to embrace coexistence.[45]

No one outside the DPRK can claim to know what North Korea's nuclear capability really is. Its leaders have, probably deliberately, left ambiguous how many nuclear weapons they have, how extensive the country's nuclear weapons production capability is, and how many of the nuclear-fuel rods they have reprocessed. Possibly, the DPRK by now—as the head of IAEA stated in December 2004—has four to six plutonium bombs.[46] Pyongyang may not be engaged in full-scale reprocessing, since that is a red line for U.S. officials who ponder attacking the North. But if it has several nuclear weapons, it has the potential to sell plutonium. That prospect, and not the still-unproved highly enriched uranium program,[47] is the real basis for international concern.

The question is this: Does the DPRK's nuclear weapons capability justify reliance on threats and pressure to terminate it? The Bush administration's actions following the Kelly trip strongly suggest that it not only believes in the virtues of coercion but also is fixed on regime change in North Korea as the end game. After the U.S. war on Iraq began, Pentagon sources spoke of sudden air strikes on Saddam Hussein's command centers as also sending a message to Kim Jong-il.[48] Other news reports cited Pentagon plans to tighten military pressure on the DPRK, including provocative flights designed to test North Korean air defenses.[49] At various times the administration has hinted that were it not for Iraq, the use of force against the DPRK might jump to the top of the list.[50] The Proliferation Security Initiative, a fifteen-country group launched by the Bush administration in May 2003 to intensify searches and seizures of ships, planes, and vehicles suspected of delivering weapons of mass destruction, is just one of several military steps short of force the Bush administration has undertaken against rogue states, with North Korea foremost in mind. In light of Bush's self-proclaimed visceral reaction to Kim Jong-il, neither these military options nor the use of nuclear weapons against North Korea can be ruled out.[51]

To be sure, the Bush administration's policy on North Korea has another leg: a negotiating posture and an aid program. It has proposed, as a precondition for any kind of security guarantee and the resumption of oil deliveries, which were suspended at the end of 2002, a complete, irreversible, and verifiable end to all North Korean nuclear weapons programs and the removal of all equipment related to them.[52] The aid program consists of substantial amounts of food delivered through the United Nation's (UN) World Food Program, as well as disaster relief—other humanitarian assistance is handled by nongovernmental organizations. But this second leg of policy has a much lower priority than the first. As one expert, now a member of the administration, wrote, the essence of U.S. policy is "hawk engagement," which is "based on the idea that engagement [with North Korea] lays the groundwork for punitive action,"[53] not reciprocal concessions. As Pyongyang's February 2005 announcement on nuclear weapons shows, it understands the American message quite well: The U.S. military moves and leaks, the rejection of direct U.S.–DPRK dialogue, the threatening language, and the preconditions the administration places on normalization of relations all spell intimidation. Anyone familiar with the way Pyongyang views the world, and the constraints its economic situation and absence of reliable allies place on its leaders' policy options, should expect that Kim Jong-il and his military-dominated leadership would regard nuclear weapons as their best bet for deterring U.S. threats. No matter that Bush and other top officials have said a number of times, the United States has no intention of attacking North Korea; in Pyongyang U.S. hegemony is the key factor in regime survival.

The problem for Washington's strategy extends beyond North Korea's reactions to the reactions of neighboring countries, starting with China and South Korea. They probably see North Korea's nuclear gambits as defensive responses to the failure of diplomacy to address its security needs. Chinese and South Korean leaders understand that what North Korea wants is security assurances from the United States and long-term aid from both it and Japan—in short, acceptance of its legitimacy as part of full-fledged normalization of relations. DPRK representatives have met with U.S. officials in both bilateral and multilateral settings, in the latter case at Six Party Talks[54] hosted by China. These talks, which have now gone through three rounds, have accomplished little because of a fairly complete breakdown of trust between the United States and the DPRK. In its February 2005 announcement Pyongyang said it was withdrawing from the talks, though Chinese authorities have indicated it will return eventually. Foreign ministry spokespersons for China and South Korea have made thinly veiled criticisms of the lack of flexibility in the U.S. position, and Beijing has gone so far as to question U.S. intelligence on North Korea's nuclear weapons program.[55] China and South Korea would like the United States to accept North Korea's proposal for direct talks. Neither country has chosen to associate with the Proliferation Security Initiative, with theater missile defense, or with the American preference for UN sanctions on North Korea, since those steps are believed likely to provoke North Korea and to risk a major blow-up on the Korean peninsula.

So far, the combined weight of Chinese, South Korean, Russian, and, to some extent, Japanese wishes, as well as the U.S. preoccupation with Iraq, have been sufficient to keep a semblance of diplomacy alive and to block the Bush administration's resort to sanctions and other forms of active containment of North Korea. That circumstance may last, however, only as long as the possibility exists that North Korea will finally cave in to U.S. demands, or until U.S. allies finally lose their patience with the North and accept the U.S. argument that engagement is a bankrupt approach. Meanwhile, even though other U.S. purposes are served by maintaining a hard-line posture, such as providing a rationale for theater missile defense in East Asia and bringing Japan into closer military coordination with the United States, it carries costs and risks. North Korea may add to its nuclear weapons arsenal, may continue nuclear exports, and even may test a nuclear weapon. It may resume ballistic missile tests. North Korea's relations with Japan are likely to deteriorate further and to become more militarized. Absent a diplomatic solution to the nuclear issue, pronuclear weapon groups in South Korea—where experimentation with the ingredients of a nuclear weapons program has occurred—and Japan are likely to become stronger. North Korea itself may become unstable and may generate many more refugees than at present.

Finally, and of immediate concern, U.S. relations with South Korea are deteriorating in large part because of Bush's North Korea policies. Anti-Americanism is on the rise there.[56] The South Korea government has distanced itself from the United States even though it has become the number-one customer in East Asia for U.S. arms[57] and has deployed troops to Iraq—in the latter case, despite public disapproval and U.S. plans for reducing its military presence in South Korea.[58] President Roh Moo-hyun has balanced these decisions with increased closeness to China. Not only has Roh vowed to step up military exchanges with China; he has also stressed a new role for South Korea as "a balancer" in Northeast Asia, which suggests a more independent foreign policy that would avoid alignment with the United States in containing China or North Korea.[59]

"The fundamental difference between Clinton's near-success in resolving the issues and Bush's stalemate," one scholar wrote recently, "lies not in Bush's unwillingness to talk or in his proposal to expand the agenda for talks but in his refusal to end the enmity between the two nations."[60] How can the enmity be ended? First, a human-security approach to North Korea is needed, based on ultimately transforming relationships between countries and peoples to meet the basic needs of ordinary people and to promote a positive context for improving human rights there. Second, a common-security framework is needed, based on enhancing the security of North Korea so that weapons of mass destruction no longer have value and North–South Korea engagement can move forward. For these approaches to work, the United States must offer a new deal to North Korea based on genuine reciprocity. It should accept direct dialogue with the North along with the Six Party Talks. The essential elements of a comprehensive deal are U.S. security assurances to North Korea, an official end to the Korean War, diplomatic recognition of the DPRK by Washington and Tokyo, and long-term economic and energy assistance to the DPRK.[61] An enhanced role for international nongovernmental organizations is also needed, not just to provide emergency relief but also to meet North Korea's long-term economic development needs. In return, the DPRK must refreeze its nuclear facilities, must open them to regular international inspections, must dismantle its ballistic-missile programs, and must terminate any and all exports of equipment and materials related to weapons of mass destruction.

North Korean spokespersons suggested many times prior to its February 2005 statement that the DPRK would be willing to make major concessions, starting with nuclear weapons, if U.S. incentives were on the table.[62] But now that the DPRK has declared itself a nuclear weapons state and, like India and Pakistan, has demanded that it be treated as one of the club, a deal with the Bush administration becomes more problematic, though not impossible.[63] Nevertheless, if a breakthrough in talks occurs, the momentum might carry over to discussions about creating a new regional (Northeast Asia) security mechanism—a permanent forum North Korea would be invited to join to regularize political and military contacts among the parties, to craft mutual-security pledges, and to regulate military transfers to both Koreas.[64] A DPRK spokesperson has indicated his country's interest in regional disarmament discussions.[65] Meanwhile, North–South Korean economic and people-to-people exchanges, which have continued and even expanded despite the political tensions, would extend to the military arena, where the most urgent business is troop withdrawals from within range of the demilitarized zone dividing the two countries. North Korea's domestic policies are slowly changing, with a new openness to private markets, consumerism, and foreign investment, mostly from South Korea. With U.S.–DPRK relations normalized, further opening, which the Chinese have been urging on the North for years, becomes more likely.

U.S. policy is out of sorts when it comes to North Korea. It is isolated from its allies is South Korea and Japan, is at odds with China and Russia, and out of touch with developments in North Korea. Every former U.S. ambassador to South Korea and special envoy to North Korea has publicly stated disagreement with the Bush policies and has urged direct negotiations to resolve the nuclear and other issues.[66] Among these former officials is Jack Pritchard, who resigned as Bush's special envoy to the North Korea talks in dismay over the administration's policy. He characterized U.S. policy as follows: "At best it can be described only as amateurish. At worst, it is a failed attempt to lure American allies down a path that is not designed to resolve the crisis diplomatically but to lead to the failure and ultimate isolation of North Korea in hopes that its government will collapse."[67]

Japan

Changes under Bush in the alliance with Japan are another important and—unlike Korea policy—understated element of the neoconservative strategy. The war on terror has enabled Prime Minister Koizumi Junichiro to strengthen the alliance and to further erode Article 9 of the constitution. Koizumi joined Bush's "coalition of the willing," pushed emergency legislation on terrorism through the Diet, and, in a major break with tradition, deployed both air and naval units of the Self-Defense Forces, first to the Indian Ocean in support of the war in Afghanistan and later to the Persian Gulf.[68] In December 2003 Koizumi took the unprecedented step of sending around 600 ground Self-Defense Forces soldiers to Iraq despite overwhelming disapproval from the Japanese public. By law the soldiers were limited to rear-guard support roles for up to one year, but Koizumi decided in December 2004 to extend the deployment for another year as a further show of support of the United States. Again, he defied public opinion.[69]

Japan took two other significant steps in support of U.S. policy. In September 2003 it joined the Proliferation Security Initiative, no doubt with North Korea's missile exports in mind. The Japanese cabinet subsequently allocated funds to deploy U.S.-built missile defenses. With the Bush Doctrine as precedent, Japan's foreign minister said that Japan had the right, in self-defense, to make a preemptive attack on North Korean missile sites.[70] Then, at the end of 2004, the Koizumi government announced new defense guidelines. The chief security threats to Japan are now said to be missiles and terrorists, but for the first time China was specifically named a potentially threatening country. The guidelines also considerably enlarge the geographic scope of Japan's security interests, which by implication also widen the area of future Self-Defense Forces deployments.[71] There is also talk, which the Japan Defense Agency seems to be behind, of relocating the headquarters of the U.S. Army First Corps from the state of Washington to Japan.[72]

Taken together, what do these steps mean? From the perspective of alliance history, they can be interpreted as simply the latest indicators of the Japanese bowing to U.S. leadership. That is, the Japanese government is showing the same loyalty to U.S. policy in the war on terror that it showed in Cold War-era conflicts. But such loyalty raises problems and creates risks of undermining Japan's relations with its neighbors. For example, when Koizumi made a surprise trip to Pyongyang in fall 2002, against U.S. wishes he extracted an apology from Kim Jong-il for the abduction of Japanese citizens and a promise to return them to Japan. The Bush administration's reaction was to exaggerate

North Korea's highly enriched uranium program, possibly to "scare Japan and South Korea into reversing their policies" of conciliation toward the North.[73] But the cost of that gambit was to undermine a promising step toward the normalization of Japan–North Korea relations. Now, instead, the chief discourse in Japan concerning North Korea is the imposition of economic sanctions—the closure of Japanese ports to North Korean ships—which again would reflect American preferences.[74]

Japan's agreement with the United States in February 2005 on Taiwan security is a second example. Perhaps not accidentally, the statement came at the same time that Pentagon and Central Intelligence Agency leaders were testifying before Congress on the growth of PRC military capabilities vis-à-vis Taiwan. Chinese leaders doubtless view these developments through the prism of growing Japanese international assertiveness in line with U.S. policies to contain China. Beijing's response was to condemn the Japan–U.S. declaration and to push through its legislature an antisecession law formalizing the use of force in case Taiwan should declare independence. Japan, China's number-one trade partner, is now part of the "Taiwan problem."[75]

Significant changes are probably in the offing in Japan's national security policies. "In essence," Richard Tanter argued, "the Bush Doctrine has been welcomed [in Japan] for the cover and opportunities it affords to accelerate already existing planning preferences"—preferences, that is, for making Japan a "normal country," one that can and should project its military power to protect its interests, just as the United States has long done.[76] Rather than embrace that kind of normalcy and instead expand its unique role as a "global civilian power,"[77] Japan seems headed toward removing constitutional and philosophical constraints that have kept it from making the kinds of security contributions Washington prefers. Thanks to the Bush Doctrine, that first step may now have been taken.[78] But each such step further distances Japan from China and both Koreas. As one Japanese commentator wrote, "By far the most important contribution Japan can make toward international peace is the establishment of a solid and peaceful relationship with China … Japanese militarization … dangerously erodes Sino–Japanese relations."[79]

Southeast Asia

The Philippines, Indonesia, and Thailand—the pivotal members of the ten-member Association ASEAN—are on the front lines of the war on terrorism.[80] Yet their most serious internal enemies are weak governing institutions, declining economic performance, and the military's corruption and penchant for interfering in politics. The two terrorist attacks that occurred in Indonesia in October 2002 and August 2003 may demonstrate a link between Jemaah Islamiyah and Al-Qaeda. But in the Philippines, the Abu Sayyaf guerrillas are an entirely different problem of long standing, and in Thailand there is no organized terrorist activity. Nevertheless, the United States has made counterterrorism its highest priority in relations with all three countries. Not only did the Bush administration send troops into combat in the Philippines on a six-month mission in 2002,[81] but it also used the terrorism issue to increase military aid and sales to the Philippines for the purpose of fighting Filipino communists.[82] Similarly, in Indonesia the Bush administration openly pressured the government of Indonesia to line up against Jemaah Islamiyah and other militant groups even before the 2002 attack in Bali. The administration's aim is clearly to overcome congressional bans on arms sales and other ties to the Indonesian armed forces imposed following the genocidal operations in East Timor. "We are starting down a path to a more normal relationship with respect to military-to-military," Powell said.[83] That goal was achieved in early 2005 with reinstatement of the Pentagon's international military education training program.[84] In Thailand, Bush rewarded its decision to send military engineering troops to Afghanistan and Iraq by granting Thailand the status of a major non-NATO ally, which entitled Bangkok to greater access than other military aid recipients to certain U.S. financing and technologies. Thailand also received over $30 million in various kinds of military assistance between September 2001 and 2004.[85]

The accent on military relations has important political consequences at odds with human-security concerns. It precludes protesting Indonesian armed forces offensives that brutally put down separatist activities such as have occurred in Aceh—Indonesian officials have openly stated that attacking separatists in the name of counterterrorism without incurring international criticism was "a blessing" conferred by 9/11 and the war on Iraq.[86] It strengthens the military's hand in each country's politics while simultaneously engaging in the fiction that working closely with the military will democratize it and will enhance its respect for human rights. And the attention and resources devoted, with U.S. support, to fighting terrorism risk turning otherwise secular Muslims into anti-American radicals.

The apparent U.S. strategy to strengthen security ties across Southeast Asia extends to ASEAN as a whole. An August 1, 2002, treaty between ASEAN and the United States promises cooperation to "prevent, disrupt and combat" international terrorism.[87] Washington gave assurances that it had no intention to base U.S. troops on Asian soil or to ignore the repression of legitimate dissent. But the dispatch of troops to the Philippines, the absence of U.S. protests of the Indonesian military's actions—only Burma's repression draws U.S. criticism—and the increase of U.S. arms sales and transfers to the region undermine those assurances.[88] The Bush Doctrine's talk of preemptive attack, moreover, has left leaders in Malaysia, Philippines, Indonesia, and Thailand cold. All of them have expressed the belief that preemption violates principles of state sovereignty and collective security under the UN.[89] And the foreign minister of Indonesia, the government so assiduously courted by Bush, has vigorously criticized the precedent set by the war on Iraq, doubtless reflecting concern that one day an Australian government might use it to justify interfering in Indonesian affairs.[90]

Bush's one-sided emphasis on terrorism has led a leading Singapore security specialist to write that "America's Asian alliances, always unequal entities, are more so now than they have been since the end of World War II."[91] The administration's attention has been drawn away from the main action in Southeast Asia: multilateral initiatives such as ASEAN+3 and regional free-trade agreements. While Bush's trade strategy, like its security strategy, centers on global arrangements with the United States as the hub, East Asian countries are forging ahead with free-trade agreements to protect their interests against WTO.[92] Free-trade agreements have either been completed or are in negotiation between Japan and Singapore; China and ASEAN; ASEAN and India; Thailand and India; and South Korea, Japan, and China, among others.[93] Some of these arrangements will promote intraregional trade, whereas others will reinforce rivalries, such as between China and Japan. ASEAN+3, however, is a vehicle for mitigating such competition while also reducing reliance on the U.S. market. Yet the United States is a virtual outsider to the ASEAN process: Unlike the "3," as well as Australia, New Zealand, and India, the United States does not have an annual summit meeting with the ASEAN leaders.

The fact that all these developments are occurring without reference to Washington is a signal of dissatisfaction with the way it defines and promotes trade liberalization and harmonization. Failing to pay attention to Asian regionalism will leave the United States as the odd man out and will feed distorted thinking about, for example, China. While the Republican right wing clamors about China's military challenge, Chinese economic expansion is really the centerpiece of the PRC's global diplomacy. Free-trade areas are just one prong of that effort, which includes major investments in Latin America—Brazil, Venezuela, and Argentina—and energy partnerships in Central Asia and, forthcoming, in Canada.

South Asia

The war in Afghanistan also led to major changes in U.S. policy toward Pakistan and India. The Bush administration was aware of the links between Pakistan's Inter-Services Intelligence and the Taliban but decided that the need of Pakistan's cooperation in the war on terror exceeded its liabilities.[94] Those liabilities are extensive. The government of General Pervez Musharraf is undemocratic and corrupt; its violations of human rights are extensive and of long standing. Pakistan's role as a supplier of nuclear weapons technology to North Korea, Iran, and Libya, which went on after as well as before September 11, 2001, has been well documented.[95] For years Musharraf shielded A. Q. Khan, the founder of Pakistan's nuclear weapons program, and allowed his global network of nuclear sales to continue.[96] Even now, U.S. intelligence reportedly has no access to Khan that might reveal the full extent of his network's operations.[97] Nevertheless, the Bush administration removed sanctions on Pakistan for its nuclear weapons tests in 1998, provided over $4 billion in aid from 9/11 to 2004 and an open door to International Monetary Fund assistance ($135 million), upgraded Pakistan's status to that of a major non-NATO ally, and refused to condemn Musharraf's rigged extension of his rule in 2002 and retaking of the army's leadership at the end of 2004. As though those steps were not enough, in spring 2005 Bush decided to complete the long-delayed sale to Pakistan of twenty-four F-16 jet fighters.

Washington has been improving ties with India as well, for both economic and strategic reasons. Economically, the Bush administration has an eye on the Indian market and India's role as a Third World leader at global trade talks. Strategically, the administration probably hopes to gain some leverage over Indo-Pakistani tensions in Kashmir but also to improve military ties with an eye on containing China. Though India elected not to send troops to Iraq, it did endorse the U.S. theater missile defense plans in East Asia.[98] Since 9/11 U.S.–India relations have been marked by military exchanges, joint sea patrols, and the resumption of military sales to India that had been suspended because of India's nuclear tests in 1998.[99] The sale of F-16s to Pakistan actually had the Indian market in mind: Bush assured the Indian government that it would also sell it over 100 combat aircraft—a boon to the Indian military, which shares the concern of some Pentagon leaders about Chinese expansionism,[100] as well to Lockheed's fortunes.[101] Moving closer to India may not be to Pakistan's liking, but it seems to have had an impact in Beijing: In April 2005 Premier Wen Jiabao's visit to New Delhi concluded with agreements to resolve their border dispute and to expand their rapidly growing trade relationship.

Conclusions

Certain themes bring together the array of specific Asia policies being carried out under the Bush Doctrine. One is that Asia is among the regions that have suffered from policy neglect. In Washington, Iraq and Afghanistan—and the war on terror generally—seem to absorb virtually all attention and resources. Policymaking that should be riveted on two potentially dangerous situations—China–Japan rivalry and North Korea's nuclear weapons—is episodic at best and dysfunctional at worst. Second, the tug of war between the State and Defense Departments that has been so visible in Iraq policymaking is also apparent in Asia policy, particularly over the choice of multilateral diplomacy or sanctions and military threats to deal with North Korea and over the depth of support of Taiwan's quest for sovereignty. A third theme is that the war on terror has brought with it, as was true during the Cold War, a preference for making U.S. power the principal instrument of foreign policy. Geoeconomics remains important under Bush, but the unilateral pursuit of strategic advantage has far greater salience. Fourth is that global issues such as the advancement of human rights and democratic rule, equitable and sustainable development, and the rule of law sit well back among U.S. priorities in Asia.

These themes draw attention to some unpleasant and potentially dangerous particulars of U.S. policy, some of which are reminiscent of the Cold War. Following the same path that got the United States into so many entangling relationships during the Cold War, the Bush administration has embraced a number of autocratic regimes on the false assumption of partnership against terrorism. Driven by supposed strategic and economic opportunities, the administration has fallen in with regimes whose methods and objectives have nothing in common with professed American values. Related to this, various U.S. partners in the war on terror—in Pakistan, Indonesia, Uzbekistan, and China, for example—have justified their repressive policies by classifying their domestic opponents as terrorists, in many instances quashing legitimate dissent. Using the war on terror as a basis for international partnerships may bring short-term advantages, such as military cooperation and oil deals. But the longer-term risks are formidable, just as they were during the Cold War: becoming party to systematic human rights violations, taking the side of friendly regimes in politically unstable situations, and increasing dependence on imported resources.

On the opposite end of such unsavory partnerships are policies of engagement that ought to be pursued. Here, the volatile situation in Northeast Asia is especially salient. Nationalism feeds that volatility: North Korea's pride and intransigence, rivalry between Japan and China and between Japan and Korea, and recent displays of anti-Americanism in South Korea. But there is opportunity here to embed nationalist rivalry in multilateral cooperative bodies. A working security mechanism supported by the United States, as suggested earlier, would also have the virtue of positively affecting South Korea's government and public, which have become increasingly alienated from the United States in part because of Bush's refusal to endorse an engagement policy with North Korea.

The United States faces serious constraints as it tries to build an antiterror coalition in Asia. Terrorism may be a commonly perceived problem, but governments such as China, Pakistan, and Indonesia do not agree with the United States about whom the terrorists are, how they should be fought, and what price in domestic political terms should be paid to conduct a war against them. In truth, the war on terror is viewed as an American priority, not the world's. And if cooperating with the Americans means sacrificing other priorities—such as staying in the nuclear weapons business for Pakistan, tolerating ethnic unrest and revaluing the *renminbi* for China, containing the military's abuses for Indonesia, or fighting corruption for Kazakhstan—these governments are simply not going to cooperate, or to cooperate fully. The more democratic among them must also attend to the wishes of their publics—thus the

Philippines' withdrawal of its troops from Iraq, India's refusal to send any, and South Korea's distancing itself from the United States even while sending troops. To make matters worse, the Bush administration's notions of preemptive attack and limited sovereignty, as well as his pro-Israel policies, leave various governments uncomfortable, particularly in Southeast Asia with its long history of western colonialism.

Thus, far from providing the glue of regional cooperation, the war on terror is more likely to be another wedge that drives many Asian countries apart from the United States. The most serious regional problems, such as the alleviation of poverty, unemployment, and environmental damage (beyond what was caused by the tsunami), will continue to receive only passing attention. Weak, impoverished states in Asia such as North Korea, Kazakhstan, and Indonesia need long-term human development assistance, trade relief, and civil-society training, not support for counterterrorism, which tends to gravitate to repressive military and police forces.[102] When the tsunami struck Asia in December 2004, it was an opportunity for the United States to lead the international relief effort and use that relief as a counterpoint to the war on terror—a war on underdevelopment, a Marshall Plan for Asia that would go beyond emergency assistance to address the two billion people living there on less than $2 a day.[103] Bush did not grasp the opportunity, instead offering a modest sum ($350 million, a good deal less than Japan's $500 million). Later, he did nearly triple that amount, and U.S. soldiers won plaudits for their relief role. But the real purpose of the aid soon became apparent—to reinstitute the International Military Training and Education program for the Indonesian army at the very time the army was restoring its iron grip on Aceh. Moreover, when one considers that in 2005 the United States is spending $5 billion a month on the wars in Iraq and Afghanistan and around $500 billion for the year on international and homeland security, its development spending is paltry and embarrassing. Ignoring Asia's legions of disempowered and despairing people is likely, as in the Middle East, to provide fertile soil for militant groups.

On the home front, as Kurt Campbell pointed out, Democrats in Congress have provided no meaningful opposition to any of Bush's foreign policies; they have "ceded the field."[104] Under the rubric of the war on terror, Bush has been able to move his agenda—global troop deployments, huge military budgets, hawk engagement in Korea, Japanese militarization, oil politics in Central Asia—with virtually no opposition or significant input from outside the inner circle. The only real foreign policy debate, such as it is, occurs within the Republicans' own ranks, and even then the subject is not Asia policy but the war in Iraq. This domestic political reality is unfortunate not just because the North–South Korean and China–Taiwan situations demand serious, ongoing diplomatic engagement. Democracy also suffers from such neglect.

Notes

1. For example, G. John Ikenberry, "America's Imperial Ambition," *Foreign Affairs* 81 no. 5 (September–October, 2002), 44–60; Samuel S. Kim, "The U.S.–DPRK Nuclear Standoff: The Case for Common-Security Engagement," *Joint U.S.–Korea Academic Studies* 14 (2004), 41–64; David C. Hendrickson, "Toward Universal Empire: The Dangerous Quest for Absolute Security," *World Policy Journal* 19 no. 3 (Fall 2002), 1–10.
2. Robert W. Tucker and David C. Hendrickson, "The Sources of American Legitimacy," *Foreign Affairs* 83 no. 6 (November–December, 2004), 18–32.
3. Prestowitz, *Rogue Nation: American Unilateralism and the Failure of Good Intentions* (New York: Basic Books, 2003).
4. An unidentified senior aide in the Bush administration said the following about the media: "We're an empire now, and when we act, we create our own reality. And while you're studying that reality—judiciously, as you will—we'll act again, creating other new realities, which you can study too, and that's how things will sort out. We're history's actors ... and you, all of you, will be left to just study what we do." Julian Berger, "Bush Wages War on the Enemy Within," *Guardian Weekly*, March 18–24, 2005, 6.
5. *Human security* as used here derives from the annual United Nations Development Program's *Human Development Report*, which has been deeply informed by the work of Indian economist Amartya Sen. Common, or cooperative, security is a concept found in many sources, including Ashton B. Carter, William J. Perry, and John D. Steinbruner, *A New Concept of Cooperative Security* (Washington, DC: Brookings Institution, 1992).
6. See, for example, William Kristol and Robert Kagan, "Toward a Neo-Reaganite Foreign Policy," *Foreign Affairs* 75 no. 4 (July–August, 1996), 18–32; and Charles Krauthammer, "The Unipolar Moment," *Foreign Affairs* 70 no. 1 (1990–91), 23–33.
7. The PNAC's founding statement and other documents may be found on its Web site, http://www.newamericancentury.org. On the origins of the PNAC, its embrace of the Reagan legacy, and its membership, see Tom Barry and Jim Lobe, "The People," in *Power Trip: U.S. Unilateralism and Global Strategy after September 11*, ed. John Feffer (New York: Seven Stories, 2003), 39–49; and Dilip Hiro, *Secrets and Lies: Operation "Iraqi Freedom" and After* (New York: Nation Books, 2004).
8. Kristol and Kagan, "Toward a Neo-Reaganite Foreign Policy," 28.
9. "The National Security Strategy of the United States" (September 20, 2002), available at www.nytimes.com/2002/09/20/international/20STEXT_FULL.html.
10. See, for example, Powell's "Remarks at Asia Society Annual Dinner," June 10, 2002, in Robert M. Hathaway and Wilson Lee, eds., *George W. Bush and Asia: A Midterm Assessment* (Washington, DC: Woodrow Wilson International Center for Scholars, 2003), 160–73; Condoleezza Rice, "Promoting the National Interest," *Foreign Affairs* 79 no. 1 (January–February, 2000), 45–62.
11. As, for example, in Powell's remarks, Hathaway and Lee, *George W. Bush and Asia*, 163.
12. Andrew J. Bacevich, "Bush and Asia: Continuity or Change?" in Hathaway and Lee, *George W. Bush and Asia* (see note 10), 32.
13. Michael Renner, "Post-Saddam Iraq: Linchpin of a New Oil Order," *Foreign Policy in Focus*, January 2003, available at www.fpif.org/papers/oil.html.
14. On U.S. deployments, see William D. Hartung, Frida Berrigan, and Michelle Ciarrocca, "Operation Endless Deployment," *Nation*, October 21, 2002, 21–24; *New York Times*, January 9, 2002, A10; and *New York Times*, September 23, 2002, A10.
15. See "Nepotism in Central Asia," editorial, *New York Times*, October 27, 2003, A22.
16. U.S. aid figures in this paragraph are from Center for Defense Information (CDI), "Arms Trade," March 21, 2003, http://www.cdi.org/news/arms-trade. Total military assistance typically includes some combination of military training, weapons sales, financing assistance, and counterterrorism support.
17. Jeff Gerth, "Bribery Inquiry Involves Kazakh Chief, and He's Unhappy," *New York Times*, December 11, 2002, A14; and Lutz C. Kleveman, "The Devil's Tears," *Amnesty Now* (Spring 2004), 18–21.
18. See, for example, Edmund L. Andrews, "New U.S. Allies, the Uzbeks: Mired in the Past," online editorial, *New York Times*, May 31, 2002. Available at http://www.nytimes.com/2002/05/31/international/asia/31UZBE.html.
19. During an official visit in February 2004, Donald Rumsfeld said that U.S. relations with Uzbekistan were "growing stronger every month." And Scott McClellan, the White House

spokesman, responded to the increasing violence by promising "close cooperation with Uzbekistan and our other partners in the global war on terror." Seth Mydans, "3rd Day of Violence Claims 23 Lives in Uzbekistan," *New York Times*, March 31, 2004, A3.

20. Lutz Kleveman, "Oil and the New 'Great Game,'" *The Nation*, February 16, 2004, 11–14. For a report that attaches less significance to the pipeline—at least as of 2002, when oil prices were low ($18 a barrel), consumption was rising rapidly, alternative routes were available, and Afghanistan was in total disarray; see Murray Hiebert, "No Big Win for Big Oil," *Far Eastern Economic Review*, January 17, 2002, 24–25.

21. Among the many reports on corruption and misrule in Central Asia linked to the war on terrorism and oil politics, see Andrews, "Spotlight on Central Asia is Finding Repression, Too," *New York Times*, April 11, 2002, A6; Todd S. Purdum, "Uzbekistan's Leader Doubts Chances for Afghan Peace," *New York Times*, March 14, 2002, A18; Muhammad Salih, "America's Shady Ally against Terror," *New York Times*, March 11, 2002, A25; and Ahmed Rashid, "Trouble Ahead," *Far Eastern Economic Review*, May 9, 2002, 14–18.

22. See Harry Harding, "Asia in American Grand Strategy: The Quadrennial Defense Review and the *National Security Strategy*," in Hathaway and Lee, *George W. Bush and Asia* (see note 9), 43–56.

23. In Rice, "Promoting the National Interest," 56–7, she favored efforts to integrate China into the world economy but said China was "still a potential threat to stability in the Asia-Pacific region," making it "a strategic competitor" rather than partner. She said that under Republican Party leadership, "containing Chinese power and security ambitions" would be the norm.

24. See Susan V. Lawrence, "Duel over Sanctions," *Far Eastern Economic Review*, November 6, 2003, 32–3. The most recent reported case of U.S. sanctions against Chinese conglomerates said to have sold Iran missile components was in January 2005. See David E. Sanger, "U.S. Is Punishing 8 Chinese Firms for Aiding Iran," *New York Times*, January 18, 2005, 1.

25. Yu Shuman, "A Tentative Analysis of the U.S. Foreign Policy after the 'Sept. 11' Event," *International Strategic Studies* (China Institute for International Strategic Studies, Beijing) no. 1 (2002), 19–27. See also Chris Buckley, "China Uses Defense Report to Renew Warnings to Taiwan," *New York Times*, December 28, 2004, A6.

26. Donald Rumsfeld, "Report to Congress Pursuant to the FY2000 National Defense Authorization Act: Annual Report on the Military Power of the People's Republic of China" (Washington, D.C.: Department of Defense, 2002).

27. See the inside account of John Keefe, "A Tale of 'Two Very Sorries' Redux," *Far Eastern Economic Review*, March 21, 2002, 30–3.

28. See Steven Mufson, "Clash with China Strengthens Hard-Liners," *Washington Post*, April 23, 2001, 6. Bush's sales list did not include the most controversial weapon, the *Aegis* combat radar-equipped destroyers, but it contained just about everything else Taiwan was able to handle, including four *Kidd*-class destroyers, eight diesel-powered submarines, twelve P-3C *Orion* submarine-hunting aircraft, and mine-sweeping helicopters.

29. CNN interview of April 24, 2001, broadcast April 25; text in NAPSNet (Northeast Asia Peace and Security Network) Daily Report, April 25, 2001.

30. This account relies mainly on Lawrence, "A New Threat," *Far Eastern Economic Review*, December 18, 2003, 16–20.

31. Powell contributed to putting U.S. policy on the right track when, during a visit to China, he referred to China's "peaceful reunification," which was an undiplomatic slap at Chen Shui-bian's bid for independence. Powell also said, to the delight of his Chinese hosts, "There is only one China. Taiwan is not independent. It does not enjoy sovereignty as a nation." Interview with Mike Chinoy of CNN International TV, October 25, 2004. Available at http://www.state.gov/secretary/rm/37366pf.htm.

32. Only Saudi Arabia and Egypt ranked higher. Congressional Research Service (CRS), *U.S. Arms Sales: Agreements with and Deliveries to Major Clients, 1996–2003* (Washington, DC: CRS, December 8, 2004), 7, http://www.fas.org/man/crs/RL32689.pdf. Taiwan has had financial difficulty affording the latest U.S. arms package, however.

33. PLA Daily, "China's National Defense in 2004" (English version), *China Military Online* [English], http://english.chinamil.com.cn/special/cnd2004/contents_02.htm.

34. These include Japan's continuing claims to the disputed islands west of Okinawa (the Senkakus or Diaoyutai), the Japanese prime minister's repeated visits to the Yasukuni war shrine, Japan's association with U.S. theater missile defense plans, and Japan's pursuit of a permanent seat on the UN Security Council (which China opposes).

35. Kim, "Northeast Asia in the Local–Regional–Global Nexus: Multiple Challenges and Contending Explanations," in *The International Relations of Northeast Asia,* ed. Kim (Lanham, MD: Rowman & Littlefield, 2004), 24, 42.
36. In fact, working with China has already had some success in the last category. In November 2002 China implemented new export controls that covered "military equipment, special production facilities, and materials, technologies and services for military purposes" as well as dual-use chemical and biological materials. Reuters, "China Tightens Rules on Military Exports," Beijing, October 21, 2002, in NAPSNet Daily Report, October 22, 2002.
37. As the former unification minister under Kim, Lim Dong-won, later said, Bush "told Kim talks with the north were off and the U.S. did not support a policy of engagement. Kim Dae-jung was stunned … He was furious." PBS "Frontline" television, "Kim's Nuclear Gamble," http:// www.pbs.org/wgbh/pages/frontline/shows/kim/et/script.html.
38. Among these gains were the Agreed Framework, a step-by-step agreement whose main components were a nuclear freeze by North Korea in exchange for oil and nuclear-energy assistance and eventual diplomatic relations; direct high-level diplomacy, such as an exchange of visits in fall 2000 by DPRK Vice-Marshal Jo Myong-rok to Washington and Secretary of State Madeleine Albright to Pyongyang; Kim Jong-il's moratorium on ballistic-missile testing; and, at the tail end of Clinton's tenure, meetings in North Korea discussing trading substantial U.S. aid for the complete termination of the DPRK's nuclear weapons and missile programs.
39. On the eve of Kim Dae jung's visit to Washington, Powell said he hoped to "pick up where the Clinton administration left off" on engaging North Korea. See Frank S. Jannuzi, "North Korea: Back to the Brink?" in Hathaway and Lee, *George W. Bush and Asia* (see note 9), 79. Over a year later Powell, in a major speech on Asia policy, said, "We wholeheartedly support South Korea's sunshine policy." Powell, "Speech to the Asia Society," June 10, 2002, in ibid., 167.
40. For the first remark, see Howard Fineman, "'I Sniff Some Politics,'" *Newsweek,* May 27, 2002, 37; and for the second, Bob Woodward, *Bush at War* (New York: Simon and Schuster, 2002), 340.
41. As former defense secretary William J. Perry said on returning from meetings with the North Korean leaders: "… I believe their primary reason is security, is deterrence … We do not think of ourselves as a threat to North Korea, but I fully believe that they consider us a threat to them and, therefore, they see this missile as a means of deterrence. I think they have a very clear logic and a very clear rationale for what they are doing. We don't always understand that rationale; we don't always understand that logic, and therefore we consider it illogical." Interview on the Public Broadcasting System, September 17, 1999; quoted in NAPS Daily Report, September 20, 1999.
42. As Cheney was quoted as saying at a policy meeting on North Korea in December 2003, "We don't negotiate with evil; we defeat it." Murray Hiebert, "How Kerry Sees Asia," *Far Eastern Economic Review,* March 18, 2004, 28.
43. Gurtov, *Pacific Asia? Prospects for Security and Cooperation in East Asia* (Lanham, MD: Rowman & Littlefield, 2002), 178.
44. "President Delivers State of the Union Address," January 29, 2002. Available at www.whitehouse.gov/news/releases/2002/01/20020129/11.html.
45. The official announcement, as translated by the BBC, may be found in NAPSNet Daily Report, February 10, 2005.
46. David E. Sanger and William J. Broad, "North Korea Said to Expand Arms Program," *New York Times,* December 6, 2004, A9.
47. See Selig S. Harrison, "Did North Korea Cheat?" *Foreign Affairs* 84 no. 1 (January–February, 2005), 99–110.
48. Thom Shanker, "Lessons from Iraq Include How to Scare Korean Leader," *New York Times,* May 12, 2003, A17.
49. See Timothy L. Savage, "Letting the Genie Out of the Bottle: the Bush Nuclear Doctrine in Asia," in *Confronting the Bush Doctrine: Critical Views from the Asia-Pacific,* ed. Mel Gurtov and Peter Van Ness (London: Routledge, 2005), 72.
50. For example, a "senior [U.S.] administration official" was quoted in 2002 as saying that "one rogue-state crisis at a time" was Bush's preferred approach, suggesting North Korea might be next on his hit list after Iraq was subdued. Online editorial, *New York Times,*

December 13, 2002. That also seems to have been the view of administration hard-liners in the afterglow of seeming victory in Iraq; see Sanger, "Administration Divided over North Korea," *New York Times*, April 21, 2003, A15.
51. See Savage, "Letting the Genie Out," 73–4; and Chung-In Moon and Jong-Yun Bae, "The Bush Doctrine and the North Korean Nuclear Crisis," in Gurtov and Van Ness, *Confronting the Bush Doctrine* (see note 46), 39–62.
52. The proposal was presented to North Korea on June 24, 2004, in Beijing. See Harrison, chair, *Ending the North Korean Nuclear Crisis: A Proposal by the Task Force on U.S. Korea Policy* (Chicago: Center for International Policy and Center for East Asian Studies, University of Chicago, 2005), 9.
53. Victor D. Cha, "Korea's Place in the Axis," *Foreign Affairs* 81 no. 3 (May–June, 2002), 79–92. Cha now heads up Asian affairs in the National Security Council.
54. The six parties are the two Koreas, the United States, China, Russia, and Japan.
55. Joseph Kahn, "China Questions U.S. Data on North Korea," *New York Times*, March 7, 2005, A5.
56. Gi-Wook Shin and Paul Y. Chang, "The Politics of Nationalism in U.S.–Korean Relations," *Asian Perspective* 28 no. 4 (2004), 119–45.
57. CRS, *U.S. Arms Sales*, 7.
58. During 2004, the Pentagon decided to redeploy about 4,000 troops from South Korea to Iraq. Roh, who had been criticized by many supporters for agreeing to send a similar number of South Korean troops there, kept his promise. He ordered around 3,000 soldiers to Iraq in mid-2004, adding to the roughly 400 already there. In return, or so it seems, an agreement was reached to redeploy U.S. forces based at Yongsan in central Seoul, an extremely valuable piece of real estate, to less visible bases to the south, and to keep the number of U.S. forces at the existing level.
59. NAPSNet Daily Reports of March 30 and April 4, 2005 from the South Korean Press.
60. Jae-Jung Suh, "Assessing the Military Balance in Korea," *Asian Perspective* 28 no. 4 (2004), 77.
61. These and some other elements of a new approach to North Korea can also be found in the Council on Foreign Relations Task Force Report, *Meeting the North Korean Nuclear Challenge* (New York: CFR, 2003); Kim, "The U.S.–DPRK Nuclear Standoff"; Gurtov, "Common Security in North Korea: Quest for a New Paradigm in Inter-Korean Relations," *Asian Survey* 42 no. 3 (May–June, 2002), 397–418; Harrison, "Time to Leave Korea?" *Foreign Affairs* 80 no. 2 (March–April, 2001), 62–78; and Harrison, *Ending the North Korean Nuclear Crisis*.
62. See, for example, the statement of Li Gun, deputy director general of the DPRK Ministry for Foreign Affairs, December 16, 2003, in NAPSNet Special Report, February 6, 2004, http://DPRKbriefingbook@nautilus.org. Li Gun's main message was "if the US fundamentally changes its hostile policy toward North Korea we could also give up our nuclear deterrent." The specific steps he said the United States must take were a nonaggression guarantee, diplomatic relations, and noninterference with North Korea's economic relations with other countries. See also Philip P. Pan, "N. Korea Says It Can 'Show Flexibility,'" *Washington Post*, June 26, 2004, 14.
63. Following a visit to North Korea and talks with senior leaders, Harrison reported that the DPRK might be willing to freeze its nuclear weapons production under certain conditions but was no longer willing to agree to a step-by-step elimination of its bombs. Joseph Kahn, "North Korea Deals a Blow to Arms Talks," *New York Times*, April 11, 2005, A8.
64. See Van Ness, "The North Korean Nuclear Crisis: Four-Plus-Two—An Idea Whose Time Has Come," in Gurtov and Van Ness, *Confronting the Bush Doctrine* (see note 46), 242–59; Suh, "The Two-Wars Doctrine and the Regional Arms Race: Contradictions in U.S. Post-Cold War Security Policy in Northeast Asia," *Critical Asian Studies* 35 no. 1 (2003), 3–32; and Francis Fukuyama, "Re-envisioning Asia," *Foreign Affairs* 84 no. 1 (January–February, 2005), 83–4.
65. See the report by Choe Sang-Hun, "North Korea Seeks Broader Talks," online editorial, *International Herald Tribune*, April 2, 2005, quoting a DPRK foreign ministry statement that proposed transforming the Six Party Talks into a regional forum that would address U.S. deployments in Northeast Asia as well as North Korea's nuclear weapons program. Available at http://www.iht.com/articles/2005/04/01/news/korea.php.

66. See, for example, Task Force on U.S. Korea Policy, *Turning Point in Korea: New Dangers and New Opportunities for the United States* (Chicago: Center for International Policy and Center for East Asian Studies, University of Chicago, February, 2003).
67. Jack Pritchard, "What I Saw in North Korea," *New York Times*, January 21, 2003, A29.
68. These paragraphs on Japan rely mainly on Richard Tanter, "With Eyes Wide Shut: Japan, Heisei Militarization, and the Bush Doctrine," in Gurtov and Van Ness, *Confronting the Bush Doctrine* (see note 46), 153–80.
69. A Kyodo news poll found that 61 percent of respondents opposed the extension and 32 percent favored it. *Japan Times*, December 11, 2004, in NAPSNet Daily Report, December 15, 2004. To assuage the public, however, the soldiers were billeted well away from populated areas, inviting the opposite criticism from some Iraqis as well as Japanese—that the soldiers were doing little good.
70. Tanter, "With Eyes Wide Shut," 161.
71. *Asahi Shimbun* (Tokyo, English ed.), December 13, 2004, online at www.asahi.com.
72. See NAPSNet Daily Report, October 28, 2004, for various *Japan Times* articles on this subject.
73. See Harrison, "Did North Korea Cheat?" 100–1. Jonathan D. Pollack's account is consistent with Harrison's assessment. Pollack writes, "The Koizumi visit [to North Korea in September 2002] in all likelihood accelerated plans for the long-deferred visit" of James Kelly to Pyongyang, where Kelly made the uranium enrichment charge. Pollack, "Learning by Doing: The Bush Administration in East Asia," in Hathaway and Lee, *George W. Bush and Asia* (see note 46), 66.
74. The ships would not be able to enter without required insurance, which few North Korean ships have. The main effect would be on fish exports, which account for most of North Korea's roughly $250 million in annual trade with Japan.
75. For a good, brief summary of the issue, see Wenran Jiang, "Japan Dips Its Toe in the Taiwan Strait," *YaleGlobal*, March 2, 2005, http://yaleglobal.yale.edu/display.article?id=5362.
76. Tanter, "With Eyes Wide Shut," 156. See also Anthony Faiola, "Japan to Join U.S. Policy on Taiwan," *Washington Post*, February 18, 2005, 8.
77. Yoichi Funabashi, "Japan and the New World Order," *Foreign Affairs* 70 no. 5 (Winter, 1991–92), 58–74.
78. John Bolton, speaking when he was U.S. undersecretary of state for arms control and international security, lauded Japan's growing assertiveness, citing its claims to the Sensaku islands. Japan "is moving in the direction of what a number of Japanese politicians and commentators call the idea of a normal nation," Bolton said. Agence France Presse, February 10, 2005, in NAPSNet Daily Report, same date.
79. Masaru Tamamoto, "After the Tsunami, How Japan Can Lead," *Far Eastern Economic Review* 168 no. 2 (January–February, 2005), 10–8.
80. On conditions in these countries, see James Hookway, "Genuine Grievances," *Far Eastern Economic Review*, August 7, 2003, 16–8; John McBeth, "The Betrayal of Indonesia," *Far Eastern Economic Review*, June 26, 2003, 14–8; and Shawn W. Crispin, "Mafia Mission," *Far Eastern Economic Review*, July 3, 2003, 19.
81. Amitav Acharya, "The Bush Doctrine and Asian Regional Order: The Perils and Pitfalls of Preemption," in Gurtov and Van Ness, *Confronting the Bush Doctrine* (see note 46), 208.
82. Bradley Graham, "New Defense Ties with Philippines," *Washington Post*, August 13, 2002, A10. "We consider [the communist rebels] a much bigger threat than the Abu Sayyaf, the Moro Islamic Liberation Front or the Jemaah Islamiyah," said a Philippines military spokesman, citing two militant Muslim groups. Carlos H. Conde, "Communist Revival Worries the Philippines," online editorial, *New York Times*, January 4, 2004. Available at http://carlosconde.com/?p=121.
83. Todd S. Purdum, "U.S. to Resume Aid to Train Indonesia's Military Forces," online editorial, *New York Times*, August 3, 2002. Available at http://www.westpapua.net/news/02/08/030802-terrorism7.htm.
84. Jane Perlez, "U.S. Takes Steps to Mend Ties with Indonesian Military," *New York Times*, February 7, 2005, A12.
85. CDI, "Arms Trade." See note 16.
86. Perlez, "Indonesia Says It Will Press Attacks on Separatists in Sumatra," *New York Times*, May 23, 2003, A11.
87. Associated Press dispatch, in online editorial, *New York Times*, August 1, 2002.

88. U.S. arms manufacturers, with all-out support from the government, have used 9/11 as a springboard for pushing sales all across East Asia, with major fighter aircraft sales to South Korea, Australia, and Taiwan topping the list. European arms dealers seem to have no chance. David Lague, "Gripes over U.S. Grip on Arms Trade," *Far Eastern Economic Review*, September 26, 2002, 14–8. This circumstance became even more apparent in early 2005, following the EU's agreement, under U.S. pressure, not to remove the embargo on arms sales to China and Bush's decision to allow the sale of Lockheed Corporation's F-16s to Pakistan to go forward (see the following discussion).
89. See Acharya, "The Bush Doctrine and Asian Regional Order," 210–1.
90. Hassan Wirajuda, quoted in Raymond Bonner, "Indonesian Criticizes U.S. over the War in Iraq," *New York Times*, December 9, 2003, A12.
91. Acharya, "The Bush Doctrine and Asian Regional Order," 221.
92. See Bernard K. Gordon, "A High-Risk Trade Policy," *Foreign Affairs* 82 no. 4 (July–August, 2003), 105–18.
93. For a comprehensive overview, see Yul Kwon, "East Asian Regionalism Focusing on ASEAN plus Three," *Journal of East Asian Affairs* 18 no. 1 (Spring–Summer, 2004), 98–130.
94. See James Risen and Judith Miller, "Pakistani Intelligence Had Links to Al Qaeda, U.S. Officials Say," *New York Times*, October 29, 2001, A1.
95. Sanger, "In North Korea and Pakistan, Deep Roots of Nuclear Barter," online editorial, *New York Times*, November 24, 2002; Joby Warrick, "Iran Admits Foreign Help on Nuclear Facility," online editorial, *New York Times*, August 29, 2003; and Patrick E. Tyler and Sanger, "Pakistan Called Libyans' Source of Atom Design," online editorial, *New York Times*, January 6, 2004. Available at http://www.hvk.org/articles/0104/46.html. Pakistan, not having signed the Nuclear Non-Proliferation Treaty, is technically not subject to its prohibition of nuclear weapons exports.
96. An excellent overview of Khan's network is by Sanger and Broad, "From Rogue Nuclear Programs, Web of Trails Leads to Pakistan," online editorial, *New York Times*, January 4, 2004. Available at http://www.freerepublic.com/focus/f-news/1050932/posts.
97. See Broad and Sanger, "As Nuclear Secrets Emerge, More Are Suspected," *New York Times*, December 26, 2004, 1.
98. Perlez, "U.S. Ready to End Sanctions on India to Build an Alliance," online editorial, *New York Times*, August 27, 2001.
99. Celia W. Dugger, "Wider Military Ties with India Offer U.S. Diplomatic Leverage," *New York Times*, June 9, 2002, A1; Joanna Slater and Murray Hiebert, "U.S. and India Stage Quiet Rapprochement," *Wall Street Journal*, December 18, 2001, A11; and Conn Hallinan, "U.S. and India—A Dangerous Alliance," *Foreign Policy in Focus*, May 12, 2003, www.fpif.org/ commentary/2003/0305india.html.
100. Concerning India's military build-up to counter China, see Amit Gupta, *The U.S.–India Relationship: Strategic Partnership or Complementary Interests?* (Carlisle, PA: Strategic Studies Institute, U.S. Army War College, 2005), 34–5.
101. Somini Sengupta, "Courting a Pair of South Asia Partners," online editorial, *New York Times*, March 27, 2005. Available at http://www.nytimes.com/2005/03/27/international/asia/27india.html. *New York Times*, April 16, 2005, B1. Without the Indian market, Lockheed's Fort Worth, Texas, production line for F-16s would have had to close down, putting some 5,000 workers out of jobs; Leslie Wayne, "Connecting to India Through Pakistan." In June and July 2005 the United States and India signed additional agreements on cooperation in space and civil nuclear power plants, the latter of which will require Congressional approval. See Lora Saalman, "Redrawing India's Geostrategic Maps with China and the United States," available at http://japanfocus.org/article.asp?id=400.
102. Jeremy M. Weinstein, John Edward Porter, and Stuart E. Eizenstat, *On the Brink: Weak States and U.S. National Security* (Washington, DC: Report of the Commission on Weak States and US National Security, Center for Global Development, June 2004), http:// www.cgdev.org.
103. On the scope of the human-security crisis in East and South Asia, see Gurtov, *Pacific Asia? Prospects for Security and Cooperation in East Asia* (Lanham, MD: Rowman & Littlefield, 2002), 13–4, 35–7. The estimate of poverty comes from the Asian Development Bank's report, *Asian Development Outlook 2000*, cited in Gurtov, *Pacific Asia?*, 13.
104. Kurt M. Campbell, "Still Searching for a Vision," in Hathaway and Lee, *George W. Bush and Asia* (see note 46), 145–6.

13
The Bush Doctrine and Democracy Promotion in the Middle East

MAHMOOD MONSHIPOURI

Since the attacks of September 11, 2001, initially, and the subsequent terrorist attacks on European targets in Casablanca, Madrid, and London, a fundamental reformulation of U.S. foreign policy has underlined the need for a new perspective on confronting the growing terrorist threat. Domestic conditions in the Middle Eastern region have increasingly come to be seen as a major source of disillusionment and violence. Support for internal reform in Arab countries has invariably become an integral part of U.S. foreign policy. Some experts have argued that the main threat to U.S. security is no longer rogue states but rather substate or transnational actors who engage in terrorist activities.[1] The George W. Bush administration's inability to target substate or transnational actors, however, has led to a linking of terrorism to rogue states. Hence, a policy has developed of acting preemptively against rogue states possessing—or believed to possess—weapons of mass destruction.

Support for internal reform most often takes the form of a call for greater democratization. This invocation of democracy as a visionary complement to the war on terrorism has drawn mixed reactions in the Middle East. On the one hand, lopsided support by the United States for Israel, the U.S. invasion of Iraq, and the abuse of prisoners at Abu Ghraib and Guantanamo Bay have all intensified national sentiments of many Arabs, who dismiss the democracy rhetoric as yet another ploy to control the region's vast oil supplies. On the other hand, Middle Eastern people have welcomed such an initiative given the repressive atmosphere under which they have lived for so many years. The ordinary people of the Middle East have never been more ready than now for such a serious engagement with reform.[2]

The more skeptical view in the Middle East is supported by the fact that the history of U.S. intervention in other parts of the world in the name of promoting democracy or fighting communist aggression in the postwar period has invited controversy. Consider, for example, the cases of U.S. intervention in the twentieth century and early twenty-first century: Iran, Korea, Guatemala,

Cuba, Laos, Vietnam, Cambodia, Grenada, Libya, El Salvador, Nicaragua, Panama, Somalia, Sudan, Yugoslavia, Afghanistan, and Iraq.[3]

Differences persist over what kinds of reform must be implemented and how extensive they should be. What is clear is that the rhetorical appeal to democracy alone is unlikely to lead to a sustainable democratic transformation. A wide variety of questions have emerged regarding the method and content of reform, given the region's intricate historical and political milieu. There is also major disagreement over the issue of whether ending the long-running Israeli–Palestinian dispute is directly linked with pressing for more freedoms.

This chapter's purpose is threefold: (1) to examine the vision of the Bush doctrine for the greater Middle East; (2) to investigate the process by which democracy will be promoted as a way of combating the terrorist epidemic and containing the proliferation of weapons of mass destruction; and (3) to analyze the practical implications of a democracy-based approach to U.S. foreign policy in the region. Although the greater Middle East covers a vast landmass stretching from North Africa to Central Asia and embracing the Caucasus, the Levant, and the Persian Gulf, I am primarily concerned here with the traditional Muslim Middle East—that is, Arab countries.

Making Sense of the Bush Doctrine

U.S. involvement in the region's internal affairs and conflicts since the 1940s has been based on promoting stability, while ignoring the human rights abuses and undemocratic systems of government from which the United States has stood to benefit. This policy, marked by inconsistencies and paradoxes, has won the United States few friends in the Middle East.[4] It also explains why today there is—at least in some parts of the region—widespread skepticism regarding its greater Middle East initiative. Feelings of impotence, humiliation, and frustration continue to pervade much of the Middle East, especially after the invasion and occupation of Iraq. This is complicated by traditions and authoritarian governments in the region that give people little opportunity to participate in their own governance. The general point here is that terrorism thrives in an atmosphere where opportunities for democratic participation are lacking.[5] Defeating terror entails attenuating the rage that fuels it, and hence the argument for democratic transformation of these societies.[6]

The U.S. "democracy promotion doctrine" in the Middle East was articulated in Bush's speech at the Twentieth Anniversary of the National Endowment for Democracy on November 6, 2003, in Washington, D.C., where he noted, "Sixty years of Western nations excusing and accommodating the lack of freedom in the Middle East did nothing to make us safe—because in the long run, stability cannot be purchased at the expense of liberty. As long as the Middle East remains a place where freedom does not flourish, it will remain a place of stagnation, resentment, and violence ready for export. And with the spread of weapons that can bring catastrophic harm to our country and to our friends, it would be reckless to accept the status quo."[7]

In another speech before the American Enterprise Institute in February 2003, Bush suggested that the allied occupation and reconstruction of Germany and Japan provided good models for the greater Middle East initiative. "After defeating enemies," the president asserted, "we did not leave behind the occupying armies, we left constitutions and parliaments ... we established an atmosphere of safety, in which responsible, reform-minded local leaders could build lasting institutions of freedom. In societies that once bred fascism and militarism, liberty found a home."[8] American-style liberty, Bush implied, could find a home via similar large-scale occupations in the Middle East.[9]

Some observers call into question the Bush administration's position on democracy promotion through wholesale occupation. The historical experience of Germany and Japan in the postwar period showed that military occupation may increase the likelihood of democratization and that wise policy choices could surely improve its chances. Critics claim, however, that their experience was unique and not easily replicable today. The outcome of such interventions, Eva Bellin finds, "is largely shaped by factors, both domestic and international, that cannot be controlled by military engineers operating within the confines of current cultural norms and conventional limits of time and treasure."[10]

Before explaining what factors contributed to both Germany's and Japan's drive toward democracy, it is important to know that the process of the emergence of democracy in these two countries in the eighty to one hundred years before U.S. troops entered their territories after World War II was a complex one; this should serve as a warning against the simplistic notion that U.S. military occupation alone could lead to democratization in other countries.[11]

Prior to the outbreak of World War II, both Germany and Japan were highly industrialized countries with advanced level of economic development that generated an impressive gross national product per capita. They were both relatively homogenous ethnically, with a significant consensus about their sense of social solidarity and national identity. After World War II, both Germany and Japan retained an effective police force, judicial system, and civil service with which to govern.[12]

Both also had extensive experience with democratic rule prior to World War II and had committed leaders, whose embrace of the democratic project helped anchor democratic projects at home. Additionally, context-specific factors such as the experience of total devastation and defeat, the fear of communist threat and takeover, and the imposed freedom of occupation bestowed by contemporary cultural norms made it possible for democracy to endure in these countries.[13] These endowments crucial to democratic outcomes—levels of economic development, ethnic homogeneity, strength of state institutions, historical experience, and elite leadership—are factors conspicuously lacking in the cases of many Middle Eastern countries.

It is also important to take into account the way in which the region's political economy presents obstacles to the transition to democracy. In the postcolonial era, Arab governments emphasized their military strength to protect their often hard-won independence. Their often violent struggle for independence, followed by a half-century of conflict with Israel within the context of the Cold War, in turn greatly fostered authoritarianism.[14] Another formidable barrier to the transition to democracy has been the "low dependence of states on citizens."[15] This is indeed in the nature of the region's rentier states, states which live off "rents"—income from oil.

In many Arab countries the most viable and best organized opposition forces are those of political Islam. Islamists now participate in elections in countries as diverse as Bahrain, Iraq, Jordan, Lebanon, Kuwait, Morocco, Palestine, Yemen, Bangladesh, Malaysia, Pakistan, and Indonesia. Strong democratic trends exist within the movements of "political Islam."[16] Alan Richards, an expert on Middle Eastern Politics, wrote that the main barriers to a transition to democracy in the Arab world are "fundamentally political."[17] External interventions leading to occupation exacerbate the situation of Middle Eastern countries. The U.S. invasion of Iraq, for instance, has strengthened the popular appeal of antidemocratic extremists such as Al-Qaeda and other *jihadi salafis*.[18] The endemic interstate and intrastate conflicts and the massive infusions of military aid into the region are major barriers to democratization and political development.[19]

The question the Bush administration now must answer is how to support local institution building and democracy promotion efforts in a region that has a dismal human rights record. With almost 300 million people, the Arab states of the Middle East and North Africa include no free country, as rated by Freedom House (Table 13.1). Free elections are not allowed in most of the Arab world. The region's well-entrenched and nondemocratic regimes have survived numerous political upheavals. Their level of economic development and economic power varies (Table 13.1). Some of these states have survived through dependency on either oil or security rents for their revenues; thus, they can be termed rentier states (e.g., Algeria, Bahrain, Iraq, Kuwait, Libya, Oman, Qatar, Saudi Arabia, Tunisia, the United Arab Emirates). Others have relied on foreign aid (i.e., Egypt, Jordan, and Yemen). Clearly, oil revenues have had "an incredibly corrupting influence," rendering these states less accountable to public pressure and demands.[20]

A growing body of evidence points to governance failures among the rentier states. These states, according to one study, are the least advanced in observing civil liberties and political rights. Their citizens are among the least able—when compared to other transitional states of the former Soviet Union and Eastern Europe—to participate in the selection of their governments.

Table 13.1 Political Freedom in the Arab World

Country	Population	GDP per Capita (ppp$)	Freedom Rating
Algeria	31.4 million	$5,308	Not free
Bahrain	700,000	$15,084	Partly free
Comoros	600,000	$1,588	Partly free
Djibouti	700,000	$2,377	Partly Free
Egypt	71.2 million	$3,635	Not free
Iraq	23.6 million	Na	Not free
Jordan	5.3 million	$3,966	Partly free
Kuwait	2.3 million	$15,799	Partly free
Lebanon	4.3 million	$4,308	Not free
Libya	5.4 million	$7,570	Not free
Mauritania	2.6 million	$1,677	Partly free
Morocco	29.7 million	$3,546	Partly free
Oman	2.6 million	$13,,356	Not free
Qatar	600,000	$18,789	Not free
Saudi Arabia	24 million	$11,367	Not free
Somalia	7.8 million	Na	Not free
Sudan	32.6.million	$1,797	Not free
Syria	17.2 million	$3,556	Not free
Tunisia	9.8 million	$6,363	Not free
UAE	3.5 million	$17,935	Not free
Yemen	18.6 million	$893	Partly free

Source: Data regarding population and gross domestic product per capita have been collected from *in the World 2003: Annual Survey of Political Rights and Civil Liberties* (New York: Freedom House, 2003), 703–4. Data regarding freedom rating are based on *Freedom in the World 2005* (New York: Freedom House, 2005).

Their media are not independent. Their main successes are confined to the rule of law and, to a lesser extent, control of corruption.[21] Although these countries control about half of the world's oil reserves, the region has higher unemployment and poverty than much of developing countries. Unemployment averages 15 percent, and one out of five people live on less than $2 per day.[22]

Women's empowerment remains in critical deficit in the region. The utilization of Arab women's capabilities through political and economic participation remains the lowest in the world as evidenced by the very low proportion of women in government both at the ministerial level and in the number of seats in parliament held by women. Gender inequality in education and economic activity is rampant throughout the Middle East. It should be noted, however, that Arab countries have made great strides in women's education. Female literacy rates have increased threefold since 1970, and female primary and secondary enrollment rates have more than doubled. Despite this progress, the female enrollment rates are lower than those for males.[23]

Moreover, Arab women remain marginalized and underutilized in all sectors of the economy and society, notably in terms of their economic, intellectual, and leadership potential.[24] Of the 25 percent unemployed, 82 percent are women. They are the most likely to be deprived of access to health and educational services because of financial pressures on families.[25]

Views regarding the link between democracy and economic growth sharply contrast. Although some emphasize good governance and accountability, others argue that an independent judiciary "would allow people to invest more freely" and that without democratization, economic changes will occur, but at a much slower pace.[26] Today, Kuwait is the only Arab country with a parliament that could effectively check decisions by the executive branch of government. Only Yemen's freedom status has improved over the past year.[27] The Middle Eastern region has by far the lowest average freedom score (5.5) of any region of the world, when compared with 4.4 in Asia, 4.3 in Africa, 3.4 among the postcommunist states, and 2.5 in Latin America and the Caribbean.[28]

Democratic movements, however, have made some strides in the Middle East. In Turkey the *Adalet ve Kalkinma Partisi* [Justice and Development Party] with Islamic roots and ideological orientation, has been in power since 2002. Restricted democracy in Iran has led to an insatiable public desire for a more open, tolerant, and democratic political system. The Persian Gulf monarchies, such as Bahrain, Kuwait, and Qatar, have taken some meaningful if rudimentary steps toward more constitutional rule. The U.S. officials have criticized Kuwait, Qatar, the United Arab Emirates, and Saudi Arabia for doing little to stop forced labor and other forms of "modern slavery," such as sexual and human trafficking (imported workers and prostitutes), within their borders.[29] There are hopeful signs of democratic struggles in both Iraq and the Palestinian occupied territories.[30]

According to the 2004 *Freedom House Survey*, since 9/11 fifty-one countries have made democratic gains, as opposed to twenty-seven countries that have had setbacks.[31] The evidence suggests that democracy now enjoys enormous support in non-Western countries and cultures. Although there is a less liberal attitude in Muslim societies than in the West toward such social issues as gender equality and gay rights, no difference exists at all when it comes to support for democratic institutions. One empirical study concludes that nearly 90 percent of the respondents in Muslim societies favor democracy, the same level of support as in the West.[32]

The importance of the Middle Eastern region should also be underscored, as well as why it figures prominently in the strategic calculation of the United States, the European Union (EU), and East Asia. The Persian Gulf region and the Caspian Basin together have by far the world's largest reserves of oil and natural gas. Since reliable access to reasonably priced energy is vitally significant to the world's great powers, Zbigniew Brzezinski noted, "Strategic domination over the area, even if cloaked by cooperative arrangements, would be a globally decisive hegemonic asset."[33]

Will the Bush doctrine bring the EU and the United States closer, or will it drive a wedge in the transatlantic alliance? The September 11, 2001, terrorist attacks in the United States laid bare the fact that the Middle East cannot be left to its own devices. To ignore this region's problems and to underestimate its potential for global disruption, Brzezinski wrote, would be "tantamount to declaring an open season for intensifying regional violence, region-wide contamination by terrorist groups and the competitive proliferation of weaponry of mass destruction."[34]

These realities have pushed the Europe and America toward a convergence of new interest: confronting the threat of Islamic extremists. Unlike the Cold War era, the menace of Islamic fundamentalism is not restricted to a certain border; it is global.[35] The mounting threat of Islamic fundamentalism in Europe is directly linked to the increasing flow of Muslim immigrants to the Europe; their attempts to promote their own cultural traditions and religious beliefs have prompted an intense debate over such issues as the headscarf and veil. Similarly, Muslims warn of Western cultural invasion, fearing the loss of their identity.[36] Muslim immigrants' participation—or their absence—in the politics and economy of the country in which they reside has also caused numerous reactions throughout the Europe.

Prior to the U.S.-led invasion of Iraq, the United States and Europe disagreed over the method of how to fight the global war on terrorism. In the aftermath of invasion, however, the talk of the international cooperation has permeated diplomatic forums. Increasingly, the United States and the EU member states have tacitly reached an agreement on oil distribution and the active role in the Middle East peace process. The upshot has been the U.S. emphasis on a sustained effort to delegitimate terrorism and to promote forces within the Muslim world intent on building and preserving modern, moderate, and democratic political institutions.[37] This may mean different things in different countries of the region. In some cases, it may only require a minimal degree of democratization in the region so that the stability of friendly and pro-West countries would not be jeopardized. To this end, a shift of approach toward countries such as Iran must be seen in this context. For now, at least, the U.S. diplomatic pressure on Iran has supplanted the threat of a use of force or preemptive strike.

Bush's foreign policy entails two new elements. First, the administration is seeking a broader engagement with the world than what was observed in his first term. This greater willingness to listen and engage the rest of the world, especially the rapprochement with the EU, indicates the drawbacks of its unilateral foreign policy toward Iraq. Secondly, a shift in rhetoric from fighting terrorism to a discussion of freedom and democracy has shaped this new foreign policy. The Bush administration was not preoccupied with a preemptive use of force to the extent that it was in its first term.

Bush's forward strategy of freedom is based on applying external pressures for internal political reform. Given the diversity of the region, a much more differentiated policy toward the Middle Eastern countries is needed. There is no coherent plan, and there cannot be a coherent strategy vis-à-vis these countries. In fact, the absence of policy cohesion has caused a fundamental difference of opinion among Middle Eastern governments and scholars concerning the definition, goals, and implications of such a doctrine.

Reactions from the Middle East

Varying groups tend to interpret the reforms associated with the Bush doctrine differently. Increasingly, the battle lines over reform within the Middle East are drawn between the pessimists and optimists. Four reactions to such initiative can be discerned throughout the Middle East.

Traditional Islamists

Conservative Islamist groups see reform as an opportunity to create pure Islamic values and political regimes while refuting liberal states; elections and democratization; and market economies and secular values. These groups favor conditional reform. While welcoming reform-oriented policies on the part of their governments, many conservatives view with skepticism the Bush doctrine. They argue that the doctrine is bound to fail to resonate deeply with the Arab street, largely because of the widely held perception in the region that the Bush doctrine is a euphemistic replacement for the war on Islam. They assert that the United States is not a right agent to initiate reform in a region where the U.S. government has routinely supported authoritarian but pro-West regimes for both political and economic reasons since the mid-twentieth century.

Protecting its access to oil as well as political regimes friendly to it, Islamic conservatives note, has for so long been the central premise around which U.S. foreign policy toward the region has taken shape. Highly suspicious of this democratic initiative, conservative Islamists take the view that the relationship between democracy and economic growth is an unproven one. To the extent that the Bush administration is unwilling to push for a more assertive policy toward nondemocratic but friendly Middle Eastern states, this pessimistic view continues.

Many observers, Islamists or otherwise, assert that the Arab–Israeli conflict—not internal reforms in the Arab world—lie at the heart of the Arabs' lack of freedom. There is widespread recognition that the resolution of Arab–Israeli conflict is equally as relevant as the progress toward reform.

The Palestinian issue has arguably become a matter of identity for the region's Arabs and non-Arab Muslims. "The contemporary political consciousness of the region," Shibley Telhami wrote, "has been largely defined in relation to Israel and Palestine."[38]

Many European governments have stressed the necessity for socioeconomic changes and modernization in the Arab world to precede any major pressure for democratization.[39] Equally important is the fact that this policy initiative runs the risk of offending and alienating these countries' leaders in the process. If this proves to be the case, the Bush administration might even be forced to abandon its initiative. Such a setback will most likely give antireform forces a momentum of sorts.[40] For now, it is argued that it will be difficult, if not impossible, to implement the Greater Middle East Initiative to establish democracy in the region unless the Palestinian–Israeli conflict is effectively resolved.[41]

Radical Islamists

Radical Islamic groups, also known as Islamic neoconservatives, lash out ferociously at anyone who proposes fundamental reform along the lines offered by secular western ideas, practices, and institutions. In fact, some *Wahhabis* and *Salafis* consider liberal democracy contrary to Islam, arguing that this type of democracy is an alien intrusion that is part of the larger pernicious influence of the Great Satan and his cohorts.[42] They advocate *ijtihad*—that is, Islamic reasoning in matters relating to Islamic law. Extremely devout and often puritanical, this group's goal is to "establish an Islamic state based on the comprehensive and rigorous application of the *Shari'a.*"[43] The members of this group are not drawn exclusively from the ranks of the *ulama* [Islamic scholars]. They regard the conservative approach, as represented by the orthodox *ulama*, as unrealistic, and they oppose modernist Islamic groups that emulate western ideas, practices, and institutions as alien to Islam.[44]

Islamic neoconservatives link the Muslim world's decline into colonialism, neocolonialism, and disunity within the Muslim world. They emphasize a constitution that is Islamic. Most of them view with skepticism the imposition of liberal democracy from outside. They argue that the Greater Middle East Initiative is a new ploy to gain access to oil—a fact that has figured prominently in U.S. foreign policy toward the Middle East since the mid-twentieth century. In fact, a major goal of U.S. foreign policy has been to ensure the access to foreign oil supplies, especially since 1971 when domestic oil production began its gradual decline. By 1996, the United States imported half of its oil.[45]

Liberal Islamists

The radical Islamists' considerations are contested by the view, shared by many Muslims, that construction of civil society and democratic institutions should be seen as global and legitimizing efforts. Turkey's dominant party, *Adalet ve Kalkinma Partisi*, is in fact an example of liberal Islam, although it is not the only party that criticized U.S. invasion of Iraq. Ali Bulaç, a Turkish Islamic thinker, argues that the superiority of western principles and institutions, such as human rights, democracy, market economy, the rule of law, have gained near universal consensus. The debate is no longer over these principles and institutions; rather, it is about the unfair distribution of the benefits derived from universal principles and institutions.[46]

Liberal Islamists tend to appeal to women and more generally to the young to reconcile the calls for reform with those of the indigenous people for reforms. This may be, they suggest, an accident, but nevertheless the move is consistent with the masses of people's desire for democracy and the fulfillment of human rights. Seeking accommodation and engagement—not isolation—is in fact an effective way to construct democratic institutions and to promote a democratic political culture.

Regardless of the ulterior motives of the Bush administration, the mounting American pressure for reforms is widely appreciated by dissenting voices in the Arab world. Though arguing that free, fair, and competitive elections are central to any types of reform, they insist that an actual separation of state and religion is unacceptable and that laws made by elected parliaments must be compatible with Islamic law.[47]

Many Islamic reformists question the U.S. detention practices in Guantanamo Bay as well as human rights abuses of the prisoners at Abu Ghraib prison in Iraq. They also question the U.S. refusal to resign the convention for the International Criminal Court. They see the U.S. pressure for domestic reform in their countries as contradictory to what its foreign policy directions.

Secularists

Secular Arab intellectuals and political leaders, who tend to embrace western values and institutions, welcome the emphasis on liberty and freedom but warn against trying to impose western models on Arab societies. In the past, secularists—known as socialists and nationalists—have always spearheaded riots, peaceful antigovernment protests, strikes, revolution, and guerrilla warfare. Today, secularists are among reform-minded groups and factions who tend to support reform.

On balance, the leaders of many Middle Eastern countries fit this description. As ardent proponents of modernizing programs, they have fiercely resisted democratization programs, in part because such agenda would jeopardize their political survival and in part because western powers have been reluctant to push for such changes given their interests in maintaining the status quo. Secularists have at times appeared as effective populist politicians. The debate among secularists is largely about how to promote reform, internally or by relying on outside sources.

The Greater Middle East Initiative

Well prior to the September 11 terrorist attacks, building democracy and supporting civil society, human rights, and the rule of law have been central elements of the Barcelona process (the Euro-Mediterranean partnership) in both its multilateral and bilateral dimensions.[48] One of the lessons of the Barcelona process is that the concept of democracy is broken down into constituent elements such as the rule of law, independence of the judiciary, transparency, accountability, and fostering civil society. This process will avoid the fear of externally directed regime change and may make it easier to bring the elites of these countries along and to create common interests to promote such objectives.[49] In reality, however, the progress of the Barcelona process in the fields of political reform or human rights sadly has been limited.[50]

In the aftermath of the September 11 terrorist attacks, however, the United States and the EU have come to define a common security threat: global terrorism. Since June 2004, the United States and the Group of Eight Industrialized Nations (G-8) have coordinated efforts to promote gradual but systematic socioeconomic and political reform in the Middle East. This attempt, known as the Partnership for Progress, is grounded on the notion that a growing pool of politically disadvantaged and economically underprivileged individuals is likely to pose a grave threat to the internal stability of their own countries. More importantly, such disillusionments would present a great menace to the international peace and stability by contributing to the burgeoning rise in the global terrorism, international crime, and illegal terrorism.[51]

The Greater Middle East Initiative (GMEI) proposes that the governments of the G-8 work toward empowering Arab citizens by increasing funding to democracy, human rights, the media, women's nongovernmental organizations (NGOs), and other NGOs in the region. A special focus is put on educational programs, women's economy, and civil society. The initiative also encourages the region's governments to lift restrictions on basic freedoms, to promote the operations of NGOs, to allow civil society growth and press freedoms, and to foster judicial reform. Furthermore, the GMEI suggests that the Helsinki model—that is, the 1975 Helsinki Accords, signed by the U.S., the former Soviet Union, and most European countries—be adopted to establish a mechanism for settling disagreements regarding human rights issues, especially as they relate to the dissident groups.[52]

Despite the G-8 official statement, no direct reference is made of the imperative of holding free elections or releasing prisoners of conscience. Preoccupied with generalities, the G-8 summit fails to lay down the specifics of how to advance such lofty goals given the diversity of countries and their political, economic, and sociocultural circumstances. With the exception of token funding for the region's NGOs, as Kaveh Afrasiabi aptly noted, "Neither the

United States nor Europe nor Japan have explicitly allocated any budget to bankroll the overall program."[53]

It is important to remember that the lack of progress in governance—especially the rule of law, political participation, civil–political rights, and accountability—and in the absence of economic reforms (e.g., liberalization, fortifying the domestic banking systems, and increased openness to foreign investment) the Greater Middle Eastern Initiative will most likely fail. This is especially true of the rentier states.[54]

The Paradox of Democracy and Security

Although the G-8 official statement has deployed the argument in favor of democratic reform in the region, it has yet to adopt a monolithic strategy toward achieving such an initiative. It is worth recalling that the relationship between democracy promotion and security enhancement is crucial to understanding the complexities of implementing democracy today in the region. Western powers, as Rashid Khalidi wrote, have never rendered the promotion of democracy integral to their Middle East policies. In fact, British and French policies were contingent on the negation of meaningful self-determination, from Palestine to Egypt and from Algeria to Iraq and Syria.[55]

Since the 1930s, the Western world has gained more access to the region's oil resources by working with dictators than with accountable democratic regimes. The 1953 coup in Iran is a notable case in point. The Central Intelligence Agency (CIA) and British agents, in collaboration with internal army generals, engineered a coup against the nationalist and constitutionally elected prime minister of Iran, Mohammad Mossadeq, who nationalized the Anglo-Iranian Oil Company. He was deposed, and the shah was restored to power shortly afterward. The United States foreign policy between 1953 and 1978 stressed a special relationship with the shah and his inner circle, while largely disregarding the needs and demands of the Iranian masses. When in the late 1970s President Jimmy Carter's concern for human rights had to be balanced against U.S. support for the shah's repressive regime, the policy of having it both ways led to contradictory policies, precipitating in the process the fall of the monarchy in Iran.[56]

Since 9/11 the Bush administration has sent mixed signals to the Saudis. On the one hand, they have argued that Saudi Arabia has done little to crack down on Islamic extremists. On the other hand, U.S. Secretary of State Condoleezza Rice praised Saudi officials for taking "some first step toward openness" in the holding of municipal elections but condemned their denying women the right to vote and the arrest of nonviolent dissidents.[57] Yet Washington is reluctant to push the Saudi royal family beyond a certain point for the fear that the Saudi government is susceptible to Islamist opposition movements. What is more, the Saudis play a constructive role in determining oil production and prices, in advancing the Arab–Israeli peace process, and in moving forward the reconstruction of Iraq.

The Bush administration has permitted its war on terrorism to dilute its democracy promotion efforts in such key countries as Pakistan, Saudi Arabia, and Kuwait.[58] Many countries around the world are using the U.S.-led campaign against terror as a pretense to justify repression of dissenting voices and activities, including those of a nonviolent kind. Restrictions on military aid have also been lifted to countries—particularly those with large Muslim populations—that have expressed support for the war on terrorism.[59]

The United States has adopted an approach toward Egypt that is similar to its approach to Saudi Arabia. Rice praised Egyptian President Mohamed Hosni Mubarak for taking some "encouraging" first steps toward democracy promotion in his country, but she insisted that "Egypt's elections, including the Parliamentary elections, must meet objective standards that define every free election, including freedom of assembly, speech and press."[60] She nevertheless refused to meet with the leaders of the outlawed Islamist organization known as *Ikhwan-al-Muslemeen* [the Muslim Brotherhood], even though it is believed to be among the most popular opposition group.[61]

The Bush administration exercises a great deal of caution when it comes to pushing Mubarak to democratize Egypt's political system, given Egypt's critical role in the Egyptian–Israeli peace treaty and its crucial role in resolving the Israeli–Palestinian conflict. Though the Bush administration urges the Egyptian and Saudi governments to press for democracy, it continues to provide them with arms and funds because they are generally regarded as allies in the war on terrorism and crucial to the region's stability.

The United States is too often resented for propping up dictatorial and corrupt regimes rather than prodding them to change their ways.[62] Osama bin Laden was the price of the U.S. victory over the Soviet Union in Afghanistan.[63] With the active encouragement of the CIA and Pakistan's Inter-Services Intelligence (ISI), the *mujahideen* played a significant part in dislodging Soviet troops from Afghanistan throughout the 1980s. The Taliban's rise to power in Afghanistan by the mid-1990s was made possible by Pakistan's ISI, which in turn was influenced by the CIA. The actions of the Taliban at that time largely served U.S. geopolitical interests.[64]

The paradox of democracy and security is generally seen as the GMEI's Achilles' heel. It indeed represents one of the most obvious obstacles to achieving the GMEI. Democratization in some Arab countries is likely to increase the internal vulnerability of political regimes, while providing unique opportunities to those Islamic groups and parties that are well organized and capable of mounting serious and legitimate challenges to the status quo. The result may be the establishment of nonsecular regimes that could potentially pose a threat to U.S. regional interests.[65]

The lack of extended and firm democratic demands among the local people is another reason for the slow pace of change. These tribal and traditional networks and foundations are in some ways symbolic of their countries' national unity and territorial integrity.[66] Pushing for reform in the cases of Pakistan, Saudi Arabia, Egypt, and the Palestinian territories is not risk free. Saudi Arabia presents a special case, where the regime combines characteristics of a traditional authoritarian regime with the modern economic power of a rentier state facing an internal Islamic opposition movement. In Kuwait, press freedom is firmly observed, yet there are no official political parties in the country. Women gained the right to vote for the first time in Bahrain in 2003.

The core Arab states such as Egypt and Algeria have typically combined authoritarian aspects of government with a strong security apparatus capable of confronting opposing Islamic groups or parties. Despite its withdrawal from Lebanon, Syrian's influence on Hezbollah, an Islamic party, may persist. Another possibility is that Lebanese politics may also plunge back into the sectarian strife that invited Syrian intervention in the first place.[67] Some observers even suggest that the fears of a new civil war in Lebanon are likely to pit anti-Syrian forces against pro-Syrian forces.[68] Although France and the United States have feuded over Iraq, Syria's occupation of Lebanon has provided them common ground.[69] The French advocated a legitimate role for Hezbollah and brought Americans along in pursuit of the larger goal of ending Syrian hegemony by pushing it out of Lebanon.[70]

Sectarian tensions and tribal games continued to define Lebanese politics. The anti-Syrian opposition bloc led by Saad Hariri, son of the assassinated former Lebanese prime minister Rafiq Al Hariri, managed to gain a final governing majority of seventy-two seats in the 128-seat parliament. But without enough Christians in their ranks, the winning coalition could collect the votes needed to expel pro-Syrian President Emile Lahoud, since each religion has carefully guarded prerogatives. On June 26, 2005, the post of parliament speaker, reserved for a Shiite, went to Nabih Berri, another ally of Syria.[71]

Far from the democracy promotion the Bush administration has claimed the elections would effect, elections revealed the underlying sectarian divisions that have long characterized the Lebanese politics under Syrian occupation.[72] The fact remains that Syrians continue to wield considerable clout in Lebanon. They could indeed make things difficult for Lebanon if the new government moves to further sever the decades-old bonds with Damascus.[73]

How significant is electoral politics in the stalled transitions in Yemen and Jordan? One expert argues that the answer is in the lack of importance of elections in Jordan: For instance, the electoral system is structured in such a way to generate particular results. In the early 1990s, new legislation was introduced whereby anything passed by the lower house must be approved by the appointed upper house. This ensured that nothing can be approved by the legislators without the king's approval. In short, the king may never need to use the veto.⁷⁴ In Yemen, a legislator has to be either in the ruling party or he is out. There is one ruling party, and the Islamist party—*Islah* [reform]—has to either ally with the ruling party or become a loyal opposition.⁷⁵ Outside the sphere of electoral politics, the Islamists and leftists engage in cooperative activity on a number of specific issues.⁷⁶

As noted already, Islamist groups could very well be the beneficiary of democratic openings in countries such as Egypt, Pakistan, and the Palestinian-occupied territories. The unintended consequences of a sudden opening of the political system render the Bush doctrine inconsistent and less cohesive. The Palestinian general elections will most likely pose a mortal threat to Mahmoud Abbas's regime. Both Israeli and American officials have tried to figure out how to preempt a Hamas election victory in the near future.⁷⁷

In the cases of the small but welfare states of the Arab countries of the Persian Gulf, the slow pace of democratic openings have led to few signs of major breakthrough. Yemen, Morocco, Tunisia, Libya, and Jordan appear to be in line with democratic initiatives and capable of absorbing the shocks of democratic reforms. Political parties, parliament, and intense competitive elections typify Yemen's political landscape. President Ali Abdullah Salah's attempts to pave the way for his son to succeed him demonstrate how limited democracy is in Yemen.⁷⁸

In Iran, the push for democratic opening is limited given the influence of a conservative clerical establishment and its hold on power. To minimize the complexity of the relationship between security and democracy, European governments have suggested working on the basis of bilateral relations with Iran, while boosting cooperation for the gradual reform in that country. The problem with this approach is that European and American national interests in curbing Iran's nuclear program tend to trump any support for the Iranian people's struggle to reform their government.⁷⁹

Western leaders argue that making bilateral relations contingent on political democratization could interrupt the internal trends transpiring toward reform there. Outside interference could prove utterly counterproductive in the case of Iran. On June 16, 2005, the eve of the ninth presidential elections in Iran, Bush declared that the electoral process there had failed to fulfill the "basic requirements" of democracy and that the "oppressive record" of the clerical rulers would undermine the legitimacy of the vote.⁸⁰ The Associated Press reported that on election day Bush's message backfired in that he motivated people to vote in retaliation. One conservative hard-line Iranian newspaper wrote that people crushed the American president's wishes by casting their votes. Likewise, even many opponents of the conservative clerical establishment, including reformist groups, objected to Bush's tone and timing.⁸¹

Another issue worthy of consideration is how change in the political climate would be introduced. Top-down political reforms appear more familiar to the Middle Eastern regimes than the idea of instantaneous democratization.

A policy of promoting political reform—rather than a large-scale democratization—via the back door may prove durable in certain cases given the seemingly conflicting imperatives of security and democracy.[82]

The Case for Multilateralism

What are the costs of the new American bid to remake the Arab world? What are the best tools or mechanisms to achieve this? The fellow members of the Quartet—the United States, the United Nations, the EU, and Russia—and their road map for the peace process in the Middle East have helped to nudge forward a stalled peace process. By working with Israel, the Palestinian Authority, Egypt, and the members of the Quartet, the United States can facilitate the Israeli disengagement from Gaza and the northern West Bank.[83]

The notions of an externally directed "regime change" and a "reordering of the region from abroad" have come to be seen as a threat not only by authoritarian-regime elites but also by cultural and social elites. This view demonstrates that even the sole superpower in the world would need a broadly cooperative strategy for promoting better governance in the states of the region.[84] Only by laying down comprehensive arrangements and multilateral strategies can the United States avoid becoming mired alone in a hegemonic quicksand.[85] The EU has the economic resources and financial means necessary to make the critical difference to the region's long-term stability.[86] A partnership between European and Arab countries and the United States will most likely revolve around the threat of radical Islamic groups, which pose a serious threat of violence and instability to the entire region.

Unilateral applications of power tend to draw active noncooperation by other powers. A clear illustration of this is the reluctance of some key allies to assist the U.S. and British occupation efforts in Iraq.[87] Multilateralism has clearly brought the EU and America closer in their position vis-à-vis Syria. The new U.S. security doctrine of promoting democracy in the region demonstrates that a multilateral pattern of action would be more effective.

In the case of Iran, U.S. unilateral acts and criticism have had an adverse effect on Iran, largely because the United States has lacked any diplomatic or economic relations with Iran—which explains why it has carried no leverage. Some experts argue that because the economy is a major concern for Iranian leadership, Washington can increase its leverage in a multilateral framework, working with states that can be persuaded to cooperate and that are in fact Iran's key trading partners: the EU, Japan, Russia, and China. Together, these states must raise the economic stakes of Iran's nuclear aspirations: "either nuclear weapons or economic health."[88]

The U.S. inclusion of Iran in the so-called axis of evil designation and its rhetoric of regime change have made the Islamic Republic suspect U.S. policies toward Iran. By contrast, the EU, the United Nations (UN), and some

NGOs are engaged with Iran and pose no threat to the stability of the Islamic Republic. They have had some modest leverage with Iran's clerical rulers. In recent years, some foreign governments and NGOs have successfully joined Iranian activists to demand the release of bloggers and Internet journalists arrested on the suspicion of espionage.[89]

It is important to recognize, as one observer reminds us, that neither U.S. repeated condemnations of Iran's clerical rulers nor the threat of military force will promote the cause of democracy there. When and if reforms come to Iran, it will most likely materialize because of the internal pressures such as the demands of its youth—not because of the outside pressure by the United States.[90]

In the Algerian case, the military took over following the cancellation of the 1992 elections in which the *Front islamique du salut* [Islamic Salvation Front], or FIS, was about to win a majority of seats in the parliament. Fearing that an FIS majority in the National Assembly would lead to the emergence of an Islamic state, the army stepped in to prevent such a change—a takeover tacitly supported by some secular groups who similarly feared Islamization and Arabization, as well as by western governments who supported a gradual, pro-western change. To this date, western countries still worry about the impact of the Algerian crisis on pro-western Arab regimes and equally fear an expected influx of people running away from the northern shores of the Mediterranean. Though the French plan for Algeria includes fostering bilateral aid and rescheduling debt, U.S. policy favors the development of more democratic system. There is no general consensus on how to deal with Algeria's case other than seeking a nonviolent solution to it.

Conclusion

Although the democratic transformation of the Middle East has become the latest vindication for U.S. foreign policy toward this region, it is not clear whether this rationale will enduringly place democratization high on U.S. foreign policy agenda. On balance, predictions regarding the remaking of the Middle East are notoriously unreliable given the region's cultural alienation, political volatility, and ethnic complexities. This unreliability stems in part from the fact that competing U.S. interests are most likely to trump the region's democratic considerations and in part because there is a widespread commitment to a strong state throughout the Arab world.

The real question remains: Will the push for democratization be steadily present in and viewed as a credible pillar of U.S. foreign policy for years to come? To the extent that free elections can result in electoral victories for Islamic parties bent on challenging U.S. military presence and policies in the region, the answer is clearly no. As noted previously, the process of democratization might promote the growth of nationalism and Islamic radicalism, which could have destabilizing consequences for the region and could run counter to U.S. interests. That is to say that genuinely fair and free elections are likely to bring governments to power that would be more critical of Israeli policies vis-à-vis the Palestinians, much more critical of U.S. policy toward the region—and especially critical of its invasion of Iraq—and far more likely to use oil in ways hostile to the U.S. interests in the region.

Applying varying benchmarks to different countries, depending on their status as friends or foes, has typically raised the suspicion among the people in the region that the U.S. government pursues double standards. It may be the case that there is no single Bush doctrine; rather, "there are many Bush doctrines."[91] Whatever the U.S. strategic calculations are, the road to building a secure and stable Middle East is through development and liberation. The Middle Eastern people, who have for a long time been in the grip of authoritarian regimes, have grown weary of their own leaders and western ulterior motives behind these new democratic initiatives. They should be given more say in the way they are governed.

It is now widely believed that the advancement of democratic participation and human rights are in fact essential safeguards against the rise of terrorism in both local and global contexts. Although a visionary pathway for democracy promotion can be mapped, it is a mistake to exaggerate its priority in view of other competing interests. No uniform model of or approach toward democracy promotion exists in the region. Success in confronting terrorism will depend on the ability of U.S. policymakers to understand its deeper causes.

The practical implications of a democracy-based approach to foreign policy are varied and many. Although there are palpable tensions between democratic changes and strategic considerations, it is clear that the old bargain with the Arab autocracies is no longer operative. Even though the costs of democratic transformation in the Middle East may be substantial, the costs of preserving the status quo are tragically greater in the longer run.

Under such circumstances, the United States has to set its own priorities, making differentiated accommodations when faced with the strategic realities of the region. Democratization is a complicated and difficult process that would entail numerous uncertain consequences. It may be practical, in contrast, to demand a higher standard of respect for human rights—especially when it comes to the rights of women, minorities, and children—in these countries.

To promote internal reform in the region requires tackling structural problems. Externally enforced democratization—as valid and legitimate a cause it may be in some cases—is likely to evoke resistance and reactions from both the political regimes and the adherents of cultural and Islamic traditions. The economic and political transformation will be sluggish at best and inconsistent at worst. But if properly implemented, the notion of combating terrorism by institutionalizing democratization is likely to substantially curtail the risks of a worldwide religious and cultural clash between the Muslim and Western worlds.

Whatever the motivation of the Bush administration is, the fact remains that the immediate and just resolution of the Israeli–Palestinian conflict more specifically and the Arab–Israeli disputes more generally, as well as a comprehensive recognition of Israel by its Arab neighbors, must be among the most basic strategic objectives of the U.S. policymakers. For change to be sustainable, the pace of democratic transformation must be gradual, systematic, and directly linked to homegrown movements.

Notes

1. Daniel Neep, "Dilemmas of Democratization in the Middle East: The Forward Strategy of Freedom," *Middle East Policy* 11 no. 3 (Fall 2004), 73–84, especially 74–5.
2. Marina Ottaway and Thomas Carothers, "The Greater Middle East Initiative: Off to a False Start," *Policy Brief*, Carnegie Endowment for International Peace 29 (March 2004), 1–8, especially 2.
3. Joseph P. Lawrence, "Some Questions about Freedom," *Zaman Daily News*, Zaman Online, http://www.zaman.com/include/yazdir.php?b1=commentary&trh=2005050&hn=16706.
4. Rashid Khalidi, *Resurrecting Empire: Western Footprints and America's Perilous Path in the Middle East* (Boston: Beacon Press, 2004), 43.
5. Carol C. Gould, *Globalizing Democracy and Human Rights* (Cambridge, UK: Cambridge University Press, 2004), 259.
6. Henry Munson, "Lifting the Veil: Understanding the Roots of Islamic Militancy," in *World Politics*, 26th ed., ed. Helen E. Purkitt (Dubuque, IA: McGraw-Hill/Dushkin, 2006), 179–81.
7. President George W. Bush (speech, Twentieth Anniversary of the National Endowment for Democracy, U.S. Chamber of Commerce, Washington, DC, November 6, 2003), http://www.cdhr.info/aquote 11060301.asp.
8. Julie A. Mertus, *Bait and Switch: Human Rights and U.S. Foreign Policy* (New York: Routledge, 2004), 63.
9. Ibid.
10. Eva Bellin, "The Iraqi Intervention and Democracy in Comparative Historical Perspective," *Political Science Quarterly* 119 no. 4 (Winter 2004–05), 595–608, see 595.
11. Khalidi, *Resurrecting Empire*, 39.
12. Bellin, "The Iraqi Intervention," 599.
13. Ibid., 601–3.
14. Alan Richards, "Democracy in the Arab Region: Getting There from Here," *Middle East Policy* 12 no. 2 (Summer 2005), 28–35, especially 30.
15. Ibid., 30
16. Ibid., 31.
17. Ibid., 33.
18. Ibid., 33.
19. James A. Bill and Robert Springborg, *Politics in the Middle East*, 4th ed. (New York: HarperCollins College Publishers, 1994), 27. See also Khalidi, *Resurrection Empire*, 71.
20. Stephen Krasner (director of the Center on Democracy, Development and the Rule of Law, Stanford University's Institute of International Studies, Palo Alto, CA), quoted in Kenneth Jost and Benton Ives-Halperin, "Democracy in the Arab World," in *Global Issues*, ed. CQ Researchers (Washington, DC: CQ Press, 2005), 181–206, especially 187.
21. Robert Looney, "The Broader Middle East Initiative: Requirements for Success in the Gulf," *Strategic Insights* 3 no. 8 (August 2004), 1–11, especially 7, http://www.ccc.nps.navy.mil/si/index.asp.
22. Jost and Ives-Halperin, "Democracy in the Arab World," 187.
23. The United Nations Development Programme (UNDP), *The Arab Human Development Report2002: Creating Opportunities for Future Generations* (New York: UNDP, 2002), 52. Also see UNDP, *Human Development Report 2004: Cultural Liberty in Today's Diverse World* (New York: UNDP, 2004), especially 225–37.

24. Ibid., 98.
25. See the report by the Canadian International Development Agency (CIDA), "Support to Gender Equality in the Middle East Region: Jordan, Lebanon, West Bank and Gaza, and Yemen." Available at http://www.acdi-cida.gc.ca/cidaweb/webcountry.nsf/VLUDocEn/NorthAfricaand-MiddleEast-Supporttogenderequality-MiddleEast.
26. Jost and Ives-Halperin, "Democracy in the Arab World," 190.
27. Ibid., 182–4.
28. Larry Diamond, "The State of Democratization at the Beginning of the 21st Century," *Whitehead Journal of Diplomacy and International Relations* 1 no. 1 (Winter–Spring 2005), 13–8, especially 16.
29. Joel Brinkley, "U.S. Faults 4 Allies over Forced Labor," *New York Times*, June 4, 2005, A5.
30. Diamond, " The State of Democratization," 17.
31. Carl Gershman, "Democracy as Policy Goal and Universal Value," *Whitehead Journal of Diplomacy and International Relations* 1 no. 1 (Winter–Spring 2005), 19–38, especially 22.
32. Ibid., 22.
33. Zbigniew Brzezinski, "Hegemonic Quicksand," *National Interest* 74 (Winter 2003–04), 5–16, especially 13.
34. Ibid., 6.
35. Mustafa Zahrani, "September 11, Globalization, and the U.S. Hegemony," in *The New International Trends*, ed. Mohammad Javad Zarif and Zahrani (Tehran: The Office of Political and International Studies, 2005), 1–61, especially 48.
36. A roundtable on "The European Union and Islamic Fundamentalism: Challenges and Policies," *Discourse: An Iranian Quarterly* 5 no. 4 (Spring 2004), 1–16, especially 3.
37. Douglas J. Feith, "On the Global War on Terrorism," in *Clashing Views on Controversial Issues in World Politics*, 12th ed., ed. John T. Rourke (Guilford, CT: McGraw Hill/Dushkin, 2006), 232–6.
38. Shibley Telhami, *The Stakes: American and the Middle East: The Consequences of Power and the Choice for Peace* (Boulder, CO: Westview Press, 2002), 101.
39. Memorandum, Tamara Cofman Wittes, "The New U.S. Proposal for a Greater Middle East Initiative: An Evaluation," Saban Cofman Middle East Memo #2, May 10, 2004, *Global Politics*, Brookings Institution. Available at http://www.brookings.edu/views/op-ed/fellows/wittes20040510.htm.
40. Marina Ottaway and Thomas Carothers, "The Greater Middle East Initiative: Off to a False Start," *Policy Brief*, Carnegie Endowment for International Peace 29, March 2004, 1–8, especially 2.
41. Hassan Hanizadeh, "G8 Leaders' Greater Middle East Dream," *Tehran Times*, opinion column, June 12, 2004, http://www.mehrnews.ir/en/NewsDetail.aspx?NewsID=86034.
42. Bernard Lewis, "Freedom and Justice in the Modern Middle East," *Foreign Affairs* 84 no. 3, (May–June 2005), 36–51, especially 48.
43. Ottaway and Carothers, "Greater Middle East Initiative," 125–30.
44. Ibid., 93.
45. Mary H. Cooper, "Oil Production in the 21st Century," in *Global Issues: Selections from the CQ Researcher*, ed. (Washington, DC: CQ Press, a division of Congressional Quarterly, Inc., 2001), 113–31, see 117.
46. For further perspective on Ali Bulac's ideas, see Wendy Kristianasen, "New Faces of Islam," *Le monde diplomatique*, http://mondediplo.com/1997/07/turkey.
47. Ottaway and Carothers, "Greater Middle East Perspective," 2.
48. Volker Paerthes, "America's 'Greater Middle East' and Europe: Key Issues for Dialogue," *Middle East Policy* 11 no. 3 (Fall 2004), 85–97, especially 86.
49. Ibid., 87.
50. Neep, "Dilemmas of Democratization," 80.
51. Kaveh Afrasiabi, "Iran and the Greater Middle East Initiative," *Iranian Journal of International Affairs* 17 no. 2–3 (Summer–Fall 2004), 255–83, especially 259.
52. Ibid., 261.
53. Ibid., 262.
54. Robert Looney, "The Broader Middle East Initiative: Requirements for Success in the Gulf," *Strategic Insights* 3 no. 8 (August 2004), 1–11, especially 9.
55. Khalidi, *Resurrecting Empire*, 16–25.

56. For further analysis of the contradictory policies of the United States toward the Middle East, see Mahmood Monshipouri, "The Paradoxes of U.S. Foreign Policy in the Middle East," *Middle East Policy* 9 no. 3 (September 2002), 65–84, especially 72.
57. Steven R. Weisman, "Rice Challenges Saudi Arabia and Egypt on Democracy Issues," *New York Times*, June 20, 2005, A2.
58. This point is particularly emphasized by Harold Hongju Koh, former assistant secretary of state for human rights in the Clinton administration; see Mertus, *Bait and Switch*, 64.
59. Ibid., 67.
60. Weisman, "Rice Challenges Saudi Arabia and Egypt."
61. Ibid.
62. Augustus Richard Norton, "America's Approach to the Middle East: Legacies, Questions, and Possibilities," *Current History*, January 2002, 3–7; See p. 4.
63. Noam Chomsky, "United States, Global Bully: Terrorism, Weapon of the Powerful" (speech, Massachusetts Institute of Technology, October 18, 2001). Available at http://www.matrix-masters.com/wtc/chomsky/bully/bully.html.
64. Michel Chossudovsky, "Who Is Osama Bin Laden?" *Global Dialogue* 3 no. 4 (Autumn 2001), 1–7, see 5.
65. Rahman Ghahramanpour, "Iran and the Doctrine of the Greater Middle East: A Strategic Assessment," *Strategic View*, The Center for Strategic Defense Research (CSDR), Tehran, Iran 9 no. 29, January 2004, 1–20, especially 10.
66. Hassan Yavari, "Iran and the Trend of U.S. Democratization in the Middle East,"*Bardash-e Awal* [The First Impression], the Islamic Republic of Iran, Center for Strategic Studies 3 no. 22–23 (November–December 2004), 133–143, especially 141.
67. Ottaway and others, "Democracy: Rising Tide or Mirage?" *Middle East Policy* 12 no. 2 (Summer 2005), 1–7, see comments by Ottaway, 3.
68. P. V. Vivekanand, "Syrians out of Lebanon: The Dynamics of Change," *Panorama: Gulf Today*, April 29–May 5, 2005, 18–23, especially 23.
69. Fuad Ajami, "The Autumn of the Autocracy," *Foreign Affairs* 84 no. 3 (May–June 2005), 20–35, especially 21.
70. Ibid., 29.
71. John Kifner, "A Fine Line between Civil War and Politics," *New York Times*, June 26, 2005, Section 4, 14.
72. Chris Talbot, "Swing to Right-Wing Christian Leader Aoun in Lebanese Elections," *World Socialist Web Site*, June 17, 2005, http://www.wsws.org/articles/2005/jun2005/leb-j17.shtml.
73. Vivekanand, "Lebanese Elections: An American Roulette," *Panorama: Gulf Today*, June 3–9, 2005, 18–23, especially 23.
74. Ottaway and others, "Democracy," comments by Schwedler, 5.
75. Ibid., 6.
76. Ibid.
77. Debka*file*, "Did Bush and Sharon Figure out How to Preempt a Hamas Election Victory?" April 11, 2005, http://www.debka.com/article.php?aid=1014.
78. Yavari, "Iran and the Trend of U.S. Democratization," 140.
79. Shirin Ebadi and Muhammad Sahimi, "In the Mullahs' Shadow," *Wall Street Journal*, June 15, 2005, A14.
80. David E. Sanger, "Bush Says Iran's Elections Ignore 'Basic Requirements,'" *New York Times*, June 17, 2005, A6.
81. Brian Murphy, "Bush Remarks May Have Spurred Iran Voters," *Associated Press*, June 19, 2005. Available at http://sfgate.com/cgi-bin/article.cgi?f=/n/a/2005/06/19/international/i132039D97.DTL
82. Neep, "Dilemmas of Democratization," 83.
83. David Makovsky, "Gaza: Moving Forward by Pulling Back," *Foreign Affairs* 84 no. 3 (May–June 2005), 52–62.
84. Volker Paerthes, "America's 'Greater Middle East' and Europe: Key Issues for Dialogue," *Middle East Policy* 13 no. 3 (Fall 2004), 85–97, especially 93.
85. Brzezinski, "Hegemonic Quicksand," 10.
86. Ibid., 12.
87. David Skidmore, "Understanding the Unilateralist Turn in U.S. Foreign Policy," *Foreign Policy Analysis* 1 no. 2 (July 2005), 207–28, especially 225.

88. Kenneth Pollack and Ray Takeyh, "Taking on Tehran," *Foreign Affairs* 84 no. 2 (March–April 2005), 20–34, especially 27–8.
89. Christopher de Bellaigue, "Think Again: Iran," *Foreign Policy* 148 (May–June 2005), 18–23, especially 22.
90. Ibid., 18.
91. See PERRspectives: Bringing Light to Darkness, "The Myth of the Bush Doctrine," March 9, 2005, http://www.perrspectives.com/blog/archives/000128.htm.

Contributors

Conrad C. Crane is director of the U.S. Army Military History Institute at the U.S. Army War College. He has authored or edited books and monographs on the Civil War, World War I, World War II, Korea, Vietnam, and the War on Terror and has written and lectured widely on airpower and landpower issues.

Jack Donnelly is Andrew Mellon Professor in the Graduate School of International Studies at the University of Denver. He has published three books, including *Universal Human Rights in Theory and Practice* (Cornell University Press, 2003) and *Realism and International Relations* (Cambridge University Press, 2000), and over fifty scholarly articles and book chapters in the field of international human rights.

David P. Forsythe is Charles J. Mach Distinguished Professor of Political Science at the University of Nebraska–Lincoln. His more than seventy-five publications on different aspects of international relations include, most recently, *The United Nations and Changing World Politics* (with Tom Weiss and Roger Coate, Westview Press, 2004, 4th ed.); *Human Rights and Diversity: Area Studies Revisited* (coedited with Patrice McMahon, University of Nebraska Press, 2003), and *The Humanitarians: The International Committee of the Red Cross* (Cambridge University Press, 2005) He is also the general editor of a new edition of *The Encyclopedia of Human Rights*.

Mel Gurtov is professor of political science and international studies in the Hatfield School of Government at Portland State University, Oregon. He is also editor-in-chief of *Asian Perspective*, an international quarterly. He has published numerous books and articles on East Asian affairs, U.S. foreign policy, and global politics. His most recent books are *Pacific Asia? Prospects for Security and Cooperation in East Asia* (Rowman & Littlefield, 2002), *Confronting the Bush Doctrine: Critical Perspectives from Asia-Pacific* (coedited with Peter Van Ness, Routledge, 2005), and *Global Politics in the Human Interest*, 4th ed. (Lynne Reinner Publishers, 1999). His latest work, to be published early in 2006, is *Superpower on Crusade: the Bush Doctrine in U.S. Foreign Policy*.

Ole R. Holsti is the George V. Allen Professor of International Affairs at Duke University. His primary teaching and research interests are foreign policy decision making and public opinion and foreign policy. Holsti is the author or coauthor of eight books. His articles have appeared in *World Politics, American Political Science Review, International Political Science Review, International*

Security, Journal of Politics, Millennium, Journal of Conflict Resolution, and *Handbook of Social Psychology.* His most recent books are *Public Opinion and American Foreign Policy,* rev. ed (University of Michigan Press, 2004) and *Making American Foreign Policy* (Routledge, 2006).

Loch K. Johnson is Regents Professor of Public and International Affairs at the University of Georgia, editor of the journal *Intelligence and National Security,* and the author of several books and more than one hundred articles on U.S. national security, including most recently *Bombs, Bugs, Drugs, and Thugs: Intelligence and America's Quest for Security* (2002). He has won the Certificate of Distinction from the National Intelligence Study Center, the "Studies in Intelligence" Award from the Center for the Study of Intelligence, and the V. O. Key Prize from the Southern Political Science Association. He has served as secretary of the American Political Science Association and president of the International Studies Association, South. Johnson was special assistant to the chair of the Senate Select Committee on Intelligence in 1975–1976, staff director of the House Subcommittee on Intelligence Oversight in 1977–1979, and special assistant to the chair of the Aspin–Brown Commission on Intelligence in 1995–1996.

Robert J. Lieber is professor of government and international affairs at Georgetown University. He is an expert on American foreign policy and U.S. relations with the Middle East and Europe. Lieber's latest book is *The American Era: Power and Strategy for the 21st Century* (Cambridge University Press, 2005). In addition, he is author or editor of thirteen books on international relations and U.S. foreign policy, and his articles have appeared in numerous scholarly and policy journals.

Edward C. Luck is director of the Center on International Organization and professor of practice in international and public affairs at Columbia University. A past president and CEO of the United Nations Association of the United States of America and one of the architects of the UN reform efforts from 1995–97, he has published widely on UN affairs, U.S. foreign policy, and a range of security and political issues. Among his publications are *Mixed Messages: American Politics and International Organization, 1919–1999* (Brookings Institution Press, 1999), *Reforming the United Nations: Lessons from a History in Progress* (Academic Council on the United Nations System, 2003), and *International Law and Organization: Closing the Compliance Gap* (with Michael Doyle, Rowman & Littlefield, 2004).

Patrice C. McMahon is assistant professor at the University of Nebraska–Lincoln. Her work has appeared in *Political Science Quarterly, Democratization,* and *Problems of Post-Communism.* She published *Human Rights and Diversity: Area Studies Revisited* (coedited with David P. Forsythe, University of Nebraska Press,

2003). Her book, *Taming Ethnic Hatred: Ethnic Cooperation and Transnational Networks in Eastern Europe* is forthcoming from Syracuse University Press.

Karen A. Mingst is Lockwood Chair in the Patterson School of Diplomacy and International Commerce and professor of political science at the University of Kentucky. She is coauthor of several books on international organizations, including *International Organizations: The Politics and Processes of Global Governance* (with Margaret P. Karns, Lynne Rienner Publishers, 2004) and *The United Nations in the Post-Cold War Era* (with Margaret P. Karns, Westview Press, 2000). She is also the author of a popular international relations textbook *Essentials of International Relations*, 3rd ed. (W. W. Norton & Company, 2004), as well as *Essential Readings in World Politics,* 2nd ed. (coedited with Jack Snyder, W. W. Norton & Company, 2004).

Mahmood Monshipouri is professor of political science at Quinnipiac University and a visiting fellow at the Yale Center for International and Area Studies. He is working on a book with the working title *Identity, Human Rights, and the Middle East in a Globalizing World*. His most recent publications are *Constructing Human Rights in the Age of Globalization* (M.E. Sharpe, 2003) and *Islamism, Secularism, and Human Rights in the Middle East* (Lynne Rienner Publishers, 1998). His most recent articles have appeared in *World Affairs, Global Dialogue, The Muslim World,* and *Human Rights Quarterly.*

Mark Peceny is professor and chair in the Department of Political Science at the University of New Mexico. His work has appeared in *American Political Science Review, International Organization, International Studies Quarterly, Political Research Quarterly,* and *Journal of Peace Research*. His book *Democracy at the Point of Bayonets* (Pennsylvania State University Press, 1999) examines the promotion of democracy during twentieth-century U.S. military interventions.

John Gerard Ruggie is the Kirkpatrick Professor of International Affairs and director of the Center for Business and Government at Harvard University's Kennedy School of Government. From 1997 to 2001 he was assistant secretary-general and chief advisor for strategic planning to UN secretary-general Kofi Annan; he continues to serve as UN special envoy for business and human rights. He has published six books, including *Winning the Peace: America and World Order in the New Era* (Columbia University Press, 1996) and *Constructing the World Polity: Essays on International Institutionalization* (Routledge, 1998). He has authored more than sixty articles in scholarly journals and books and has provided numerous op-ed and television commentaries around the world.

Andrew Wedeman is associate professor of political science at the University of Nebraska–Lincoln, where he is also director of International Studies and director of Asian Studies. Recent publications include *From Mao to Market: Rent Seeking, Local Protectionism, and Marketization in China* (Cambridge University Press, 2003) and articles in *Journal of Contemporary China* and *China Review*. His article "The Intensification of Corruption in China" was awarded the 2004 Gordon White Prize for the most original article in *China Quarterly*.

Jon Western is a Five College Assistant Professor of International Relations at Mount Holyoke College and the Five Colleges, Incorporated, where he teaches courses on American foreign policy, international relations theory, and international security. He is the author of *Selling Intervention and War: The Presidency, the Media, and the American Public* (Johns Hopkins University Press, 2005). His articles on U.S. foreign policy, military intervention, and international security have appeared in *International Security, Security Studies, Global Dialogue, International Affairs, Ethnopolitics,* and *Harvard International Review*.

Index

A

ABC News/*Washington Post*, 143, 159, 160
Abdullah, Adullah, 225, 226, 227
Aberbach, Joel, 176
Abrams, Elliot, 288
Abu Ghraib prison, 134, 201, 202, 204, 209, 313, 322
Abuses of power, *see* Secret intelligence accountability
Acheson, Dean, 63, 66, 73
Act of Chapultepec, 62
Acton, Lord John, 262
Adams, John Quincy, 33
Ad hoc coalitions, 114, 116
Advanced technology, 10
Afghanistan–U.S. relations, 5, 7, 14, 18, 23, 25, 105, 106, 107, 110, 113, 116, 119, 127, 128, 129, 130, 143, 185, 200, 209, 215, 216, 265; *see also* Democracy promotion, U.S. efforts toward
Afrasiabi, Kaveh, 323
Africa, 134, 273, 275
African slave trade, 194
African Union, 136
AIDS epidemic, 143
Albright, Madeleine, 41
Algeria, 195, 196, 263, 326, 329
Al-Jaafari, Ibrahim, 234
Al-Kahtani, Mohamed, 201
Allende, Salvador, 179
All-volunteer military, 116
Al-Qaeda, U.S. policy toward, 19, 107, 119, 126, 130, 156, 159, 169, 186, 187, 229, 265, 316
Al-Sistani, Ayatollah Ali, 233
Amalgamated security communities, 94
American Civil Liberties Union (ACLU), 203, 204
American Enterprise Institute (AEI), 39
American exceptionalism, *see* Exceptionalism, American
American Revolution, 271
Ames, Aldrich H., 180, 183, 188
Amnesty International (AI), 205
Anarchic international orders, 84–85; *see also* Hierarchy in anarchy
Annan, Kofi, 51, 52, 128, 228

Anti-Ballistic Missile (ABM) Treaty, 116, 264
Antiterrorism, 98; *see also* War on Terrorism
Arab world, *see* Middle East–U.S. relations
Arafat, Yasir, 271
Arbour, Louise, 205
Argentina, 95, 269, 302
Aristide, Jean-Bertrande, 243
Armitage, Richard L., 222
Article 2(4), origins of
    conclusion, 75–76
    cynicism perspective, 60–64
    domestic politics and, 73–75
    exceptionalism perspective, 64–67
    idealism perspective, 56–60
    introduction, 51–56
    realism perspective, 67–73
Article 2(7), 38
Article 51, 53, 69, 70
Article 53(1), 59
Article V, 119, 264–265
Article X, 74, 75
ASEAN (Association of South East Asian Nations), 136, 289, 300–302; *see also* Southeast Asia–U.S. relations
Asian Development Bank, 128
Asia-Pacific Economic Cooperation forum, 289
Asia policy
    Association ASEAN, 134, 272, 279, 300–302
    Central Asia, 24, 290–291
    conclusions, 303–305
    freedom status and, 318
    introduction, 17, 25, 287–288
    North–South Korea engagement, 153, 297–299
    Project for a New American Century (PNAC), 288–290
    South Asia, 302–303
    U.S.–China relations, 291–293
    U.S.–DPRK relations, 294–297, 298
    U.S.–Japan relations, 90, 142, 299–300
Aspin-Brown Commission (1994), 180, 185, 186
Association of South East Asian Nations (ASEAN), 136, 289, 300–302; *see also* Southeast Asia–U.S. relations

Atomic energy, 71
Atran, Scott, 108
Aussaresses, Paul, 195
Australia, 69, 250
Austria, 133
Azerbaijan, 290
Aznar, José Maria, 266

B

Baathist Party, 107, 155
Baccus, Rick, 199
Bacevich, Andrew, 289
Baghdad, 114, 115, 130, 147, 150, 156, 157, 159, 160
Baker, James, 118, 119, 289
Baldwin, David, 3
Balkins, 246–247, 255, 256, 275
Baruch, Bernard, 71
Bay of Pigs (1961), 179, 180, 183
Beijing, 17, 292
Belgium, 117
Bellin, Eva, 315
Bemis, Samuel Flagg, 32
Berlin Wall, 186
Bibby, John, 178
Biden, Joseph, 220
Bin Laden, Osama, 25, 259, 325
Biological and Toxins Weapons Convention (1972), 126
Biological/chemical weapons, 145
Blair, Tony, 20, 266
Boland Amendments, 183, 185
Bolivia, 24, 69
Bolton, John, 39, 45, 120
Bonn Summit (2001), 225, 226, 227, 228, 232
Borah, William, 35
Bosnia–U.S. relations, 88, 112, 113, 125, 133, 221, 246, 247, 255
Bouchard, Edwin, 62
Brahimi, Lakhdar, 128, 130, 228
Brandeis, Louis, 176
Brazil, 69, 302
Bremer, Paul, 231, 244
Bricker Amendment, 38
Britain, *see* Great Britain–U.S. relations
Brooks, David, 271
Brzezinski, Zbigniew, 319
Buchanan, Patrick, 142, 165
Bush, George W. (administration), 31, 32, 40, 45, 52, 61, 118, 160, 174, 188, 215, 251, 270, 288; *see also* specific topics
Bush Doctrine
  in Asia, 287–305
  debates over the future, 119–120
  dominance, unilateralism, and ad hoc coalitions, 112–119
  efficacy of force, 106–112, 131
  European–American relations and, 264–266
  introduction, 7, 105–106
  in the Middle East, 98, 313–331
  public opinion on, 168

C

Campbell, Kurt, 305
Canada, 43, 45, 269
Caribbean, 33
Carnegie Endowment for International Peace, 110, 111
Carr, E. H., 141
Carter, Jimmy, 142, 324
Casualty of war, *see* Enemy detainees, U.S. policy toward
CBS News/*New York Times*, 143, 157
Cedras, Raoul, 243
Central America, 33, 185
Central Asia–U.S. relations, 24, 287, 290–291; *see also* Asia policy
Central Intelligence Agency (CIA), 107, 132, 174, 179, 180, 182, 184, 186, 197, 199, 324
Chalabi, Ahmed, 231, 233, 234
Chavez, Hugo, 24
Chechnya, 222
Chemical/biological weapons, 145
Chen Shui-bian, 293
Cheney, Dick, 159, 197, 203, 288
Chicago Council on Foreign Relations (CCFR) survey, 143, 144, 147, 150, 151, 153
Chile, 37, 43, 179, 210, 269
China–U.S. relations, 8, 11, 16, 17, 18, 59, 60, 90, 91, 136, 141, 288, 291–293, 328; *see also* Asia policy
Chirac, Jacques, 120, 262, 264, 276, 283
Church, Albert III, 202
Church and Pike Committee (1974), 180, 184
Churchill, Winston, 64
CIA, *see* Central Intelligence Agency (CIA)
Civil War, 86, 271
Clark, Wesley, 113
Clarke, Richard A., 187
Cleland, Max, 220
Climate change politics, 44
Clinton, Bill (Administration), 4, 32, 40, 41, 112, 163, 186, 220, 221, 270, 288
Clinton National Security Strategy, 252

CNN/*USA Today*/Gallup, 159
Coercive interrogation, 197, 199–200, 201; *see also* Enemy detainees, U.S. policy toward
Coercive power, 7–12
Cohen, Eliot, 288
Cold War, U.S. policy toward, 3, 5, 32, 35, 36, 38, 53, 55, 123–124, 262
Collection of analysis, 178
Collective security model, 92
Columbia, 153, 272
Common security communities, 93
Communism, 124
Comprehensive Test Ban Treaty, 40, 267
Concert system model, 91–92
Congo, 135, 273
Congress, *see* U.S. Congress
Congressional Budget Office (OBO), 14
Connally, Tom, 61, 73
Constitution, U.S., 37, 136, 151, 173
Convention Against Torture, 38
Convention on the Elimination of All Forms of Racial Discrimination, 38
Converse, Philip, 141
Cooper, John Milton, 34
Côte d'Ivoire, 135
Counterintelligence, 178, 183
Covenant of the League of Nations, *see* League of Nations
Covert action, 178, 179
Crane, Conrad, 23
Cronin, Bruce, 91, 93, 94, 135
Cuba–U.S. relations, 42, 43, 124, 197, 236, 253, 256, 272
Curran, John Philpot, 188
Cynicism perspective, on Article 2(4), 54, 60–64
Czech Republic, 266, 275

D

Dahl, Robert, 3
Darfur genocide, 24, 46
Declaration on Principles of International Law Concerning Friendly Relations and Co-operation among States (1970), 88
Declaration on the Granting of Independence to Colonial Countries and Peoples (1960), 88
Defense Intelligence Agency, 180
Defense Planning Guidance (1992), 112
Defense spending, 8–10, 14–15, 278
De Gaulle, Charles, 262
Democracy promotion, U.S. efforts toward
  Afghanistan, congressional support for, 220
  Afghanistan, grand strategy arguments for, 220–222
  Afghanistan, multiethnic government for, 223–228
  Afghanistan, nation-building strategy for, 222–223
  domestic politics, liberal hegemony and, 218–219
  Germany, Vietnam, and Cuba, 235–236
  introduction, 97, 215–218
  Iraq, regime change in, 133, 228–231
  Middle East peace process, 314–320
  strategic interactions of democratization, 232–235
Democratic Party, 74, 142, 163, 203, 204, 220
Denmark, 266
D'Estaing, Valery Giscard, 269
De Tocqueville, Alexis, 141, 270
De Villepin, Dominique, 280, 283
Dewey, Thomas, 62
DeWine, Mike, 186
Dillon, Douglas, 166
Diplomatic history, 32
Discrimination, 194
Dobbins, James, 227
Domestic mobilization, 134
Domestic politics, on Article 2(4), 55–56, 73–75
Dominance, in military power, 112
Dominican Republic, 124
Dominion model, 93, 95
Donnelly, Jack, 3
Dower, John, 251, 254
DPRK–U.S. relations, 294–297, 298
Duelfer, Charles A., 159
Dulles, John Foster, 62, 63, 65, 68, 70, 71, 263
Dumbarton Oaks negotiations, *see* Article 2(4), origins of
Dunleavey, Michael, 199
Durbin, Richard, 203

E

Eagleton, Clyde, 58, 62, 68
East Asia, 17, 272, 297; *see also* Asia policy
East Timor, 301
Economic interests, 150
Economic power, 14–18
Ecuador, 24
Eden, Anthony, 65
Egypt, 97, 198, 263, 269, 325, 326, 327
Eisenhower, Dwight D., 38, 62, 166, 173, 263
Elections, 133

342 • Index

Empire, defining, 81, 82–83, 94, 95, 119; *see also* Sovereign inequality
Enemy detainees, U.S. policy toward
 conclusion, 209–210
 domestic reaction to, 202–204
 international reaction to, 204–209
 introduction, 193–195
 reality of Bush policy, 196–202
 relevance of history: French-Algerian war, 195–196
Environmental groups, 45
European–American relations
 capability of radical change, 282
 foreseeable future, 283
 introduction, 261–262
 sources of conflict, 262–272
 sources of solidarity, 272–281
European Defense Agency (EDA), 277
European Union (EU)
 capability of radical change, 282
 foreseeable future, 283
 introduction, 261–262
 Middle East peace process and, 319–320, 323, 328
 multilateral institutions and, 136
 sources of conflict, 262–272
 sources of solidarity, 272–281
 sovereign inequality and, 87, 94
 U.S. public opinion on, 141
 U.S. unilateralism and, 39
Exceptionalism, American
 on Article 2(4), 54–55, 64–67
 historical/conceptual context of, 32–37, 193, 195, 270–272
Exemptionalism, American, 37–39, 99

F

Fahim, Marshal, 226, 227
Fallujah, 108, 156
Federal Bureau of Investigation (FBI), 132, 174, 180, 187, 199
Federalist Paper 51, 176, 186
Ferguson, Niall, 94
Financial controls, 87
Financial Times, 203
First responders, 132
Fischer, Joschka, 227, 280
Fleischer, Ari, 222
Foreign Intelligence Surveillance Court, 187
Fourteen Points, 254
Fowler, Wyche, 177
Fox News, 143

France–U.S. relations, 20, 21, 43, 59, 61, 96, 116, 117, 120, 195, 196, 209, 210, 255, 256, 262, 263, 265, 266, 268, 272, 275, 276, 278, 283
Franks, Tommy, 114
Freedom House Survey (2004), 316–318
Freedom of Information Act, 203
Freedom status, 316–318
French–Algerian War, 195–196
Frum, David, 131

G

Gaddis, John Lewis, 116, 136, 137
Gailani, Pir Sayed Ahmad, 226
Gallup Organization, 143, 145, 157, 159, 169
Garner, Jay, 115
Gelfand, Lawrence, 34
General Agreements on Tariffs and Trade (GATT), 35, 95
General Assembly (GA) Resolution 1514, 88
General Assembly (GA) Resolution 2625, 88
General Framework Agreement for Peace (GFAP), 246, 247
Geneva Conventions for Victims of War (GCs), 195, 197, 198, 208, 209
Genocide, 194, 202
George III, King of England, 176
German Confederation of 1815, 87
Germany–U.S. relations, 37, 43, 61, 116, 117, 123, 130, 133, 235, 248–250, 254, 261, 266, 272, 276, 278
Gingrich, Newt, 46
Gitmo detainees, 199, 200, 201, 203, 204, 205, 206, 207, 208
Glennon, Mike, 55
Global business community, 44
Global protection regimes, 90
Global warming, 142
Gonzales, Alberto, 197, 202, 203
Goodhart, A. L., 72
Goodrich, Leland M., 62, 72
Gore, Al, 221, 264
Goss, Porter, 186
Graham, B., 186
Graham-Porter Committee (2001), 180
Grant, Ulysses S., 252
Great Britain–U.S. relations, 16, 20, 21, 114, 128, 130, 169, 194, 199, 204, 250, 256, 263, 266, 267, 272, 276, 278, 283, 324, 328; *see also* United Kingdom
Greater Middle East Initiative (GMEI), 323–324, 325
Great Power status, 89–90, 91
Greece, 72

Grenada, 124
Grew, Joseph C., 62, 63
Gross domestic product (GDP), 15, 276
Group of Eight Industrialized Nations (G-8), 281, 323, 324
Guantanamo Bay, 87, 98, 195, 197, 313, 322
Guatemala, 84, 210
Gulf War, 10, 113, 118, 124, 130, 143, 155

H

Haiti, 125, 133, 135, 221, 243–246, 255, 256
Halifax, Earl of, 64
Hambro, Edvard, 62, 72
Hamilton, Lee H., 176, 177
Hardt, Michael, 82
Hariri, Saad, 326
Hawaii, 33
Haynes, William J. II, 202
Hegemony, U.S., 3–7, 93, 94, 218
Helms, Jesse, 51, 270
Helsinki Accords (1975), 323
Heritage Foundation, 39
Hierarchical security systems, 91–94
Hierarchy in anarchy
    conceptions of empire, 82–83
    conclusion, 99–100
    defining, 83–85
    forms of, 94–95
    Great Power status and, 89–90
    introduction, 81
    models of hierarchical security systems, 91–94
    outlaw states and, 90–91
    reading of the war in Iraq, 95–99
    sovereign inequalities and, 85–89
Hobbes, Thomas, 273
Hobsbawm, Eric, 195
Holbrooke, Richard, 110
Holsti, Ole, 134
Holy Alliance, 90
Holy Roman Empire, 82, 83, 87
Homeland Security, 132
Horton, Scott, 204
House Intelligence Oversight Committee (2001), 180
House Permanent Select Committee on Intelligence (HPSCI), 184, 187, 188, 189
Hughes, Karen, 120
Hull, Cordell, 57, 58, 60, 64, 67, 74
Human Development Index (2004), 128
Humanitarian intervention, 87, 90, 98, 128
Human rights, 20, 38, 193, 194, 200–201, 206, 322

Human Rights Watch (HRW), 205
Hungary, 266, 275
Hunt, E. Howard, 183
Hussein, Saddam, U.S. policy toward, 20, 53, 107, 109, 114, 115, 130, 147, 151, 155, 157, 159, 160, 216, 228, 229, 230
Huston Plan, 173

I

Idealism, American, 271
Idealism perspective, on Article 2(4), 54, 56–60
Ikenberry, John, 134
Illegal drugs, 150, 153
Illegal immigration, 150
Immelt, Jeffrey, 44
Imperfect unions, 87
Imperialism, 32, 82–83, 193
India, 91, 272, 302, 303
India–Pakistan conflict, 142, 144
Indochina, 263
Indonesia, 24, 300, 301, 304, 305
Inequalities, *see* Sovereign inequality
Inouye-Hamilton Committee (1987), 180
Intelligence, congressional oversight for, *see* Secret intelligence accountability
Intelligence Accountability Act of 1980, 182
Intelligence Identities Act of 1983, 181
Intelligence Reform and Terrorism Prevention Act of 2004, 184
Inter-American Conference on Problems of War and Peace, 69
Intercontinental ballistic missiles (ICBMs), 11
Intermediate Range Nuclear Forces (INF) Treaty, 124
International Atomic Energy Agency (IAEA), 115, 295
International Committee of the Red Cross (ICRC), 199, 201, 203, 206, 207, 208, 209
International Convenant on Civil and Political Rights, 38
International Criminal Court, 19, 39, 40, 46, 116, 126, 264, 267, 322
International Criminal Tribunal for Former Yugoslavia, 255
International humanitarian law (IHL), 197, 199, 200
International Law, 86
International Monetary Fund, 6, 281, 303
International Red Cross, 206
International relations theory, 1, 3, 81
International Security Assistance Force (ISAF), 128

International security systems, models of, 91–94
Interrogation, coercive, 197, 199–200, 201; see also Enemy detainees, U.S. policy toward
Iran-Contra affair (1987), 174, 180, 182, 184, 186, 188, 189
Iran–U.S. relations, 8, 11, 37, 111, 136, 153, 230, 279, 327
Iraqi Independent Electoral Commission, 130
Iraqi National Congress, 230, 231, 233
Iraqi nationalists, 107
Iraq–U.S. relations, 14, 18, 20, 21, 23, 41, 44, 53, 124, 125, 133, 162, 167, 200, 278; see also Iraq War; Terrorism (9/11 terrorist attacks); War on Terrorism
Iraq War; see also specific topics
    common reading of Bush's war, 95–99
    U.S. military power and, 105–106, 110, 113, 115–116, 116
    U.S. promotion of democracy and, 215, 216, 217, 218, 228–231, 233, 234, 319
    U.S. public opinion on, 143, 150, 153–164, 169
Irish Provisional Authority in Northern Ireland, 199
Islamic reactions, 316, 319, 320–322, 326, 327, 329
Islamiyah, Jemaah, 301
Israeli–Palestinian conflict, 142, 144, 153
Italy, 61, 113, 114, 266, 276
Ivory Coast, 273

J

Japan–U.S. relations, 16, 17, 24, 61, 90, 91, 130, 133, 142, 151, 235, 250–252, 254, 255, 269, 299–300, 328; see also Asia policy
Jebb, Gladwyn, 76
Jim Crow laws, 38
Johnson, Lyndon B., 173, 255
Jordon, 326
Judge Advocate General (JAG), 199
Junichiro, Koizumi, 299
Justice for peace, principle of, 57

K

Kabul, 128, 227
Kagan, Robert, 41, 43, 46, 117
Karimov, Islam, 290, 291
Karpinski, Janis, 201, 202
Karzai, Kandahari Pashtun Hamid, 216, 218, 225, 226, 227, 232, 233

Kay, David, 159
Kazakhstan, 290, 304, 305
Kean Commission (2001), 180, 185
Kellenberger, Jacob, 207, 209
Kellogg, Frank B., 61, 62
Kellogg-Briand Pact of 1928, 54, 61, 62, 63, 274
Kelly, James, 294
Kelsen, Hans, 62, 75
Kennan, George F., 141
Kennedy, John F., 38, 166, 271
Kennedy, Paul, 119
Keohane, Robert, 32
Kerry, John, 220, 231
Khalidi, Rashid, 324
Khalilzad, Zalmay, 232, 288
Khan, A. Q., 111, 302
Kim Dae-jung, 294
Kim Jong-il, 294, 295
Kirk, Grayson, 68
Kissinger, Henry, 263, 268
Koran, 207
Korea, 17, 162, 163, 182, 183, 185, 255
Korean Air Force, 10
Kosovo–U.S. relations, 41, 43, 88, 113, 125, 126, 157, 221, 246, 255
Krauthammer, Charles, 41
Kristol, William, 43
Kurds, 156, 167, 233
Kuwait, 92, 114, 124, 133, 143, 155, 273, 318, 325
Kyoto Treaty, 116, 126, 264, 267
Kyrgyzstan, 21

L

Lahoud, Emile, 326
Latin America, 24, 60, 69, 97, 134, 272, 302
Law of Nations, 87
Law of the Sea Treaty, 39
League Convenant, 54
League of Nations
    Article 2(4) and, 55, 56, 62, 274
    sovereign inequality and, 87–88
    state stabilization and reconstruction, 254
    U.S. unilateralism and, 34–35
Lebanon, 21, 86, 326
Leffler, Melvyn, 32
Legal restraint, vitiating, 197–198
Liberal culture, in guiding policy, 218–219
Liberia, 135, 273
Libia, 110
Lindsey, Lawrence, 167

Lippmann, Walter, 67, 141
Lipset, Seymour Martin, 271
Locarno Treaty, 61
Lodge, Henry Cabot, 34, 74
London, 313
Los Angeles Times, 143, 188
Luck, Edward C., 5, 136
Lynch laws, 38

M

Maastricht Treaty, 274
MacArthur, Douglas, 250, 254
Machiavelli, Niccolo, 273
Madison, James, 166, 176, 186
Madrid, 313
Maine, Henry, 86
Malaysia, 301
Mandela, Nelson, 208
Mandelbaum, Michael, 268
Manifest destiny, 194
Mansfield, Mike, 179
Mao Zedong, 26
Marshall Plan, 274, 305
Marten, Kimberly Zisk, 256
McCain, John, 220
McCubbins, Mathew D., 175
McKinley, William, 33, 193, 253
McNamara, Robert, 166
McPherson, James, 253
Mead, Walter Russell, 132, 271
Mexican War, 151, 163
Mexico, 43, 69, 241, 269
Middle East–U.S. relations; *see also* specific topics
    the Bush Doctrine and, 108, 118, 199, 314–320
    conclusion, 329–331
    democracy and security paradox, 222, 324–328
    doctrinal differences today and, 42
    Greater Middle East Initiative (GMEI), 323–324
    introduction, 20, 25, 313–314
    multilateralism and, 131, 134, 328–329
    reactions from, 145, 151, 153, 163, 320–322
    sources of solidarity and, 273, 279
Military intelligence, 174; *see also* Secret intelligence accountability
Military power, U.S. security policy and; *see also* Article 2(4), origins of
    debates over the future, 119–120
    dominance, unilateralism, and ad hoc coalitions, 112–119
    efficacy of force, 106–112
    introduction, 5, 6, 10, 12–14, 105–106
    post-conflict operations and, 242–251
    state stabilization and reconstruction, 241, 256
    strategic supremacy and, 7–12
Miller, Geoffrey, 199, 200, 202
Minority rights regimes, 87
Mitterrand, Francois, 263
Molotov, Vyacheslav M., 64
Monroe, James, 33
Monroe Doctrine, 33, 63, 69, 89
Moo-hyun, Roh, 297
Morgenthau, Hans, 141
Mossadeq, Mohammad, 324
Mubarak, Mohamed Hosni, 325
Mueller, John, 143
Multilateral institutions
    ad hoc coalitions and, 112, 113
    9/11 and, 126–127
    change in goals, 130–132
    Cold War issues, 123–124
    the dilemma of goals, 132–134
    the dilemma of means, 134–137
    introduction, 4, 123, 267
    Middle East peace process and, 328–329
    new era multilateral involvement, 137
    post–Cold War issues, 124–126
    U.S. exceptionalism and, 37
    UN Security Council Resolution 1368 and, 127–130
Multilateralism, *see* Multilateral institutions
Munich Olympics, 269
Musharraf, Pervez, 111, 226, 302
Muslims, 194, 321
Myers, Richard B., 109

N

Narcoterrorism, 24
Nationalism, American, 194, 195
National Security Act of 1947, 182
National Security Council (NSC), 180, 185
National Security Strategy, 131, 151, 252, 265
National Security Strategy Document, 229, 265
National Student Association, 182
NATO, *see* North Atlantic Treaty Organization (NATO)
Nazi Germany, 37, 142, 250, 272
NBC News/*Wall Street Journal*, 143
Negri, Antonio, 82
Netherlands, 263

New Deal, 35
Newsweek, 143
New York Times, 179, 203, 207
New York Tribune, 253
New Zealand, 63, 69, 70, 75, 76
Nicaragua, 133, 182, 183
Nicaragua v. the United States, 39
Nixon, Richard, 39, 142, 173
Noel, Cleo, 269
Nongovernmental organizations (NGOs), 44, 205, 323, 329
Noriega, Manuel, 242
North Africa, 90, 316
North Atlantic Council, 127
North Atlantic Treaty Organization (NATO)
    Bush Doctrine and, 105, 112, 113, 115, 116, 118
    European–American relations and, 263, 264, 265, 278, 280–281
    multilateralism and, 123, 125, 126, 127, 129, 130, 136
    post-conflict operations and, 246
    transnational civic politics and, 43
    U.S. public opinion on, 141
    unilateralism doctrine and, 36, 40
Northern Alliance, 223, 224, 225, 226, 227, 232
North Korea–U.S. relations, 7, 8, 11, 17, 25, 110, 153, 185, 272, 279, 288, 294–299; see also Asia policy
Norway, 71
NSC-68, see Bush Doctrine
Nuclear Non-Proliferation Treaty of 1968, 124
Nuclear proliferation, 109–110, 142, 145
Nunn Lugar Cooperative Threat Reduction Program, 111
Nye, Joseph, 3, 4

O

Office of the Coordination for Reconstruction and Stabilization, 241, 252
Ogul, Morris, 178
Oil-energy related issues, 25, 153, 263, 287, 290, 291, 319
Oil for Food scandal, 136
Operation Blacklist (1945), 250, 251
Operation Eclipse (1942), 249
Operation Iraqi Freedom (2005), 12
Operation Joint Endeavor (1997), 247
Operation Just Cause (1989), 242
Operation Uphold Democracy (2003), 244
Oppenheim, Lassa, 86
Organization of American States, 136
Organization of Economic Cooperation Development (OECD), 97, 99
Ottoman Empire, 90
Oudeh, Daoud, 268, 269
Outlaw states conception, 90

P

Pact of Paris, 54, 61, 62, 63
Pakistan–U.S. relations, 24, 111, 226, 272, 279, 302, 303, 304, 325, 326, 327
Palestine, 321, 327
Panama, 6, 33–34, 124, 242–243
Papas, Thomas, 201, 202
Paraguay, 69
Partisanship, 163
Partnership for Progress, 323
Pasvolsky, Leo, 60, 70
Patriot Act, 174, 187
Patten, Chris, 275
Peacekeeping policies, see Stabilization and reconstruction, U.S. policy toward
Peace of Westphalia, 86
Pearl Harbor, 35, 142, 151, 164, 169
Pentagon, 7, 217, 229
People's Liberation Army Air Force (PLAAF), 9
Perelli, Carina, 130
Perle, Richard, 131, 288
Permanent Five (P-5) veto, 124, 129
Pershing, John J., 248
Persian Gulf, 10, 113, 118, 124, 130, 143, 155, 318
Pew Research Center for the People and the Press, 108, 116, 143, 157, 159
Philippines, 33, 248, 300, 301, 305
Pike and Church Committee (1974), 180, 184
Platt Amendment, 236
Pluralistic security communities, 93
PNAC (Project for a New American Century), 288–290
Poindexter, John M., 189
Poland, 114, 266, 275
Polarity, defining, 84
Political power, 18–21
Poos, Jacques, 275
Portugal, 266
Post-Cold War issues, 124–126
Post-conflict operations, see Stabilization and reconstruction, U.S. policy toward
Potsdam Declaration, 254
Powell, Colin, 20, 118, 119, 127, 166, 220, 221, 226, 288, 291, 294, 301
Power literature, see U.S. power, overview of
Preemptive warfare, 40

Presidential Directive (PDD) 25, 125
Prestowitz, Clyde, 287
Prisoner abuse, *see* Enemy detainees, U.S. policy toward
Prisoner of war (POW), 198
Project for a New American Century (PNAC), 288–290
Protection/guarantee model, 86, 91
Protective imperialism, 32
Public opinion, on foreign policies
    America's role in the world, 145–147
    conclusions, 164–169
    extensive research, 143
    goals for American foreign policy, 147–151
    introduction, 141–142
    Iraq and, 153–164
    threats to vital U.S. interests, 143–145
    use of American armed forces abroad, 151–153
Putin, Vladimir, 185, 279

Q

Qaddafi, Muammar, 110
Qanooni, King Ynus, 224, 226, 227, 232, 233

R

Rabbani, Berhanuddin, 227
Race relations, 37–38
Ramcharan, Bertie, 205
Rand Corporation, 135
Rapid Reaction Force, 278
Reagan, Ronald (Administration), 38, 39, 98, 142, 155, 182, 184, 271, 276, 288
Realism perspective, on Article 2(4), 55, 67–73
Reconstruction, *see* Stabilization and reconstruction, U.S. policy toward
Recruitment rates, 14
Red Crescent Movement, 206
Reisman, Michael, 54
Renan, Ernest, 195
Report on Nuclear Security, 111
Republican Party, 74, 142, 163, 166, 202, 203, 204, 220, 252
Rhodes, Edward, 133
Rice, Condoleezza, 19, 45, 117, 120, 187, 220, 288, 292, 324
Robinson, Mary, 205
Roosevelt, Franklin D., 35, 53, 54, 56, 59, 60, 63, 66, 67, 73, 166, 173, 193, 254, 271
Roosevelt, Theodore, 32, 33, 34
Root, Elihu, 74

Ruggie, John, 3, 99, 124
Rumsfeld, Donald, 43, 118, 156, 157, 197, 199, 201, 202, 205, 288, 292
Russia, 8, 111, 112, 222, 279, 328; *see also* Soviet Union–U.S. relations
Rwanda, 6

S

Salah, Ali Abdullah, 327
Sanchez, Ricardo, 200, 202
Sartre, Jean-Paul, 196, 202
Saudi Arabia, 318, 324–325, 326
Schlesinger, Arthur, Jr., 142, 151, 165
Schröder, Gerhard, 117
Schwartz, Thomas, 175
Scowcroft, Brent, 167
Secret intelligence accountability
    barriers to effective oversight, 188–189
    conclusion, 189–190
    congressional oversight agenda for, 187–188
    controversies/stimulus for, 179–182
    failures and scandals, 185–187
    frequency of intensity for, 182–185
    inside the extent of, 178–179
    introduction, 173–174
    philosophy of, 176–178
    sharing of secret power, 174–176
Secular Arab reactions, 322
Senate Armed Services Committee (2005), 109
Senate Foreign Relations Committee (1945), 60, 63, 65, 69, 70; *see also* Article 2(4), origins of
Senate Foreign Relations Committee (2002), 110, 270
Senate Intelligence Oversight Committee (2003), 180
Senate Select Committee on Intelligence (SSCI), 184, 187, 188, 189
Servitudes (legal obligations), 86–87
Shah, King Zahir, 216, 224, 226, 232
Shiite Muslims, 107, 131, 156, 167, 326
Shinseki, Eric, 156, 157, 167
Shirzai, Gul Agha, 227
Siam, 91
Silberman-Robb Commission (2002), 180
Simpson, Gerry, 90
Singapore, 302
Sirat, Abdul Sattar, 226
Smaller scale contingencies (SSCs), 247
Snyder, Jack, 110
Social power literature, 3
Society for Historians of American Foreign Relations, 32

Soft power resources, 4
Solana, Javier, 275
Somalia, 6, 115, 133, 221, 244
South Asia–U.S. relations, 302–303; *see also* Asia policy
Southeast Asia–U.S. relations, 90, 134, 142, 153, 272, 289, 300–302; *see also* Asia policy
South Korea–U.S. relations, 17, 72, 133, 153, 288, 294–299; *see also* Asia policy
South Vietnam, 235
Sovereign inequality
    changing conceptions of, 88–89
    conceptions of empire, 82–83
    conclusion, 99–100
    defining hierarchy in anarchy, 83–85
    forms of, 85–88
    forms of hierarchy in anarchy, 94–95
    Great Power status and, 89–90
    introduction, 81
    models of hierarchical security systems, 91–94
    outlaw states and, 90–91
    reading of the war in Iraq, 95–99
Soviet Union–U.S. relations, 5, 6, 35, 41, 43, 59, 60, 63, 93, 111, 123, 124, 125, 261, 263, 279
Spain, 114, 266, 276
Spanish-American War of 1898, 33, 151, 163, 193, 253
Stabilization and reconstruction, U.S. policy toward
    the Balkins, post-conflict operations in, 246–247
    dilemma of end states, 251–256
    Germany, post-conflict operations in, 248–250
    Haiti, post-conflict operations in, 243–246
    introduction, 241–242
    Japan, post-conflict operations in, 250–251
    Panama, post-conflict operations in, 242–243
    the Philippines, post-conflict operations in, 248
Stamp Act, 176
Stassen, Harold E., 66, 71
State stabilization, *see* Stabilization and reconstruction, U.S. policy toward
Stettinius, Edward R., 51, 57, 60, 65, 68, 76
Stimson, Henry L., 166
Stoiber, Edmund, 117
Strategic Arms Limitation Treaty I (SALT I), 124
Sub-Saharan Africa, 24, 90
Sudan, 5, 273
Suez Canal, 72, 263
Suicide attacks, 107–108
Sullivan, Mark, 271
Sunni Muslims, 107, 131, 156, 167
Superordinate authority, in international orders, 84–85, 91
Supreme Council for the National Unity of Afghanistan, 224
Sweden, 204
Syria, 86, 91, 230, 326

T

Taft, Robert A., 36, 67
Taft, William Howard, 166
Taiwan, 10, 17, 24, 153, 292, 293
Taliban, U.S. policy toward, 25, 107, 127, 129, 130, 197, 198, 222, 223, 226, 265, 325
Tanter, Richard, 300
Telhami, Shibley, 321
Terrorism (9/11 terrorist attacks); *see also* Iraq–U.S. relations
    Asia policy and, 287
    efficacy of force and, 110, 118, 119, 126, 130–131, 271
    Middle East and, 313, 319–320, 323, 325
    public opinion and, 141, 142, 145–147, 169, 264, 265
    unilateralism and, 41
Thailand, 300, 301
Time, 143
Torture, defining, 201
Trade deficits, 142, 150
Transatlantic relationship, *see* European Union (EU)
Transition operations, *see* Stabilization and reconstruction, U.S. policy toward
Transnational civic politics, 42–45
Treaties of protection/guaranteeing powers, 86, 91
The Troubled Partnership (Kissinger), 263
Truman, Harry S., 32, 38, 51, 54, 56, 58, 60, 63, 66, 73, 173
Turkey, 43, 72, 114, 117, 118, 318, 322

U

Ukraine, 21
U.S. Agency for International Development (USAID), 244, 245

Index • 349

U.S. Army Fourth Infantry Division, 114
U.S. Congress
   enemy detainees and, 194
   intelligence accountability of, 174,
     175, 176, 177, 179–180, 189
   policy preferences of, 40, 270
   promotion of democracy in
     Afghanistan and, 220
U.S. Constitution, 37, 136, 151, 173
U.S. Department of Defense (DOD), 187,
   205, 233, 244, 245, 252
U.S. Department of Justice (DOJ), 244
U.S. *Foreign Policy: Shield of the Republic*
   (Lippmann), 67
U.S. Marine Corps, 13, 14
U.S. military, *see* Military power, U.S. security
   policy and
U.S. National Guard, 13, 14, 116
U.S. nuclear arsenal, 11
U.S. power, overview of; *see also* Sovereign
   inequality
   Bush policies in practice, 21–25
   coercive power, 7–12
   conclusion, 25–26
   hegemonic power, 3–7
   introduction, 1–2
   sustainability of hegemonic power,
     12–21
U.S. State Department, 199, 201, 231, 233,
   241, 245, 252
UN (United Nations)
   Charter of the, 5–6, 51–76
   European–American relations and,
     267
   Genocide Convention, 38
   multilateral commitments and,
     135–136, 328
   principle of sharing power and, 174
   promotion of democracy and, 228
   sovereign inequality and, 88
   state stabilization and reconstruction,
     241
   U.S. foreign policy and, 105, 112, 127,
     264
   U.S. public opinion on, 150, 167
   U.S. unilateralism and, 35, 39
UN Assistance Mission in Afghanistan, 128
UN Commission on Human Rights, 116
UN Convention Against Torture and
   Degrading Treatment, 195, 198, 200
UNDP (United Nations Development
   Program), 128
UN Genocide Convention, 38

UN High Commissioner for Refugees
   (UNHCR), 128
UN High Level Panel on Threats, Challenges
   and Change, 136
UN Human Rights Commission, 205
Unilateralism doctrine, American historical/
   conceptual contexts of
   on change and continuity, 32
   conclusion, 45–46
   doctrinal differences today, 39–42
   on exceptionalism, 32–37
   on exemptionalism, 37–39, 99
   introduction, 31
   transnational civil politics and,
     42–45
   use of military force and, 106, 113,
     116
United Kingdom, 53, 59, 60
United Nations (UN), *see* UN (United
   Nations)
United Nations Development Program
   (UNDP), 128
Universal Declaration of Human Rights, 38
UNMOVIC, 115
UNSCOM, 115
UN Security Council; *see also* UN (United
   Nations)
   Articles 2(4) and, 5–6, 51–76
   Cold War issues and, 124
   European–American relations and,
     265, 266, 273–274
   multilateral commitments and,
     136, 137
   post-Cold War issues and, 125, 126
   transnational civic politics and, 43
   U.S. public opinion on, 153
   U.S. unilateralism and, 35
UN Security Council Resolution 1368,
   127–130
UN Security Council Resolution 1510, 128
Uruguay, 95
Use of military force, *see* Military power, U.S.
   security policy and
USSR, *see* Soviet Union–U.S. relations
Uzbekistan, 290, 291, 304

V

Vandenberg, Arthur, 67, 70, 72
Védrine, Hubert, 41, 264
Vendrell, Francesc, 228
Venezuela, 302
Versailles Conference, 66, 249, 254

Vietnam War, U.S. policy toward, 14, 32, 37, 124, 142, 163, 173, 179, 235, 241
Von Moltke, Count Helmuth, 241

W

Waever, Ole, 93
Wall Street Journal, 188, 203
Waltz, Kenneth, 83, 85
War in Iraq, *see* Iraq War
War of 1812, 151, 163
War on Terrorism; *see also* Terrorism (9/11 terrorist attacks)
    insurgency by Bush, 107–109
    multilateral participation and, 127
    sovereignty inequality and, 98
War Powers Act of 1973, 151
Washington, George, 33, 166, 176
Watergate scandal (1973), 182, 183
Watson, Adam, 93
Weapons of mass destruction (WMD), U.S. policy toward, 96, 105, 109, 110, 111, 112, 115, 145, 159, 169, 180, 185
Wen Jiabao, 303
Westfalian system, 85
Wilson, Woodrow, 34, 35, 59, 62, 67, 73, 132, 166, 193, 253, 271
Winn, Peter, 95
WMD (weapons of mass destruction), *see* Weapons of mass destruction (WMD), U.S. policy toward
Wolfowitz, Paul, 19, 112, 120, 157, 230, 288
Wood, Leonard, 248, 253
Woods, Bretton, 35
World Bank, 6, 128, 130, 167, 290
World Economic Forum (2003), 118
World Food Program, 128
World Trade Center, 7, 217, 229
World Trade Organization (WTO), 35, 269, 270, 281
World War I, 34, 151, 166, 193, 194, 248, 253, 272, 274
World War II, U.S. policy toward, 5, 37, 90, 142, 145, 151, 166, 173, 194, 235, 249, 272, 274, 315

Y

Yalta summit, 57, 64, 66
Yemen, 318, 326
Yom Kippur War, 263
Yugoslavia, 125, 126, 246, 255

Z

Zakara, Fareed, 127, 133
Zedong, Mao, 26